Out to Eat

London 2001

Lonely Planet Publications
Melbourne, London, Paris, Oakland

Lonely Planet ***Out to Eat – London***

1st edition – September 2000

Published by Lonely Planet Publications

Lonely Planet Offices
Australia PO Box 617, Hawthorn, Vic 3122
USA 150 Linden St, Oakland, CA 94607
UK 10a Spring Place, London NW5 3BH
France 1 rue du Dahomey, 75011 Paris

Series publishing manager: Adrienne Costanzo
Editor: Courtney Centner
Layout & series design: Wendy Wright
Mapping: Alison Lyall
Cover design: Simon Bracken
Photographs: Simon Bracken

ISBN 1 86450 083 2

Printed by The Bookmaker International Ltd
Printed in China

London Underground map reproduced with the permission of the London Transport Museum.

Lonely Planet books provide independent advice. Lonely Planet does not accept advertising in its books, nor do we accept payment in exchange for listing or endorsing any restaurant. Lonely Planet reviewers do not accept discounts or free meals in exchange for positive coverage of any sort.

Dis-moi **où** tu manges, je te dirai ce que tu es.
Tell me **where** you eat and I will tell you what you are.
with apologies to Brillat-Savarin

OUT TO EAT – PEOPLE

This book is the result of more than a year's planning, hundreds of meetings, and the creative efforts of a hungry team that includes experienced food writers, food-mad editors, designers, cartographers, guidebook authors, and a sprinkling of publishers. Fuelled by equal parts Alka Seltzer and passion for good food, the core **team of writers** comprised: Ryan Ver Berkmoes, David Ellis, Steve Fallon, Imogen

Franks, Andrew Humphreys, Kath Kenny, Simon Richmond, Maureen Stapleton, Anna Sutton and Sara Yorke.

For **additional assessments**, thanks to Jolyon Attwooll, Neal Bedford, Sarah Bennett, Paul Bloomfield, Katrina Browning, Joanna Clifton, Ciara Clissman, Liz Corcoran, Gordon Damzen, Robert Devcic, Paul Edmunds, Teresa Fisher, Lorna Gallagher, Janet Gower, Michelle Hawkins, Charlotte Hindle, Mark Honan, Claire Hornshaw, Chris Horton, Katharine Leck, Sarah Long, Claudia Martin, Thornton McCamish, Rebecca Packham, David Rathborne, Nicky Robinson, Corinne Simcock, Dorinda Talbot, Bryn Thomas, Sam Trafford, David Wenk and Georgina Wintersgill. Thanks also to everyone at Lonely Planet and the entire reviewing team for their recommendations.

Features by Ryan Ver Berkmoes, Neal Bedford,

Specialist Lonely Planet Authors

Simon Richmond wrote 'On Your Plate – Japanese' and reviewed restaurants. Andrew Humphreys also reviewed restaurants and wrote 'On Your Plate – Middle Eastern'.

Courtney Centner, Steve Fallon, Imogen Franks, Simon Heng, Andrew Humphreys, Simon Richmond and Anna Sutton.

From the Out to Eat team
This book was coordinated by Courtney Centner, and edited and proofed by Courtney Centner and Janet Austin, with assistance from Carolyn Holbrook, Dan Goldberg and Emma Miller. The maps were designed by Alison Lyall.

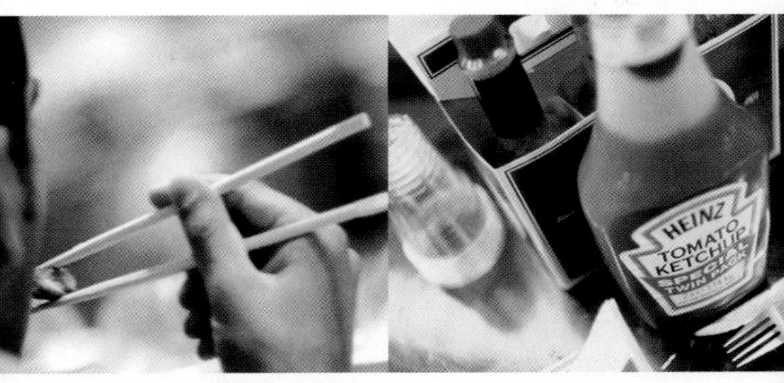

Thanks to super programmer Dan Levin and Production Services, Paul Clifton for cartographic words of wisdom and David Kemp for expert design advice. Thanks also to Imogen Franks for endless support and enthusiasm, Sara Marley for dining companionship and journal clippings, the ideas and expertise of Mike Rothschild, and Nikki Anderson and Adam McCrow for obtaining the London Underground map. Sue Galley, Katie Cody, Donna Wheeler and Katharine Day did a little bit of everything. Glossary and map veteran Rhys Graham did his thing, Joceyln Harewood checked maps and Elissa Coffman remained calm under contracts. Restaurant Services checked facts and figures. Finally, thanks to Simon Bracken for continual cover work, the clever 'techie boys' for ever-ready know-how and Valerie Tellini, Brett Pascoe and all the gang at LPI.

Coordinating Author

A lifelong lover of food (his mum says he had a real passion for strained bananas at age 1), Ryan Ver Berkmoes has honed his culinary expertise in worldwide travel that has included extensive time in the USA, Russia, Germany and Canada as a Lonely Planet guidebook writer. Other assignments have sent him looking for the best Parisian cafe, Italian village market and Thai waterfront fish restaurant. With his journalist wife, Sara Marley, Ryan was thrilled to eat his way across London. In fact he was heard to say at the outset, 'You're going to pay me to find the best restaurants in London? What's the catch?'

Satsuma (p 80)

Map Contents

Introduction

Lonely Planet has been synonymous with excellent independent travel advice for more than 25 years. Travellers look to Lonely Planet for straight talk and guidance without pretension. This holds especially true with the guides to the UK. Every new edition of Britain is accompanied by howls of anger from those it exposes as overrated. The London guide regularly gets an abundance of press coverage for its candid take on all things good and bad in the capital.

But even in a guidebook solely devoted to London, there's only so much room for our favourite past-time: eating. With over 8000 London restaurants vying for our attention, we decided that a celebrated city deserves a great guide dedicated to dining out. The book draws on the vast resources of local knowledge at Lonely Planet's London office. Insights are added by Lonely Planet guidebook authors, those seasoned travellers who bring their in situ knowledge of other cuisines and cultures that they've acquired from years on the road. After journeying to the far corners of the earth, our authors know the difference between an authentic dish and a poor imitation.

The sum of all this experience is a team of reviewers who are passionate about food and won't settle for mediocrity. After devouring hundreds of meals and tossing back untold glasses of wine, all the while noting myriad details such as service, décor and ambience, the *Out to Eat – London* team has gathered the best of the best for this guide. We recommend every restaurant in this book, but we also tell you if a place falls short of perfection in any area.

With such a huge number of places to choose from, we applied a variety of standards to the restaurants that made the final cut. Whether it's a place to take your lover, a warm refuge on a rainy day (and there's no shortage of those), a Sunday retreat that handles noisy families with aplomb, or an upscale dining room where your business associates will think you're a high-flier, *Out to Eat – London* is there with recommendations so you won't go wrong.

And we didn't just focus on the old stand-bys or the famous names: in the best Lonely Planet tradition we scoured London from Bloomsbury to Brixton, from Hammersmith to Hampstead and beyond, for our favourite restaurants – cheap, expensive and in between. We found top-notch ethnic eateries that represent the polyglot of cultures found in London today, and fine little neighbourhood joints are here alongside the noteworthy names of London dining.

In addition to the knowledgeable reviews, *Out to Eat – London* listings include a wealth of vital details such as noise levels, vegetarian options, smoking restrictions, al fresco dining and availability of wheelchair access. Wondering whether that restaurant really uses certified organic ingredients? We tell you. Got a hankering for fish and chips beyond compare? We save you from fruitlessly trawling the waters.

Eating out in London is as hard to characterise as the city itself, although a few points are universal. The food is better than it used to be, although there are still too many places coasting along serving sub-standard fare that wouldn't pass muster in other major cities. Prices are still too high: modest meals easily cost two people £100 or more. And you often have to book a table and endure other formalities just to get a quick bite out. London still has some way to go before going to a restaurant is a carefree and fairly priced undertaking. But with our insight, you'll be well on your way to a good meal, no matter what kind of experience you want.

To be fair and impartial, *Out to Eat – London* reviewers dined anonymously and did not accept discounts or free meals in exchange for positive coverage.

Finally, and very importantly, *Out to Eat – London* – like every other Lonely Planet guidebook – is free from advertising. This means an uncluttered read for you and uncompromised opinion from us. With more than 350 independently appraised places to choose from, we hope that you'll soon find new favourites that fast become old favourites.

Ryan Ver Berkmoes

A Guide to the Guide

Organisation
Out to Eat – London is organised according to locality. The names of the chapters represent convenient groupings of areas (ie Central, North & North-West, South-East, etc) and do not refer to actual named districts. Within the chapters the listings are organised alphabetically and according to area. Features are sprinkled throughout the book.

Best
Because *Out to Eat* includes such a diversity of listings, there are no 'stars', or points scored out of 20. But there are places that we would especially steer you towards in the 'Best' lists at the beginning of each chapter. Likewise, there are certain dishes, tastes or experiences that we'd walk miles to have again – we've collected them together in themed lists such as 'The Breakfast Brigade' and 'Riverside Pubs'.

The Listings
Each review offers a snapshot of one reviewer's experience of one or more visits to the restaurant, bar, pub or cafe. We emphasise that the opinion outlined in each listing should be taken as a guide only, and not as hard evidence of what you may expect. Dishes are seasonal, prices change, staff and owners move on. The reviews attempt to encapsulate the spirit of a place and provide an opinion on whether the place delivers what it promises.

Every listing is a recommendation. The bottom line for inclusion is that the food must be good.

Lesser known cuisine terms are explained in the Glossary on p 266.

Cuisine Most of the cuisine titles are self-explanatory – French, Moroccan, Thai, etc. A little less self-evident are the cuisine terms 'international' and 'modern British'.

international – the kitchen prepares more or less ethnically authentic dishes from various cuisines. You might find, for example, classic versions of phat thai, osso buco, vindaloo and cassoulet all together on the same menu.

modern British – see the feature 'From Vile to Vogue – A History of British Dining' on p 30.

Certified Organic As a result of the swiftly growing interest in organic food, we've listed the words 'certified organic' in the margin of a review if the restaurant can guarantee that it uses certified organic ingredients. Also, see the feature 'Manic Organic' on p 231.

Licensing A restaurant with a BYO (Bring Your Own) licence allows you to bring alcohol that you have purchased elsewhere to be served with your meal. Almost all restaurants with a BYO licence allow only bottled wine to be brought in and served. 'Unlicensed' means that it is illegal to consume alcohol on the premises.

Map Reference Each listing is cross-referenced to a numbered map.

Telephone Numbers We have listed the area code '020' before each telephone number, but 020 does not need to be dialled if you are calling from within London. The area code is only required if you are calling from outside London.

Transport In the margin of each review we've listed the tube/rail station or bus line closest to your restaurant destination. And, conveniently, there is a map of the London Underground on p 304.

Price Fields Price fields show the complete range of prices on each restaurant's menu, eg, 'starter: £5-£11', where £5 is the price of the least expensive starter on the menu and £11 is the most expensive. Prices were correct at the time of research.

Set Menu/Banquet Special menus and banquets available are indicated beneath the price fields. Again, prices were correct at the time of research.

Credit Cards Abbreviations show credit and debit facilities offered by the restaurant.
AE: American Express, BC: BankCard, DC: Diners Club, JCB: Japanese Credit Bureau card; MC: MasterCard; V: Visa Card; SW: Switch.

Wheelchair Access Restaurants equipped with a toilet that has been purpose-built or adapted for wheelchair access are the only listings carrying the words 'wheelchair access'. 'Access' suggests that wheelchairs will also easily get into the restaurant and have ease of movement once inside. Unfortunately we can't guarantee this, and we urge you to telephone ahead to confirm facilities.

Entertainment Any in-house entertainment (eg, dance, live music, performances) is indicated beside each listing.

Cuisine Glossary/Special Order – A Glossary for All Tastes
There are two glossaries: one explains lesser-known cuisine terms mentioned in the listings and the other describes special dietary needs.

Indexes Restaurants are grouped into four indexes – alphabetical index by special features, index by cuisine, index of vegetarian restaurants and index by area. So whether you're looking for all of the recommended Japanese restaurants in the book, all of the restaurants recommended in Brixton, or all of the restaurants that are totally smoke free, you'll be able to find them.

Tipping & VAT Many restaurants now add a 'discretionary' service charge to your bill, and technically this should be clearly advertised so that you do not mistakenly add an additional tip. In places that don't automatically add the service charge you're expected to leave a 10% to 15% tip, unless the service was unsatisfactory. Restaurant menus will already include 17.5% value-added tax (VAT) in their prices.

Write to us

Things change – prices go up, opening hours change, good places go bad and bad places go bankrupt – nothing stays the same. So, if you find things better or worse, recently opened or recently closed, please tell us and help make the next edition even more accurate and useful.

Every morsel of information you send will be read and acknowledged by the appropriate author, editor or publisher. The best contributions will be rewarded with a free Lonely Planet book and excerpts may appear in future editions of *Out to Eat – London*, so please let us know if you don't want your letter published or your name acknowledged.

Write to us:
Lonely Planet Out to Eat
10a Spring Place
London NW5 3BH
email: out2eat@lonelyplanet.com.au

Symbols

Totally smoke free.

Smoking Text accompanying this symbol explains whether there are smoking restrictions, separate smoke-free dining areas or smoking throughout.

Vegetarian Options

Each restaurant has been rated for the quality and range of vegetarian dishes (those that contain no meat, including fish and seafood) on offer on the *regular* menu. 'Carrot' icons indicate the rating. If there is no carrot icon, the restaurant does not offer a satisfactory selection of vegetarian dishes on their regular menu. Bear in mind that most kitchens will (when given at least a day's notice) create interesting vegetarian dishes and cater for other diners with special needs (eg halal, kosher, gluten-free, low-fat). There's a glossary of special dietary terms on p 260.

Various and/or interesting vegetarian options.

All-vegetarian menu or excellent vegetarian options.

Quiet Noticeably quiet, even when busy.

Mid-range Medium noise, not noticeably quiet, and you can generally hear conversation at your own table without straining.

Noisy Can be very noisy when busy (either due to music or the acoustics of the space). You may have to raise your voice considerably to be heard in conversation.

Romantic Make a date. Something about this place makes romance seem very likely.

Open fireplace Open fireplace for chilly days or nights.

Outdoors Outdoor dining options for fine days or nights.

Parking Free private parking on premises or valet parking.

Business Exercise the expense account. This place is suitable for business occasions. Expect professional table service, compatible clientele, adequate table spacing and comfortable noise levels.

Aldwych

Bloomsbury

Chinatown

Covent Garden

CENTRAL

Edgware Rd

Euston

Fitzrovia

Holborn

Leicester Square

Marble Arch

Marylebone

Mayfair

Oxford Circus

Piccadilly

Regent's Park

St James's

Soho

Strand

Trafalgar Square

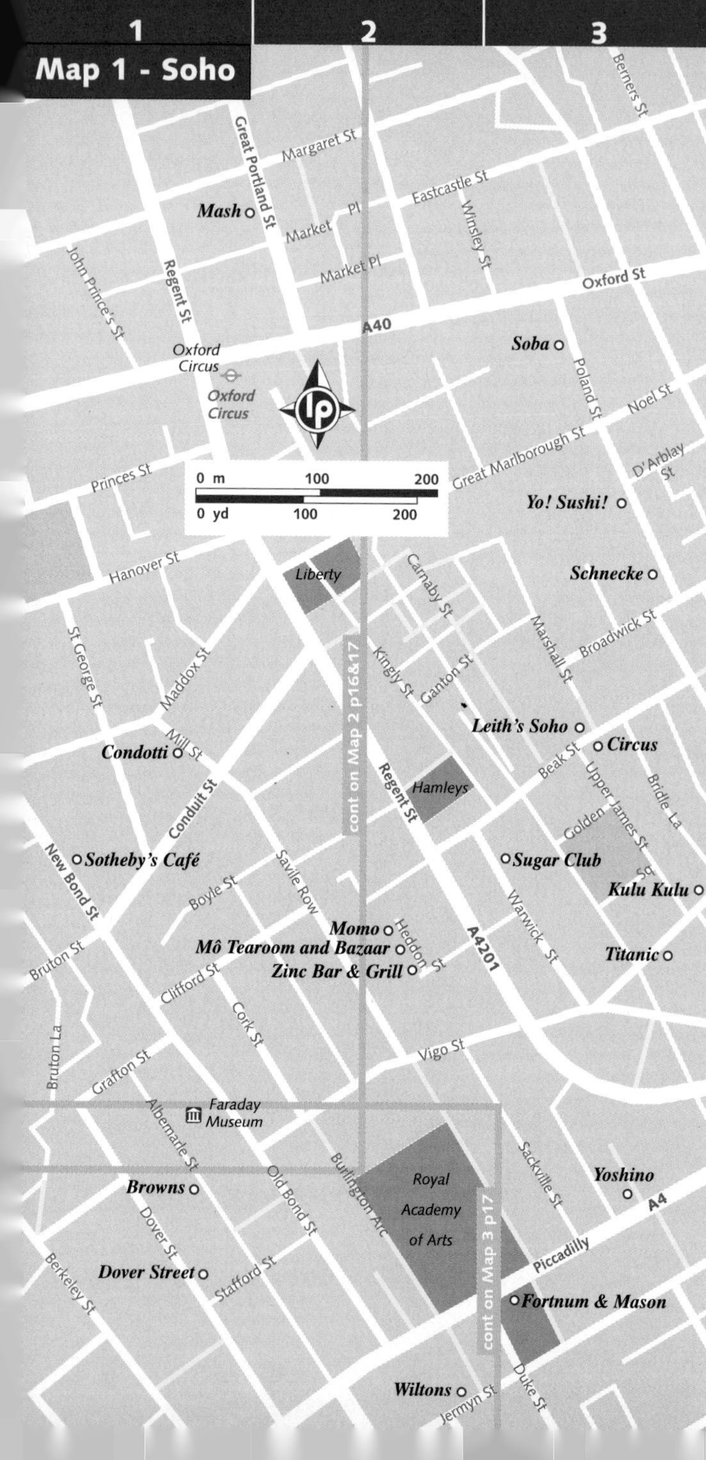
1
2
3
Map 1 - Soho
Great Portland St
Margaret St
Mash
Market Pl
Market Pl
Eastcastle St
Winsley St
Berners St
John Prince's St
Regent St
Oxford St
A40
Oxford Circus
Oxford Circus
Soba
Poland St
Noel St
Princes St
Great Marlborough St
D'Arblay St
0 m 100 200
0 yd 100 200
Yo! Sushi!
Hanover St
Liberty
Carnaby St
Schnecke
St George St
Maddox St
Kingly St
Ganton St
Marshall St
Broadwick St
cont on Map 2 p16&17
Leith's Soho
Condotti
Mill St
Circus
Beak St
Upper James St
Bridle La
Conduit St
Regent St
Hamleys
Golden Sq
New Bond St
Sotheby's Café
Savile Row
Sugar Club
Kulu Kulu
Boyle St
Momo
Heddon St
A4201
Warwick St
Mô Tearoom and Bazaar
Titanic
Bruton St
Zinc Bar & Grill
Clifford St
Cork St
Vigo St
Bruton La
Grafton St
Faraday Museum
Albemarle St
Burlington Arc
Royal Academy of Arts
Sackville St
Yoshino
Browns
Old Bond St
A4
Dover St
cont on Map 3 p17
Piccadilly
Dover Street
Stafford St
Berkeley St
Fortnum & Mason
Wiltons
Jermyn St
Duke St

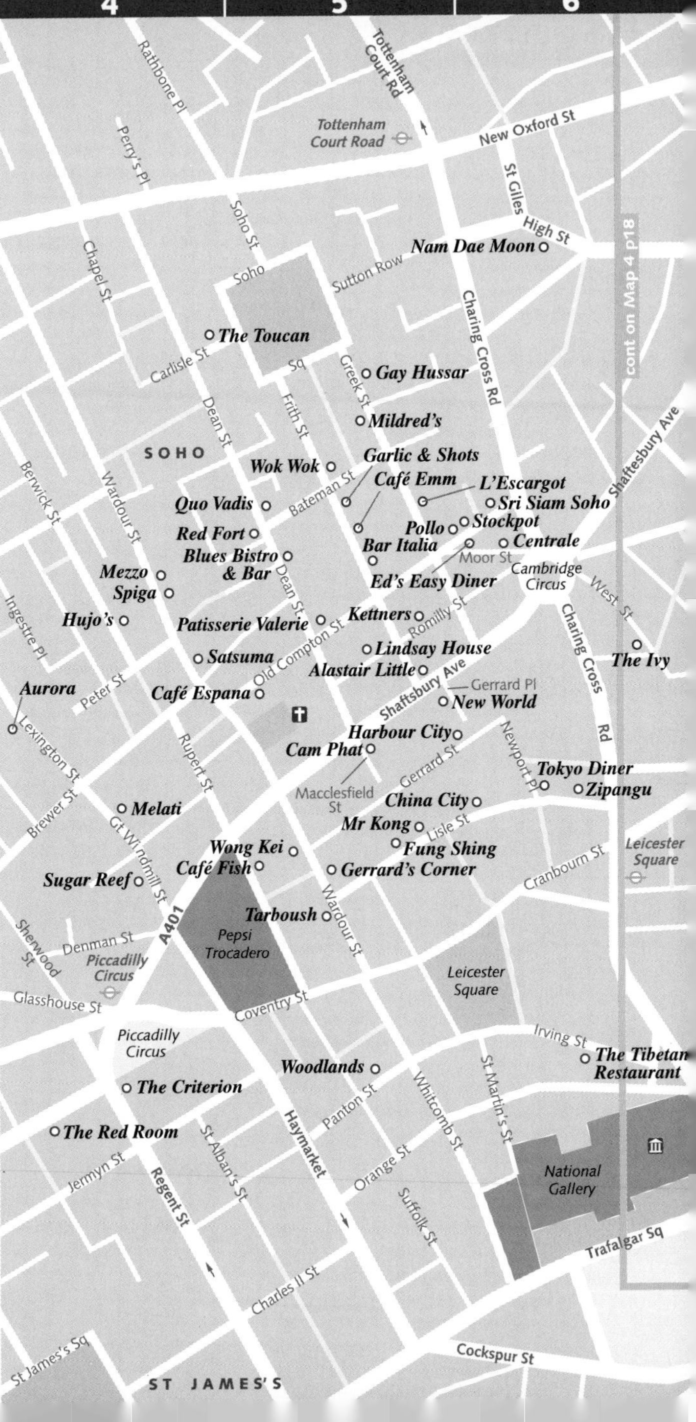
4
5
6
Tottenham Court Rd
Rathbone Pl
Perry's Pl
Tottenham Court Road
New Oxford St
St Giles High St
Soho St
Chapel St
Soho
Sutton Row
Nam Dae Moon
cont on Map 4 p18
Charing Cross Rd
The Toucan
Carlisle St
Sq
Greek St
Gay Hussar
Dean St
Frith St
Mildred's
SOHO
Shaftesbury Ave
Berwick St
Wardour St
Wok Wok
Garlic & Shots
Café Emm
L'Escargot
Quo Vadis
Bateman St
Sri Siam Soho
Red Fort
Pollo
Stockpot
Bar Italia
Centrale
Blues Bistro & Bar
Moor St
Mezzo
Cambridge Circus
Spiga
Ed's Easy Diner
West St
Ingestre Pl
Hujo's
Patisserie Valerie
Kettners
Romilly St
Charing Cross Rd
Old Compton St
Lindsay House
The Ivy
Satsuma
Alastair Little
Aurora
Peter St
Café Espana
Shaftsbury Ave
Gerrard Pl
New World
Lexington St
Harbour City
Newport Pl
Rupert St
Cam Phat
Tokyo Diner
Gerrard St
Zipangu
Macclesfield St
Brewer St
Melati
China City
Gt Windmill St
Mr Kong
Lisle St
Leicester Square
Wong Kei
Fung Shing
Café Fish
Gerrard's Corner
Sugar Reef
Cranbourn St
Tarboush
Wardour St
A401
Pepsi Trocadero
Sherwood St
Denman St
Piccadilly Circus
Leicester Square
Glasshouse St
Coventry St
Irving St
Piccadilly Circus
The Tibetan Restaurant
Woodlands
The Criterion
Panton St
Whitcomb St
St Martin's St
The Red Room
St Alban's St
Haymarket
National Gallery
Jermyn St
Regent St
Orange St
Suffolk St
Trafalgar Sq
Charles II St
St James's Sq
Cockspur St
ST JAMES'S

Map 2 - Marylebone

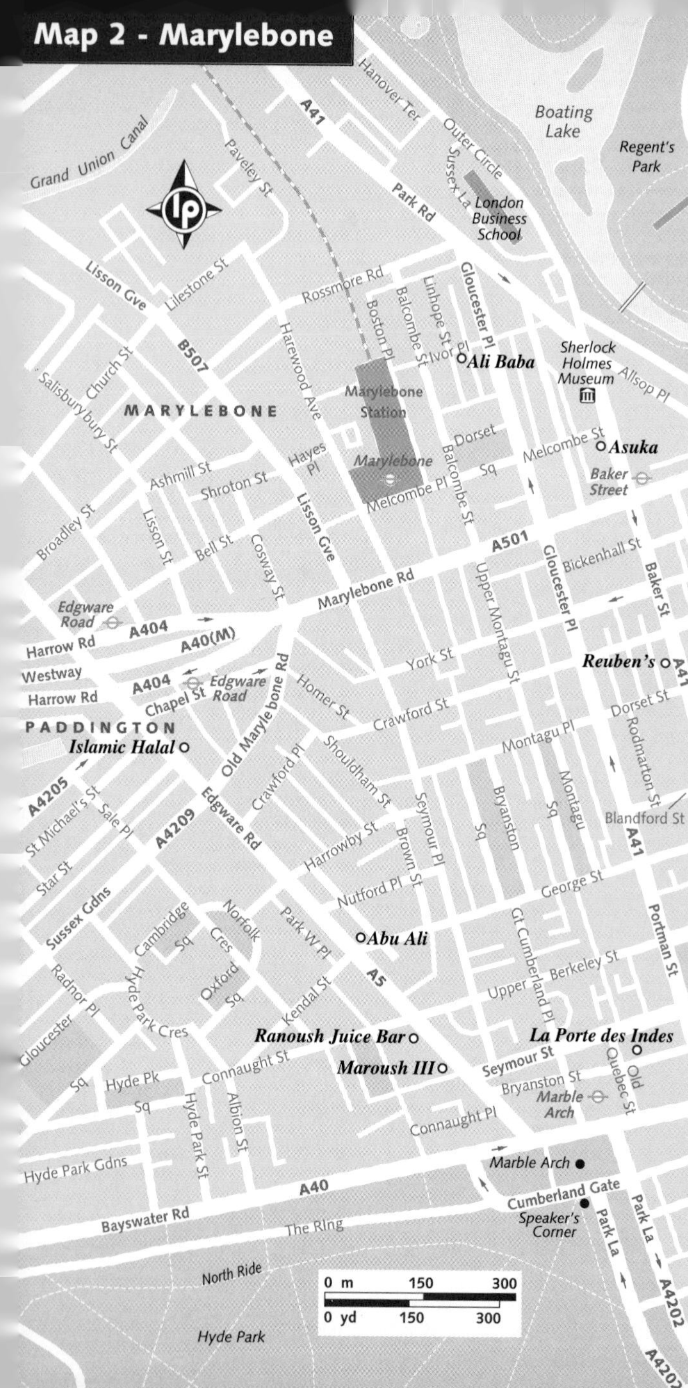

Map 3 - Mayfair

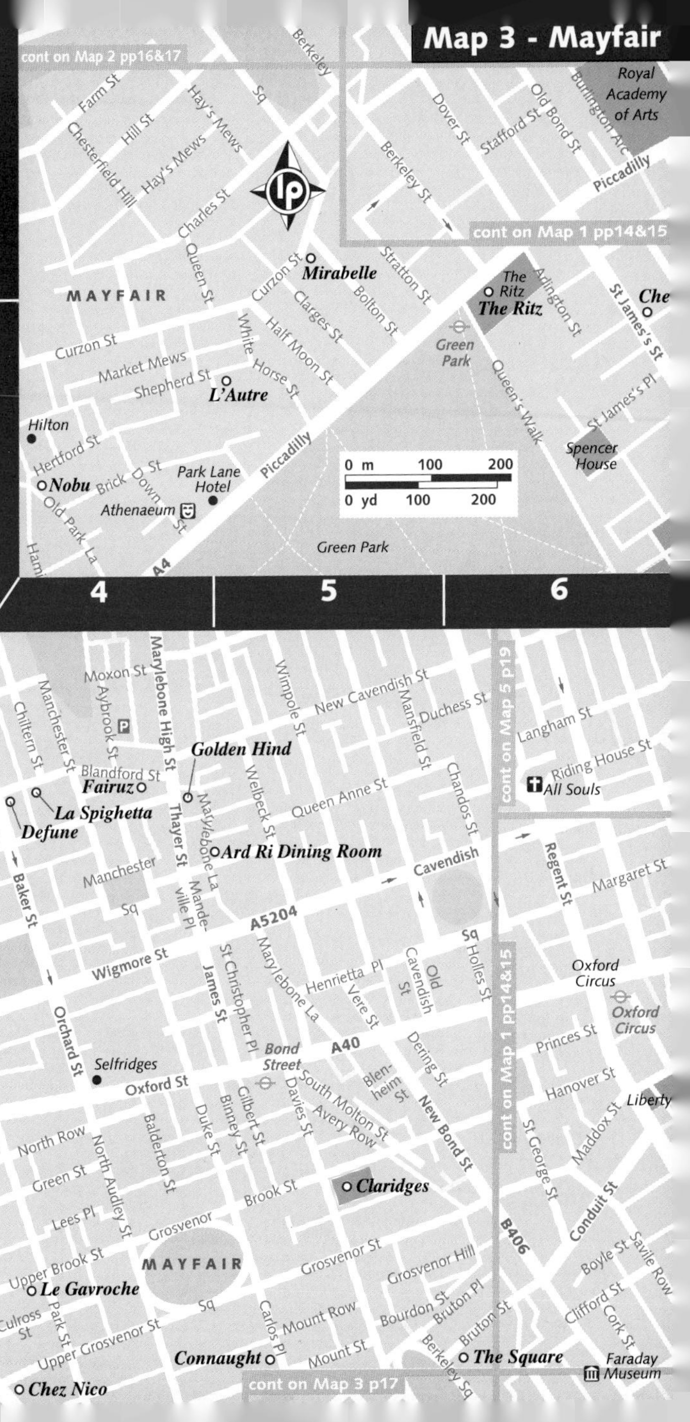

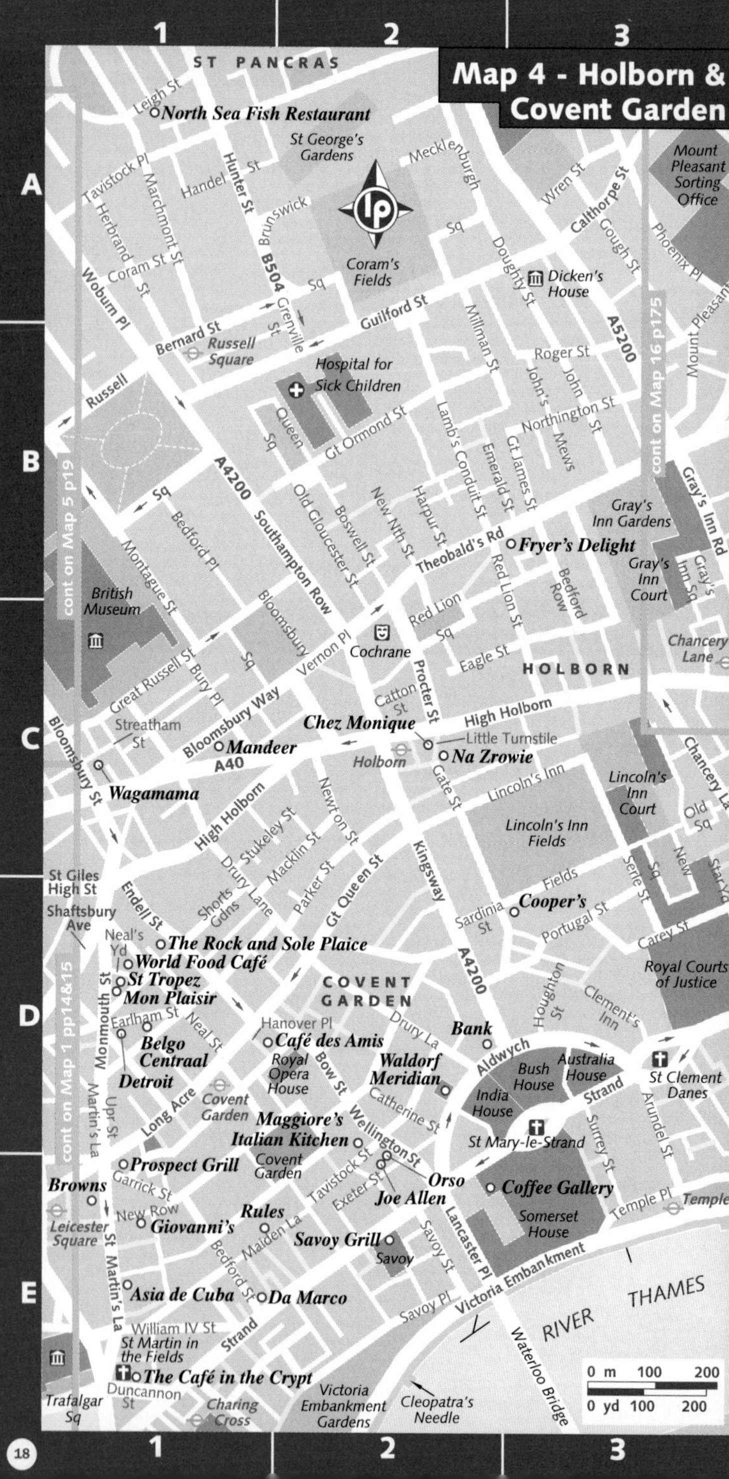
Map 4 - Holborn & Covent Garden
ST PANCRAS
North Sea Fish Restaurant
St George's Gardens
Coram's Fields
Dicken's House
Mount Pleasant Sorting Office
Russell Square
Hospital for Sick Children
British Museum
Fryer's Delight
Gray's Inn Gardens
Gray's Inn Court
Cochrane
Chancery Lane
HOLBORN
Chez Monique
Mandeer
Little Turnstile
Na Zrowie
Holborn
Wagamama
Lincoln's Inn Court
Lincoln's Inn Fields
Cooper's
Royal Courts of Justice
The Rock and Sole Plaice
World Food Café
St Tropez
Mon Plaisir
COVENT GARDEN
Belgo Centraal
Detroit
Café des Amis
Royal Opera House
Bank
Waldorf Meridian
Bush House
Australia House
India House
St Clement Danes
St Mary-le-Strand
Maggiore's Italian Kitchen
Covent Garden
Prospect Grill
Browns
Orso
Joe Allen
Coffee Gallery
Leicester Square
Giovanni's
Rules
Savoy Grill
Savoy
Somerset House
Temple
Asia de Cuba
Da Marco
RIVER THAMES
St Martin in the Fields
The Café in the Crypt
Trafalgar Sq
Charing Cross
Victoria Embankment Gardens
Cleopatra's Needle
Waterloo Bridge
0 m 100 200
0 yd 100 200
cont on Map 5 p19
cont on Map 16 p175
cont on Map 1 pp14&15
A
B
C
D
E
1
2
3

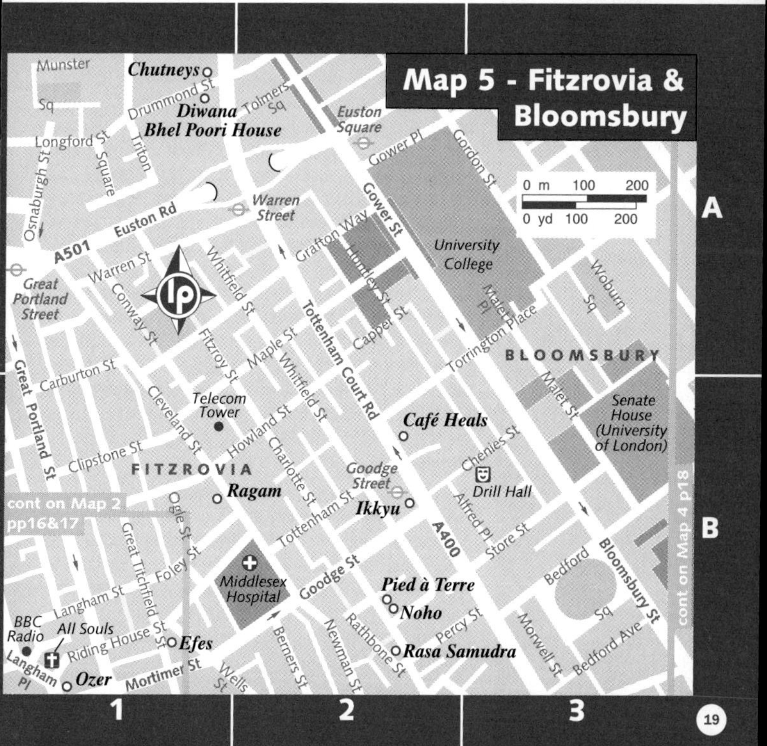

Map 5 - Fitzrovia & Bloomsbury

Munster Sq
Chutneys
Drummond St
Diwana Bhel Poori House
Tolmers Sq
Euston Square
Longford St
Osnaburgh St
Triton Square
Euston Rd
Warren Street
Gower Pl
Gordon St
Gower St
A501
Warren St
Great Portland Street
Conway St
Whitfield St
Grafton Way
Huntley St
University College
Malet Pl
Woburn Sq
Fitzroy St
Maple St
Tottenham Court Rd
Capper St
Torrington Place
BLOOMSBURY
Carburton St
Great Portland St
Cleveland St
Telecom Tower
Howland St
Whitfield St
Malet St
Senate House (University of London)
Café Heals
Chenies St
Clipstone St
FITZROVIA
Charlotte St
Goodge Street
Drill Hall
Ragam
Tottenham St
Ikkyu
Ogle St
Great Titchfield St
Foley St
A400
Alfred Pl
Store St
Bedford Sq
Bloomsbury St
Middlesex Hospital
Goodge St
Langham St
Pied à Terre
Noho
BBC Radio
All Souls
Riding House St
Efes
Berners St
Newman St
Rathbone St
Percy St
Rasa Samudra
Morwell St
Bedford Ave
Langham Pl
Ozer
Mortimer St
Wells St

0 m 100 200
0 yd 100 200

A
B
1
2
3

cont on Map 2 pp16&17

cont on Map 4 p18

BEST

- **The Criterion**
  Decadent décor, sumptuous sustenance
- **The Ivy**
  Book well ahead. Need we say more?
- **La Spighetta**
  Quality Italian at reasonable prices
- **Lindsay House**
  A utopian experience
- **Mr Kong**
  Three floors of top-notch Chinatown eating
- **New World**
  Seats over 700 diners for dim sum delicacies
- **Pâtisserie Valerie**
  Long-loved French treats
- **Rules**
  Old-fashioned favourites circa 1798
- **Wiltons**
  Distinguished British cuisine
- **Woodlands**
  Authentic South Indian vegetarian cookery

Kettners (p 72)

Central

Gaudy, noisy and popular, Soho has long been London's centre for a night out. From high-end restaurants and eclectic cafes, to trendy nightclubs so cutting edge that they close before the masses hear about them, the heaving, narrow streets of Soho are lined with myriad diversions. The area was once a royal hunting ground, and back in the dark days of the 1980s illegitimate activity far outweighed the rest. Though the streets have now been cleaned up, purveyors of vice still lurk in the shadows.

Restaurants in Soho open and close at a dizzying pace, although old stand-bys such as Mr Kong in Chinatown can soldier on for decades. London's prices are at their highest here and in the adjoining and equally popular areas of Covent Garden and Mayfair. The former was once home to a market, but Covent Garden has been gentrified for so long that few remember that it was once London's main source of wholesale produce. The reopening of the Royal Opera House is just one more reason Covent Garden's streets are jammed at night with pre- and post-theatre crowds. The restaurants can be as trendy or as famous as those in Soho, but overall the mood is more relaxed and the atmosphere less frenzied. Calmer still is Mayfair, traditionally the most exclusive London area, where the dining can be as subdued as the engines of the many Rolls Royces gliding along the streets.

In contrast Marylebone and Edgware Rd feel much more like typical London areas with their mixture of cultures and incomes. The restaurants and pubs here cater first to locals while still happily welcoming visitors. Prices are more reasonable and patrons are more concerned with seeing what's on their plate as opposed to seeing and being seen by others.

Bank

Modern French

☎ **020 7234 3344**
1 Kingsway WC2

Map 4 D2
Tube: Holborn or Temple
Wheelchair access

Smoking throughout

Bank is one of the more reliable of London's mega-restaurants. A mirror wall expands the long space, with a trendy bar out front and an open-view kitchen, to warehouse proportions. Poster-paint seaside murals are a fun touch and a latticed ceiling of sheet glass hangs dramatically over it all. Although we found the chewy salt cod fritters (£6.75) overloaded with salt, the seafood here is generally best. The house fish (a classy halibut) and chips (£18.50) is reliable and comes with creamy mushy peas. The seared mullet is moist, plentiful and well-matched with Asian greens. The rubbery roast rabbit (£13.50) had clearly bounced around too many fields, but a starter portion of tagliatelle (£8) was splendidly mushroomy. Yes, the tables are crammed together and the noise can overwhelm conversation, but service is courteous and you've just got to admire a place that runs the gamut of meals from fry-up breakfasts to post-theatre suppers and does it with class.

Open: Mon-Fri (breakfast 7am-11.30am), noon-3pm, Mon-Sat 5.30pm-11.30pm, Sat & Sun brunch 11.30am-3.30pm, Sun 5.30pm-10pm; reservations essential; licensed

starter: £4.75-£16.50
main: £9.50-£19
dessert: £4.80-£6.50
Prix fixe £13.90-£17.50

AE DC MC V

The Coffee Gallery

International

☎ **020 7848 2527**
Courtauld Institute, Somerset House, Strand WC2

Map 4 E2
Tube: Temple or Charing Cross
Wheelchair access

No smoking inside

Pavement tables

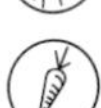

Reached via a spiral staircase just past the entrance to the Courtauld Gallery, The Coffee Gallery is a handy escape from the bustle of the Strand. There's no signage on the street, so most of the customers are from the immediate vicinity: visitors to the museum, students from the Courtauld Institute of Art and workers from government offices in and around Somerset House. Due to fire regulations, food can be heated but not cooked on the premises so much of the menu consists of simple but carefully prepared cold fare such as sandwiches, quiche served with salad and bread (£4.40), salads and cakes, including the exquisite lemon tart (£2.60). Though appealing year-round, the restaurant comes into its own in summer when the sunken courtyard is filled with tables and you can eat alfresco in one of the quietest spots in central London.

Open: Mon-Sat 10am-5.30pm, Sun noon-5.30pm; reservations advisable; unlicensed

main: £3.50-£5
dessert: £1.25-£2.60

cash only

Map 5 B2
Tube: Goodge Street
Wheelchair access
Nonsmoking tables available

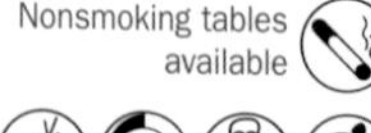
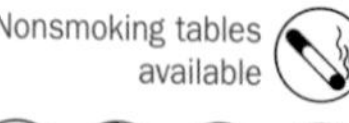

Café Heal's
International

☎ 020 7636 1666, ext 250
Level 1, Heal's,
196 Tottenham Court Rd W1

With cool mauve walls and beige leather banquettes, Café Heal's is as fashionable as the department store it calls home. If you find yourself dining alone or are short on conversation, a wide selection of newspapers and design magazines are on hand. The daily set menu is the way to go, as á la carte tends to be a bit pricey. Spicy tomato and lentil soup is the perfect starter on a rainy afternoon, and hot smoked salmon with soy noodles and bok choy also warms the cockles. Leave room for chocolate cake and cream (£3.25) or strawberry tart with amaretti crumble (£3.95). Service can be excruciatingly slow, so make sure you've time to spare on your shopping schedule.

starter: £3.75-£7.50
main: £8-£10
dessert: £3.95
Set menu £9.50
AE MC V; SW

Open: Mon-Wed 10am-5.30pm, Thurs 10am-8pm, Fri 10am-6pm, Sat 9.30am-6pm, Sun noon-5.30pm; reservations advisable; licensed

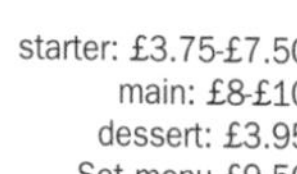

Map 4 C1
Tube: Tottenham Court Rd

Wagamama
Japanese

☎ 020 7323 9223
4a Streatham St WC1

Canteen dining doesn't get much more trendy than at Wagamama, where steaming noodle dishes are served up for the eager masses. Although there are now three other outlets around London, you'll still find yourself queuing up in the evening to get into this, the original Wagamama, a basement hall tucked away near the British Museum. The food isn't textbook Japanese – what you'd expect from a restaurant whose name can be translated as 'willful' – but is still good in its own right. If it's your first visit, take the pain out of ordering from the wordy menu by opting for one of the three 'positive eating' set meals combining a huge bowl of ramen (in either a chicken and pork or vegetarian stock) with gyoza dumplings and a choice of juice. Our chicken ramen (£5.40) had generous chunks of grilled meat, but the zasai gohan (£5.70) rice dish needed a dash of chilli for zest. Wagamama isn't a place to linger, but it's always fun while it lasts. *Also at 101a Wigmore St W1 ☎ 020 7409 0111, 26-40 Kensington High St W8 ☎ 020 7376 1717, 11 Jamestown Rd W1 ☎ 020 7428 0800 and 10a Lexington St W1 ☎ 020 7292 0990.*

starter: £2.95-£4.70
main: £4.70-£7.50
'Positive eating' set meals £8.25-£9.75
AE DC JCB MC V; SW

Open: Mon-Sat noon-11pm, Sun 12.30pm-10pm; reservations not accepted; licensed

CHINATOWN

Cam Phat
Chinese/Vietnamese

☎ 020 7437 5598
12 Macclesfield St W1

Map 1 C5
Tube: Leicester Square

 Smoking throughout

Although essentially another formulaic Chinatown eatery, Cam Phat does offer something slightly unique: Vietnamese cuisine. Look for the subtle 'v' next to a dish and you won't be disappointed. We opted for tender beef with lemongrass and green peppers (£4.70). Traditional Chinese dishes were also available and proved equally tasty: the egg fried rice (£1.70) came in generous portions, ensuring there were no unsatisfied appetites at meal's end. The ambience is typical of Chinatown – big tables covered by white tablecloths, bright overhead lights and quick service – but the staff are refreshingly attentive and well informed, and were in no hurry for us to leave. We enjoyed a tasty meal at our own leisure, paid a reasonable price for both the food and the house red (£9.50), and left certain that if dining in Chinatown again, we would return for a taste of Vietnam.

Open: daily noon-1am; reservations accepted (only for groups of 8 or more); licensed

starter: £1.70-£5.00
main: £3.30-£16
dessert: £1.50-£3.80
Set menu £8-£17
AE DC JCB MC V

Wagamama

CHINATOWN

Map 1 C6
Tube: Leicester Square
Nonsmoking tables available

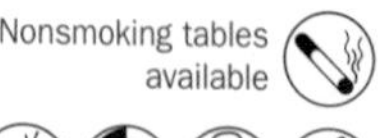

China City
Chinese

☎ 020 7734 3388
White Bear Yard, 25a Lisle St WC2

Why choose China City above the multitude of Chinese restaurants in Chinatown? Because it's hidden away from the crowds of central London, making it a great place to escape to. The simple and stylish white décor and courtyard fountain make a refreshing change from the usually tacky Chinatown ambience, and the food wins hands down for price and portion sizes. We just had to try the crispy aromatic duck with pancakes (£11.50) and found it suitably tender and rich in flavour, although there could have been more greens. The stir-fried pork with vegetables (£5.50) was nicely balanced and there were plenty of prawns in the sweet and sour king prawns (£7), but the accompanying rice was a tad gluggy. Try to avoid being seated under the air-conditioning vent – it's not the most comfortable way to spend an evening.

starter: £1.70-£5
main: £4.50-£25
dessert: £1.50-£3
Set menu £8.50 & £9.50 (2 or 4 people) or set banquet £14 & £18 (2 or 4 people)
AE DC MC V; SW

Open: Mon-Sat noon-11.45pm, Sun 11.30am- 11.15pm; reservations advisable; licensed

Map 1 C5
Tube: Leicester Square
Smoking throughout

Fung Shing
Chinese

☎ 020 7437 1539
15 Lisle St WC2

Since the 1980s, Fung Shing has been regarded as a culinary cut above the rest, serving upmarket Chinese cuisine at prices to match. Forget sweet and sour chicken, although it is available: this is the sort of place that serves abalone, ostrich, pigeon and venison. Seafood is the speciality and the starter of steamed razor clam cooked in garlic sauce (£3.50) is a minuscule delicacy. The pan-fried turbot (£16) is crispy at the edges and doused with a zingy ginger and garlic sauce. A more traditional choice is the stewed duck hotpot in plum sauce (£9.50), tinged with the distinctive flavour of coriander. Soak up the sauce with a bowl of sticky boiled rice (£1.70). Fung Shing's plain interiors are customary for Chinatown, but for a bright contrast book a table in the canary-yellow room at the back. Service is efficient, if a little robotic.

starter: £3.50-£16
main: £6-£60
dessert: £2.50-£4.50
Set menu £32 (for 2 people)
AE DC MC V; SW

Open: daily noon-11.30pm; reservations advisable (especially Fri & Sat evening); licensed & BYO (corkage £5/bottle)

CHINATOWN

Harbour City

Cantonese

☎ **020 7439 7859**
46 Gerrard St W1

Map 1 C5
Tube: Leicester Square

 Smoking throughout

This three-story Chinatown restaurant has maintained consistently good standards over its 13 years of existence, while many of its neighbours have waxed and waned or changed hands. The speciality here is dim sum, served from 11am to 5pm daily and ordered from a separate menu, with not a trolley in sight. Ensconced in the white but spartan 1st-floor dining room, we opted for prawn dumplings (£2 for 4), scallop dumplings (£2.20 for 4) and barbecued pork cheung fun (£2.40), each of which was fresh and succulent. The baked fresh crabs with ginger and spring onions arrived in their shells (£8.50) and were messy but delicious. They were accompanied by a generous portion of chiu chow fried rice (£6) topped with wilted greens, prawns, scallops and squid. Washed down with Tsing Tao beer, lunch can be excellent value.

Open: Mon-Sat noon-11.30pm, Sun 11am-10.30pm; reservations advisable; licensed & BYO (corkage £5/bottle)

starter: £5.50-£10.50
main: £7.50-£25
dessert: £2.50
Set menu £12.50/person (min 2 people)

AE DC JCB MC V; SW

Mr Kong

Chinese

☎ **020 7437 7341**
21 Lisle St WC2

Map 1 C5
Tube: Leicester Square

 Smoking throughout

It seems that not a pence of profit at Mr Kong is ploughed back into the interior – a serviceable array of functional tables jammed into three floors. Fortunately all the effort goes into the food, which is offered on three different menus. The best of the lot, the Chef's Special menu, has an attached sheet called 'To-Day Chef's Special' that looks suspiciously permanent. But ignore these quibbles and try the seafood curry (£9) which comes with a rich coconut sauce or the steak with black pepper and garlic (£7.80) that arrives still sizzling. If the prospect of scanning several hundred items over multiple menus proves daunting, there are set menus that draw from some of the more interesting items. Menu B (£19 per person) includes a fine satay chicken over crispy seaweed and crispy duck with pancakes. Hardcore Chinese menu aficionados can opt for separate items such as various incarnations of pig intestine and jelly fish. This part of Soho is riddled with Chinese restaurants, but Mr Kong rises above the rest.

Open: daily noon-2.30am; reservations accepted; licensed

starter: £1.90-£12.50
main: £5.80-£25
Set menu £16, £19 or £22/person (min 4 people)

AE DC JCB MC V; SW

CHINATOWN

Map 1 C5
Tube: Leicester Square
Separate smoke-free dining available

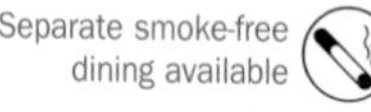

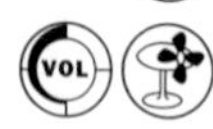

New World
Chinese

☎ 020 7734 0396
1 Gerrard Place W1

New World has a 20-page menu packed with everything from fried beef ho-fun with chilli and black bean sauce (£3.60) to pork and yam in a hotpot (£6.15) and several styles of abalone (from £12.50). But many other Soho Chinese joints can boast long menus, too. What the competition can't boast are wheeled carts and lots of them. Everyday from 11am to 6pm fleets of dim sum trolleys circulate through the vast dining room bearing scores of little dishes, most of which cost £1.55. There's no menu and no need to know the names as you can point and choose based on what you see. Various steamed dumplings, sautéed greens, deep-fried meats, stir-fried noodles and much more parade past. The whole vast place seems lifted right out of Hong Kong and the many dining Chinese families are a great endorsement. Since there are more than 700 seats, you'll never have to linger long on the worn red carpet in the entry.

starter: £2-£5
main: £6-£14
dessert: £2-£4
Set menu £11

AE DC JCB MC V; SW

Open: daily 11am-midnight; reservations accepted (except Sunday); licensed

COVENT GARDEN

Asia de Cuba

Asian/Cuban fusion

☎ 020 7300 5588
45 St Martin's Lane WC2

Map 4 E1
Tube: Leicester Square
Wheelchair access

 Smoking throughout

The giant chess pieces and gold molar seats in the St Martin's Lane Hotel sets the Daliesque tone for Asia de Cuba. Dragging our attention away from the Philippe Starck-designed interior (pillars decorated with books, TVs, arty photos and potplants) the matey waiter informs us that the menu is a 'share concept' – two starters and one main is ideal. The fusion of tropical and oriental is apparent in dishes like the tunapica (£9.50), spicy and fruity tuna tartare on wonton crisps, and the house calamari salad (£9.50), teaming slightly rubbery squid with a zesty salad including banana and heart of palm. Another unlikely combo of five-spiced sirloin steak with a pink grapefruit salad (£22.50) works well and is nicely presented, just like our knockout tequila and lime sorbet with pineapple and strawberries, which looks so fetching we don't know whether to eat it or wear it.

Open: Mon-Fri noon-2.30pm, Mon-Wed 6pm-midnight, Thurs-Sat 6pm-1am, Sun 6pm-10.30pm; reservations advisable (essential Fri & Sat); licensed

starter: £8.50-£12.50
main: £15.50-£34
dessert: £7.50-£9.50

AE DC MC V; SW

Belgo Centraal

Belgian

☎ 020 7813 2233
50 Earlham St WC2

Map 4 D1
Tube: Covent Garden
Wheelchair access

 Smoking throughout

Whether it's the ride in the cage elevator down to the subterranean beer halls, the chatter of strangers at the communal tables, the waiters dressed as Trappist monks or the Belgian graffiti sprawled boldly on tangerine walls, there's something wacky about Belgo Centraal. The menu's main staple is mussels, served by the kilo in a variety of sauces, from classic, uncomplicated marinières (£11.95) to saffron, coriander and cream subtly flavoured with beer (£12.95). The menu also features a good black pudding with caramelised apples and tart sherry vinegar sauce, and wild boar sausages with stoemp and forest fruits (£7.95). Puddings rely heavily on Belgian chocolate – the gooey biscuit and chocolate cheesecake with dark chocolate sauce is a must. And with more than 100 varieties of beer to choose from, you'll certainly need that elevator to come back up for air! *Also Belgo Noord 72 Chalk Farm Rd NW1 ☎ 020 7267 0718 and Belgo Zuid 124 Ladbroke Grove W10 ☎ 020 8982 8400.*

Open: daily noon-3.30pm, Mon-Thurs 5.30pm-12.30am, Fri & Sat 5.30pm-1.30am, Sun 5.30pm-11.30pm; reservations advisable; licensed

starter: £3.95-£6.95
main: £9.95-£19.95
dessert: £3.95-£4.95
Set menu £15.95

AE DC JCB MC V; SW

Map 4 E1
Tube: Leicester Square
Wheelchair access
Nonsmoking tables available
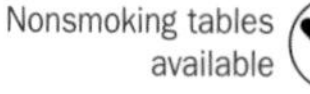

Browns
Traditional English

☎ 020 7497 5050
82-84 St Martin's Lane WC2

No one could ever accuse Browns of being cutting edge, but to those who grew up on a diet of Enid Blyton moving on to Somerset Maugham and Graham Greene, it certainly has appeal. Occupying a former courthouse, Browns' high ceilings with languid fans, potted palms, wicker chairs and a magnolia colour scheme suggest a colonial retreat. What ho! Pot roasted lamb (£9.95), steak and Guinness pie (£8.95), confit of duck (£9.45) and roast on a Sunday: the menu certainly does little to challenge expectations, but it's unfair to call it 'glorified pub grub' when the dishes are so well done. Just stay away from the pastas and all that Frenchy stuff – this is not the place for that. Do try the excellent puddings though, particularly the sticky toffee (£4.25) and bread and butter (£4.25). Sadly, no lashings of ginger beer, but the wine list is decent and there's a fine long bar at which to sit and mourn the setting of the sun on the empire of old. *Also at 47 Maddox St, Mayfair, W1 ☎ 7491 4565 and 114 Draycott Avenue, Chelsea, SW3 ☎ 7584 5359.*

starter: £3.65-£6.50
main: £8.25-£16.95
dessert: £4.25
Pre- & post-theatre set menu £9.95 or £12.95 or Sun lunch £12.95
AE DC JCB MC V

Open: Mon-Thurs noon-midnight, Fri & Sat noon-12.30am, Sun noon-11pm; reservations advisable; licensed

Map 4 D1
Tube: Covent Garden
Smoking throughout

Pavement tables
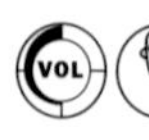

Café des Amis
Modern European

☎ 020 7379 3444
11-14 Hanover Place WC2

Tucked down a narrow alley, sleek Café des Amis calls itself French, but in this age of rampant globalism that description fades right after the French subheadings on the menu. Les Pains includes a nice oily ciabatta (£1.95) and Les Entrées feature a mozzarella salad with rocket and some delectable aubergine croutons (£5.75). Les Petits ou Grands Plats has an array of variably sized dishes such as a rich, three-onion risotto (£5.85/£9.95) and Les Plats' range of meat and fish dishes includes a crispy, yet still moist, roasted halibut (£16.95) atop the increasingly ubiquitous but tasty garlic mash. We left the wine choice to the waiter who rewarded our faith with an excellent tasting and well-priced Spanish Lorinõn Crianza 1996 Rioja (£9.60). The theatre menu served before 7pm and after 10pm is an excellent deal at £10.50/£13.50 for two/three courses. We told the staff we had a 7.30pm curtain and we finished right on time.

starter: £4.75-£8.50
main: £7.95-£16.95
dessert: £4.25-£6.25
Set menu £12.50 or £15, theatre menu £10.50 or £13.50
AE DC JCB MC V

Open: Mon-Sat 11.30am-11.30pm; reservations advisable; licensed

Detroit **☎ 020 7240 2662**
Modern British **35 Earlham St WC2**

Map 4 D1
Tube: Covent Garden
Entertainment: DJ Thurs-Sat

 Smoking throughout

For the hipper London socialites, the basement bar and restaurant Detroit is certainly a place to be seen. The cavernous interior, sandstone walls and circular designs adorning the ceiling are reminiscent of a 1960s sci-fi film set. The bar is the venue's focal point and boasts a superb cocktail list. Off to the side, a small dining area provides the sustenance to soak up any alcohol intake. The generous platter of Scotch smoked salmon with anchovies in oil and vinegar (£5.25) received well-earned praise, and the vegetarian lasagne stefano (£8) was full of interesting flavours – Jerusalem artichokes, aubergines and mushrooms layered between sheets of pasta and topped with freshly grated parmesan. A side portion of fries (£3.50) seemed pricey but when they arrived there were more than enough to feed two hungry people. The service is relaxed and unpretentious – refreshing for this type of bar and restaurant, making it a good place to chill.

Open: Mon-Sat 5pm-midnight; reservations advisable; licensed

starter: £4.50-£5.50
main: £8-£11.50
dessert: £4.50
(£10 min) AE DC MC V; SW

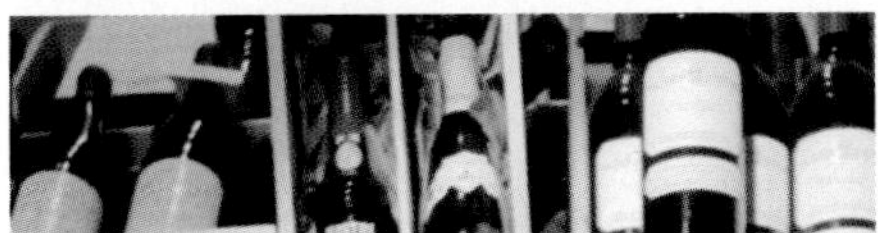

Giovanni's **☎ 020 7240 2877**
Italian **10 Goodwin's Court, 55 St. Martin's Lane WC2**

Map 4 E1
Tube: Leicester Square
Dress code: collared shirt

 Smoking throughout

Hidden away down an 18th-century alleyway, this small Italian restaurant is popular with the stars who appear at Covent Garden and the English National Opera. Roberto Alagna and Angela Gheorghiu, the current darlings of the opera scene, had their first date at Giovanni's and they continue to make frequent visits. The atmosphere of romance is almost palpable – in fact, young Chilean tenor Tito Beltran, a regular, has been known to belt out a few arias for the assembled diners. If he's not in town you can try his favourite dish, rosetta alla Tito Beltran: rolled breast of chicken with spinach, tomato and pecorino (£9.50). The menu has a distinct Sicilian influence, with spicy pasta sauces and wines which are deep, flavourful and pricey, with few choices under £20 a bottle.

Open: Mon-Fri noon-3pm, 6pm-11.30pm, Sat 6pm-11.30pm; reservations essential; licensed

starter: £4.50-£10
main: £8.50-£18
dessert: £5
AE JCB MC V; SW

From Vile to Vogue – A History of British Dining

Prior to the late 1700s, most London menus featured boiled hunks of meat served with boiled potatoes in public taverns and inns. Some would say that such fare remained the norm in London until recently, but in reality London dining has been revolutionised during the past 200 years.

The French, popularly derided by the British through the ages, were revered for their cooking. Having a French chef was considered *de rigueur* at the private dining clubs in Pall Mall during the early 1800s. The middle of the 19th century saw the beginning of the concept of having a meal out as entertainment in itself, rather than just a way to get a meal while away from home. Economic conditions, however, meant that less than 10% of Victorian London could routinely opt to dine out.

If London's first fine food came from the French, later waves of immigrants from Italy and Switzerland helped further diversify British menus. During the 20th century Asian and Indian immigrants brought spices and exotic flavours to London's tables, and there has been an explosive growth of these cuisines with many uniquely British variations.

Dining in London reached a new level of importance with the economic boom of the 1980s. Discussing a meal, talking about the hot new restaurants and which chef had created the best menu became conversational staples to rival football. And everyone was using the expression 'modern British'.

Modern British is a vague term that we all use, though it really tells us little more about what sort of food you can expect than other recent monikers such as 'modern European'.

Typically, modern British food includes traditional staples like smoked fish, shellfish, root vegetables, game and other meats and even common fare like bangers, and combines the ingredients in ways that accentuate their flavour, a concept perhaps missing from old British fare. Influences are drawn from many of the immigrant cultures now established in Britain. Curry, pesto, chilli and coriander are just a few of the many flavours you'll encounter doing their bit to enliven even the simplest meals.

Dishes like wild greens with field mushrooms and a balsamic drizzle; seared scallops with orange-seasoned black pudding; roast pork with chorizo on rosemary mash; and blackberries with lemon curd and shortbread biscuits are the kind of foods served at the so-called gastropubs – those places with talented chefs in the kitchen and daily changing blackboard menus. And, of course, modern British fare is also found at many of the stylish, new restaurants matching fresh surrounds with contemporary menus.

Ryan Ver Berkmoes

COVENT GARDEN

The Ivy

Modern European

☎ **020 7836 4751**
1 West St WC2

Map 1 C6
Tube: Leicester Square

Free valet parking on Sun

Smoking throughout

For the grand central of London luvviedom, The Ivy is surprisingly unpretentious. The snappy service is friendly and unobtrusive and the menu as ready to dabble in world cuisine – such as sashimi (£11.50) or Thai-baked sea bass (£21.75) – as British standards. We pass from the neat bar to the panelled dining room – a place where Celia Johnson might have had a tryst with Trevor Howard in another age – to tuck into starters of crisp asparagus and artichoke, fresh and liberally truffled (£8.75), and a creamy onion and cider soup (£5.75). The shepherd's pie (£10.75) is a classic round of mince and potato in a sea of glistening gravy, while the kedgeree (£10.25) includes mushrooms and salmon and a touch too much curry powder. Round it all off with more comfort foods, like the spot-on sticky toffee pudding (£6.25). Scoring a reservation at one of the seatings is the trickiest part.

Open: Mon-Sat noon-3pm, Sun noon-3.30pm, daily 5.30pm-midnight; reservations essential; licensed

starter: £5.75-£28.50
main: £9-£36.50
dessert: £5.25-£12.50
Set lunch Sat & Sun £16.50

AE DC MC V; SW

The Ivy

Map 4 E2

Tube: Covent Garden

Entertainment: pianist Mon-Sat 8.30pm-midnight

Nonsmoking tables available

Joe Allen

American

☎ 020 7836 0651
13 Exeter St WC2

Back in New York City some years ago, a quiet guy named Joe Allen hit upon a simple but profitable concept: serve solid comfort food in a relaxed brick-walled setting and keep the joint open late. Joe has exported his American concept (and his name) to both Paris and London. The Covent Garden hangout, like its Big Apple namesake, attracts a theatre crowd, along with a smattering of homesick Yanks. The black-bean soup (£4) is always a winner, as are American-style salads like traditional Caesar (£4.50) and daily specials such as roast chicken with coriander (£8). With later hours, a broader menu and more famous names at the tables, the original New York Joe's still has the edge. But if you want a great hamburger (they're not listed on the menu, but they'll make one for you if you ask), or want to celebrate Thanksgiving in London, this is the place to head for.

starter: £4-£10
main: £6.50-£12
dessert: £4.50
AE MC V; SW

Open: Mon-Sat noon-12.45am, Sun 11.30am-11.30pm; reservations essential; licensed

---

Map 4 D2

Tube: Covent Garden

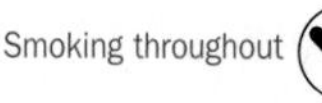

Smoking throughout

Pavement tables

Maggiore's Italian Kitchen

Traditional Italian

☎ 020 7379 9696
17-21 Tavistock St WC2

This rustic-style Italian restaurant in the heart of theatreland has changed owners, and both menu and operation are going to be revamped. It's still busy and popular nonetheless, with entertaining service. Start with a selection of country-style breads and olives to whet the appetite, followed by monkfish baked in foil (£12.95) – as long as you like a lot of lemon and rosemary – or lamb chops with rosemary and garlic (£10.50). The best dish on the menu is the moreish pot-roasted chicken with Italian bacon, mushrooms and red wine (£9.95). Delicious roast potatoes and spinach make a great accompaniment. The lemon tart (£4.95) is excellent, and the zabaione (£4.95) warm and well flavoured, if a little under-whipped.

starter: £3.45-£5.95
main:£7.95-£15.95
dessert: £3.95-£4.95
AE DC MC V; SW

Open: daily noon-4pm, Mon-Sat 5pm-11.30pm, Sun 5pm-10.30pm; reservations advisable (Fri & Sat); licensed

Mon Plaisir

French

☎ **020 7836 7243**
21 Monmouth St WC2

Map 4 D1
Tube: Covent Garden
Dress code: collared shirt

 Smoking throughout

Mon Plaisir was founded by a French couple in 1943 and passed on to waiter Philippe Lhermitte, who still presides with son Alain. The restaurant has three handsome dining areas with exposed brick walls; a more secluded loft accommodates four additional tables. The three-course pre-theatre menu includes a glass of wine and cup of coffee, but the á la carte menu is so good you'll be tempted to stray from the budget path. The grilled fish changes daily, joined by traditional fare such as escargot or veal shank with morel mushrooms (£13.95). Vegetarians are offered daily specials like risotto with goat's cheese and spring onions (£6/£11.50 starter/main). Vin maison (red or white) goes for just £8.95, plus there's a great selection of reds. Mon Plaisir is a rare example of continuity on the London restaurant scene.

Open: Mon-Fri noon-2.30pm, Mon-Sat 5.50pm-11.30pm; reservations essential; licensed

starter: £5.20-£13
main: £11-£16
dessert: £5.50
Set menu £11.95 & £14.95
AE DC MC V

Orso

Italian

☎ **020 7240 5269**
27 Wellington St WC2

Map 4 D2
Tube: Covent Garden

Nonsmoking tables available

Once the darling of media types, Orso now seems to be resting on the rucola (rocket) – not laurel – leaves of its modern-ish Italian cuisine, attracting rather noisy suits and suburbanites who want to catch a West End spectacle (whether on or offstage). The food is reliable and good. Baccalà (£7.50) is a salty and very flavourful preliminary delight perched on an island of bitter spinach in a sea of stewed tomatoes and white beans. The warm wild mushroom and spinach salad (£8) turns out to be Chinese black mushrooms, the grilled scallops (£13.50) in a delightful marriage bed of roasted red peppers and (of course) rocket are excellent, though a tad gritty, and the risotto (£8) is studded with rock prawns and richly flavoured with saffron and yet more rocket.

Open: daily noon-midnight; reservations advisable; licensed

starter: £4.50-£8.50
main: £11.50-£13.50
dessert: £4-£5
Set lunch £15 & £17 or pre-theatre dinner £14.50 & £16.50
AE MC V; SW

The Rock & Sole Plaice

Map 4 E1

Tube: Covent Garden or Leicester Square

Certified organic

Smoking throughout

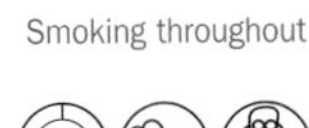

Prospect Grill

American

☎ **020 7379 0412**

4-6 Garrick St WC2

Prospect Grill offers a setting of dark-wood booths separated by frosted glass partitions, an American style menu and quiet jazz on the stereo – in other words, it's a little bit of Manhattan smack in the middle of London. The mid-priced menu offers organic and free-range meat and a range of fresh fish. Regular specials like grilled swordfish steak in coriander salsa (£12.25) and free-range pork chops (£10.25) are delicious, as is the £13.95 organic steak (rump, filet or sirloin, depending on the butcher's supply). Lighter fare tends to be overpriced – a tuna burger at £11.50 seems a bit much for what you get. The only downside to Prospect Grill (for local office workers) is that it tends to be a bit *too* reliable – the menu hasn't varied much in the several visits we've made to this understated restaurant.

starter: £3.95-£6
main: £9.95-£14.95
dessert: £3.95-£4.25

AE MC V; SW

Open: Mon-Fri 11.45am-3.30pm, 5.45pm-midnight, Sat 11.45am-midnight; reservations advisable; licensed

The Rock & Sole Plaice

British/Fish

☎ 020 7836 3785
47 Endell St WC2

Map 4 D1
Tube: Covent Garden

Smoking throughout

Pavement tables

One of London's oldest fish and chip shops (est. 1871), the Rock & Sole Plaice is a Covent Garden institution, enjoying a constant stream of customers at both its takeaway and restaurant. Its reputation for London's finest fish and chips is certainly well deserved. The succulent cod (£6) was crisply battered and garnished with lemon and parsley, while the thick chips (£2) were freshly made and not at all greasy. For the more adventurous fish eater, the range of specialities includes dover sole, scotch salmon and tuna steak. Vegetarians can have a pastie or cream cheese vegetable slice (£4), plus a host of extras like baked beans and of course mushy peas (80p). House wine starts at £7 a bottle and beers at £2. You can sit upstairs and lap up the atmosphere or relax downstairs amid the aquarium mosaics that adorn the walls – wherever, you can be sure of quick, friendly service and top quality fish and chips.

Open: Mon-Sat 11.30am-10.30pm, Sun 11.30am-10pm; reservations accepted; licensed

starter: £1.50
main: £6-£12
dessert: £1.50

MC V; SW

Rules

British

☎ 020 7379 0258
35 Maiden Lane WC2

Map 4 E1
Tube: Covent Garden

Smoking throughout

The dark mahogany booths, heavy curtains, extensive wine list and monied hush of the business clientele all whisper that, yes, you are in 'London's Oldest Restaurant' (established 1798). So it's a shock when your waiter takes out a computer hand pad to electronically send the order to the kitchen; the high prices are another reminder that you're in the 21st century. Still, you are dining in a place that welcomed Charles Dickens and countless other luminaries, and the service is of a high standard. As you would expect from a place steeped in such history, the menu offers traditionally prepared fish (salmon and brill with vermouth sauce, £14.95) along with classic game cookery (foie gras, deer, pigeon, grouse), much of the latter bred especially for the restaurant on Scottish moors. Traditionalists will love it, but sensitive vegetarians should probably keep walking.

Open: Mon-Sat noon-11.30pm, Sun noon-10pm; reservations advisable; licensed

starter: £6-£18
main: £14.95-£26
dessert: £6.50
set menu from 3pm-5pm, Mon-Fri, £19.95

AE DC JCB MC V

COVENT GARDEN

St Tropez

Modern European

☎ 020 7379 3355
1a Shorts Gardens WC2

Map 4 D1
Tube: Covent Garden or Leicester Square
Smoking throughout

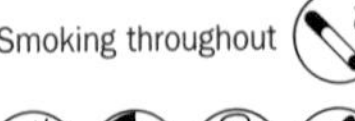

In an area of town packed with overpriced or dodgy dining choices, this Covent Garden newcomer distinguishes itself with well-prepared, fairly priced dishes. The restaurant's name betrays the stylish Mediterranean influence, with options appealing to all tastes. Choices range from a charcuterie platter (£10.95) to roasted monkfish (£11.50) and roasted vegetables on couscous for a very reasonable £6.75. House specialities include a sinful chorizo chicken, the meat and sausage swimming in a blue cheese sauce with mushrooms on roasted vegetable rice (£8.85). But the real bargain is the set meal at £14.95, available both at lunch and dinner. The three-course menu offers fish, fowl and meat choices, and includes a glass of the decent house wine. The restaurant has a distinct 'scene' on weekends, when it is packed with a lively thirty-something crowd, so it might not be for those who want a quiet dining experience.

starter: £3.75-£10.50
main: £5.50-£18.50
dessert: £3.25-£4.95
Set lunch £14.95
AE DC MC V; SW

Open: Tues-Fri noon-3pm, 6pm-11pm, Mon &Sat 6pm-11pm; reservations advisable; licensed

World Food Cafe

International vegetarian

☎ 020 7379 0298
Level 1, 14 Neal's Yard WC2

Map 4 D1
Tube: Covent Garden

The World Food Cafe features vegetarian dishes from India to South America, catering to curious tourists as well as the local community of reiki practitioners, masseurs and 'rolfing' fans (don't ask – it's something to do with 'movement integration'). There's a choice of light meals, including Mexican tortilla, Greek salad and Egyptian felafels (£5.85), or larger dishes such as Turkish meze and Mexican refried beans (£7.85). The latter come in massive serves (with perhaps too much hummus and beans for even the biggest admirers) and everything is served with fresh salad. Desserts might include artfully sculptured mango ice cream with fresh fruit (£3.25) – tasty, but unlikely to satisfy the sweet toothed. At tea time try carrot cake with a pot of tea or coffee (£2.45 after 2.30pm Mon-Fri). Grab a barstool at the bench that surrounds the open-plan kitchen for a view of all the action, or tables by french windows for a bird's-eye view of the village life below – and don't leave without a peek at the famous fishtank toilets.

light meals: £4.25-£5.85
main: £7.85
dessert: £3.25
MC V; SW

Open: Mon-Sat noon-5pm; reservations accepted for groups of 7 or more; BYO (corkage 95p/bottle)

Abu Ali
Lebanese

☎ **020 7724 6338**
136-138 George St W1

Map 2 D2
Tube: Marble Arch

 Smoking throughout

 Pavement tables

There's an Arabic word, *baladi*, which means literally something like 'of the land', though you could translate it more loosely as 'working class'. Well, Abu Ali is baladi through and through. It's the kind of place you find in the backstreets of the low-rent quarter of a Middle Eastern town. In this West End of London incarnation, a sparse interior of chipped formica and peeling linoleum is enlivened by a TV blaring the latest Nile-pop hits and a roaring brazier used to supply glowing coals for the sheesha pipes favoured by the mostly Arab male clientele. Food is basic; there are some 25 streetfood staples as starters, like fuul* (£2.50), torshi (salty-sour pickled vegetables, £2) and fried haloumi (£3), and a refrigerated counter of skewered meats from which to choose for main courses. All the meats are grilled and served with salad. Meal over, this is the place to try a sheesha for yourself; the tobacco is soaked in apple juice, giving it a sweet aftertaste, and though expensive at £5, the smoke lasts a good half-hour.

Open: daily 9.30am-11.30pm; reservations not accepted; unlicensed

starter: £2.50-£3
main: £5-£7
dessert: £2

cash only

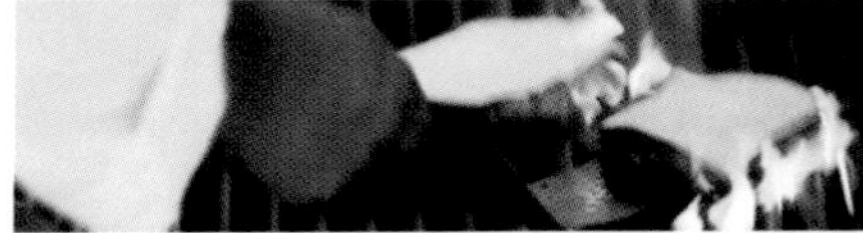

Islamic Halal
Middle Eastern

☎ **020 7724 1909**
228 Edgware Rd W2

Map 2 C1
Tube: Edgware Road

 Smoking throughout

  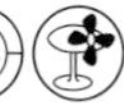

This kebab house is deservedly popular. There's little to distinguish it from the dozen or so other Middle Eastern cafés on Edgware Rd, but Islamic Halal (which claims to be London's first eatery to exclusively serve food entirely under Islamic strictures) is everything you'd want: it's clean, it's cheap, and it's fast. Stick to the basics and you won't go wrong: a starter of baba ghanoush, followed by a lamb pita sandwich and a soft drink will still get you change from a £10 note. The Turkish coffee is super strong and will give you the much-needed kick-start in the middle of a tiring day (make sure they don't serve you the weaker filtered stuff).

Open: daily noon-1am; reservations not accepted; licensed

starter: £2-£4
main: £3-£7
dessert: £3

cash only

EDGWARE RD

Map 2 D2
Tube: Marble Arch

Smoking throughout 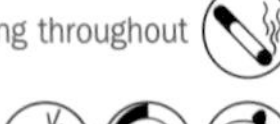

Maroush III
Lebanese

☎ 020 7724 5024
62 Seymour St W1

Maroush is an Arab London institution – its first felafels hit the deep-fryer more than 25 years ago. The original (still largely catering to the oil-rich, with belly dancing and music until 5am and a £48 per head minimum charge) has since been joined by several sister restaurants. Maroush III is for the non-sheikhs among us; it has the same menu as Maroush I but no entertainment overheads and a more western atmosphere. Diners are mainly non-Arab, who order from the menu by numbers rather than trip over the Arabic names. Starters run to an impressive 40 plus, but fatayer bi sabahekh (lemon-soaked spinach pastries, £3.60) was bland and we regretted not going for something more adventurous – the beid ghanam (£4.50), grilled lamb testicles, perhaps? Maroush stuffed lamb (£10.50) was much better, with meat so tender it fell from the bone at the nudge of a knife. Portions leave little room for dessert but a banquet-sized fruit platter and a tray of baklava is served to every table – generous, even allowing for the £2 per person cover charge. *Maroush, 21 Edgware Rd W2 ☎ 020 7723 0773, Maroush II, 38 Beauchamp Place, Knightsbridge SW3 ☎ 020 7581 5434 and Maroush IV, 68 Edgware Rd W2 ☎ 020 7224 9339.*

starter: £3.60-£4.50
main: £10-£18
dessert: £2.50-£5
AE DC JCB MC V

Open: daily noon-11.45pm; reservations advisable (especially Fri & Sat evenings); licensed

---

Map 2 D2
Tube: Marble Arch

Smoking throughout 

Ranoush Juice Bar
Lebanese

☎ 020 7723 5929
43 Edgware Rd W2

One of the best things about the Edgware Rd is that it stays open late. Ranoush makes the perfect pitstop for a post-pub or club binge. Bright and mirrored, the interior is dominated by a large, long counter filled with all the standards (tabouli, hummus, labna, felafel, stuffed vine leaves etc), ordered by the plate (all £3.50). Chicken liver sandwiches (£2.50) are good and the no-fat, garlicky shwarma (lamb or chicken, £3) is some of the best in town. Freshly squeezed juices (£1.25-£1.50) include all the usuals plus more exotic ingredients like grape, mango and melon, or they'll do you a cocktail for £1.75. Most of the trade is takeaway but there are a few tables and counter seats for those who are slowing down.

main: £1.50-£9
cash only

Open: daily 9am-3am; reservations not accepted; unlicensed

On Your Plate **Middle Eastern**

Granted, if you look in your *A-Z*, the Edgware Rd and neighbouring Bayswater may appear to be in London, but the reality is that they are in fact two far-flung suburbs of Beirut and Cairo. If you want to pick up your copy of the Arabic daily *Al Ahram*, cash a cheque at the Bank of Kuwait or catch Egyptian league football on TV in a boisterous smoke-filled cafe, then this is where you come. It's an insular world and one little visited by most Londoners. But that is changing. In recent times Maghrebi and Middle Eastern and all things Asian have become hip. London's club scene has caught on to the sound of the tabla, and ethnic-techno diva Natacha Atlas, of Egyptian-Moroccan roots, is flavour of the moment with the cutting-edge crowd. Along with the sounds come the tastes – it may owe more to hype and celebrity diners than its poor-show North African cuisine but **Momo** is still the place everyone wants to be. And now there's **Ozer**, the stylish, media-friendly Turkish haute-cuisine joint recently opened in the West End.

With couscous and kebabs in the spotlight, maybe more Londoners will now discover what a wealth of excellence their city possesses when it comes to Middle Eastern dining. Restaurants like **Al Waha** and **Fairuz** are serving Lebanese cuisine that is on a par with the best that London's Indian, Thai or Japanese establishments have to offer. London may lack the Mediterranean sun but there are still few more pleasurable dining experiences than to fill a table with a spread of meze and languorously dip and pick while emptying a bottle of arak. Anyone prepared to travel north-east to Dalston can sample some of the best Turkish cooking north of the Black Sea – the premises themselves are on the basic side and vegetarians don't get much of a look in, but for top-quality charcoal-grilled meat, places like **Mangal** and **Istanbul Iskembecisi** are a revelation. The Iranians also do wonders with kebabs, marinating the meat, pounding it flat and slow-grilling it over an open flame. Plenty of fresh herbs like parsley, tarragon and mint, and spices like sumac, add zest and flavouring.

With the current fad we can probably expect to see the opening of more Middle Eastern restaurants in London – that will be welcome. But they will have to be good to match what we already have.

Andrew Humphreys

A freelance travel writer specialising in the Middle East, Andrew lived and worked in Egypt for several years. He has authored or co-authored Lonely Planet guides to Cairo, Egypt, Israel, Jerusalem, the Middle East and Syria.

Chutneys

Indian vegetarian

☎ 020 7388 0604
124 Drummond St NW1

Map 5 A1
Tube/rail: Euston
No smoking at lunch, nonsmoking tables available at dinner

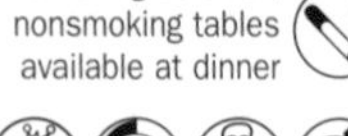

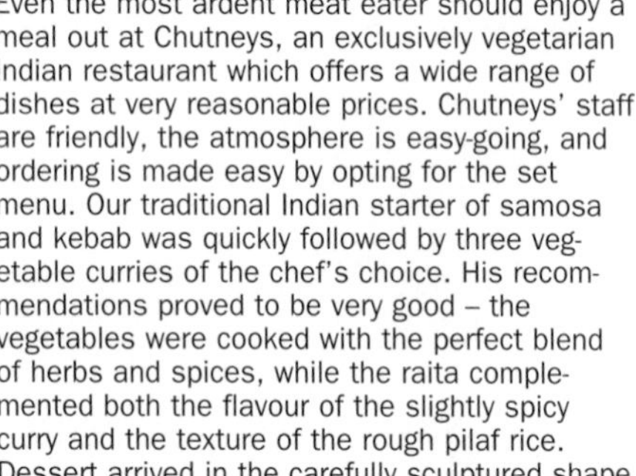

Even the most ardent meat eater should enjoy a meal out at Chutneys, an exclusively vegetarian Indian restaurant which offers a wide range of dishes at very reasonable prices. Chutneys' staff are friendly, the atmosphere is easy-going, and ordering is made easy by opting for the set menu. Our traditional Indian starter of samosa and kebab was quickly followed by three vegetable curries of the chef's choice. His recommendations proved to be very good – the vegetables were cooked with the perfect blend of herbs and spices, while the raita complemented both the flavour of the slightly spicy curry and the texture of the rough pilaf rice. Dessert arrived in the carefully sculptured shape of pistachio kulfi, providing an entertaining finish to a tasty and interesting meal.

starter: £2.30-£2.50
main: £4.50-£10
dessert: £1.60-£1.80
Set menu £9.95
MC V

Open: Mon-Sat noon-2.45pm, 6pm-11.30pm, Sun noon-10.30pm; reservations advisable; licensed

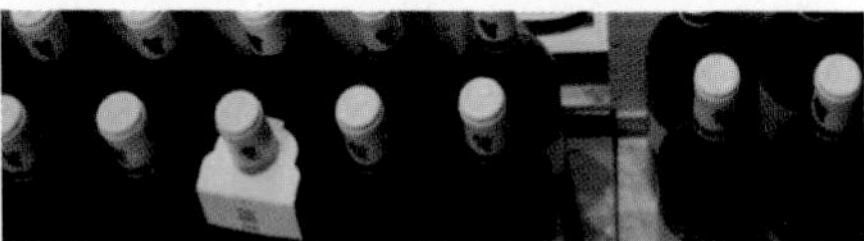

Diwana Bhel Poori House

Indian vegetarian

☎ 020 7387 5556
121-123 Drummond St NW1

Map 5 A1
Tube/rail: Euston
Nonsmoking tables available

Diwana's reputation as top dog among the doyens of Drummond St has been formed over years of dishing up superb vegetarian food. Tear into the enormous lentil and rice deluxe dosa (£4.60) and you'll see why: the spiced potato filling with coconut chutney and hot lentil and vegetable sambhar is well worth savouring. The chewy cheese and vegetable kofta malai (£4.95) offers a bit more substance and has a rich but mild sauce. For the really ravenous, the Diwana thali (£6.20) is a full meal, comprising a range of vegetable dishes and lentil dhal, as well as rice, breads, a starter and shrikhand – a syrupy dessert of cheese, spices and sugar. If the heat leaves your tongue tingling try a sweet yoghurt lassi (£1.50), the best oral fire extinguisher this side of Bombay (or Brick Lane, at least).

starter: £2.30-£2.50
main: £4.60-£6.20
dessert: £1.50-£1.70
Chef's special £4.80 or lunch buffet £4.50
AE DC MC V; SW

Open: daily noon-midnight; reservations accepted Tues-Thurs only; BYO (no corkage)

Efes I

Turkish

☎ 020 7636 1953
80-82 Great Titchfield St W1

Map 5 B1
Tube: Great Portland St

 Smoking throughout

 Pavement tables

A reputation garnered over 25 years as one of London's best Turkish grills means that the banquet-style rows of tables in Efes' deceptively vast interior are always kept busy. Favoured by large parties and groups, shared set meals are popular and keep the table filled with a succession of mixed meze, salads, mixed grill, a fruit platter, baklava and coffee, all for £17 per head. Ordered off the menu, starters are disappointing and we'd recommend giving the meze a miss and heading straight for the grills. Portions are huge and the beautifully smoky meat comes with all the trimmings. Yogurtlu kebab (£7.20), for example, was heaped pieces of lamb, chicken, kofta and doner kebab, plus onion and tomato in a rich yoghurt sauce. This is heavy dining. Wash it down with Efes beer – not actually the restaurant's own brand but the most popular brew in Turkey – and you may just be able to squeeze in one of the gorgeous confections of filo pastry, almonds and syrup. *Also Efes II 175-177 Great Portland St W1 ☎ 020 7436 0600.*

Open: Mon-Sat noon-11.30pm; reservations accepted; licensed

starter: £3.50-£3.95
main: £6.20-£11
dessert: £1.75-£2
Set menu £16 or £17/ person (min 2 people)

AE DC JCB MC V

Ikkyu

Japanese

☎ 020 7636 9280
67a Tottenham Court Rd W1

Map 5 B2
Tube: Goodge St

  No smoking at the counter

An unobtrusive doorway on Tottenham Court Rd leads to a convivial robatayaki* basement restaurant that could be a stone's throw from Tokyo's Ginza. It's a popular place and deservedly so. After choosing either a counter seat – from where you can view the chefs busily at work – or one of the regular tables, consider the extensive menu's wide range of sushi, sashimi and yakitori (sticks of grilled chicken, vegetables or fish). We went for the tuna roll and New York roll sushi (£2.80), with the rice and sesame seeds on the outside, the seaweed and salmon on the inside. As with the crispy-battered tempura served atop rice in a lacquered box (£6) and the healthy chunk of grilled salmon (£6.80), both presentation and quality were excellent. For a bit of fun, try the DIY hand-roll sushi set (£35), enough fish, vegetables, sheets of dried seaweed and sushi rice for three people. Otherwise, let the experts prepare some of the best-value Japanese food you'll find in London.

Open: Mon-Fri noon-2.30pm, 6pm-10.30pm, Sun 6pm-10pm; reservations advisable (especially weekends); licensed

starter: £1.10-£4.50
main: £3.10-£24.50
dessert: £2.50-£3.50
Set menu £6.50-£7.50

AE DC JCB MC V

noho

Modern Pan-Asian

☎ **020 7636 4445**
32 Charlotte St W1

Map 5 B2
Tube: Goodge St
Wheelchair access

Smoking throughout 

Pavement tables

Noho is a cool oasis in Media Land's hot-to-trot streets: wooden floors, gold suede chairs and banquettes, terracotta walls, ambient music and menus ready and waiting on the tables. The menu is more than manageable, even though it spans Thai, Indonesian and Malay cuisine. The 'noho mix' (£8.50) for two is a great way to sample nearly all the starter dishes: steamed dumplings, chicken satay, spring rolls, prawns and zesty Thai fish cakes. Our portions of seafood rice noodles and stir-fried chicken with cashew nuts and chilli (£5.25) were generous, but the hidden treasure was the santan salad (£3.50) of cucumber, pineapple, red onion, radish, chilli and coconut milk. It looked like fruit and vegetables covered in pink milk, but the contrasting tastes and textures were fabulous. The 'outros' (desserts) offered a delicate exit – rambutans stuffed with pineapple segments (£2.75), and the unobtrusive service complemented the whole evening. Smooth operators.

starter: £4-£9.50
main: £5-£7.95
dessert: £2.75-£2.95

AE DC JCB MC V; SW

Open: daily noon-11.30pm; reservations essential; licensed

Pied à Terre

Contemporary French

☎ **020 7636 1178**
34 Charlotte St W1

Map 5 B2
Tube: Goodge Street or Tottenham Court Road

Smoking throughout

Despite losing one of its Michelin stars (it now has one), Pied à Terre still scales heights of culinary ecstasy that other restaurants only dream about. An audacious platter of amuse-gueule – including a caramelised quail's egg and a shot glass of carrot purée with a frothy anise foam – set the tone for a spectacular meal. The boudin* of guinea fowl with french beans, drizzled in cep vinaigrette and topped with a nob of foie gras, is a triumph of taste and texture. The pot-au-feu of lamb, which came with a spoon to sup up all the good juices, is an event in itself. We're almost too delirious with the memory of it all to mention the succulent venison with juniper, never mind the raspberry sablé or the exquisite petits fours. The restaurant disappoints in its plain and windowless décor and a set up so cramped that it's a miracle the waiters keep so cheery. The thing is, if we're going to squeal with delight, we want to do so without alarming our fellow diners.

Set lunch £19.50 or
set dinner £39.50
dessert: lunch £3.50,
dinner £10.50

AE DC JCB MC V; SW

Open: Mon-Fri 12.15pm-2.15pm (last orders) Mon-Sat 7pm-10.45pm (last orders); reservations advisable; licensed & BYO (corkage £25/bottle)

Ragam — ☎ 020 7636 9098
South Indian — **57 Cleveland St W1**

Map 5 B1
Tube: Goodge St

 Smoking throughout

This outwardly nondescript place (complete with standard curry-house furniture and prints) is nonetheless remarkable and, indeed, praised by various gastronomic luminaries for its exceptional yet cheap south Indian specialities. Idlis (£3.50), steamed rice dumplings, are best dunked in a hot, thin sambhar – lentil and vegetable soup – and coconut chutney, as are the crisp masala vadai (£2), fried, chilli-tinged gram flour and onion doughnuts. A range of dosas (filled rice and lentil-flour pancakes) and other south Indian staples complete the snack menu, familiar dishes such as chicken dansak (sweet and sour chicken and lentil curry, £4.50) and prawn vindaloo (very hot, cooked with a vinegar marinade, £4.50). Smiling and efficient service, and the provision of regulation Kingfisher and Cobra beers, round off Ragam's deserved reputation as a Fitzrovia institution.

Open: daily noon-3pm, Sat-Wed 6pm-10.30pm, Thurs & Fri 6pm-11pm; reservations advisable (Fri & Sat); licensed

starter: £1.50-£4.50
main: £2.95-£7.95
dessert: £1.95-£2.50
AE MC V

Rasa Samudra — ☎ 020 7637 0222
Indian — **5 Charlotte St W1**

Map 5 B2
Tube: Goodge St

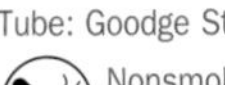 Nonsmoking tables available

Owned by the same folks behind the two notable Rasa restaurants, Rasa Samudra specialises in the complex vegetarian and fish cooking from the coastal Kerala region of south-west India. Starters include a mellow banana boli (£4.25) which, despite the name, uses the banana's overgrown cousin the plantain, dipped in spices and then fried. The accompanying ginger peanut sauce is perfect. Samudra rasam (£4.95), a shellfish soup in a rice base, is tangy and complex. There's a long list of vegetarian curries; we jumped in for the veluthulli curry (£6.25), which was hot and spicy and warmed every part of the throat going down. There was more spice to come with the koyilandu konju masala (£12.95) – juicy prawns in a thick sauce that hinted of ginger. Rasa Samudra is easily in the top tier of London's Indian restaurants, and the Kerala-inspired décor is as tasteful as the food. *Also Rasa W1 6 Dering St, W1 ☎ 7629 1346, Rasa 55 Stoke Newington Church St, N16, ☎ 7249 0344.*

Open: Mon-Sat noon-3pm, 6pm-11pm; reservations advisable; licensed

starter: £4.25-£7.50
main: £8-£15
dessert: £2.50-£3.50
Set menu £22.50 or £30
AE DC MC V; SW

HOLBORN

Map 4 D3
Tube: Holborn

Smoking throughout

Cooper's

Modern British

☎ 020 7831 6211
49a Lincoln's Inn Fields WC2

Tucked away near the Olde Curiosity Shoppe, north of the Royal Courts of Justice, Cooper's is the haunt of legal eagles during the day and romantics at night. The dining room has warm terracotta and mahogany tones, white linen tablecloths and a relaxed ambience. The menu changes daily, capitalising on market supplies of fresh produce. Our smoked salmon with fiery horseradish cream and griddled potatoes (£7.95) was full of flavour, but although the chorizo, red peppers and poached egg salad (£5.95) had plenty of colour, it lacked spice. The medium-rare fillet of Scotch beef with potatoes and roasted shallots (£14.50) was grilled to perfection, and our seared salmon with courgettes, potatoes and coral butter (£9.50) was moist and tender. The cheeseboard (£5) offered a selection of 14 high-quality French cheeses served with crunchy celery and water biscuits.

starter: £3.50-£7.95
main: £8.50-£14.75
dessert: £4.25-£5
AE MC V; SW

Open: Mon-Fri noon-3pm, 5.30pm-10.30pm; reservations advisable; licensed

---

Map 4 C1
Tube: Holborn

Mandeer

Indian/Vegetarian

☎ 020 7242 6202
8 Bloomsbury Way WC1

Established in 1960, Mandeer claims to be the only Ayurvedic restaurant in the world. The tasty and balanced food is prepared according to the principles of Ayurveda, an ancient Indian holistic tradition of medicine. Meat, fish, preservatives and colourings are excluded, and many dishes are vegan. Everything we sampled in our thali shree and thali Mandeer deluxe was light in both texture and flavour. No heady spice concoctions here: the hottest item, a tangy yoghurt and chickpea soup, would have been described as mild on most Indian menus. Health benefits apart, Mandeer is a great place to come for an intimate chat; you couldn't wish for a more restful setting, with low-hanging copper lanterns, Hindu deities, golden tables and classical Indian music playing in the background.

starter: £2.60-£5.50
main: £3.75-£5.85
dessert: £2.25-£2.50
Thalis £9.25-£14.75 or lunchtime buffet £3.90
AE DC JCB MC V; SW

Open: Mon-Sat noon-3pm, 5pm-10pm; reservations advisable; licensed & BYO (corkage £2/bottle)

Na Zdrowie

Polish

☎ 020 7831 9679
11 Little Turnstile WC1

Map 4 C2
Tube: Holborn

 Smoking throughout

Hidden away in a tiny lane at the back of Holborn tube station, Na Zdrowie is first and foremost a drinking haunt, but one with an exceptionally varied food menu. The selection of predominantly Polish dishes changes daily, though you'll always find firm favourites such as platcki (£3.95) – fluffy potato fritters served with sour cream – and kielbasa (£4.95) – spicy, greasy and completely delicious pan-fried sausage. For the more diet-conscious there's a choice of salads (£3.50) or the option of beetroot soup (£2). It's relatively easy to find a table until 6pm on a weekday, but any later and the post-work crowd starts pouring in, and drinking takes precedence over food. If the tables are full, resign yourself to sampling the liquid menu: with 40 Polish vodkas (£1.50-£2.50 per shot) and seven Polish beers to choose from, it's not too much of a hardship.

Open: Mon-Fri noon-9pm, Sat 6pm-9pm; reservations not accepted; licensed

main: £1.95-£5.95
dessert: £2.50-£2.75
MC V; SW

World Food Cafe (p 36)

Map 1 C6
Tube: Leicester Square
Separate smoke-free dining available

Tokyo Diner
Japanese

☎ 020 7287 8777
2 Newport Place WC2

If the test of a good Japanese restaurant is that it pulls in the native crowd, then Tokyo Diner passes with flying colours. But the beauty of this cheap and cheerful place is that you don't need to know a thing about Japanese cuisine to enjoy what it offers, thanks to a menu that gives the lowdown on everything from how best to slurp noodles to the addictive nature of 'bland' (it's their word) Japanese curry. The steaming bowls of soba or udon noodles (£4.90) can always be relied on, as can the nigiri sushi platter (£7.50), with very generous slices of fish. We also tried the tasty chicken kara fry bento (£11.50), one of nine traditional set meals in a lacquered box. Nice touches include Japanese newspapers hanging by the till, a student special lunch deal for £3.50 (2.30pm-5.30pm) and a no-tipping policy.

starter: 60p-£3.50
main: £3.90-£12.90
Bento box set meals £8.30-£12.90
JCB MC V; SW

Open: daily noon-midnight; reservations not accepted; licensed

Map 1 D5
Tube: Leicester Square
Smoking throughout

Woodlands
South Indian vegetarian

☎ 020 7839 7258
37 Panton St SW1

If you love Indian food, but you're bored by the usual offerings, Woodlands will give your taste-buds a treat. It's all freshly made, with no sign of the bog-standard sauces you get at some less-upmarket establishments. With clean, modern décor and abstract paintings on the walls, it has a band of loyal followers – in fact the main problem is resisting complete gluttony. Masala dosa – a pancake filled with spiced peas and potatoes – was filling but not stodgy. Delhi royal thali (£11.95) was a huge affair – a pile of fluffy rice and rotis surrounded by dhal, channa masala, dahi vada, mutter paneer in a rich tomato gravy, vegetable korma and dessert. Bottled beers (£2.25) were perfectly chilled, and a sweet lassi tempered spices perfectly. Service is attentive and swift, and good advice was given when requested. The only gripe was that the service charge was hidden in the middle of the bill, so watch out for it if you don't want to pay twice!

starter: £2.95-£4.25
main: £4.50-£13.25
dessert: £2.75
Lunch buffet Mon-Fri £5.99
AE DC MC V; SW

Open: daily noon-2.30pm, Mon-Sat 5.30pm-10.30pm, Sun 6pm-10.30pm; reservations advisable; licensed

LEICESTER SQUARE

Zipangu

Japanese

☎ 020 7437 5042
8 Little Newport St WC2

Map 1 C6

Tube: Leicester Square

 Smoking throughout

Amid the gleaming chrome and glass pleasure palaces of modern Leicester Square, Zipangu harks back to the district's sleazier era, with its stained carpets, cosy corners and plastic tartan tablecloths. There's just enough Asian whatnots spread around the restaurant's three levels to persuade you that they really do serve Japanese food here, even if, as when we visited, the young English waitress drew a blank when asked for wasabi. All fears evaporated when the food arrived, as the chef's 40 years of experience showed through in well-executed, nicely presented classic Japanese dishes such as agedashi-dofu, lightly fried cubes of tofu topped with grated radish and spring onions. The house speciality is that old standard chicken teriyaki (£4.50); more adventurous diners should sample natto* (£2.50), sticky, stringy fermented soybeans.

Open: Mon-Sat noon-11.30pm, Sun noon-10.30pm; reservations not accepted on Sat; licensed

starter: 90p-£3.80
main: £3.90-£5.50
dessert: £2.50
Set menu £5-£12 or course menu £9-£14

MC V; SW

MARBLE ARCH

MARBLE ARCH

La Porte des Indes

Indian

☎ 020 7224 0055
32 Bryanston St W1

Map 2 D3

Tube: Marble Arch

Entertainment: Live jazz during Sun brunch

  Smoking throughout

The opulent interiors of La Porte des Indes ('gateway to India') are spectacular – a grand marble staircase, 40-foot waterfall, exotic fresh flowers and towering palm trees. Start in the Jungle Bar, based on the Raffles Hotel in Singapore, where tigers stare through the tropical foliage on the walls.The menu draws much of its inspiration from the French/Creole cuisine of Pondicherry. The poulet rouge (£10.75) is a mild dish of grilled shredded chicken served in yoghurt and red spices with a buttery sauce. The Parsee fish (£7.90), sole fillets in a mint and coriander chutney and steamed in banana leaves, is an aromatic delicacy. The separate vegetarian menu features unusual dishes such as crisp, fried lotus roots tossed with green chillies (£11). But our favourite is the rougail d'aubergine (£9.50), fleshy aubergine brought to life with chilli, ginger and zesty lime.

Open: Mon-Fri noon-2.30pm, Mon-Sat 7pm-midnight, Sun noon-3pm, 6pm-10.30pm; reservations advisable; licensed & BYO (corkage £2.50/bottle)

starter: £4.50-£9.90
main:£9.80-£19.20
dessert: £3.50-£6.50
Dinner maison £31 & £33, royal vegetarian £29 & £31, Mon-Fri lunch buffet £16.75 or Sunday brunch £17.50

AE DC JCB MC V; SW

Ali Baba

Egyptian

☎ 020 7723 7474
32 Ivor Place NW1

Map 2 B2
Tube: Baker St

Smoking throughout

Pavement tables

Fronted by a takeaway section, the dining area resembles a family parlour; a wall unit supports a massive TV tuned to Egyptian soaps, a vacuum cleaner stands in the corner and mama is shouting down the phone to some distant relative in Cairo. The food, though basic, is good if ordered wisely; stick to the Egyptian dishes. Main courses are disappointing – over-parsleyed kofta (£6) and shish kebab (£6) were dry, while the tomato sauce with the bamiya (okra, £5) was a bit too over-powering. But the Egyptian streetfood staple of fuul* (£2.50) was excellently done, the mashed black-eye beans nicely flavoured with garlic, lemon and cumin. The felafel (£2.50) was fresh, and mincemeat and rice-stuffed vine leaves (£4) were also good. Ali Baba is possibly the only place in London serving koshari (£4), a starchy but satisfying mix of black lentils, rice, macaroni and fried onions with hot sauce. Order for the table to share and everyone should go away happy.

starter: £2-£5.50
main: £5-£7
dessert: £2-£2.50
cash and cheque only

Open: daily noon-11.30pm; reservations accepted; BYO (no corkage)

The Ard Ri Dining Room

Irish

☎ 020 7935 9311
Level 1, The O'Conor Don, 88 Marylebone Lane W1

Map 2 C5
Tube: Baker St or Bond Street

Smoking throughout
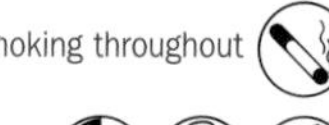

The Ard Ri Dining Room is situated on the 1st floor of the O'Conor Don, an established Irish pub that avoids the commercialism of today's ever-increasing chain establishments. The restaurant is a relatively small room, although high ceilings provide a spacious feel. A good pint of Guinness was our preparation before approaching the Irish cuisine on offer, this being a rare culinary opportunity to sample a main ingredient of your meal beforehand. The caesar salad with crispy bacon (£5.50) was a palatable starter, and a good base for the beef and Guinness casserole with mashed potato (£9) – a very tasty, uncomplicated main with an appreciated home-cooked feel. Or go for the bowl of steamed Irish mussels (£8.80), complemented by a plate of chips. For dessert, be tempted by the warm Guinness cake.

starter: £3.50-£6.75
main: £8.20-£16.95
dessert: £2.75-£4.95
AE MC V; SW

Open: Mon-Fri noon-2.30pm, 6pm-10pm; reservations advisable; licensed

Defune

Japanese

☎ **020 7935 8311**
61 Blandford St W1

Map 2 C4

Tube: Baker Street or Bond Street

 Smoking throughout

This small, authentic Japanese restaurant has a downstairs sushi bar and a discreet upstairs dining room. The best reason for coming here is the chefs' expert preparation of fresh fish, so bag a seat at the sushi counter. A photo menu simplifies ordering and tempts you to be adventurous by describing some of the seasonal options as 'challenging' – for example, uni (sea urchin), with its butterscotch-coloured, brains-textured flesh. The individual sushi are served directly onto the counter, without a plate, with a generous mound of gari. Don't be afraid to use your fingers – this is why the waitress brings a finger towel in a tiny wicker basket. Best value are the platters of nigiri sushi (£14.50), including eight different types of sushi, or sashimi (£17). Set lunches can include tempura, yakitori, salads and piping-hot agedashi dofu. Try the cook-at-the-table beef shabu-shabu or sukiyaki (£19.80), with enough meat for two.

Open: Mon-Sat noon-2.30pm, 6pm-10.30pm; reservations advisable (especially evenings); licensed

starter: £2.70-£12
main: £6.20-£19.80
dessert: £3.40
Set lunch £12.50-£15

AE DC JCB MC V; SW

Fairuz

Lebanese

☎ **020 7486 8108**
3 Blandford St W1

Map 2 C4

Tube: Bond St

 Smoking throughout

Elegant and sophisticated with a voice once described as silk and fire, Fairuz is Lebanon's most famous chanteuse. She's a class act, and so is this restaurant that bears her name. Large glass windows create a light and airy yet intimate interior, made even more pleasant by friendly and welcoming service from the Lebanese staff. The menu follows the usual pattern of hot and cold meze and charcoal grills, but there are also a couple of fishy dishes and some vegetarian mains, including baked aubergine and a daily special of okra stew (both £8.95). Everything we tried was fresh and very delicious, with even the most basic dishes like hummus (£3) and labna* (£3.50) enlivened with olive oil, pine nuts, herbs and spices. Best of all was another Fairuz speciality, farrouj musakkhan (£11.95) – tender marinated chicken smothered in fried onions, baked in a parcel of flat bread. Dessert would seem to be unnecessary but the meal is rounded off by complementary fruit and baklava.

Open: Mon-Thurs noon-11pm, Fri &Sat noon-11.30pm, Sun noon-10pm; reservations accepted; licensed

starter: £3-£4.75
main: £8.95-£14.50
dessert: £3.50
Meze £14.95/person (min 2 people) or set menu £24.95/person (min 2 people)

AE DC MC V; SW

MARYLEBONE

La Spighetta

Italian

☎ 020 7486 7340
43 Blandford St W1

Map 2 C4
Tube: Baker Street
Nonsmoking tables available

Like Soho's La Spiga, La Spighetta is a cheaper offshoot of Zafferano, the highly regarded modern Italian restaurant in Knightsbridge. This is the best value and least formal of the trio, discreet yet stylish with small tables and terracotta floors. La Spighetta fits the bill for many occasions: a date, a business lunch or a get-together with friends. You'd be hard pressed to find better Italian fare anywhere in central London at these prices. Starters are particularly good – the tuna carpaccio (£6) is delicately textured with a sharp lemony tang, and the grilled goat's cheese served on a bed of cardoon (a celery-like vegetable) (£5) is subtly sweet. The tagliolini in a tomato and crab sauce (£7.50) and pizza with spicy salami (£7) are of trattoria quality but lack the finesse of the starters. To finish, the espresso was gratifyingly short and strong.

starter: £3-£7
main: £6.50-£11
dessert: £5

AE DC JCB MC V; SW

Open: daily noon-2.30pm, Mon-Fri 6.30pm-10.30pm, Sat & Sun 6.30pm-11pm; reservations advisable (especially Thurs-Sat); licensed

Reuben's

Kosher

☎ 020 7486 0035
79 Baker St W1

Map 2 C3
Tube: Baker St
Nonsmoking tables available

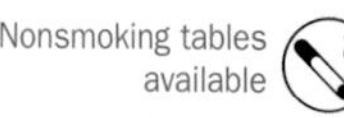

Pavement tables

The unfussily decorated basement restaurant at Reuben's is an incredibly popular place to go for family celebrations and special occasions. The service is friendly, particularly so if you're one of the many regulars. All the old favourites are on the menu, and there's absolutely no skimping on the portions. The food is excellent quality, but don't expect any surprises. The menu promises that 'you'll never want chopped liver again' but, despite this doom-laden prophecy, it was delicious: rich and oniony (£4.25). The chicken soup (£3.25) was no disappointment either. Main courses were a bit dull. However, the steak à la Reuben's (£15.95), with its sweet brandy sauce, is tender and tasty. Desserts are a mixed bunch: the apple strudel (£2.45) is rich with cinnamon and fruit, but the chocolate mousse (£2.95) is heavy on the chocolate and light on the mousse. If you're not after a meal of these proportions, there's a street-level diner (with wheelchair access) where you can get a quick bite.

starter: £2.95-£5.95
main: £8.95-£18.95
dessert: £2.25-£4.75

MC V

Open: Mon-Fri noon-3pm, Mon-Thurs 5pm-10pm, Sun 11am-10pm; reservations advisable; licensed

Chez Nico

Classical French

☎ 020 7409 1290
90 Park Lane W1

Map 2 E4
Tube: Hyde Park Corner

 Smoking throughout

At Chez Nico you instantly sense the wealth in the sumptuous décor, the well-heeled clientele (some of whom are so doddery we fear they might not make it through to brandy and cigars), and the superfluity of staff whisking silver trays hither and thither. It's easy to see why starters, such as the exemplary parmesan risotto (£10), are firm fixtures on the menu. We're more than happy with the silky chicken liver parfait (£11), teamed with neat dollops of tart grape chutney, and the iceberg white fillet of cod (£9.50), on a bed of upmarket puréed peas, works a treat. Chez Nico might be famous for its classical French cuisine but, cream-heavy desserts apart, many dishes have a lightness of touch that's very appealing, especially if you want to go the full three courses at dinner for £48. Given the cooking's quality, the final bill is good value and causes us to overlook the ailing flowering plant on the table and, at times, over-intrusive service.

Mon-Fri noon-2pm, Mon-Sat 7pm-11pm; reservations advisable (essential for dinner); licensed

starter: £7-£22
main: £9-£24
dessert: £8
Set dinner £48 or gastronomic menu £62-£75

AE DC MC V

Condotti

Italian

☎ 020 7499 1308
4 Mill St W1

Map 1 C1
Tube: Oxford Circus

 Smoking throughout

An Italian restaurant of the Pizza Express ilk, Condotti is a pleasant, albeit unexciting, venue for a meal out in Mayfair. Entry through a dark glass door makes you wonder what you will find on the other side, but don't get too excited as this restaurant doesn't exactly buzz with atmosphere. It is spacious and streamlined – even verging on the clinical – but the staff are friendly and efficient, and the pizzas are well worth the visit. The garlic bread (£1.95) was literally dripping in garlic butter, and the American pizza (£7.75) was piled high with pepperoni. While the La Reine (£7.90) gave only a cursory nod to olives (three!), it made up for it with a generous helping of cheese. A bottle of house red (£10.75) was finished off at our leisure and a reasonable bill sent us happily on our way. The final verdict? This place may lack spark but for great pizza, good wine and ease of chat, you can't go far wrong.

Open: Mon-Sat noon-midnight; reservations advisable; licensed

starter: £1.95-£9.95
main: £6.50-£8.10
dessert: £2.75-£4.25

AE DC JCB MC V; SW

Map 2 E5

Tube: Green Park

Dress code: jacket & tie

Smoking throughout

The Connaught

Classical French/Traditional British

☎ 020 7499 7070
16 Carlos Place W1

The Connaught, with its hushed mahogany-panelled dining room and tail-coated waiters, is caught in a glorious time warp. Grand Gallic fare and traditional British cooking (such as steak and kidney pie) sum up the menu and dishes are delivered with such a sense of occasion that in a less formal establishment they would be greeted with a round of applause. We chose the excellent smoked trout, served with a good squeeze of lemon and a dollop of horseradish) and a dish of warm artichoke and asparagus with cheese for starters. The rendez-vous du pecheur, a sumptuous medley of fish and seafood served with a mushroomy sauce, and filet mignon followed. What really tickled us, however, was when a French waiter wheeled up the dessert trolley and announced that among other offerings, 'we have zee roly-poly pudding'. It was a tough choice, but we finally opted for a sublime sherry trifle that had just the right amount of boozy sponge, gooey custard and fruit and two deliciously thick inches of whipped cream.

starter: £8.50-£32
main: £22-£45
dessert: £6.60-£12
Set lunch £28.50, set Sun lunch £35 or set dinner £58

AE DC MC V; SW

Open: daily 7.30am-10am, 12.30pm-2.30pm (last orders), 6.30pm-10.45pm (last orders); reservations advisable (essential Sat & Sun); licensed

Dover Street Restaurant & Bar

French/Mediterranean

☎ 020 7629 9813
8-10 Dover St W1

Dover Street Restaurant & Bar has been a jazz venue for over 20 years, and following a recent refurbishment is now London's biggest jazz restaurant. The atmosphere is buzzing, even on a Monday night, and the restaurant attracts big names in jazz, soul and swing. Dinner prices include an entertainment cover charge, and for once the menu is on par with the show. The crowd is a mix of foot-tapping jazz buffs and people simply enjoying a good night out, attentively waited on by the well-informed, dinner-suited staff. The smoked haddock and poached egg with a creamy chive sauce (£5.50) reminds you how lavish haddock can be. Although the venison with oyster mushrooms looked tempting, we chose the best end of roast lamb (£14.95) – the meat was crusted with herbs and mustard, and the aubergine caviar was juicy. The wine list is well structured and ranges from the house wine for £12.50 to a bottle of Krug Grande Cuvée champagne for £120.

Open: Mon-Fri noon-3.30pm, Mon-Thurs 5.30pm-3am, Fri & Sat 7pm-3am; reservations advisable; licensed

Map 1 E1
Tube: Green Park
Entertainment: live music, DJ & dancing nightly, Mon: jazz, Tues: Latin, Wed-Sat: jazz, rhythm & blues or soul

 Smoking throughout

starter: £4.95-£8.95
main: £9.95-£15.95
dessert: £4.50
Set lunch £6, £8 or £10, set dinner Mon-Tues £17.95, Wed & Thurs £22.95 or Fri & Sat £25.95
AE DC MC V; SW

L'Autre

Polish/Mexican

☎ 020 7499 4680
5b Shepherd St W1

How this small restaurant came to serve dishes as incongruous as borscht and burritos is a tale too complex to tell here, but both the food and the atmosphere in this charming mock-Tudor corner of Mayfair work very well together. Salt herring in a lightly soured cream with apple and dill (£3.50) shows how flavours can blend on a palate rather than do battle, and the refreshingly tangy borscht with mushroom-filled piroshki (£2.95) is as Polish as the polka. Beneath the taut skin of the kielbasa (£7.95) lurked the tastes of garlic, herbs and smoke, but a plate of mixed piroshki (£9.95) proved a bit much for a lunchtime main course; piroshki are not 'Polish dim sum', as they are often described, but heavy, almost gluey 'ravioli' that get rather tiresome after three or four. And the Mexican element? Well, it's all here, but we stayed east – not south – of the border.

Open: Mon-Sat noon-2.30pm, 5.30pm-10.30pm, Sun 5.30pm-10pm; reservations advisable (dinner); licensed

Map 3 B5
Tube: Green Park

 Smoking throughout

 Pavement tables

starter: £2.75-£4.50
main: £6.50-£11.50
dessert: £3.25
AE MC V; SW

Le Gavroche
Modern French

☎ 020 7408 0881
43 Upper Brook St W1

Map 2 E4
Tube: Marble Arch
Dress code: jacket
Smoking throughout 

When Albert Roux opened his haute cuisine restaurant in 1967 he cheekily named it after the street urchin in Les Misérables. If only the little kid could have eaten such food. Leave the à la carte with its terrine de foie gras (£26.90), coquilles St Jacques (£24.60), and tournedos au poivre (£33.80) to those fatter wallets and suit up instead for the set lunch (£38.50) – a steal when you consider it includes a half bottle of good wine. A heavenly lobster soufflé arrived first, followed by monkfish bathed in a buttery lemon sauce. The pan-fried entrecôte steak topped with roquefort was the best we've ever eaten. To finish we chose from a delectable selection of ices – ginger, vanilla, and pear and port among them – scooped out of silver containers at our table. The dining room is reassuringly old fashioned and comfortable, the clientele discerning and the service impeccable. Faultless. *Note: there is a minimum charge of £38.50/person for lunch and £60/person for dinner.*

starter: £15.80-£33
main: £27.80-£34.60
dessert: £11.80-£23.40
Set lunch £38.50 or set dinner £60
AE DC JCB MC V; SW

Open: Mon-Fri noon-2pm (last orders), 7pm-11pm (last orders); reservations essential; licensed

Mirabelle
French

☎ 020 7499 4636
56 Curzon St W1

Map 3 A5
Tube: Green Park
Entertainment: pianist Tues-Sat evening, Sun lunch
Smoking throughout

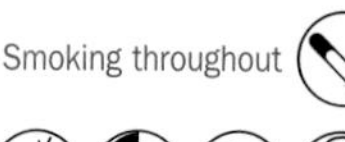

We are talking Mayfair, and we are talking le doyen Marco Pierre White, but what a place for a splurge! There's the doorman, for a start, and then there's the elegant lounge where you absolutely must linger for a fresh fruit and champagne cocktail (£7.50). A maître d' escorts you onward through the sophisticated piano bar and underneath a huge glittering disco ball into the classic, white-pillared dining room. Starters are superb – truffled cabbage soup with seared foie gras (£8.50) and tarte tatin of endive with caramelised scallops (£11.50). Simple mains proved excellent – lemon sole with chives (£18.95) and quail cooked in chicken broth (£12.50). Pudding is a must. The caramel soufflé is sublime (£7.50) and the cheeses are just as fine (£7.50). The wine list is formidable and, yes, we could have stretched to a bottle of the 1847 Chateaux D'Yquem (£30,000) but spent the money on our taxi home instead.

starter: £6.50-£11.50
main: £12.50-£25
dessert: £7.50
Mon-Sat set lunch £14.95 or £17.95, Sun set lunch £14.50-£17.50
AE DC MC V; SW

Open: Mon-Fri noon-2.30pm, Mon-Sat 6pm-11.30pm, Sun noon-3pm, 6pm-10.30pm; reservations advisable; licensed

MAYFAIR

Mô Tea Room and Bazaar

Moroccan

☎ **020 7734 3999**
23 Heddon St W1

Set back from Regent St, this intimate Moroccan tearoom will revive the weariest of West End shoppers. Multicoloured glass lights hang from the wooden ceiling, and smoking pipes, copper urns and all manner of North African artefacts make it a paradise for anyone who was a magpie in a former life. The first decision is where to sit, with leather cushions, wooden benches covered in mirrored throws and authentic camel saddles to choose from. Tea is the drink to go for: try the strong and sweet mint tea (£1.50) or wild blackberry and apple iced tea . Make up your own sandwich by choosing the bread, filling and dressing – olive bread with le méchoui (tomato and pepper dressing) and hummus is a succulent combination (£3.50). There's also a good range of salads and traditional pastries. Customers will either feel energised to continue a shopping mission or be inspired to get on the next flight to Marrakesh.

Open: Mon-Sat 11am-11pm; reservations not accepted; licensed

Map 1 D2
Tube: Piccadilly

Smoking throughout

Pavement tables

main: £2-£5.25
dessert: £2-£2.50
AE JCB MC V; SW

Momo

Moroccan

☎ **020 7287 0404**
25 Heddon St W1

Momo is as much about entertainment as it is about food – a place to rub shoulders (literally, in the low and cramped seats) with super-model lookalikes and 'people in black' admiring the faux-Moorish décor of carved wooden windows and circular brass tables. Try the bourek d'agneau (£6.50), slender 'spring rolls' of lamb and almonds, or chorba (£5.50), a savoury vegetable and noodle soup, but give the limp and oily whole sardines roties à la charmoula (£6.50) a miss. For main courses the emphasis is on various tajines and couscous; we chose the couscous maison (£15) for a sampling of meats, as well as the pastilla au pigeon, an overly sweet pigeon pie in filo pastry. Desserts run the usual North African gamut of filo pastry, nuts and honey. However, there is an unusual, sweet couscous seffae (£5.50), with raisins, almonds and cinnamon. One of the staff, who are mostly French and quite charming, will wash your hands with orange-blossom water before dinner – an unusual experience.

Open: Mon-Fri 12.30pm-2.15pm, Sat 12.30pm-2.30pm, Mon-Sat 7pm-11.15pm, Sun noon-3pm, 7pm-10.15pm; reservations essential; licensed

Map 1 D2
Tube: Piccadilly
Wheelchair access

Smoking throughout

Patio & pavement tables

starter: £5.50-£13.50
main: £9.75-£15.50
dessert: £5.50
set lunch £11.50 or £14.50
AE DC MC V; SW

Map 3 B4
Tube: Hyde Park Corner
Wheelchair access
Dress code: collared shirt
Nonsmoking tables available

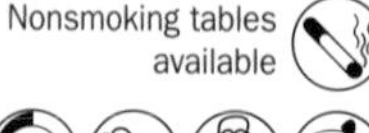

Nobu

Japanese

☎ 020 7447 4747
Level 1, Metropolitan Hotel, 19 Old Park Lane W1

Much has been made of California-based chef Matsuhisa Nobuyuki's fusion-style Japanese cuisine, and although his London operation is a tad pretentious, it's difficult to fault on any other level. Trust in the chef's judgement was amply rewarded by the omakase lunch menu (£40), a banquet of seven kaiseki-influenced dishes on steroids, kicked off in style with an ice-cooled bowl of salmon in wasabi sauce. The seared tuna sashimi salad (£13.50), a signature dish, was lifted by a zesty soy sauce, and although the pan-fried halibut took a while to arrive, the fish burst with flavour and looked fantastic. An elegant platter of sushi led to the spectacular finale of a strawberry chawan-mushi – a creamy, heavenly dessert supported by an intriguing cast of tropical fruit. On a democratic note, it's first come, first served if you want to sit at the sushi bar.

starter: £2.75-£14
main: £12.75-£22.50
dessert: £7-£9
Chef's choice menu lunch from £40 or £60 or set lunch £23.50-£25
AE DC JCB MC V; SW

Open: Mon-Fri noon-2.15pm, 6pm-10.15pm, Sat 6pm-11.15pm, Sun 6pm-9.45pm; reservations essential; licensed

---

Map 2 E6
Tube: Green Park
Wheelchair access
Smoking throughout (cigars at bar only)

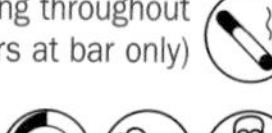

The Square

Modern French

☎ 020 7495 7100
6-10 Bruton St W1

We expected the food to be seriously good at Philip Howard's two-star Michelin restaurant, but we didn't think we'd be treated to such a culinary happening. Delightful amuse-gueule left us in toe-curling anticipation of courses to come: layers of paper-thin lasagne stuffed with crab, a creamy mousseline of scallops and salmon, and a playful medley of John Dory, plump gnocchi and chanterelle mushrooms. The menu offers plenty of meatier dishes, too, including saddle of lamb and tournedos Rossini, and a curtain call of devilish desserts. All this in an airy, modern dining room, beautifully appointed with well-spaced tables decked in crisp linen. The only niggle we had was with the service that, while gracious and friendly, was a mite slow. You might not be doing your wallet any favours by the end of your meal here but, rest assured, your taste buds will be doing cartwheels.

Set lunch £20 & £25 or set dinner £45
AE DC JCB MC V; SW

Open: Mon-Fri noon-2.45pm (last orders), Mon-Sat 6.30pm-10.45pm (last orders), Sun 6.30pm-10pm (last orders); reservations essential; licensed & BYO (corkage £25/bottle)

Sotheby's Café
Modern British

☎ **020 7293 5077**
34-35 New Bond St W1

Map 1 C1
Tube: Bond Street

This elegant oasis of tranquillity in the heart of the West End is *the* place to have 'luncheon with mother' or to glimpse how the other half lives. Style and simplicity are the keynotes, from the crisp white linen, silver service and mirrored walls hung with Cecil Beaton photographs to the daily changing menu of good, modern British cuisine. The signature dish is a generously proportioned lobster club sandwich (£10.50), but the succulent char-grilled tuna with puréed aubergine, slow-roasted tomatoes and crunchy green beans (£13.95) has fabulous textural variety. Leave room for temptations like the chocolate, quince and almond tart with clotted cream (£4.50). As expected, the wine list is impeccable, selected by Sotheby's wine expert. The cafe is also good for breakfast (salmon and eggs rather than bacon and eggs of course) and for proper English afternoon tea.

Open: Mon-Fri 9.30am-4.45pm; reservations accepted; licenced

starter: £4.50-£6.95
main: £9.95-£13.95
dessert: £4.50-£5.50

AE DC MC V; SW

Zinc Bar & Grill
Modern British/French

☎ **020 7255 8800**
21 Heddon St W1

Map 1 D1
Tube: Piccadilly

 Smoking throughout

 Terrace tables

Conran's classy Zinc Bar & Grill, popular with suits and showgoers, nestles in a secluded courtyard five minutes walk from Piccadilly. Felt banquettes line the walls and marble tables dot the convivial dining room, separated from the bar by glass panelling that leaves diners the option of conversation. From the unadventurous, sturdy menu we chose carrot and coriander soup (£4.25), with marbled texture and Indian resonance, and smoked salmon with crème fraîche (£7), delectably crisp. Entrecôte béarnaise (£13.50) and peppered rib of beef (£12.50), though succulent, didn't quite maintain the standard; both cuts could have been leaner. Commanding form returned with dessert, superconcentrated, pristine dark chocolate mousse (£5) and superb mixed berries with Jersey cream (£5), the fruit fresh and flavourful as if plucked straight from the bush. Decent service, stylishly presented classics, central location – this brasserie delivers.

Open: Mon-Wed noon-11pm, Thurs-Sat noon-11.30pm; reservations advisable (especially weekday lunches); licensed

starter: £4.25-£9
main: £7.95-£15
dessert: £4.50-£5
Menu Prix Fixe £11.50 (£14 noon-7pm)

AE DC JCB MC V; SW

OXFORD CIRCUS

Mash

Modern European

☎ 020 7637 5555
19-21 Great Portland St W1

Map 1 A1
Tube: Oxford Circus
Wheelchair access
Entertainment: DJ Wed, Thurs & Sat evenings
Smoking throughout 

Mash is meant to refer to the savoury gloop of vegetables that accompanies many dishes but here it may just refer to the huge bar area that gets thronged to bursting with black-clad professionals after work. There's a microbrewery at the back and the main beers are fine although the much trumpeted peach (£3.20 a pint) was that in name and colour only. Upstairs, the vast open dining area gets mobbed by the crowds from the bar below. The changing menu is of the nearly undefinable modern European, including a well-balanced tuna confit with cannellini beans (£6), and a somewhat overwrought woodfired pizza groaning under smoked swordfish (£9.90). The roasted chicken with wild mushrooms and the all-too-often ignored Swiss chard (£12) is a better choice among the mains. The staff – when you find them – are less ruffled than the patrons, but it took three requests to get what turned out to be some wondrous and fruity olive oil to go with our bread.

starter: £4.50-£6
main: £9-£15.50
dessert: £3.50-£5.50
AE DC MC V; SW

Open: Mon-Fri noon-3pm, Mon-Sat 6pm-11pm, Sat & Sun noon-4pm; reservations advisable (for restaurant only); licensed

Mash

CENTRAL

Ozer

Modern Ottoman

☎ 020 7323 0505
4-5 Langham Place W1

Map 5 B1
Tube: Oxford Circus

 Smoking throughout

This elegant newcomer has already received plenty of praise from the critics, and deservedly so. The restaurant is always busy with both business and social diners alike enjoying what is loosely described as modern Ottoman cuisine. Seared tuna in a spiced filo crust (£8.50) is a delight – the tender fish, served rare, is accompanied by a confit of ginger, fig and lime, giving plenty of necessary zest. Main courses will please lovers of lamb. We chose the shoulder, which had been gently roasted and basted (£14), served with an unusual kumquat and limequat marmalade. The sea bass bathed in fish stock and Turkish tea (£16) was very tempting. Desserts are also unusual – the dill sorbet (£4.50) had a refreshing hint of apple. Service is of a high standard, if at times a little too attentive.

Open: Mon-Fri noon-2.30pm, Mon-Sat 6pm-11pm; reservations advisable; licensed

starter: £6.50-£12
main: £13.50-£17.50
dessert: £4.50-£7
Set lunch £14.95 or £17.95
AE DC JCB MC V; SW

PICCADILLY

The Criterion

Modern French

☎ 020 7930 0488
224 Piccadilly W1

Map 1 D4
Tube: Piccadilly

 Smoking throughout

The transition from the tawdry neon lights of Piccadilly to Marco Pierre White's opulent haven couldn't be more marked. The lavish interior has an Ottoman feel, with marble walls, potted palms and an ornate gilded mosaic ceiling – you could be forgiven for thinking that you had unwittingly stepped onto the set of *Lawrence of Arabia*! The food is equally sumptuous, with terrine of salmon rillette (£9.75) a light fresh starter, followed by roast lamb with a rosemary and tomato jus (£14.95), perfectly cooked and beautifully presented. The roast tuna (£14.95) is rich in flavour and complemented by a lemon and sage sauce. To complete this eating extravaganza there's a range of international delights for dessert (£6.75) and a dauntingly extensive and expensive wine list which the attentive staff are happy to decipher. For the quality of the food, the crispness of the service and the unusually decadent location, the Criterion experience is sensibly priced.

Open: Mon-Sat noon-2.30pm, 5.30pm-11.30pm, Sun 5.30pm-10.30pm; reservations essential; licensed

starter: £8.50-£18.50
main: £13.50-£24.50
dessert: £6.75
Set menu £14.95 or £17.95
AE DC MC V; SW

The Red Room

Modern British

☎ **020 7851 2464**
Waterstone's, 203-206 W1

Map 1 E4
Tube: Piccadilly
Wheelchair access
Entertainment: jazz on Sun
Certified organic
Nonsmoking tables available

Ever get hungry checking out cookbooks in a bookshop? They have a solution for that at the vast Waterstone's in the old Simpson's department store – they've installed a fine restaurant in the basement. The seasonally changing menu hops around the modern British milieu. Golden beetroot salad (£4.75) makes a feature of this little used vegetable. The roast cod with mashed potato (£13.75) is topped with chorizo which provides the right counter-balance to the smooth flavours of the fish and potatoes. Other items are all well prepared and presented, including smoked haddock fishcake (£12.50) paired with fine chips. The rhubarb tart (£5) comes with rhubarb ice cream that would thrill any fan of this, another underused, vegetable. Service is as professional as the presentation. Before dinner, check out the bar on the store's 5th floor for great views over west London.

starter: £4.75-£9.80
main: £12.50-£14.25
dessert: £5-£5.50
Set menu £15.50-£18.50
AE JCB MC V; SW

Open: Mon-Sat noon-3pm, 5.30pm-9pm, Sun noon-4pm; reservations advisable; licensed

Yoshino

Japanese

☎ **020 7287 6622**
3 Piccadilly Place W1

Map 1 E3
Tube: Piccadilly
Lunch: no smoking, dinner: separate smoke-free dining available

With a discreet entrance off Piccadilly, stark contemporary design, classical music in the background and an almost all Japanese clientele, Yoshino could be an exclusive club. The friendly staff and low prices immediately soften the effect, as does the draft Kirin beer served in chilled glasses. Menus change regularly, but always feature home-made items, including excellent tofu (£4.90), ice cream (£2.80) and natto* (£2.80). This is also one of the few Japanese restaurants we've found that often serves oden*, a dish that tastes much better than it looks. The beautifully presented Yoshino no Zen (£9.80) course includes three tasty appetisers, grilled mackerel, fresh pink tuna sashimi decorated with a tiny yellow chrysanthemum, a hearty miso soup flavoured with aubergine and a bowl of rice. The flickering lights of hibachi (mini ceramic stoves) on the tables and cool jazz music create a sophisticated atmosphere at dinner, but Yoshino gets our vote any time of day.

starter: £2.40-£4.90
main: £9.80-£19.90
dessert: £2.80
AE DC JCB MC V; SW

Open: Mon-Fri noon-2pm, Sat noon-2.30pm, Mon-Sat 6pm-10pm (last orders 9pm); reservations not accepted (lunch), reservations advisable (weekend evenings); licensed

REGENT'S PARK

Asuka
Japanese

☎ 020 7486 5026
Berkeley Arcade,
209a Baker St NW1

Map 2 B3
Tube: Baker Street

 Smoking throughout

Asuka is hidden within a small shopping arcade opposite Baker St tube station. The small sushi bar at the front of the restaurant is popular with local Japanese businesspeople, which is always a good sign. The interior is typically Japanese, with white walls, dark wooden furniture and low seating. The evening à la carte menu can be very expensive, but the three-course set dinner menu is very good value (£23.90) and offers some fine choices. The prawn and asparagus salad could have done with a few more prawns, but the main dish, an Asuka box, was a far greater success. The different compartments contained sushi, tempura, salmon, pork and salad – a superb introduction for those unaccustomed to Japanese food, especially when washed down with sake. Service is gracious and attentive.

Open: Mon-Fri noon-2.30pm, Mon-Sat 6pm-10.30pm; reservations advisable; licensed

starter: £3.20-£7.50
main: £5.50-£28
dessert: £3.50
Set dinner £23.90

AE JCB MC V

High Tea

Given the important role that tea has always played in English culture, it should be no surprise that going out for 'afternoon tea' is something dear to the heart of many Londoners. These days, however, it's more of a special occasion than a daily ritual.

A traditional set tea comes with a selection of delicate sandwiches (cucumber and smoked salmon are favourites), scones with jam and cream, and rich desserts. Oh, and lots and lots of tea.

The following are some of the best places to go for afternoon tea:

Brown's Hotel 30 Albemarle St, Mayfair W1
☎ 020 7493 6020 (Map 1 E1)
Brown's dispenses tea in the Drawing Room daily from 3pm to 6pm, with a pianist to soothe away any lingering stress from the bustling streets outside. A sizable tea will set you back £17.95 per person.

Claridge's Hotel Brook St, Mayfair W1
☎ 020 7629 8860 (Map 2 E5)
This landmark hotel serves tea in its grand 18th-century foyer daily from 3pm to 5.30pm. It'll cost you £18.50 a head for a set tea or £25 if you want champagne thrown in.

Fortnum & Mason 181 Piccadilly, Piccadilly W1
☎ 020 7734 8040 (Map 1 E3)
The celebrated Fortnum & Mason serves afternoon tea for £13.50 and high teas for £16.50 and £18.50 (with champagne) from Monday to Saturday between 3pm and 5pm.

Waldorf Meridien Aldwych, Covent Garden WC2
☎ 020 7836 2400 (Map 4 D2)
Tea at the Waldorf is served in the splendidly restored Palm Court on weekdays between 3pm and 5.30pm for £18 and £21 (with champagne). On Saturday from 2.30pm to 5.30pm and on Sunday from 4pm to 6.30pm you can take part in the old-fashioned ritual of tea dancing (booking is essential, £25/£28). Tea dancing, an afternoon tea which includes dancing to light waltzes played by a band, reached its peak in the 1950s. Today tea dancing is mostly found in its traditional form at venues like the Waldorf, where patrons can while away the afternoon. However, the term 'tea dancing' has been revived by clubs which have techno, rave and other sessions on Sunday afternoons.

Orangery Kensington Palace, Kensington Gardens W8
☎ 020 7376 0239 (Map 10 D5)
The graceful Orangery in Kensington Gardens is a superb place to have a relatively affordable set tea; prices range from £6.50 with cucumber sandwiches or scones to £12.50 with champagne. It's open daily from 10am to 6pm, April to September (10am to 4pm the rest of the year).

The Ritz 150 Piccadilly W1
☎ 020 7493 8181 (Map 3 A6)
The Ritz is probably the best known place to take tea, although these days it's become something of a production line – the splendour of the surroundings notwithstanding. Afternoon tea is served daily between 2pm and 6pm and costs £24.50 per person. You need to book a month ahead for weekdays and a ridiculous three months ahead for weekends; reserved sittings are at 3.30pm and 5pm. A strict dress code applies.

Savoy the Strand WC2
☎ 020 7836 4343 (Map 4 E2)
The Savoy serves tea in its enormous Thames Foyer daily between 3pm and 5.30pm. It costs £18.50 (or £28 including champagne).

Ryan Ver Berkmoes and Steve Fallon

Che
International

☎ **020 7747 9380**
23 St James's St SW1

Map 3 B6
Tube: Green Park
Wheelchair access

 Smoking throughout

Che's menu whisks diners from Thailand to Penzance, makes a pit stop in Egypt, but, surprisingly, fails to land anywhere remotely near Cuba. This doesn't seem to matter to the cosmopolitan businessy clientele who come here for the design and impressive artwork as much as the food. Che boasts eight Warhol Marilyns and a huge Lichtenstein in a former 1960s banking hall with creamy mosaic walls, lofty ceilings and views onto swanky St James's. We started with a well-seasoned salmon tartare with crème fraîche (£8), and pappardelle with asparagus and a buttery chervil sauce (£9). The steak (£16.50) and seared yellow fin tuna (£16) are done competently. Skip the comforting desserts (sticky toffee pudding and the like) and move right onto the cigar course. This is where Che excels, with a choice of over 80 Havanas. The smoking lounge is at the back of the achingly hip and noisy downstairs bar, where there's even a photograph of Snr Guevara.

Open: restaurant Mon-Fri noon to 2.45pm (last orders), Mon-Sat 6pm-11pm (last orders), bar 11am-11pm; reservations advisable; licensed

starter: £4.50-£14.95 (restaurant cover charge £1.50/person)
main: £10-£24, bar £2.50-£14.50
dessert: £6.50-£9
Sat brunch (bar) £4.50-£11.50

AE DC MC V; SW

Wiltons
British

☎ **020 7629 9955**
55 Jermyn St SW1

Map 1 E2
Tube: Green Park or Piccadilly Circus
Dress code: jacket & tie

 Smoking throughout

When visiting Wiltons, you enter an Olde England time warp. As a long-standing hangout for Tory Members of Parliament and hereditary peers, it is the classic spot for both fresh seafood and political intrigue. Oysters run at more than £2 apiece, making a starter plate of a dozen more expensive than a main course elsewhere in town. But while other restaurants serve pre-made prawn cocktails, Wiltons offers fresh langoustines, which are shelled and cooked to order to preserve their sweetness (£17). Dover sole, a speciality of the house, is prepared in several ways. Wiltons provides its own unique form of entertainment (beyond spotting celebrities and office workers plotting their discreet affairs). The waiters seem to have come straight from a West End theatre: portly, vested men who can convey approval or disapproval of your choice for dinner with a lightly raised eyebrow. Go ahead, order the champagne.

Open: Mon-Fri, Sun 12.30pm-2.30pm, daily 6.30pm-10.30pm; reservations essential; licensed

starter: £4.95-£18
main: £8.50-£24
dessert: £5
Sun set menu £19.75

AE DC JCB MC V; SW

Alastair Little
Modern British

☎ 020 7734 5183
49 Frith St W1

Map 1 C5
Tube: Leicester Square

Smoking throughout

It's easy to like Little's low-key restaurant – an oasis of calm amid the bustle of Soho – which has been serving up reliably good nosh since 1986. Starters are spot on, with lots of robust flavours – smoked eel, ham and horseradish top a fluffy potato pancake, and a delicious fruity mouthful of tomato chutney rounds off a tasty terrine maison. Mains, roast halibut and spring lamb among them, are well-cooked, simple and satisfying – so satisfying, in fact, that we were tempted to call it a night. A glance at the desserts, however, convinced us to forge ahead: the apple and amaretti tart with crème fraîche is sensational. Lunchtime is for media types, evenings more convivial and relaxed, which is just as well given the laid-back service. By the way, the ceiling lighting is a work of art. *Also at 136a Lancaster Rd, Ladbroke Grove W11 ☎ 020 7243 2220.*

Set lunch £25 or set dinner £33
AE DC JCB MC V; SW

Open: Mon-Fri noon-3pm (last orders), Mon-Sat 6pm-11pm (last orders); reservations advisable; licensed

Aurora
Modern European

☎ 020 7494 0514
49 Lexington St W1

Map1 C4
Tube: Oxford Circus

Smoking throughout

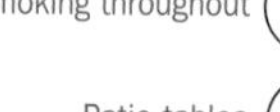

Patio tables

Bohemian but chic Soho lurks behind Aurora's inconspicuous doorway. The exposed floorboards, low ceilings, comfortable sofas and solid candlelit tables packed close together create an aura of intimacy in which to peruse the Modern European menu. Ease into the cosy twilight warmth by trying the roasted red onion and butternut squash soup (£3.95). Tantalise your taste buds with spicy Thai potato cakes and tomato salsa (£6.25) followed by delicate sea bass fillets accompanied by roasted potatoes and peppers (£12.50). As you choose from a selection of ephemeral cakes (£4.25) washed down with coffee, Aurora will seduce you, encouraging you to chill out and forget the time – but the two evening sittings mean that you may be hurried back onto the streets when you'd rather snuggle in for the night.

starter: £3.95-£6.50
main: £10.25-£13.50
dessert: £4.25
MC V; SW

Open: Thurs & Fri 12.30pm-3pm, 6.30pm-10.30pm, Mon-Wed noon-3pm, 6.30pm-10.30pm, Sat 1pm-3pm, 6.30pm-10.30pm; reservations advisable; licensed

Bar Italia

Italian

☎ 020 7437 4520
22 Frith St W1

Map 1 B5

Tube: Leicester Square

 Smoking throughout

 Pavement tables

This legendary institution has been keeping the caffeine levels of Soho's artists, hipsters and layabouts buoyant for more than 50 years. Now run by the original owner's grandson, Bar Italia hasn't diverged from its simple formula of espressos and snacks: try ciabatta, focaccia or croissants with a limited range of fillings (mozzarella, tomato, basil, avocado and salami – £2-£5) or mushroom and ham quiches (£2-£3). And it's OK to order a cappuccino (£1.40), but only if it's before 10am (this *is* Soho after all). With a television suspended in one corner, diners keep themselves entertained watching music videos or sports matches (depending on the manager's current whim), while boxing fans admire the photographs of great pugilists which take up most of the available wall space. If the London weather allows, grab a gelato on your way out. Insomniacs take note: Bar Italia is open around the clock.

Open: daily 24 hours (closed Mon 3am-7am); reservations not accepted; unlicensed

main: £2-£5
dessert: £1-£3

cash and cheque only

Blues Bistro & Bar

International

☎ 020 7494 1966
42-43 Dean St W1

Map 1 B5

Tube: Leicester Square or Piccadilly

 Smoking throughout

Blues Bistro & Bar claims to serve American food. But any menu with items like tandoori pumpkin soup (£4.25) and Thai fish curry (£11.25) will have a hard time playing in Peoria. Concept quibbles aside, Blues does a good job of plying the jabbering Soho masses with a range of global dishes. The house salad (£4.95) may be a yawner but the caesar salad is lavished with huge anchovies and lots of garlic croutons (£4.95). Linguine with prawns (£12.50) is spicy and has a rich coriander flavour, and the definitely American New York steak (£13.95) comes with some fine mashed potatoes that may attract the unwanted attentions of neighbouring forks. The pecan tart with banana ice cream (£4.25) yielded a dreamy 'wow.' By 9pm the open dining room is heaving with diners and spillovers from the small bar. Service is untroubled by the mobs.

Open: Mon-Thurs noon-midnight, Fri noon-1am, Sat 5pm-1am, Sun 5pm-midnight; reservations advisable; licensed

starter: £5.50
main: £7-£12.50
dessert: £4.25
Mon & Tues set dinner £10

AE MC V; SW

Map 1 B5
Tube: Tottenham Court Road
Smoking throughout

Café Emm
International

☎ 020 7437 0723
17 Frith St W1V

Tucked away from the heady sights and sounds of Leicester Square and its lavish counterparts on Frith Street, Café Emm is a frugal haven for trendy but unpretentious diners in the know. The clientele varies from huddled clusters of gossiping friends to party revellers burning the candle at both ends. Go for the gargantuan portions of Cumberland sausages and mash or the delectable stuffed red bell peppers with wild rice, mushrooms and cheese heaped with salad on the side – both are £5.50 and both look a million dollars. If you can manage a dessert, the pecan cheesecake is delicious (£4.20). Do as the waiters do at brash, boisterous and bohemian Café Emm – dress down to impress.

starter: £3.40-£5.40
main: £5.50-£7.20
dessert: £4-£4.50
MC V; SW

Open: Mon-Fri noon-3pm, Sun-Fri 5.30pm-11pm, Sat 5pm-midnight; reservations advisable (especially lunch); licensed

Café Fish

Café Espana

Spanish

☎ **020 7494 1271**
63 Old Compton St W1

Map 1 C5

Tube: Leicester Square or Piccadilly Circus

 Smoking throughout

If you can snag one of the front tables by the window, there's little better place for a lazy afternoon feed, lingering over a spread of small picky dishes and a bottle of the quite decent Spanish wine. Favourites among the starters include the spicy albóndigas* (£3.95) and patatas bravas (£1.95), gorgeous calamares fritos (£4.50) with pleasing restraint on the batter, and the heaped dish of mussels. Order plenty to share and forget the mains, which in our experience are not a highlight. An exception here is the show-stopping paella (£19.50), which is described as being for two but kept four happy on our last outing. Café Espana is always packed, and there are no reservations, but the staff will give you a time to come back if you want to wait it out in the pub.

Open: daily noon-midnight; reservations not accepted; licensed

starter: £1.95-£4.95
main: £5.95-£9.95
set menu £4.95

MC V; SW

Café Fish

Fish

☎ **020 7287 8989**
36-40 Rupert St W1

Map 1 D5

Tube: Piccadilly

Wheelchair access

 Smoking throughout (canteen), smoke-free dining available (restaurant)

The location off Shaftesbury Ave, wide selection of seafood, generous opening hours, stylish black and white tiled floors and French-bistrot feel all combine to make Café Fish an excellent choice for a West End feed – provided you like fish and shellfish. Depending on where you sit, you'll be offered a slightly different menu. In the bar and canteen area, the list of dishes is shorter and the prices cheaper than in the restaurant proper. If you're looking for intimacy opt for the latter, as the canteen's communal seating may not be the intimacy you had in mind. From the two-course canteen set menu (£11.50), the steamed mussels were good though they could have done with more garlic. But the crème brûlée was a treat – creamy and fluffy with a thin, crispy sugar crust. From the à la carte menu, the char-grilled seabass (£13.10) with a touch of lemon olive oil was perfectly cooked and very fresh. Our verdict: it's worth paying a little more for the fish, but don't skip dessert.

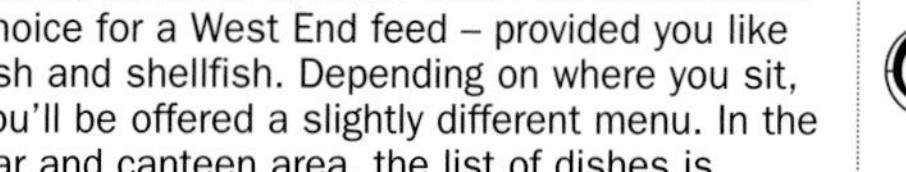

Open: canteen daily noon-10.30pm, restaurant Mon-Fri noon-3pm, 5.30pm-11.30pm, Sat noon-11.30pm, Sun noon-10.30pm; reservations not accepted (canteen), reservations essential (restaurant); licensed

starter: £3.75-£19.75
main: £6.75-£20.50
dessert: £3.95
Canteen set menu £7.50-£15.50 or restaurant set dinner £18.50

AE DC JCB MC V; SW

Centrale

Italian

☎ 020 7437 5513
16 Moor St W1

Map 1 B6
Tube: Leicester Square or Tottenham Court Rd

Smoking throughout 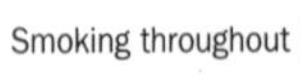

We've been eating at Centrale since university days in the mid-80s, when its cheap eats/big helpings were a boon to making a student grant go that bit further. Times have changed, but Centrale hasn't – it still has that shabby boho Soho feel of the 50s. Centrale is always packed, and loud. Patrons are crammed onto banquette seating at formica-topped tables and, if you are only two, you'll most likely end up sharing space with others. Although the menu contains plenty of meat and potato dishes like steaks (£7), escalopes (£4.50-£6.50) and grilled chicken (£3.75-£5.50), most regulars come for the pasta. Rigatoni alfredo (£4) with a creamy-garlicky-tomatoey sauce and plenty of mushrooms is our personal favourite, and the vongole (£4.20), a slippery mound of garlicky clams entwined in spaghetti, is also good. Go easy on your BYO wine – there are no loos. Portions are as huge as they've always been and rarely do we manage to clear our plates. Perhaps that's why the choice of desserts is so shabby – nobody ever gets that far.

starter: £2-£4
main: £2.50-£7
dessert: £1.20-£1.50
cash and cheque only

Open: Mon-Sat noon-9.30pm; reservations not accepted; BYO (corkage £1/bottle)

Circus

Modern British

☎ 020 7534 4010
1 Upper James St W1

Map 1 C3
Tube: Piccadilly

Smoking throughout

The setting is sleekly minimalist, but there's maximum attitude amongst the clientele at Circus. This is one of Soho's 'buzziest' venues – and proud of it. The good news is that the food's pleasing, and the three-course pre-theatre menu is a winner at £17.50. Stick to the (high-class) basics: salads feature mustard greens and potatoes or pan-fried foie gras, while mains like Dover sole and wild rabbit with roast pumpkin are expertly prepared and presented. You'll spot many a media type dining on an expense account here, and if you like to be able to taste what you're eating, be forewarned: Circus virtually encourages diners to light up post-prandial cigars. You can experience some of this heady atmosphere at a discount by checking out the popular basement bar scene.

starter: £6-£15
main: £12.50-£22
dessert: £4.75-£6.50
Set menu £10.50 or £17.50
AE DC MC V; SW

Open: Open: Mon-Fri noon-3pm, Mon-Sat 5.45pm-midnight; reservations essential; licensed

Ed's Easy Diner

American

☎ **020 7434 4439**
Old Compton St W1

Map 1 B6
Tube: Leicester Square

 Smoking throughout

 Pavement tables

Ed's Easy Diner does its best to be an authentic American diner – it's filled with formica and chrome, the Beach Boys are on the jukebox and the short-order cooks wear crisp white uniforms with matching paper hats. Ed's menu features basic diner fare, with cheeseburgers and fries (this American-style diner doesn't call them chips) taking centre stage. Both are big and greasy, the dual goals of diner fare. Ed's shines brightest in its fountain selections – shakes (£2.50), malts (£2.75) and sundaes (£3.25), smothered in whipped cream and chocolate fudge. Ed's is a fun place to eat. The kids will love it. *Also at 38 Shaftesbury Ave, Piccadilly Circus W1 ☎ 020 7287 1951, 362 King's Rd, Chelsea SW3 ☎ 020 7352 1956, The 02 Centre, 255 Finchley Rd, Hampstead NW3 ☎ 020 7431 1958, Brent Cross Shopping Center, Brent Cross NW4 ☎ 020 8202 0999, and Blue Water Shopping Mall, Water Circus, Greenhithe, Kent ☎ (01322) 380939.*

Open: Mon-Thurs 11.30am-11.30pm, Fri & Sat 11.30am-1am, Sun 11.30am-midnight; reservations not accepted; licensed

main: £3.65-£5.50
dessert: £2.95-£4.20

AE MC V; SW

Garlic & Shots

International

☎ **020 7734 9505**
14 Frith St W1

Map 1 B5
Tube: Tottenham Court Road

 Smoking throughout

 Courtyard tables

Garlic & Shots is a drinking den masquerading as a 'garlic restaurant'. Literally everything on the menu reeks of the stuff and it's also a great place to go for a serious drink, with 101 different combinations of shots on offer (£2.50). The décor may be dingy but the service is casual and friendly. We had a garlic vodka (£2.50) and garlic beer (£1.80) while waiting for starters of artichokes (£2.95) and curry shrimp (£4.20). Neither was particularly interesting, but the 'coyote's day dream' (£10.90) – fillet of lamb cooked in vodka, tequila and cactus – and 'garlic blues delight' (£11.90) – monkfish with coriander, lime, cranberry, white wine and horseradish – are excellent. Wash it all down with a bottle of house red (£8.95) before sampling the garlic and honey ice cream (£3.50), by which time your taste buds will be well past their sell-by date. A good but garlicky night out.

Open: Mon-Wed 5pm-11.15pm, Thurs-Sat 6pm-12.15am, Sun 5pm-10.45pm; reservations accepted (only for groups of 6 or more); licensed

starter: £1.50-£5
main: £8-£12.95
dessert: £3.50-£3.80

MC V; SW

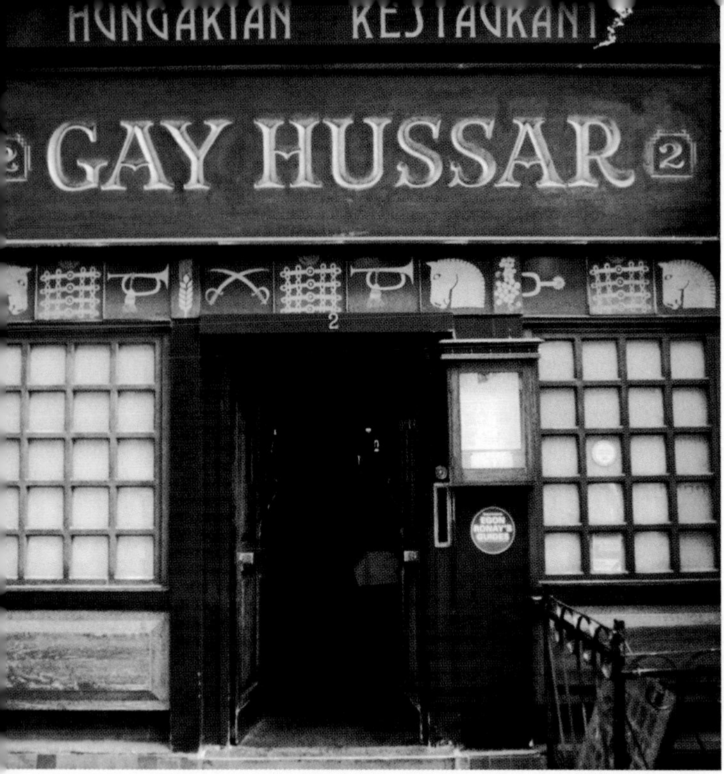

Map 1 B5
Tube: Tottenham Court Road

Smoking throughout 

starter: £3.40-£6.80
main: £11.50-£16
dessert: £3.20-£4.50
Set menu £15 or £18

AE DC JCB MC V; SW

Gay Hussar

Hungarian

☎ 020 7437 0973
2 Greek St W1

If you're after the Soho of the early 1950s – when paprika was thought risqué and the word 'gay' meant 'merry' – this is your destination: an old-style Hungarian eatery where the walls are covered in sepia-toned hunting scenes and there's meat, meat and more meat on the menu. It being winter, we eschewed the chilled wild cherry soup (£3.85) for the házi pástétom (£3.75), a grainy, home-made pâté, and mushroom soup (£3.40), which suffered from a lack of forest mushrooms . We followed with kacsa sült (£16), a crispy though somewhat dry roast duck with all the trimmings, and cigány gyors tál (£13.50), a 'Gypsy quick dish' of pork medallions, onions and green peppers. For dessert there's dobos torta (£3.50), cream layer cake, and somlói galuska (£4.25), a mountainous sponge with chocolate and whipped cream. The brief wine list includes a decent Villányi merlot (£13.50) and a top-rated Tokaji Aszu (£4 a glass), an amber nectar fit for the gods.

Open: Mon-Sat 12.15pm-2.30pm, 5.30pm-10.45pm; reservations advisable; licensed

Gerrard's Corner

Chinese

☎ 020 7437 0984
30 Wardour St W1

Map 1 D5
Tube: Leicester Square

 Smoking throughout

That old chestnut about eating where the locals eat is never truer than in Chinatown. The Chinese share one of the world's seminal cuisines and they know their food. That Gerrard's Corner is always packed with ethnic Chinese Britons and their relatives and friends from China or Hong Kong speaks volumes for the authenticity of its dishes. Most daytime diners are here for the dim sum (£2.50-£5); old favourites like ha gau, siu mai, pai gwat and char siu bow* are a lot more than just acceptable (though sadly the dishes are served directly from the kitchen and not offered from steaming carts as they should be). For more substantial dishes, or for dinner, order the sweet and creamy deep-fried oysters (£8.50), the braised duck with black mushrooms (£9/£16 half/whole duck) or a bean curd dish like mapo doufu* (£5.80). Thankfully, the chefs are parsimonious with the monosodium glutamate.

Open: Mon-Sat noon-11.30pm, Sun 11am-10.15pm; reservations advisable; licensed

starter: £2.50-£6
main: £5.80-£18
dessert: £2-£3
Set menu £18-£22

AE MC V; SW

Hujo's

Mediterranean

☎ 020 7734 5144
11 Berwick St W1V

Map 1 C4
Tube: Tottenham Court Road

Smoking throughout

Hujo's stands apart from the current crop of olive-oil-toting restaurants thanks to its low-key, friendly service and the part-familiar, part-original and frequently changing menu. The vibe is both hip and relaxed: warm yellow walls act as a shop window for up-and-coming artists, and there's a truly international drinks list (New Zealand and Chilean whites, Argentinean and Italian reds, German and English beers). Start with the warm salad of marinated wild mushrooms with walnuts and new potatoes (£5.25), or deep-fried potato skins with sour cream and onions (£5.25) – light enough to stimulate rather than spoil the appetite. Salmon fish cakes (£7.25) are less inspired, though the accompanying sautéed greens are a succulent delight. Seared tuna steak (£9.25), pan-fried to perfection, is matched by lightly herbed corn fritters. Opt for the two-course matinée menu, and enjoy.

Open: Mon-Sat noon-midnight; reservations advisable (especially Fri & Sat evenings); licenced

starter: £3.45-£5.25
main: £6.45-£10.25
dessert: £2.95-£3.95
matinée menu £7.25

AE DC MC V; SW

Map 1 C5
Tube: Leicester Square
Entertainment: pianist nightly
Smoking throughout

Kettners
International

☎ 020 7734 6112
29 Romilly St W1

Having sated the culinary cravings of Napoleon III, Auguste Kettner moved to London and founded his eponymous hotel in 1867. Many years have passed, and Pizza Express mogul Peter Boizot is now in charge, but customers keep returning to the beautifully decorated establishment. Now a Soho institution, Kettners retains the feel of a decadent hotel. Considering there are over 50 varieties of champagne on offer, as well as a pianist accompaniment, the menu may come as something of a surprise: pizza is the speciality, and salads and burgers make up the rest of the menu. The leek, rosemary, mozzarella and tomato pizza (£8.10) is light and very tasty, while the mozzarella and tomato salad comes with delicious dough balls (£1.95). The desserts range from home-made apple pie (£4.25) to a Kettners knickerbocker glory (£4.25). If you're looking for atmosphere (rather than adventurous cuisine) Kettners is a great find.

starter: £1.95-£9.95
main: £6-£15
dessert: £3-£4.50
AE DC JCB MC V; SW

Open: daily noon-midnight; reservations not accepted; licensed

---

Map 1 D3
Tube: Piccadilly

Kulu Kulu Sushi
Japanese

☎ 020 7734 7316
76 Brewer St W1

This small, convivial kaiten-zushi* (conveyor-belt sushi bar) is now so popular that at peak times a sign does the rounds on the revolving belt warning that the maximum stay is 45 minutes. The atmosphere is more laid-back than this implies, and the food for the price is pretty much unrivalled. Apart from a couple of fancy sushi rice rolls, coated in bright orange roe, the dishes don't shoot off wildly into the realms of nouvelle Japanese cuisine. What you get is generous cuts of fish and seafood, all impressively fresh. There's plenty to satisfy non-fish fans too, including aubergine cooked in miso (£1.80), with a deliciously nutty toffee flavour, and crunchy french beans (£1.80) coated in roasted sesame seeds. Dessert can be a slice of ripe melon or a sweet rice bun wrapped in a peppery shisho leaf (£1.80).

starter: £1.20
main: £1.20-£3
dessert: £1.80
JCB MC V; SW

Open: Mon-Fri noon-2.30pm, Sat noon-4pm, Mon-Sat 5pm-10pm; reservations not accepted; licensed

On Your Plate **Japanese**

Japanese cuisine in London is not what it once was, which is all for the best. You no longer need a Swiss bank account or a degree in Asian studies to enjoy sushi, tempura, noodles and a host of other dishes at the capital's growing band of low-cost, easy-access Japanese restaurants. With the improved availability of authentic ingredients, and even supermarkets getting into the bento-box business, there has never been a better time to explore the culinary delights of Japan.

For those who hanker after all the trappings of a traditional Japanese meal (steaming hand towels, elegant ceramics, beautiful presentation of food), this can be had at several generally pricey restaurants, including **Tatsuso** in the City and the sushi bar **Defune** just off Baker St. Tradition has all but been tossed out the window, though, at London's more high-profile operations.

In the mid-1990s, the groovy Bloomsbury noodle bar **Wagamama** matched contemporary design and technology with a demystification of Japanese dishes and a deflation of their cost, thus creating a new genre. This has spawned several wannabes, including Soho's **Satsuma**, and has led to the craze for kaiten-zushi – conveyor-belt delivered sushi – taken to its ultimate limit by the robots of **Yo! Sushi**.

It's not all gimmicks and cut prices. Gourmands should treat their taste buds to the fusion cuisine of the designer kaiten-zushi bar **Itsu**, or the contemporary chic of **Nobu**, both of which provide better value for money and novelty than many long-established, expense account options. The sophistication and quality of Piccadilly hideaway **Yoshino** is married with a refreshing informality and raffish approach to the classics. What's more, Yoshino is easily affordable, as are our top two tips for inexpensive *natsukashi* (nostalgic) Japanese dining: Tottenham Court Rd stalwart **Ikkyu** and relative newcomer **Tokyo Diner**.

Simon Richmond

Sydney-based writer Simon Richmond developed a taste for sushi and soba during 2½ years spent working in Tokyo. Among other places, he's written books about Japan, Central Asia and South America, and contributed to newspapers and magazines around the world, including the Independent, *the* Guardian *and the* Telegraph.

Map 1 C3
Tube: Oxford Circus
Nonsmoking tables available

Leith's Soho

Modern European

☎ **020 7287 2057**
41 Beak St W1

If you have a deeply held belief in the delights of your own conversation and shun the distractions of interesting décor or a surprising menu, Leith's Soho is the place for you. Good food and excellent service are guaranteed. Starters are mainly fish related, but there are some good choices for vegetarians. The plate of smoked salmon, crab mayonnaise, oyster tempura and Bloody Mary vinaigrette (£8.50) was packed with different textures and fun to nibble through, and you couldn't go wrong with the juicy wild duck with assorted fruity, sticky accompaniments (£14). While the green Thai coconut fish curry (£17) was deliciously delicate, it only got as far as Calais on its trip to Thailand. All was forgiven when the white-chocolate pudding with pistachio ice cream (£5.75) arrived – light, fluffy and a perfect mix of flavours.

starter: £6.50-£11.75
main: £12.75-£19.50
dessert: £4.75-£6.75
AE MC V; SW

Open: Mon-Fri noon-2.30pm, Mon-Sat 6pm-11.00pm; reservations advisable; licensed

Map 1 B5
Tube: Tottenham Court Road
Smoking throughout

L'Escargot: The Ground Floor Restaurant

French

☎ **020 7439 2679**
48 Greek St W1

The Ground Floor Restaurant at L'Escargot may not be quite as sumptuous – or expensive – as the Picasso Room upstairs, but it's still a classy dining experience. Everything from the Chagall prints to the prim napery and the 40-page wine list speaks of measured opulence. This theme continues on the menu, a classically Gallic selection displaying all the passion for rich flavours – and disdain for vegetarianism – you'd expect. The signature escargot en coquille sets each snail atop a smear of savoury mash (£6.75), but L'Escargot does originals as well: the smoked haddock and curry soup (£6.75) is an inventive triumph of textures and spices. The caramelised skate and potato salad (£6.75) is flavoured beautifully, and fans of hearty cooking will swoon over the indecently rich roast breast and confit leg of duck (£12.95), or the slow-cooked confit shoulder of lamb (£12.95). And if you should faint from sheer excess, a member of the obliging staff will doubtless restore you to your seat without fuss.

starter: £6.75-£10.75
main: £12.95-£16.95
dessert: £5.95
AE DC JCB MC V; SW

Open: Mon-Fri 12.15pm-2.15pm, Mon-Sat 6pm-11.30pm; reservations advisable; licensed & BYO (corkage £14/bottle)

Lindsay House

Modern British

☎ 020 7439 0450
21 Romilly St W1

Map 1 C5
Tube: Leicester Square

 Smoking throughout

You need to be 'in the know' about Lindsay House. The front looks like a residential house – you could mistake people ringing the doorbell for visiting friends. And Chef Patron Richard Corrigan would be the ideal friend to have. The staff are friendly and accommodating to the point of being telepathic. The daily changing set menu is full of surprises. Whet the appetite with an *amusette* of lentils velouté with juniper cream. Then go for the robust red snapper, accompanied by merguez sausage with marjoram, or the roast cod served with ratatouille of shellfish and tortellini of crab. The pre-dessert, lightly warmed muscat grapes in chilled rosemary and vanilla custard, could have easily been a dessert in its own right. But then came the inventive combination of chilled coconut rice pudding, warmed gingerbread and hot roast pineapple – a delightful taste bud twister. At meal's end, a tray of dainty truffles accompanies coffee. The Lindsay House experience is like being cocooned on an expertly run cruise liner – the kitchen is down below, silently navigating you through a voyage of culinary utopia.

Open: Mon-Fri noon-2.15pm, Mon-Sat 5pm-11pm; reservations essential; licensed

Set lunch menu £23, set dinner £42 or menu gourmand £62

AE DC JCB MC V; SW

Melati

Indonesian

☎ 020 7437 2745
21 Great Windmill St W1

Map 1 C4
Tube: Piccadilly

 Smoking throughout

Whispers from doorways vie for your attention here in one of the bawdier parts of Soho. But inside warm and inviting Melati, it's the promise of pleasurable dining that beckons. The cramped tables are spread over two small floors, but the staff are adept at negotiating the obstacles and will soon have a Tiger beer (£2.50) in front of you. Indonesian cuisine – often a poor relation to vaunted Thai cookery – shines here. The satay chicken (£5.95) is nicely grilled and has a silky peanut sauce with just the right kick. The Indonesian national dish nasi goreng (£5.95) is a delectable platter of stir-fried rice, chicken and egg right from the wok. Ikan bumbu Bali (£7.65) takes fresh white fish and bathes it in a very spicy but light sauce. You'll want to wash it down with more Tiger, which should be kept handy for the numerous other spicy items on the long menu.

Open: Sun-Thurs noon-11.30pm, Fri & Sat noon-12.30pm; reservations advisable (Wed-Sat); licensed

starter: £2.95-£5.95
main: £4.95-£7.85
dessert: £2.92-£3.50
Set menu £16.50, £19.50, £21.50 or £24.50

AE JCB MC V; SW

Mezzo

Modern European

☎ 020 7314 4000
100 Wardour St W1

Map 1 C4
Tube: Piccadilly
Entertainment: live music daily (Sun-Tues free, Wed-Sat diners free before 10pm, £5 after 10pm)
Smoking throughout

The grand success of Terry Conran's Soho baby is largely due to its something-for-everyone concept. As you enter there's the hopping bar cheek by jowl with Mezzonine, the Asian-fusion brasserie. Next door is Mezzo Café, serving very tempting pastries and snacks to the cappuccino crowd. We're here for the main event – the glam, modern jazz, 350-seater dining room, with sweeping staircase, crustacean bar and army of efficient waiters. Before the crowds arrive it has the feel of a shopping mall food court, but later the place starts to swing to good live music. The food? Well, it's uneven. A Tuscan bean soup with lardon (£5.50) is hearty and satisfying; the pigeon on a corn pancake is pretty, but insipid (£11). The pork and sole were both generous and proficient but lacked pizzazz, while the dessert – chocolate mousse and orange brûlée – was a lush, delicious partnership. Come for the atmosphere, the variety and just to say you've been.

starter: £5-£12
main: £11.25-£29.50
dessert £4.50-£6.50
Prix fixe £12.50 & £15.50 (lunch & pre-theatre 6pm-7.15pm)
AE DC JCB MC V; SW

Open: Mon-Fri noon-3pm, Mon-Thurs 6pm-midnight, Fri & Sat 6pm-1am, Sun 12.30pm-3pm, 6pm-11pm; reservations advisable; licensed

Mildred's

International

☎ 020 7494 1634
58 Greek St W1

Map 1 B5
Tube: Tottenham Court Road
No smoking inside
Pavement tables

Named after Joan Crawford's thriving restaurant in the movie *Mildred Pierce*, Mildred's serves heroically healthy food to its generally young, vegetarian-inclined clientele. A small and informal place, with a 1950s primary school look (the changing artwork on the walls is a bit more sophisticated – and for sale), it has a bubbly atmosphere that's no doubt helped along by the organic wines, beer and champagne on the menu. Most dishes have Mediterranean or eastern leanings, though there's always the veggie burger of the day with fries to provide a dose of the West. Non-vegetarians are catered for, too – we lov the tiger prawn stir-fry (£6.20) which includes plenty of plump prawns, enormous bean sprouts, crisp mange tout and an extra-spicy satay sauce. Mildred's is worth visiting for coffee and cake alone – the coffee was just right and we swooned over the plum cheesecake, which had a divinely smooth topping and perfectly moist biscuit base.

starter: £1.50-£3.75
main: £5.20-£6.90
dessert: £2-£3.30
cash and cheque only

Open: Mon-Sat noon-11pm, Sun noon-5pm; reservations not accepted; licenced

Mildred's

Nam Dae Moon

Korean

☎ 020 7836 7235
56 St Giles St WC2

When a craving for north Asian food strikes, most Londoners opt for sushi or tempura – not Korean, perhaps assuming that the tastes are limited to those Choson few of garlic, grills and pickles. Nam Dae Moon serves these in spades – it wouldn't be the most authentic Korean restaurant south of Koreatown in Finchley if it didn't. Good starters include bulgogi* (£8), the superior galbi* (£8.50) and a dish or two of marinated chicken, cuttlefish or pork (£7-£7.80), cooked on a barbecue *à table* and eaten with namul, the ubiquitous side dishes of kimchi, pickled radish and beansprouts (all £2). But try something different like bibimbab (£7.50), rice served in a sizzling cast-iron pot topped with thinly sliced beef, cooked preserved vegetables and flavoured with chilli-laced soybean paste. Or go for the pricey but superb haemul jungol (£25), a Korean 'bouillabaisse' of fish and shellfish in a spicy stock that should be shared by several. Service here is exceptionally pleasant and helpful.

Open: Mon-Sat noon-2.30pm, 6.00pm-10.30pm, Sun 5pm-10pm; reservations advisable (dinner); licensed

Map 1 A6

Tube: Tottenham Court Rd

Entertainment: karaoke in basement Mon-Sat 9pm-2am

 Smoking throughout

starter: £2-£5
main: £5.50-£18
dessert: £3.50
Set lunch £6.50, dinner £20 or £25

AE JCB MC V

Pâtisserie Valerie

French

☎ 020 7437 3466
44 Old Compton St W1

Map 1 C5
Tube: Leicester Square

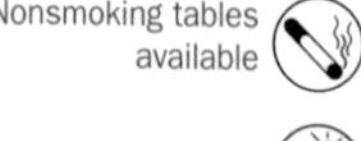
Nonsmoking tables available

Pavement tables

The Old Compton St branch is *the* Pâtisserie Valerie, established in 1926 by a Belgian lady who knew a thing or two about cakes. Take a seat at one of the red laminated tables in the shabby-chic downstairs room if you want to join the more Boho literary aficionados; a notepad, newspaper or book is *de rigueur* as you settle down for the afternoon. The newer upstairs room is lighter but less atmospheric, with the best tables by the windows. The menu offers various savoury options for a light dinner or lunch – a platter of chicken goujons (£6.50), quiche (£4.95) or a croque monsieur (£4) – but the real treats are sweet. Choose a gâteau, eclair, pastry, tarte, biscuit (£1.20-£3.20), chocolate or, best of all, a doughnut filled with crème pâtissière (£1.40) from the tantalising display counters, order a cup of tea (£1.70) – the coffee, in the Franco-Belgian tradition, is on the weak side – and sit back and enjoy.

main: £3.25-£6.95
dessert: £1.20-£3.20
AE DC MC V; SW

Open: Mon-Fri 7.30am-10pm, Sat 8am-10pm, Sun 9.30am-7pm; reservations not accepted; licensed

Pollo

Italian

☎ 020 7734 5917
20 Old Compton St W1

Map 1 B6
Tube: Leicester Square or Tottenham Court Rd

Smoking throughout

Everything about Pollo breathes authentic Italian, from the staff and décor to the robust wine glasses. Prices are a bargain for the generous portions of pasta and hearty pizzas, so you may find yourself at the back of a queue when you enter. This never lasts long though, as the bustling and frantic staff (but surprisingly friendly and cheeky) will seat you anywhere there is room. While the atmosphere is convivial, the actual food can sometimes leave a bit to be desired, as if it has been waiting longer than you have. The napoli (£3.25) was a lukewarm concoction of over-cooked noodles and a bland tomato sauce, but the tagliatelle 'Zia Rosa' (£3.40) was hot, creamy and delicious, and well worth going back for. So if you're looking for an inexpensive, filling, unpretentious and lively Italian, Pollo is for you.

starter: £1.95-£3.40
main: £3.50-£4.95
dessert: £1.60-£2.40
cash or cheque only

Open: daily noon-midnight; reservations not accepted; licensed

Quo Vadis
Modern European

☎ 020 7437 9585
26-29 Dean St W1

Map 1 B5
Tube: Leicester Square

 Smoking throughout

Originally set up by Marco Pierre White, Damien Hirst and Matthew Freud, Quo Vadis was best known for its display of Hirst's art. Times have changed. Despite the Pierre White spin paintings and lizard skeletons on the ceiling, the atmosphere is comfortable with mellow lighting, leather banquettes, a parquet floor and tables with crisp, white cloths. Quo Vadis offers modern European food with a good choice of fish and roasts. Beautifully presented, the baked cod is topped with pastry, moist and flaky inside, and surrounded by tasty mouthfuls of courgette fritter, fennel and cherry tomato (£12.50). The creamy nougatine quo vadis, with its raspberry coulis (£6.00), was gorgeous. The service was impeccable and the lack of music welcome. There are daily specials and a separate vegetarian menu.

Open: Mon-Fri noon-2.30pm, Mon-Sat 5.30pm-11.45pm, Sun noon-3.30pm, 5.30pm-10.30pm; reservations essential; licensed

starter: £4.50-£20
main: £8.50-£18
dessert: £6

AE DC JCB MC V; SW

Quo Vadis

Red Fort

Indian

☎ 020 7437 2115
77 Dean St W1

Map 1 B5
Tube: Leicester Square

Smoking throughout

Red Fort's resplendent menu promises 'a princely welcome', and you won't be disappointed. Forget steaming in at midnight after having sunk 10 pints – this is an altogether different experience. The food is prepared in the (perhaps mythical) style of the Nawabs of Avadh: that's to say, slow-cooked in clay pots sealed with dough. Starters include beautifully presented murg malai zafrani kebabs (£5.95), chargrilled chicken draped with cream, cheese and saffron. There's good old chicken tikka for the less adventurous, and plenty of delicious and surprising choices such as maachi tamater (£12.50) – fish stewed in tomatoes, onion and fenugreek. Vegetarian options are good, although the subz biryani (£8.95) was rather heavy on the basmati rice and light on the vegetables. You won't be at a loss when it comes to picking a Merlot to go with your murg: the menu imaginatively suggests wines to go with the various dishes.

starter: £4.95-£5.95
main: £8.95-£16.95
dessert: £4.95
Set buffet lunch £14.95, set dinner £35 or set vegetarian dinner £25

AE DC MC V; SW

Open: daily noon-2.45pm, Mon-Sat 5.30pm-11.30pm, Sun 6pm-11pm; reservations advisable; licensed

---

Satsuma

Japanese

☎ 020 7437 8338
56 Wardour St W1

Map 1 C4
Tube: Leicester Square
Wheelchair access

This super-trendy and surprisingly affordable Japanese noodle bar is functional, fast and easy-going, thanks to its ever-smiling staff and warm-toned, minimalist décor. The speciality is bento, a traditional assorted set meal served in a rather grand lacquered box. If you're unfamiliar with Japanese food this is a great way to find out what you like. The seafood bento (£12.90) is delicious and includes salmon, prawn, crabsticks fried in breadcrumbs, California rolls, gyoza, miso soup and rice – a culinary variety show! The noodle family extends to Chinese-style soup noodles, thick white wheat-flour noodles, buckwheat and wok-fried Chinese style noodles. The simple vegetable option (£4.90) comes with fresh shiitake mushrooms and shredded seaweed. Green food is definitely the colour to go for: the matcha (green tea) ice cream (£2.50) will refresh the parts vanilla just can't reach!

starter: £3.50-£8
main: £4.90-£13.50
dessert: £2.50-£4.50

AE DC JCB MC V; SW

Open: Mon-Thurs noon-11pm, Fri & Sat noon-11.45pm, Sun noon-10.30pm; reservations not accepted; licensed

Schnecke

Alsatian

☎ **020 7287 6666**
58-59 Poland St W1

Map 1 B3

Tube: Oxford Circus or Tottenham Court Rd

Wheelchair access

 Smoking throughout

'Alsace My Ass' is the slogan at Schnecke, and where you put the accent on the phrase greatly varies the meaning. However, the meaning of Schnecke itself isn't in doubt: it's a vast, heaving place from the Belgo folks which is ideal for rowdy groups. Although the schtick is Alsatian, that's a mere ruse. The beer is Kolsch, the crisp, fruity beer popular in Cologne, Germany, far from Alsace. Authentically served in tiny glasses a bit larger than test tubes, they keep coming until you yell 'halt!' The menu is the most Alsatian aspect of the three-floored place, centring on flambéed tarts, which are very well cooked. The cracker-thin crusts are baked in a wood-fire oven and layered with toppings like flavoured cheeses. Stick to the basic gratinée version (£6), a traditional combination of cheese, onions and bacon, as fancier variations don't work as well. Service – vital to keep the Kolsch coming – is as cheerful as the crowds.

Open: Mon-Sat noon-11.30pm, Sun noon-10.30pm; reservations accepted for large groups; licensed

starter: £2-£4
main: £5-£10
dessert: £2-£4

AE DC JCB MC V; SW

Soba

Japanese

☎ **020 7734 6400**
38 Poland St W1

Map 1 B3

Tube: Oxford Circus

 Nonsmoking tables available

This is dining for modern times: a long, communal yellow table and black lacquer benches dominate the room, while fibreglass walls decorated with Japanese calligraphy complete the picture. Customers are a mixed bag of inner city types and out-of-town shoppers. The noodle stir-fry with seafood, chicken and tofu isn't so different from the one you might make at home, given a little expertise, but for £5.30 who's complaining? The soups (£5.30-£5.50) are huge hotpots of delicious ingredients such as large slabs of teriyaki-marinated lean chicken, shiitake mushrooms and buckwheat noodles. Our starter of salt and pepper squid (£3.75) was expertly executed, and even the plain old dish of Chinese greens with oyster sauce was a tasty treat (£2.95). Our only gripes were that the side servings were smallish, the dishes were sometimes overly salty and the food wasn't 'too hot', despite the menu warnings.

Open: Mon-Fri noon-3.30pm, 5.30pm-11pm, Sat noon-11pm; reservations advisable (especially for dinner); licensed

starter: £2.80-£3.90
main: £5.30-£5.90

MC V; SW

Map 1 C4
Tube: Leicester Square

Smoking throughout

Spiga
Italian

☎ 020 7734 3444
84-86 Wardour St W1

Sleek and chic Spiga has expensive looks – warm cream décor, quality linen and cutlery, smart clientele, attentive service – but it's surprisingly affordable. A basket of sliced ciabatta bread was brought instantly to our table, accompanied by a dish of peppery olive oil, and delicious smells drifted from the open kitchen. The menu changes monthly, but always features wood-fired pizza and freshly made pasta, with a choice of large or small portions for several dishes. The antipasto vegetariano (£5.50) was a small but intensely flavoursome combo of grilled peppers, courgettes, aubergines and onions, a no-contest winner against the more pedestrian carpaccio di manzo (£5.50) of raw beef, rocket and parmesan. Our pizza (£8.50) lacked sufficient toppings for its broad size, but the angel-hair pasta (£8.50) in a chilli and olive oil sauce sprinkled with prawns and rocket hit the spot. Leave room for dessert – we had pastiera di grano (£4.50), a light, sweet ricotta and candied fruit tart, but lusted after the wickedly indulgent tiramisu (£4.50) as soon as we saw it.

starter: £4.50-£6
main: £7-£13.50
dessert: £4.50
AE DC MC V; SW

Open: daily noon-3pm, Sun-Tues 6pm-11pm, Wed-Sat 6pm-midnight; reservations essential; licensed

Sri Siam

Sri Siam

Thai

☎ **020 7434 3544**
16 Old Compton St W1

Map 1 B6
Tube: Leicester Square

Smoking throughout

Traditional Thai cooking combined with contemporary good looks and an enviable address guarantee that Sri Siam Soho is always buzzing. And since food can be ordered up until 11.15pm, it's a good spot for a late bite. Polished wooden floors, bright walls and well-spaced tables give an uncluttered feel. But beware of 'banquet syndrome' if you decide to tackle the set menus – you'll be full before the main course arrives. A starter or two (stir-fried mussels with fresh lemongrass and a dash of chilli, or the excellent hors d'oeuvres) and a main are probably ample for most people. The high point of set menu II (£16.99 per person) is the spicy tom kar goong (a creamy, custard-yellow prawn soup flavoured with coconut, lime and galangal); the main chicken dish was disappointing (not enough chicken) and the dessert choice (ice cream or sorbet) a little predictable.

Open: daily noon-3pm, Mon-Sat 6pm-11.15pm, Sun 6pm-10.30pm; reservations advisable (especially weekends); licensed

starter: £4.90-£6.30
main: £6.80-£10.50
dessert: £3-£4
Set menu £13.99, £15.50, £16.99 or £19.99

AE DC MC V; SW

Stockpot

European

☎ **020 7287 1066**
18 Old Compton St W1

Map 1 B5
Tube: Leicester Square

 Smoking throughout

 Pavement tables

On the shrieking pink frontline of Old Compton St, Stockpot remains stalwartly unfashionable. But, really, who cares when the food is this cheap? Diners here are taking the day off from preening and being seen at nearby Balans or Café Bohème, and taking advantage of a commendable formula of simple food (reasonably) well done and served in a relaxed atmosphere. Pine floors and white walls plastered with theatre posters make for a pleasant interior, with good seating at the front where you can observe the Soho streetlife. (Avoid being banished to the basement.) The menu changes daily but revolves around a good selection of salads (£2.95-£3.50), one or two pastas (£2.50-3.50), a few vegetarian dishes and lots of meat and potatoes. We always come away happy after no-frills dining on the likes of grilled liver and bacon (£3.10) or a turkey dinner with stuffing (£4). *Also at 40 Panton St SW1 ☎ 020 7839 5142, 6 Basil St, Knightsbridge SW3 ☎ 020 7589 8627, 50 James St W1 ☎ 020 7486 9185, and 273 Kings Rd, Chelsea SW3 ☎ 020 7823 3175.*

Open: Mon-Sat 11.30am-11.30pm, Sun noon-11pm; reservations not accepted; licensed

starter: 95p-£2.30
main: £2.50-£5.60
dessert: £1-£1.85
Set lunch 11.30am-5.30pm £3.75-£4.50

cash only

Map 1 C3
Tube: Piccadilly
Smoking throughout

Sugar Club
Asian Fusion

☎ 020 7437 7776
21 Warwick St W1

When chef Peter Gordon opened the Sugar Club in a townhouse in Notting Hill's All Saints Rd, he offered London something rare and new: a menu that reflected the influence of both his native New Zealand and the more subtle flavours of Australasia. This wild mix, dubbed 'Asian fusion' in the food press, attracted worldwide attention, and the fuss continued when Gordon moved the Sugar Club to these stylish new premises in Soho. Traditional choices like rump steak, duck and lamb are cooked to absolute perfection, and fish dishes are laced with chilli, ginger or soy sauces. Where else in London can you get smoked kangaroo salad with peanuts and coriander (£8.10)? It's nearly impossible to pass up dessert, as the daily tarts and cheese choices practically beg you to take the plunge. The Sugar Club doesn't come cheap, but you're paying the price not only for fame, but also for perfection.

starter: £6-£12
main: £11-£21
dessert: £5.50
AE DC JCB MC V; SW

Open: daily noon-3pm, 6pm-11pm; reservations essential; licensed

---

Map 1 D4
Tube: Piccadilly
Wheelchair access
Smoking throughout

Sugar Reef
Pan-American

☎ 020 7851 0800
42-44 Great Windmill St W1

From the street, it's quite possible to mistake Sugar Reef for one of its more risqué neighbours, with its dark tinted glass doors, cheeky leather-clad bouncer and enormous disco glitter ball. The glitter ball theme is continued inside but provides comforting dappled lighting and, together with a polite welcome from staff, customers are safe to assume they have indeed entered a restaurant. Bubble-gum pink walls hung with movie star portraits complete the dream-zone décor. In fact, the only subtle thing about Sugar Reef is the cuisine. The soda bread is fresh and bouncy, and the roast cod with herb crust and olive mash (£12.50) melts on the tongue. The only vegetarian option, mushroom and asparagus risotto (£7.50), uses jumbo mushrooms but flavours are carefully balanced to avoid mushroom overkill. Wine by the glass is good quality but the very extensive wine list makes it more appealing to go for a bottle. If you're watching your weight have a cigar for pudding – there are 20 varieties to choose from.

starter: £5.50-£10.50
main: £8-£21.50
dessert: £5.50
AE DC MC V; SW

Open: restaurant Mon-Fri noon-3pm,Mon-Sat 6pm-midnight, bar/club Mon-Wed 6pm-1am, Thurs-Sat 6pm-3am; reservations advisable; licensed

Tarboush

Lebanese

☎ 020 7287 1220
11 Wardour St W1

Tarboush is hidden above the Insomnia bar, which is appropriate as its vibrant interior would certainly cause some sleepless nights. The extensive Lebanese menu caters for a multitude of tastes, and the helpful waiting staff are on hand to advise. Chicken livers served with crispy pita bread (£2.95) made a hearty starter, even though the meat seemed a little overdone and the chilli sauce was nowhere near fierce enough for our tastes. Tawayeh (£6.95) was described on the menu as tender lamb slices and turned out to be chunks which had been slowly cooked with tomato, onion and garlic, creating a deliciously strong flavour; this time the promised chilli made its presence felt. For dessert we decided on a cold milk pudding, flavoured with rosewater, to refresh the palate. Tarboush is great value for the West End, and the loyal clientele of 20-somethings would seem to agree.

Open: restaurant Mon-Sat noon-2am, Sun noon-11.30pm, bar Mon-Thurs noon-2am, Fri-Sat noon-3am, Sun noon-11.30pm; reservations advisable (Fri & Sat); licensed

Map 1 D5

Tube: Leicester Square or Piccadilly

Entertainment: belly dancer Fri & Sat evenings

Smoking throughout

starter: £2.95-£5.50
main: £6.95-£14.95
dessert: £2.25-£3.25
Set menu £4.95-£7.95 (noon-5pm), £9.95 (5pm-7pm), £14.95 feast

MC V; SW

The Tibetan Restaurant

Tibetan

☎ 020 7839 2090
17 Irving St WC2

The word discreet isn't usually associated with Leicester Square, but this place is easy to miss. The décor has a hint of Santa's grotto, the large mirrors successfully disguising the actual size of the room while retaining a friendly snug feeling. Bland spring rolls (£1.90) served with a fiery chilli sauce were an inauspicious start, but happily the more traditional Tibetan dishes redeemed everything, as did the cup of complimentary Tibetan tea. The vegetable momo (£4.95) exceeded all our expectations of a dumpling. Baleb (Tibetan bread, £2.50) turned out to be similar to a pancake, and made a great accompaniment to the beef noodle soup with green vegetables (£4.85), leaving space only for a dessert of fresh fruit. While it's obviously not, as it claims, the only Tibetan restaurant in London, if you're looking for somewhere inexpensive The Tibetan Restaurant is an original choice.

Open: Mon-Sat noon-3pm, 5pm-10.45pm; reservations advisable; licensed

Map 1 D6

Tube: Leicester Square

Smoking throughout

starter: £1.80-£2.10
main: £4-£5.50
dessert: £1.90-£2.40
Set menu £9.70-£13.50 or vegetarian set menu £8.70-£10.50

MC V

Soba (p 81)

Titanic

British

☎ 020 7437 1912
81 Brewer St W1

Map 1 D3
Tube: Piccadilly
Wheelchair access
Entertainment: DJ Mon-Sat 11pm, magician Wed-Sat

Smoking throughout

The entrance to Marco Pierre White's Titanic is purposefully inconspicuous, but the ballroom-sized dining room is anything but understated – in fact you can't help wondering who's come here just for the food. The menu is straightforward and not always reliable, but it offers variety, with everything from soup to sushi. Accordingly, the gnocchi (£6.95) was bland and uninspiring, but the duck salad (£7.95) was flavoursome and well presented. Traditional British meat and fish dishes make up many of the main courses and, price aside, the roast pig (£12.50) and fish and chips (£11.95) come recommended. At around 9pm, as the volume rises and observation takes the place of conversation, enjoy the delights of delicate chocolate swiss roll (£5.95) or sharp lemon tart (£5.95), and watch the place come alive. It would be difficult to describe Titanic as a serious gastronomic experience but what it lacks in subtlety it more than makes up for in atmosphere.

starter: £5.75-£8.95
main: £10.50-£24.95
dessert: £5.95
AE DC MC V; SW

Open: Mon-Fri 5.30pm-11pm, Sat 5.30pm-11.30pm; reservations advisable (especially weekends); licensed

The Toucan

Irish

☎ 020 7437 4123
19 Carlisle St W1

Map 1 B4
Tube: Tottenham Court Road

 Smoking throughout

Unusually for an Irish theme bar in London, the Craic wins out at the Toucan, a diminutive bar marvellously located in the thick of Soho. You'll also find a great lunchtime menu (available until 10pm, but don't count on having enough elbow room to eat during the evenings) featuring simple dishes like Irish stew and mushroom risotto. The few tables are squeezed into the cellar section of the bar – a warmly lit comfort zone that seems a million miles away from the frantic pace of the streets above. Friendly, prompt service brought us half a dozen Galway Bay oysters (£7) – they didn't squirm but were a sensational taste of sea and metal nevertheless. Less fishy folk might like the meaty, mushroomy, gravy-rich Guinness pie (£5.50), which comes with creamy mashed potato (comfort food par excellence). There are no desserts on the menu, but you can always make do with a perfectly poured Guinness or one of the 38 Irish whiskies (from £1.60 to £40 per shot) on offer.

Open: Mon-Sat 11am-11pm; reservations not accepted; licensed

main: £2-£7
MC V; SW

wok wok

South-East Asian

☎ 020 7437 7080
10 Frith St W1

Map 1 B5
Tube: Tottenham Court Road
Wheelchair access

 Nonsmoking tables available

Wok wok is big, functional and has excellent service – all of which make it a useful address for lunch or dinner. Upstairs is light and airy, downstairs darker and more intimate. The restaurant describes its cuisine as South-East Asian but most of the dishes are Vietnamese and Thai. Starters range from that predictable favourite chicken satay (£4.50) – a little on the sweet side – to more exciting Vietnamese ricepaper rolls (£4.75), recommended for their enticing texture and tangy flavour. Of the main courses we tried – phat thai (£6.90), south Vietnamese chicken curry (£7.75) and Shanghai noodles (£6.95) – the phat thai fried noodles with chicken and prawns was the firm favourite. You may find better South-East Asian food and more intimate settings in the neighbouring streets, but if you haven't booked a table, are in a hurry or simply fancy a no-nonsense meal in comfortable surroundings, wok wok comes into its own.

Open: Mon-Wed noon-11pm, Thurs-Sat noon-midnight, Sun 5.30pm-10.30pm; reservations advisable; licensed

starter: £3.95-£5.95
main: £6.95-£11.95
dessert: £3.75-£3.95
Set lunch £6.95
AE DC JCB MC V; SW

Wong Kei

Chinese

☎ 020 7437 6833
41-43 Wardour St W1

Map 1 D5
Tube: Leicester Square

Smoking throughout 

Wong Kei has been lambasted for its below-par service and food, and like all legends the truth is somewhat more subtle: the service is simply brisk and the 1960s-style Chinese cuisine merely mediocre. But if you're starving and broke, or looking to chase away a mid-winter cold, this is the place to fill up for under £10. The restaurant sprawls over three floors and four rooms, and seating is at a communal round table with about 11 other strangers. The old maxim 'order from the board' applies here, if only to avoid handling the sticky bills of fare, and avoid anything with a glutinous 'sauce'. Nothing seems made to order anyway: ask for the won ton soup and shrimp or chicken fried rice, and the food will arrive two minutes later. The bill for a meal and copious amounts of hot, weak tea will run to about £6.

starter: £3-£6
main: £4-£7
dessert: £2
Set menu £12 (for 2 people)
cash only

Open: daily noon-midnight; reservations not accepted; licensed

Yo! Sushi

Japanese

☎ 020 7287 0443
52 Poland St W1

Map 1 B3
Tube: Oxford Circus
Entertainment: DJ downstairs Fri & Sat

Pavement tables

Yo! Sushi brings some of the best and worst of cutesy, gadgety Japan to London. Among the best: the unlimited supplies of fizzy or pure tap water just a button's press away at every table (£1); the complimentary massages from the friendly staff; the roaming house robot which brings drinks and warm sake past you so regularly that he begins to look like an old friend; the body-warming miso soup (£1.50) with plenty of fresh spring onions; and, lastly, the colour-coded plates – a pricing system for dummies. Among the worst: the way the sushi conveyer belt brings those damn colour-coded plates (£1.50-£3.50) just inches under your nose, tempting you to 'take me' at every passing; the relentless and ridiculous marketing spin-offs – Yo! Sushi T-shirts, watches, Yo! Yos; the strawberry and cream maki rolls; and, finally, the way the staff can't help but tell you about the 'terribly funky' party downstairs (Yo! Below). Oh, another good point: the cooks roll up the sushi from a kitchen smack in the middle of the oval-shaped train track – so you know it's fresh.

sushi plates: £1.50-£3.50
dessert: £1.50-£3.50
AE DC JCB MC V; S

Open: daily noon-midnight; reservations not accepted; licensed

The Savoy Grill ☎ **020 7836 4343**
British/French **The Savoy WC2**

Map 4 E2
Tube: Charing Cross
Dress code: jacket & tie

 Smoking throughout

The Savoy Grill thrives on tradition and a menu that's as conservative as its upper crust clientele. After a perfectly pleasant jerusalem artichoke soup, laced with truffle and an all right caesar salad with a hunk of hickory smoked salmon, we did the right thing and ordered the roast beef. This proved to be a performance of military precision and it's no surprise that Winston Churchill used to be a regular here. An advance guard of tail-coated waiters parked a huge silver trolley next to our banquette, while reserves were brought in to carve the roast (nicely pinky red), dish out vegetables (cracking roast potatoes) and spoon out the red wine shallot sauce. The dining room is lofty and woode-panelled, with starched linen table cloths and place settings just so. This is the sort of place to take great uncle Cedric for a treat, but remember to put on your best bib and tucker and reserve your stiff upper lip for the bill.

Open: Mon-Fri 12.30pm-2.30pm (last orders), Mon-Sat 6pm-11.15pm (last orders); reservations essential; licensed

starter: £6.75-£22
main: £16-£36
dessert: £8-£9
Pre-theatre menu £20 & £27.75

AE DC JCB MC V; SW

Yo! Sushi

TRAFALGAR SQUARE

Map 4 E1
Tube/rail: Charing Cross
Nonsmoking tables available 

The Café in the Crypt

British

☎ 020 7839 4342
St Martin-in-the-Fields, Duncannon St WC2

Surely one of the best-situated eateries in London, this friendly church cafe is jam-packed every lunchtime, with regulars ranging from hungry students to devout old ladies still sprightly enough to negotiate the steep staircase. Join the queue for the self-service selection of quiche, salads and hot daily specials. Despite the canteen style there's nothing institutional about the fresh and flavoursome poached salmon served with butter sauce and generous plateful of nicely cooked peas, carrots and new potatoes (£6.10). The créme caramel (£1.95) is melt-in-the-mouth just as it should be. But don't expect to linger over your dessert – even if you're not in a hurry, the person waiting for your table probably is. Before you leave, have a browse round the adjacent bookshop or catch one of the lunchtime concerts in the church.

main: £5.50-£6.10
dessert: £1-£1.95
cash or cheque only

Open: Mon-Sat 10am-8pm, Sun noon-8pm; reservations not accepted; licensed

The Café in the Crypt

Chelsea

Earl's Court

Fulham

CENTRAL SOUTH-WEST

Hammersmith

Knightsbridge

Olympia

Pimlico

South Kensington

Victoria

West Kensington

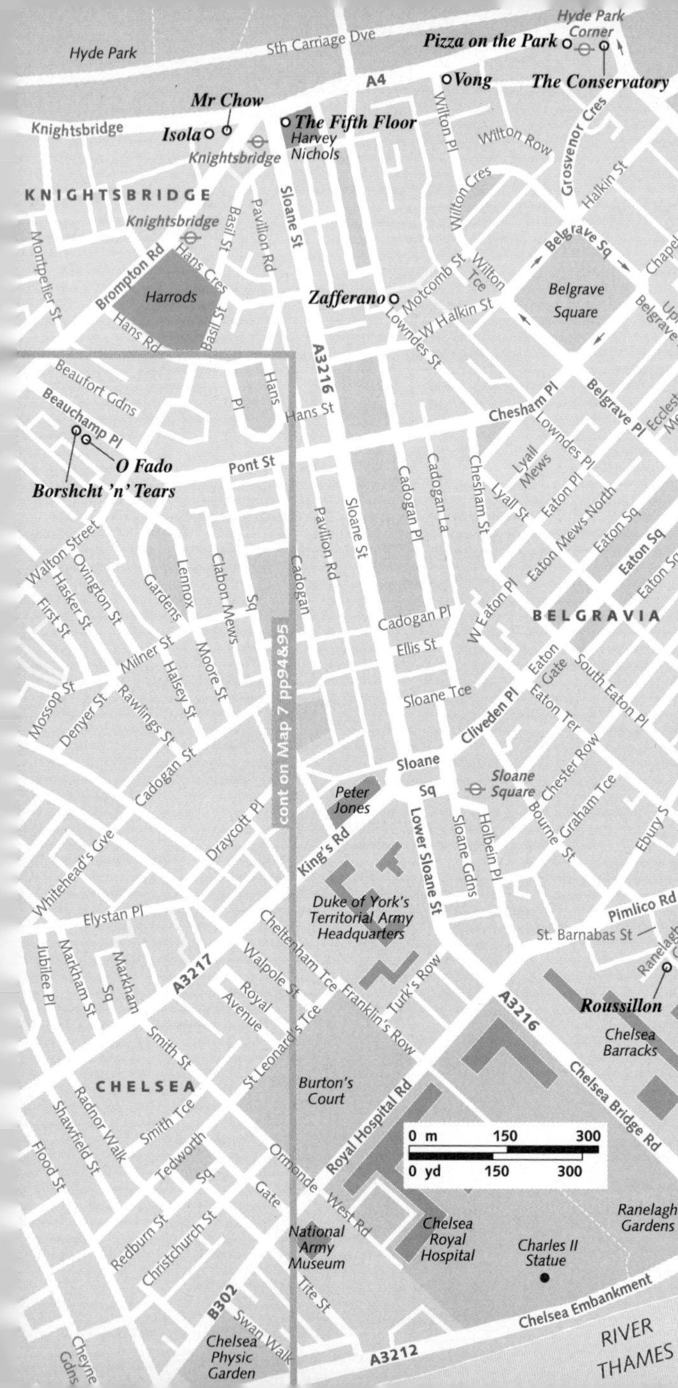

Hyde Park
Sth Carriage Dve
Hyde Park Corner
Pizza on the Park
The Conservatory
A4
Vong
Mr Chow
Isola
The Fifth Floor
Harvey Nichols
Knightsbridge
KNIGHTSBRIDGE
Harrods
Zafferano
Belgrave Square
BELGRAVIA
O Fado
Borshcht 'n' Tears
cont on Map 7 pp94&95
Peter Jones
Duke of York's Territorial Army Headquarters
Roussillon
Chelsea Barracks
CHELSEA
Burton's Court
National Army Museum
Chelsea Royal Hospital
Charles II Statue
Ranelagh Gardens
Chelsea Physic Garden
RIVER THAMES
0 m 150 300
0 yd 150 300

Map 6 - Knightsbridge & Around

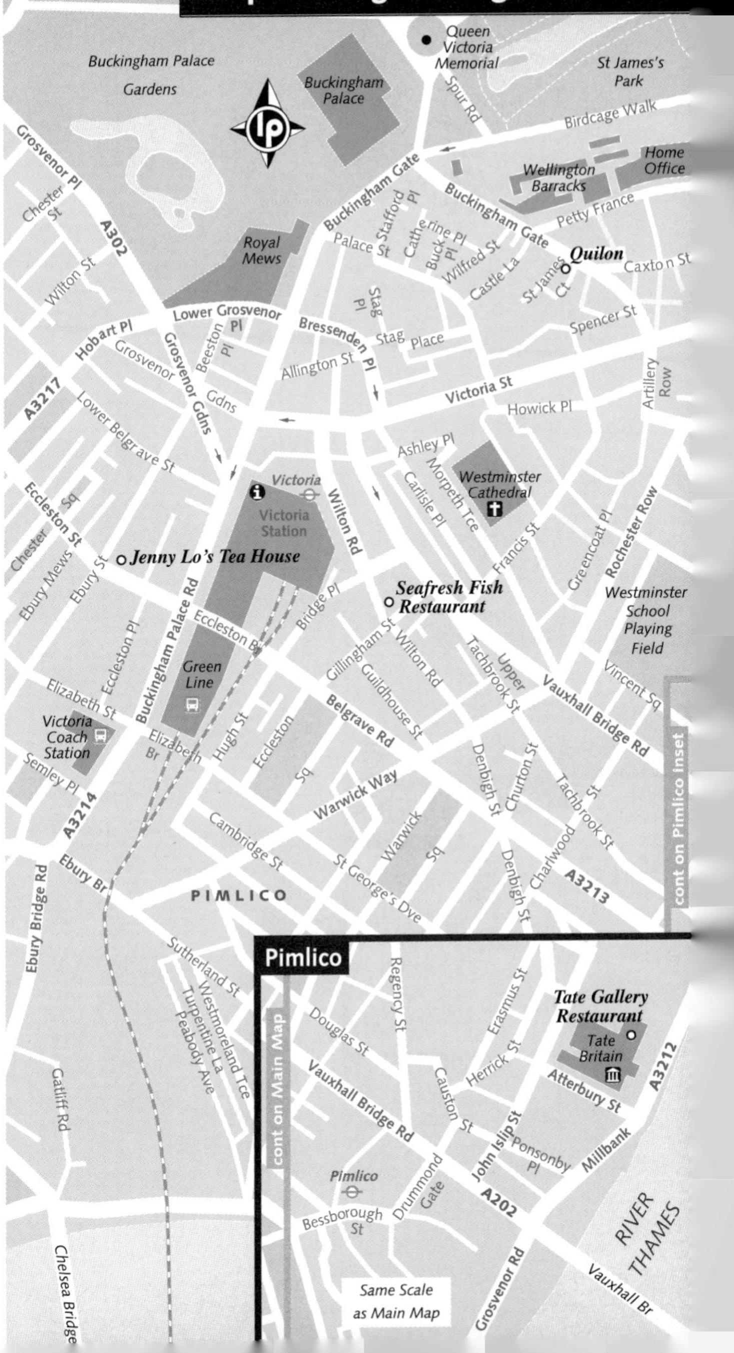

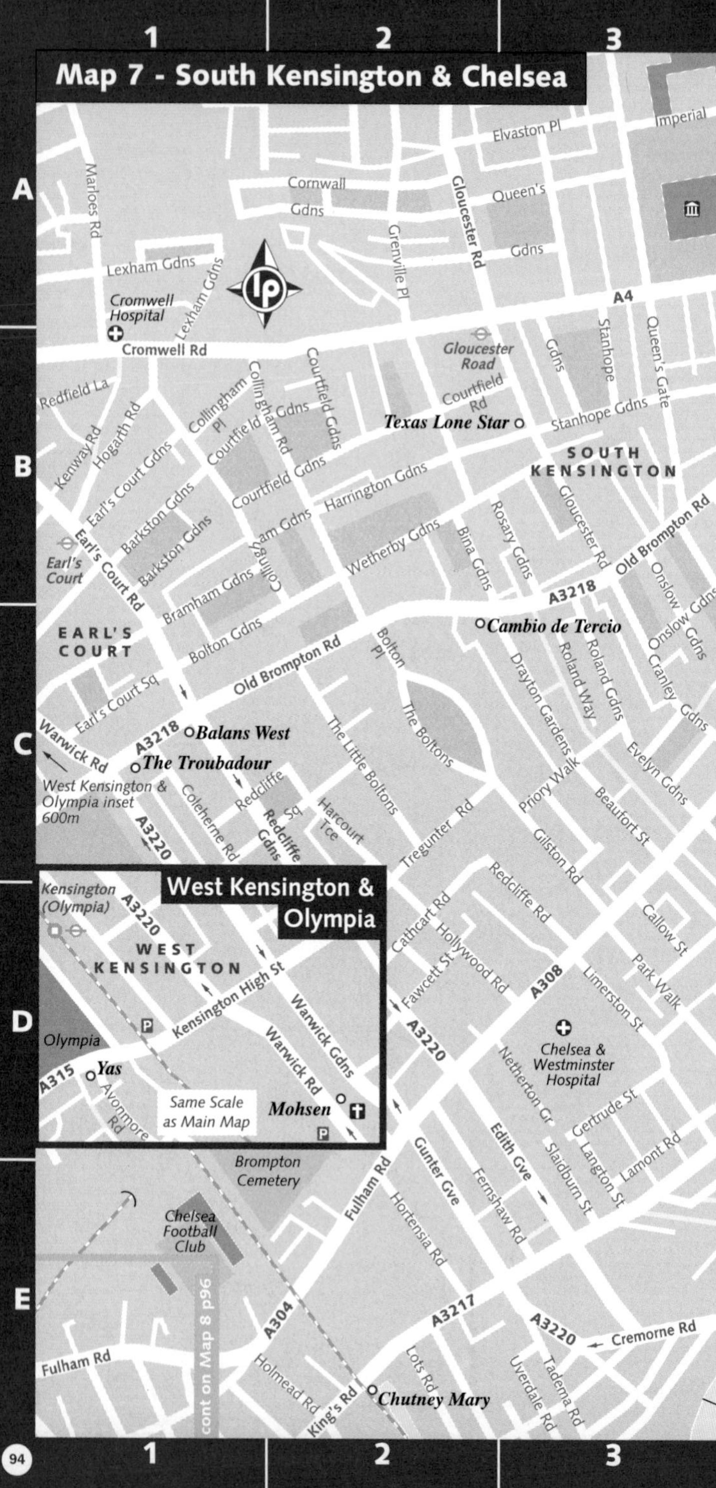

Map 7 - South Kensington & Chelsea
Imperial
Elvaston Pl
Cornwall Gdns
Queen's Gdns
Gloucester Rd
Grenville Pl
Marloes Rd
Lexham Gdns
Cromwell Hospital
Cromwell Rd
A4
Gloucester Road
Courtfield Rd
Stanhope Gdns
Queen's Gate
Texas Lone Star
SOUTH KENSINGTON
Redfield La
Hogarth Rd
Kenway Rd
Earl's Court Gdns
Collingham Pl
Collingham Rd
Courtfield Gdns
Harrington Gdns
Barkston Gdns
Earl's Court
Earl's Court Rd
Bramham Gdns
Wetherby Gdns
Bina Gdns
Rosary Gdns
Old Brompton Rd
A3218
Onslow Gdns
Cambio de Tercio
EARL'S COURT
Bolton Gdns
Bolton Pl
Roland Way
Roland Gdns
Cranley Gdns
Drayton Gardens
Earl's Court Sq
The Boltons
Warwick Rd
Balans West
The Troubadour
The Little Boltons
Evelyn Gdns
West Kensington & Olympia inset 600m
Coleherne Rd
Redcliffe Sq
Redcliffe Gdns
Harcourt Tce
Priory Walk
Beaufort St
Tregunter Rd
Gilston Rd
A3220
West Kensington & Olympia
Kensington (Olympia)
WEST KENSINGTON
Kensington High St
Warwick Gdns
Olympia
A315
Yas
Avonmore Rd
Same Scale as Main Map
Mohsen
Cathcart Rd
Hollywood Rd
Redcliffe Rd
Callow St
Fawcett St
Park Walk
A308
Limerston St
Chelsea & Westminster Hospital
Netherton Gr
Gertrude St
Edith Gve
Langton St
Lamont Rd
Slaidburn St
Brompton Cemetery
Fulham Rd
Gunter Gve
Fernshaw Rd
Chelsea Football Club
Hortensia Rd
cont on Map 8 p96
A304
A3217
A3220
Cremorne Rd
Holmead Rd
Lots Rd
Uverdale Rd
Tadema Rd
King's Rd
Chutney Mary

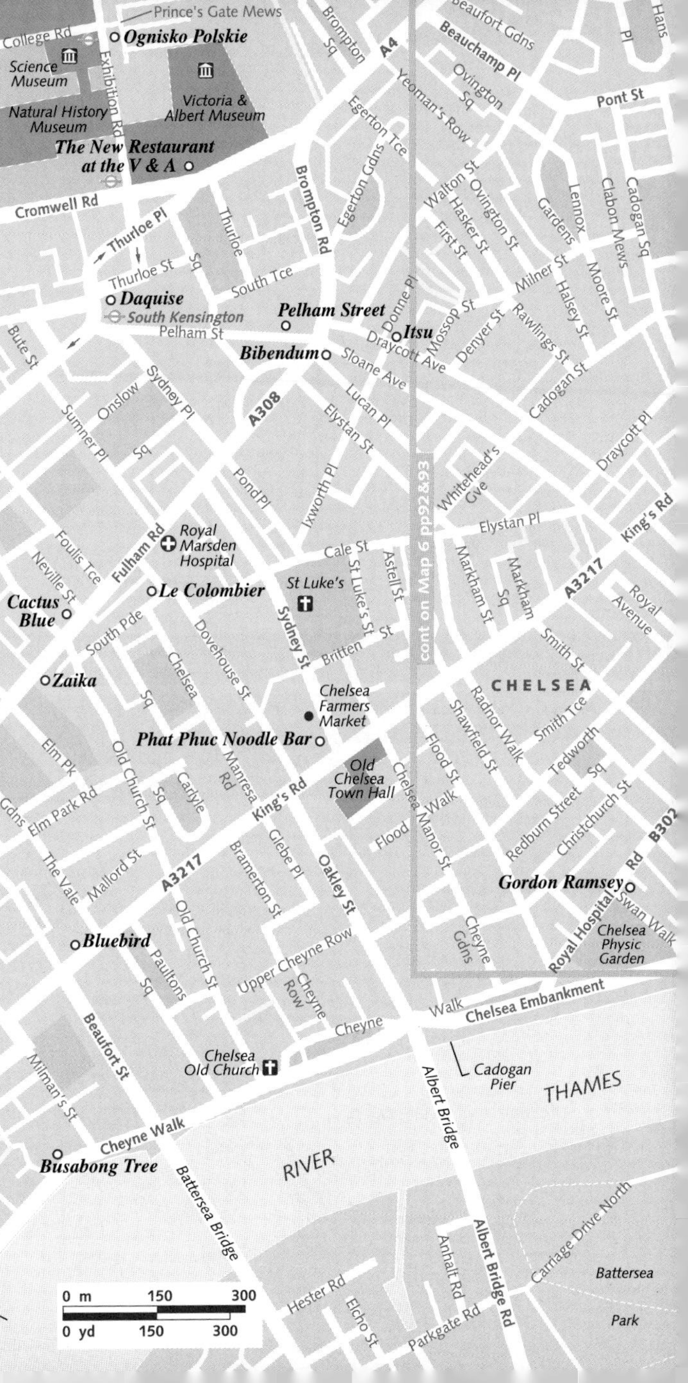

Ognisko Polskie
Science Museum
Natural History Museum
Victoria & Albert Museum
The New Restaurant at the V & A
Daquise
South Kensington
Pelham Street
Itsu
Bibendum
Royal Marsden Hospital
Le Colombier
Cactus Blue
St Luke's
Zaika
Chelsea Farmers Market
Phat Phuc Noodle Bar
Old Chelsea Town Hall
CHELSEA
Gordon Ramsey
Chelsea Physic Garden
Bluebird
Chelsea Old Church
Cadogan Pier
THAMES
RIVER
Busabong Tree
Battersea Park
cont on Map 6 pp92&93
0 m 150 300
0 yd 150 300

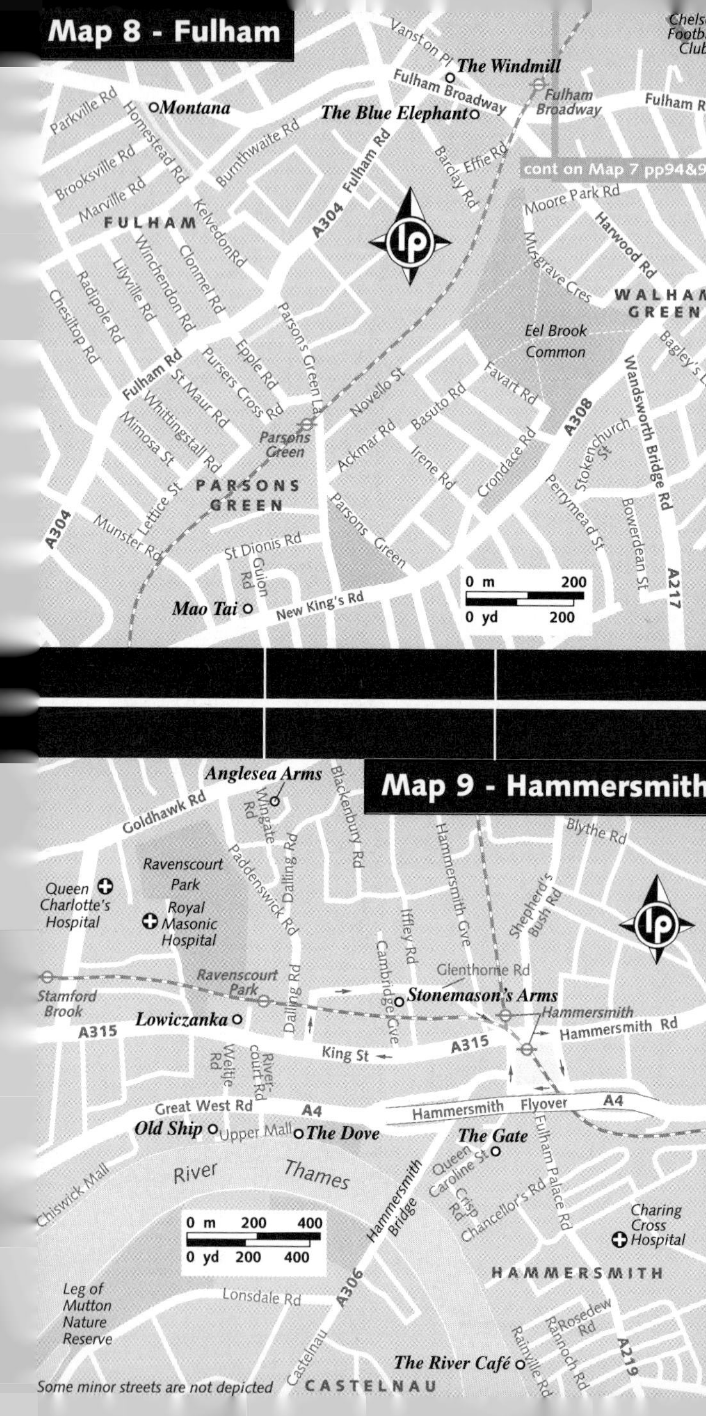

cont on Map 7 pp94&95

Central South-West

BEST

- **Mohsen**
  Excellent, unfussy Iranian home cooking
- **Montana**
  Accomplished American ambrosia
- **Roussillon**
  Superb ingredients, fine service
- **Vong**
  Where French and Thai meld masterfully
- **The Windmill**
  Pampers vegetarians with amiable staff and an enticing menu
- **Zaika**
  A palate-expanding experience in elegant surrounds

Chelsea, South Kensington and Knightsbridge are London's richest areas, yet in many ways they are also its least colourful. Home to hordes of expats living in corporate flats, the pavements echo with the sound of tourist mobs parading past the snazzy shops and swarming lemming-like into Harrods. The most common accent you'll hear around the Gloucester Rd tube stop, home to scores of hotels catering to the bus-tour set, is American. When the accent is British, it's likely to be from the posh end of the range, and the dozens of expensive and established restaurants along Fulham and Kings Rds are always ready to service this well-heeled crowd. (The Baron's Court area is a chaotic counterpoint that suits the many resident Australians just fine.)

Further out, however, in places such as Fulham and Olympia the areas are less homogenous; these districts have a mix of residents from working class to upper management. And while most of the action is generated by and for locals, you'll still find some restaurants that are worth the trip, like Fulham's elegant Montana, sumptuous Blue Elephant and charming Windmill.

Bluebird

Modern European

☎ 020 7559 1000
350 King's Rd SW3

Map 7 D4
Tube: Sloane Square
Wheelchair access
Entertainment: pianist nightly 6pm-11pm
Smoking throughout

Once the state-of-the-art home of the famous bluebird car, this fabulous Art Deco building is now one of the gastro-canteens of the Conran empire. If you arrive early, tickle your taste buds with a wander round the ground floor food hall with its tastefully presented delights. Upstairs, the restaurant is spacious and bright. The interior is eclectic, with stone floors, grey leather chairs and black and white photos incorporating the theme of the car. The menu has a strong emphasis on seafood and also contains specialities from the wood-burning stove, such as the cured salmon with tomatoes, red onion and coriander (£12.50). The goat's cheese tart (£9.50) is more than ample, delicately flavoured and complemented by roast peppers. We recommend a finish with the explosive flavours, colours and textures of the pavlova and passionfruit (£5).

starter: £6-£12.50
main: £9.25-£29
dessert: £4.50-£5.75
Lunch/pre-theatre menu £12.75 or £15.75
AE DC JCB MC V; SW

Open: Mon-Fri noon-3.30pm, Sat & Sun 11am-4.30pm, daily 6pm-11pm; reservations advisable; licensed

Busabong Tree

Thai

☎ 020 7352 7534
112 Cheyne Walk SW10

Map 7 E4
Tube: Fulham Broadway
Smoking throughout

Garden tables

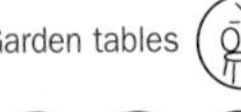

There's no mistaking the romance of old (well, mid-80s) Siam in Busabong Tree's boxy but evocative interior of wicker chairs, silk hangings and, yes, indoor pond. Once seated beneath a prospering potted palm by a fairly abrupt waiter, we took up an offer of prawn crackers (£2.80), which were more grainy than delicate and came with a very oily peanut sauce. The starters were more successful: we happily dispatched some perfectly marinated chicken satays (£4.80) and a bowl of tom yum kai (£4.90), a sweetly volatile brew packed with sinus-clearing fresh lime and lemongrass. Tempted by the 'passion killer' (prawns sautéed in fish sauce with garlic, £14.95), we opted instead for fried succulent peppercorn chicken (£7.95), dryly spiced with pepper, ginger and coriander. We couldn't get enough of a deliciously rich, coconutty version of that old crowd-pleaser Penang beef curry (£7.95). After the curry, peeled lychees on ice (£2.95) were a welcome cold shower for the taste buds.

starter: £4.20-£7.95
main: £4.95-£14.95
dessert: £2.95-£4.50
Set lunch £9.95
AE DC MC V; SW

Open: daily noon-3pm, Mon-Sat 6pm-11.15pm; reservations advisable; licensed

Cactus Blue

South-West American

☎ 020 7823 7858
86 Fulham Rd SW3

Cactus Blue is sophisticated Tex-Mex food in a tequila slammer atmosphere. The bar area, with overlooking mezzanine, is the perfect space for top-shelf Friday night drinks, but there's also a slightly quieter eating area out the back. The food is generally thoughtful, from the sparse designer nachos (count the corn chips on your fingers, £5.25) to near-perfect baked short ribs with mustard bourbon sauce (£5.45). Try the mesa tapas sampler (£9.95) because while it's hit and miss – our silver dollar crab cakes were marred by pieces of shell – the hits are superb and often original. The Peking duck tortilla wrap sounds dodgy, but is actually a succulent sausage roll with exquisite ginger and jam flavours. Tequila-marinated beef fajita (£11.95) is sweetened with black beans and the fajitas come rolled up in a banana leaf. Staff are friendly, if a little confused in the racket. You'll feel dizzy just looking at the list of tequilas (from £5), so if you prick yourself on a cactus, retire to the bar: the sublime vodka margarita (£5.25) will dull the pain.

Open: Mon-Fri 5.30pm-midnight, Sat & Sun noon-midnight; reservations advisable; licensed

Map 7 C4

Tube: South Kensington

Entertainment: live jazz Tues & Wed 9pm

 Smoking throughout

starter: £3.95-£6.95
main: £9.95-£13.95

AE DC MC V; SW

Chutney Mary

Anglo-Indian

☎ 020 7351 3113
535 King's Rd SW10

Don't have so much as one pint of lager before you visit Chutney Mary. Go in fresh and enjoy a G&T, for this place is class. It's even nicely decorated. The food is a mix of traditional Indian, Anglo Indian and a regularly changing selection of regional specialities. To start, try one of the top-notch staples including samosas (£5-£6) or 'flavour of the month' baked crab with mustard and red chilli (£8.50). We thoroughly enjoyed the lobster with mango, tamarind and coconut (£19), and spicy lamb shanks (£12.75), while the Goan green curry à la carte (£11.50) was good value. The best pudding on the menu was a lovely spiced bread and butter pudding (£6), not too sweet. We swapped a lot of spoons, so we reckon the tasting menu (£32) is the best way of sampling all the unusual flavours and combinations.

Open: Mon-Thurs 12.30pm-2.30pm, 7pm-11.30pm, Fri & Sat 12.30pm-2.30pm, 6.30pm-11.30pm, Sun 12.30pm-3pm, 7pm-10.30pm; licensed

Map 7 E2

Tube: Fulham Broadway

Entertainment: jazz Sun lunch

 Separate smoke-free dining available

starter: £5.25-£8.50
main: £11.50-£14
dessert: £4-£6
Set lunch £12.50

AE DC MC V

CENTRAL SOUTH-WEST

Map 7 D6
Tube: Sloane Square

Smoking throughout 

Gordon Ramsay

French/Mediterranean

☎ 020 7352 4441
68 Royal Hospital Rd SW3

Gordon Ramsay's rough diamond reputation proceeds him but, as far as his cooking is concerned, we can confirm that the accolades are richly deserved. Whatever the kitchen dramas, all in the intimate, elegantly beige dining room is well mannered. Service is flamboyantly Gallic (like the food), yet convivial rather than poncey. There are only set menus and gourmands will want to go for the £70 seven course dinner, including Ramsay's signature dishes of lobster pasta (in this case, tortellini) and salad of scallops and new potatoes. The three course lunch and dinner menu (£55) is very tempting, but you certainly won't be short-changed by the briefer £28 option, which comes, like everything else, with all the haute cuisine trimmings. A sublime foie gras terrine is marbled with swirling layers of duck meat, the gamey venison ideally matched with wild mushrooms and celeriac. Desserts are very fine, but fromage fans are well advised to graze from the trolley of at least 15 premium French cheeses and get their sugar fix from the marvellous petits fours.

Set lunch £28 & £55
or set dinner £55 & £70
AE DC MC V; SW

Mon-Fri noon-2.30pm, 6.45pm-11pm; reservations essential (one month in advance); licensed

Itsu

Japanese

☎ 020 7584 5522
118 Draycott Ave SW3

Map 7 B5
Tube: South Kensington
Certified organic

Smoking at the bar only

Take a cool Japanese idea – the conveyor-belt delivery of plates of sushi (known as kaiten-zushi) – apply designer Chelsea chic, and the result is Itsu. We settled into a cosy ground-floor booth beside one of the two conveyor belts, gave our drinks orders to the waiter (there's also a self-service area for drinks), and worked our way from the white (£2.50) to the gold-edged plates (£3.50). The sushi is mostly of the fancy variety, such as rolls of smoked salmon and avocado coated with black roe (£2.95) or prawn with Asian pesto (£2.95), but it's the other creations that catch the eye as they rattle by. The beetroot-cured salmon, for example, topped with a drizzle of dill sauce (£3.25), was a harmonious combination of flavours more Russian than Japanese. Not everything works – the mango-filled brandy snap (£2.95) lacked snap – but as the restaurant's slim manifesto says, 'it's an attitude rather than a cuisine', and Itsu has bags of it.

Open: Mon-Sat noon-11pm, Sun noon-10pm; reservations not accepted; licensed

starter: £2.50-£3.50
main: £2.50-£3.50
dessert: £2.50-£3.25
AE MC V; SW

Le Colombier

French

☎ 020 7351 1155
145 Dovehouse St SW3

Map 7 C4
Tube: South Kensington

Smoking throughout

Terrace tables

The flavours and aromas of fine French cuisine are alive and well at this delightful restaurant tucked between King's Rd and Fulham Rd. With its chic, modern interior and comfortable atmosphere, it's popular not only with the denizens of Chelsea and Fulham, but also with diners from further afield. Specialising in traditional Gallic cooking, Le Colombier prepares snails, oysters, fish and meat with home-style flair. The chicory, roquefort and walnut salad (£5.20) is a light introduction to main dishes such as tender monkfish wrapped in bacon (£14). If it's a romantic occasion, the plump oysters (£13 for nine) are sure to win hearts. At Le Colombier the Chelsea prices seem justified, considering the high standard of service and vibrant surrounds.

Open: daily noon-3pm, 6.30pm-11pm; reservations accepted; licensed

starter: £3.90-£12.50
main: £9.80-£19.90
dessert: £4.90
Set menu £13 (until 7.30pm)
AE DC MC V; SW

Map 7 C5
Tube: Sloane Square or South Kensington

Smoking throughout 

Courtyard tables 

Phat Phuc Noodle Bar

Vietnamese

☎ 0976 276 808
The Chelsea Courtyard, 151 Sydney St SW3

Phat Phuc (meaning happy Buddha) is a wonderful concept – a Vietnamese-style street stall in the tranquil surroundings of Chelsea Courtyard. Seating is outdoors, either on a bench or at the counter. Simply place your order and sit back and enjoy a live cookery demonstration. Only two dishes are prepared each day: steaming bowls of meat or vegetarian pho, a clear Vietnamese broth filled with delicate spices, noodles, fresh coriander and spring onions. The vegetable pho (£4) is packed with thin rice stick noodles, tasty tofu, three types of oriental mushroom and green vegetables, while the beef pho (£4) is simpler fare with fat, slippery noodles. Visit the neighbouring farmer's market if you want some drinks to take along.

main: £4-£4.50
cash only

Open: Mon-Sat noon-3.30pm; reservations not accepted; unlicensed

---

Map 7 C4
Tube: South Kensington

Smoking throughout

Zaika

Indian

☎ 020 7351 7823
257-259 Fulham Rd SW3

If you're after a late-night vindaloo and a few pints of lager, Zaika isn't for you. It's without a doubt a cut above your average curry house, in décor – sophisticated, candle-lit and spice-coloured – as well as cuisine. Chef Vineet Bhatia has broken the mould with his new interpretations of old favourites. Diners who love Indian food but are tired of formula curries will love his combinations of flavours and textures. The biryani-style risotto (£4.95), with red onion, coriander and topped with crispy prawn, and the chicken masala, with curry leaves and coconut, are exceptional. The spiced seafood (£12.50) was slightly too pungent, overpowering the delicate fishy flavours, but the ensuing plateful of chocolate samosas (£3.95) and skewer of juicy tandoori-roasted fruit with mango kulfi (£3.95), swiftly delivered by the highly attentive waiters, more than compensated.

starter: £4.95-£7.50
main: £9.50-£14.50
dessert: £3.95
Jugalbandi set menu £22/person (min 2 people)
AE MC V; SW

Open: Mon-Fri noon-2.30pm, Mon-Sat 6.30pm-10.45pm, Sun noon-2.45pm, 6.30pm-10pm; reservations advisable (especially evenings); licensed

EARL'S COURT

Balans West ☎ **020 7244 8838**
International **239 Old Brompton Rd W5**

Map 7 C1
Tube: Earl's Court
Certified organic

 Smoking throughout

 Pavement tables

Balans is probably the most influential restaurant on the gay scene to have opened in Britain in the last decade. Inspired by the success of their flagship on Old Compton St, Soho, proprietors Prady Balan and David Taylor have expanded their empire to include Balans West in Earls Court and Balans Knightsbridge opposite the Brompton Oratory. You'll love the reliability of Balans' bountiful breakfasts: 'Breakfast with a capital 'B' breakfast comes with two free-range eggs, sausage, bacon, mushrooms and tomatoes on toast (£5.50) – perfection on a plate. The blueberry pancakes (£5.25) are overflowing with fresh fruit, maple syrup and pecan maple butter (or with bacon and maple syrup – it's up to you). But there's more to Balans than just breakfast – they offer everything from noodles to grills to bangers and mash. With a good selection of coffees, teas and juices, snappy service and handsome waiters, this is the place to meet, eat and be seen.

Open: Sun-Thurs 8am-midnight (breakfast Mon-Fri 8am-noon), Fri & Sat 8am-2am; reservations not accepted; licensed

starter: £1.50-£5.25
main: £6.95-£10.95
dessert: £3.25-£4.95

AE JCB MC V; SW

Balans West

The Blue Elephant

Thai

☎ 020 7385 6595
4-6 Fulham Broadway SW6

Map 8 A2
Tube: Fulham Broadway
Wheelchair access
Nonsmoking tables available

The Blue Elephant's neon sign provides intrigue to what's on offer inside, and upon entering you won't be disappointed by the extravagant décor – exotic plants, running water and a scented aroma. Whether conversant with Thai cuisine or a first timer, the Royal Thai banquet menu is a worthy choice, and every set menu dish can be ordered and enjoyed separately. The banquet begins with mouthwatering chicken satay, pork satay and paper prawns, deliciously complemented with five flavoured sauces. The optional choice of soup that follows breaks up the courses well. Beware or enjoy the very hot tom yum goong – forewarning is provided on the menu and by the friendly staff. The main course introduces six dishes with rice and vegetable accompaniments. Our favourite is the massaman, slowly braised lamb in a gentle medium-spiced sauce. Even after the filling main course, we appreciated the fresh fruit and ice cream for dessert.

starter: £5.75-£7:50
main: £8.50-£13.95
dessert: £3-£5
Set lunch £10 & £15, dinner £29, £34 or £45
AE DC MC V

Open: Mon-Fri noon-2.30pm, 7pm-12.30am, Sat 6.30pm-12.30am, Sun noon-3pm, 7pm-10.30pm; reservations advisable; licensed

Mao Tai

Chinese

☎ 020 7731 2520
58 New Kings Rd SW6

Map 8 B1
Tube: Parsons Green, then bus 22
Nonsmoking tables available

It's no surprise why a cosmopolitan crowd flock to this perennially good Chinese restaurant. Terracotta walls adorned with various oriental displays create a warm and stylish atmosphere filled with the buzz of expectant and satisfied diners. Salt and pepper soft-shell crab (£6.50) and bang bang chicken (£4.85) are stand-out starters. Succulent shreds of chicken covered with a beautifully dry Sichuan peanut sauce are excellently counterbalanced by a crisp cucumber salad. Spicy tangerine pork with water chestnuts (£7.50) again hits the mark, the fruit working surprisingly well with the tender meat and mixed vegetables to refresh the heat of the chilli. The service at Mao Tai is friendly and incredibly fast, making it one of the best Chinese restaurants in the capital.

starter: £4.50-£7.85
main: £5.50-£17.50
dessert: £3.50-£5.50
Set menu £23.70/person (min 2 people)
AE DC JCB MC V; SW

Open: Mon-Fri noon-3pm, Sat & Sun 12.30pm-3pm, daily 7pm-11.30pm; reservations advisable; licensed

Montana — ☎ 020 7385 9500
American — **125-129 Dawes Rd SW6**

From a distance Montana shines. The white table settings and large wine glasses sparkle against the rich ochre walls, enticing you inside. But you can't just wander in, as the equally sparkling cuisine means that booking is essential. The ever-changing menu draws from North America, a trait shared with its cousins Idaho and Canyon. The rich flavours of the Southwest predominate but other regions get their due as well. Smoked salmon fishcakes (£7) are a rich alternative to the norm, while the New England seafood chowder (£6) would do any Bostonian proud (the key is getting just the right hint of black pepper). Everything comes with a selection of whole-grain breads that surprise with chillies and other flavourings. The Cajun-spiced northern albacore tuna (£14) is a hearty grilled fish, nicely teamed with coriander cream and a delicate red bean burrito. Service is smooth and professional, and the wine list has several good choices below £15. On most nights there's some combination of live jazz, piano and/or vocalists.

Open: Mon-Fri 7pm-11pm, Fri noon-3.30pm, Sat & Sun noon-11pm ; reservations advisable (essential weekends); licensed

Map 8 A1

Tube: Fulham Broadway, then bus 295

Entertainment: Jazz, piano and vocals Wed-Sun evenings, Sat & Sun lunch

 Nonsmoking tables available

starter: £5-£8
main: £9-£16
dessert: £5
Fri set lunch £10 or £12

AE MC V; SW

The Windmill — ☎ 020 7381 2372
Vegetarian — **486 Fulham Rd SW6**

The great ambience of this vegetarian and vegan restaurant is enhanced by an imaginative menu, packed with punchy flavours. The starter of rice noodle spring rolls is served with the surprisingly non-combative tastes of pickled ginger, sweet chilli dip, shoyu and a seaweed and noodle salad (£4.50). Of the mains, the leek and artichoke roulade with red pepper coulis (£7.50) ensures a full range of taste sensations, and dessert can be a delightfully creamy vegan ice cream (£3.25). The overall Windmill experience is only improved by the staff, who are adept at gauging moods. While we received friendly, unobtrusive service and enjoyed a fully relaxing evening, the birthday girl at the next table was served pudding by a singing waiter dressed as a chimpanzee.

Open: Mon-Sat 11am-11pm, Sun 3pm-11pm; reservations advisable (especially Fri & Sat evening); licensed & BYO (corkage £4/bottle)

Map 8 A2

Tube: Fulham Broadway

 Nonsmoking tables available

starter: £2.75-£4.75
main: £6-£7.95
dessert: £2-£3.75

AE MC V

The Anglesea Arms

Modern British

☎ 020 8749 1291
5 Wingate Rd W6

Map 9 A2
Tube: Goldhawk Rd or Ravenscourt Park

Smoking throughout 

Pavement tables 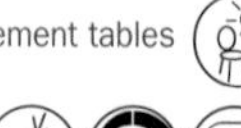

The Anglesea Arms is in a relative backwater between Shepherd's Bush and Hammersmith. It's an all-too-rare independent pub serving fine ale, decent wine and innovative, food. There are only a handful of tables in the bar area, so, despite the traditional dark wooden interior, it still feels spacious. On a balmy evening there was plenty of supping and chatting going on outside, while inside, there wasn't a free seat. It only took an ale's wait to get a table, with a view of the busy kitchen. Starters include an unusual but lovely marinated fetta salad (£4.95) and a sweet onion and emmental tart (£3.95). The calf's liver with pancetta and rosemary is nicely done (£8.95), as is the wild mushroom risotto with parmesan and rocket (£7.50). Home-made puddings include a ricotta cheesecake and an amply rich chocolate mousse/cake/sorbet (both £3.95). With proper coffee and decent service, it's well worth the trip out west.

starter: £3.95-£6
main: £7-£10
dessert: £3.95-£5
DC MC V; SW

Open: Mon-Sat 12.30pm -2.45pm, 7pm-10.45pm, Sun 1pm-3.30pm, 7pm-10.30pm; reservations not accepted; licensed

The Gate

Modern British vegetarian

☎ 020 8748 6932
51 Queen Caroline St W6

Map 9 B3
Tube: Hammersmith

Smoking throughout 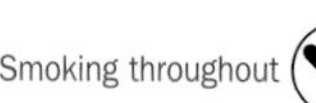

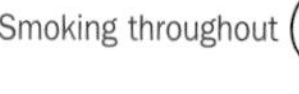

Courtyard tables 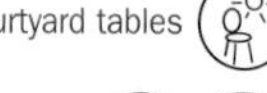

This vegetarian haven has a menu so delicious it should convert even the most confirmed meat-lover. The premises are rented from the neighbouring church, lending the décor a village hall atmosphere despite the eclectic pop art which adorns the bright yellow walls. The small menu changes monthly, and all the dishes are interesting, varied and beautifully presented. The butternut gnocchi (£4.90) and goat's cheese and pear salad (£4.90) are rich and flavoursome – a far cry from the stereotypical wholegrain, low-fat image of many a vegetarian restaurant. The mains such as rocket panzerotti (£8.90) are equally sumptuous – fresh rocket pasta filled with grilled aubergine and oven-dried tomatoes topped with shaved parmesan and a tangy sage and lemon butter. Innovative desserts include nectarines in filo (£4.75) and blackberry and kirsch brûlée (£4.25). Our animal friends agree: if only all vegetarian restaurants were as good as the Gate.

starter: £3.50-£5.75
main: £7.25-£9.75
dessert: £3.25-£5
AE DC MC V; SW

Open: Mon-Fri noon-3pm, Mon-Sat 6pm-11pm; reservations advisable; licensed

Riverside Pubs

If you've eaten your fill and need a pint to wash it down, head to a riverside pub for a bit of London tradition and a great view of the Thames.

Trafalgar Tavern Park Row, Greenwich SE10
☎ 020 8858 2437 (Map 21 A3)
The hugely popular Trafalgar Tavern serves an inviting pint. Sit in the place where Dickens downed a few ales (the Trafalgar is mentioned in *Our Mutual Friend*) and enjoy the view of the Millennium Dome and the sweeping bend of the Thames.

Prospect of Whitby 57 Wapping Wall, Wapping E1
☎ 020 8481 1095 (Map 19 A2)
The 400-year-old pewter bar of the Prospect of Whitby has served pints to sailors since 1520, and propped up the likes of Samuel Pepys and the infamous hanging Judge Jeffreys. It's not surprising that the pub is firmly listed on the tourist trails.

Captain Kidd 108 Wapping High St, Wapping E1
☎ 020 8480 5759 (Map 19 B1)
The all-wood interior of this converted warehouse and large garden area make this one of the best pubs on the Thames. The grim scaffold laments the hanging of the pub's namesake in 1701.

Anchor Bankside 34 Park St, Southwark SE1
☎ 020 7407 1577 (Map 20 A3)
There has been a tavern on this site for around 1000 years, proving the popularity of the location. Samuel Johnson rented a room and wrote part of his dictionary here, in the inventively named Samuel Johnson Room.

The Dove 19 Upper Mall, Hammersmith W6
☎ 020 8748 5405 (Map 9 B2)
The Dove retains its 17th-century heritage well and has not succumbed to change to pull the punters. It's a beautiful little place, with low-beamed ceilings and ageing woodwork providing a welcoming feel.

Old Ship 25 Upper Mall, Hammersmith W6
☎ 020 8748 2593 (Map 9 B1)
The large lawn easily accommodates the swarm of drinkers that flock here in summer. And the bar is big enough to allow you to get your drinks quickly and comfortably.

City Barge 27 Strand on the Green, Chiswick W4
☎ 020 8994 2148 (Map 24 B2)
Perched right on the river, the City Barge is split between the old low-beamed ceiling bar and the newer expansion. A pub has been on this site since 1484 and part of the Beatles film *Help!* was shot here.

The Bell & Crown 72 Strand on the Green, Chiswick W4
☎ 020 8994 4164 (Map 24 A2)
The Bell & Crown, with its airy conservatory, allows you to enjoy the river on the coldest of days. And the outside benches and river wall provide pews for views of Kew on warm summer days.

Neal Bedford

Lowiczanka

Polish

☎ 020 8741 3225
238-246 King St W6

Map 9 A1
Tube: Ravenscourt Park
Wheelchair access
Entertainment: Eastern European band Fri-Sun evenings
Nonsmoking tables available

Patio & pavement tables

With theatre shows and other attractions sharing the Polish Centre space, Lowiczanka offers diners a lively and affordable opportunity to experience Central and Eastern European food. Dining is on the first floor in rather dated but not unpleasant surroundings (the time warp feeling is accentuated by the 1970s and 80s pop music playing in the background). The food comes in large portions, but is competent rather than inspired. Expect plenty of sauerkraut and what many people would consider to be over-zealously boiled potatoes (ours collapsed into mush upon contact with a fork). The clear borscht comes with a tasty fried pancake roll filled with pork, while the grilled fillet of chicken (£7.50) is doused in a creamy 'Warsaw' sauce overflowing with mushrooms. You can wash down your meal with strong Polish beer or a selection of vodkas (£1.50 per shot). There's also a self-service cafe on the ground floor, where food prices are about 25% cheaper.

starter: £2.50-£4.50
main: £5.90-£10.50
dessert: £1.50-£3.50
AE MC V; SW

Open: daily 12.30pm-3pm, Sun-Thurs 6.30pm-10pm, Fri & Sat 6.30pm-11.30pm; reservations advisable (weekends); licensed

---

The River Café

Modern Italian

☎ 020 7381 8824
Thames Wharf, Rainville Rd W6

Map 9 B3
Tube: Hammersmith
Dress code: collared shirt
Smoking throughout

Expensive and illustrious, The River Café lays claim to London's finest modern Italian cuisine, but we're not so sure. Expanded twice, this restaurant achieves in popularity what it has lost in intimacy. The industrial interior sports a space-age stainless steel bar and a light, airy dining space. An inventive, mostly fish-based menu promises flamboyant reincarnations of Tuscan classics, but the food is functional when it ought to be exquisite. A substantial wood-roasted widgeon (£22) satisfied more than the bland-tasting char-grilled scallops (£23). Roast pheasant salad (£11) came with enough dandelions to feed a dozen rabbits but the bruschetta con granchio (£13.50) is a winner, blessed with the delicate flavour of chicory, oil and lemon. Chocolate nemesis (£7) looked frothy and light from a distance but proved impossibly rich. Try to book for an 8pm seating because, due to the restaurant's site in a residential area, guests must leave by 11pm.

starter: £8-£13.50
main: £20-£28
dessert: £6-£7
AE DC JCB MC V; SW

Open: Mon-Sat 12.30pm-2.15pm, Mon-Thurs 7pm-9pm, Fri & Sat 7pm-9.15pm; reservations essential; licensed

Stonemason's Arms

Modern British

☎ **020 8748 1397**
54 Cambridge Grove W6

Map 9 A2
Tube: Hammersmith
Wheelchair access

 Smoking throughout

The Stonemason's is one of the new breed of gastropubs popping up all over London. The refurbished interior is light and airy, yet still retains a pub atmosphere. Service in the restaurant is pretty lax, and you'll need to fight with the crowds to order food at the bar and pay immediately, but the menu is exciting and delicious. The fresh goat's cheese salad is substantial, with flavoursome olives and a tangy raspberry vinaigrette (£5.90). The mains are beautifully presented and include unusual dishes such as ostrich fillet (£11.50) smothered in a rich pepper sauce. In marked contrast, the halibut (£10) is simply prepared, served on a bed of spinach with the added punch of red cabbage soaked in balsamic dressing. This is great food in a relaxed and unpretentious pub environment.

Open: Mon-Sat noon-11pm, Sun noon-10.30pm; reservations advisable; licensed

starter: £3.50-£7.90
main: £5.50-£10.70
dessert: £3.50
AE MC V; SW

KNIGHTSBRIDGE

Borshcht 'n' Tears

Eastern European

☎ **020 7584 9911**
46 Beauchamp Place SW3

Map 6 B1
Tube: Knightsbridge
Entertainment: nightly live music 8pm-1am (which may include vocals, balalaika, violin, guitar, accordion)

 Nonsmoking tables available

The best thing about Borshcht 'n' Tears is that it's refreshingly unpretentious. Decked in red wallpaper, with live music every night, the long split-level dining room is cosy and engaging. The menu and paper placemats, reproduced virtually unchanged since the 1970s, poke fun at communists, capitalists and famous Russians. We started with borshcht (£3.15) which was disappointingly watery. But the accompanying piroshki (£2.95), small pasties filled with minced meat, were just right – juicy with a soft shell. Beef stroganoff (£10.55) consisted of thin slivers of tender beef in a creamy sauce doused liberally and to great effect with tarragon. The accompanying rice and vegetables were less memorable. Rated on gastronomic merits alone, this place is expensive, but on a wintry night, eating heavy Slavonic fare to the strains of a polka and accompanied by generous shots of vodka proved thoroughly enjoyable.

Open: daily 5.30pm-1am; reservations advisable; licensed

starter: £2.50-£5.85
main: £6.50-£12.50
dessert: £3.45
AE JCB MC V; SW

The Conservatory at the Lanesborough

International

☎ 020 7259 5599
1 Lanesborough Place, Hyde Park Corner SW1

Map 6 A3
Tube: Hyde Park Corner
Wheelchair access
Entertainment: pianist daily 3.30pm-6pm, Sun-Thurs 6.30pm-11.30pm, jazz trio and dinner dance Fri & Sat 6.30pm-midnight
Smoking throughout

This elegant, glass-domed restaurant is surely one of the most beautiful dining rooms in the capital, with towering palm trees, tinkling piano music and warm, attentive service all adding to the period charm. But there's nothing old fashioned about the food. The menu borrows from Mediterranean and Asian cuisine as well as updating some traditional British dishes and ingredients. Succulent strips of garlic roasted lamb, served with swede in a rich gravy (£20.50), had infinitely more class than the meat-and-two-veg still favoured in many British hotel dining rooms. Imaginative vegetarian dishes such as torte provençale (£20.50) ensure that non-meat eaters won't feel like also-rans, and desserts such as banana brioche with cool pear sorbet (£5) are equally inspiring. A leisurely evening in these classically beautiful surroundings will always feel like a special occasion.

starter: £6.50-£19
main: £13.50-£49
dessert: £6.50-£8.50
Set lunch £26.50, set dinner £32, £39 or £44
AE DC JCB MC V; SW

Open: Sun-Thurs 7am-11.30pm, Fri & Sat 7am-midnight; reservations advisable (especially Fri & Sat); licensed

The Fifth Floor

Modern British

☎ 020 7235 5250
Harvey Nichols SW1

Map 6 A2
Tube: Knightsbridge
Wheelchair access
Nonsmoking tables available

The Fifth Floor is a cut above your average in-store restaurant. At lunchtime, the cool, understated dining room is full of bejewelled lady shoppers clutching their Harvey Nichols purchases; by night, the adjoining bar is reputedly one of London's most sophisticated pulling joints. Bold, sun-drenched colours, well-matched textures and strong, earthy flavours are the hallmarks of chef Henry Harris' robust yet modish cuisine, translating into such dishes as buffalo mozzarella with thyme, lemon and anchovy (£8.25) and crab salad with herb omelette and roasted peppers (£10.50). The flavoursome main course of turbot steak with ceps (£19.75) is griddled to perfection, and the desserts come with individual wine suggestions. Indeed, the wine list is exemplary, drawn from the neighbouring wine department. Alternatively, for a light snack, choose between Japanese fast food at Yo! Sushi, or salads, sandwiches and traditional English tea at the conservatory-style cafe – you'll find it all on the Fifth Floor.

starter: £6.50-£16.50
main: £10-£36.25
dessert: £5.25-£7.50
Set lunch menu £23.50
AE DC JCB MC V; SW

Open: Mon-Fri noon-3pm, Sat & Sun noon-3.30pm, Mon-Sat 6.30pm-11.30pm; reservations advisable; licensed

Isola

Italian

☎ 020 7838 1044
145 Knightsbridge SW1

Map 6 A1

Tube: Knightsbridge

Wheelchair access

 Smoking throughout

Isola is the stylish new kid on the restaurant block, courtesy of Oliver Peyton of Atlantic and Mash fame. It boasts two huge floors, a massive glazed façade and plenty of chrome, gloss and red leather upholstery to suit the smart, well-heeled crowd – very impressive. Fresh, quirky combinations make for some great starters – we love the marinated sea bass with crab and diced apple (£8.50) and a summery avocado and fennel salad wrapped in tuna carpaccio (£8.50). The fillet of lamb flavoured with orange and served with capers and sautéed aubergines (£18) was *almost* great, and the overstuffed ricotta raviolo (£12) didn't hit the mark – too much of a pasty mouthful. We finished with a slightly barmy mascarpone and basil ice cream with stewed fruit. The Italian wine list is extensive and the service attentive (if a little frenetic). Downstairs dining, in Osteria d'Isola, is less formal, offering communal dishes, such as grilled quail with polenta (£14), from which you can serve yourself and your friends.

Open: daily noon-3pm, Mon-Sat 6pm-midnight, Sun 6pm-10.30pm; reservations advisable; licensed

Set lunch £19 & £23 or set dinner £50

AE DC MC V; SW

Mr Chow

Chinese

☎ 020 7589 7347
151 Knightsbridge SW1

Map 6 A1

Tube: Knightsbridge

 Smoking throughout

A visit to Mr Chow is like a step back in time to the 1970s – the long, narrow dining room has brown banquettes and once 'mod' touches. But the gardenias at the front are fragrant and new, and the ingratiating Italian waiters are younger than the décor. The media-savvy Mr Chow – whose address book you just know reads like a 1975 issue of *Hello* – limits his menu to a single page, but the waiters strongly encourage you to sit back and let them do the ordering. It's not actually a bad idea, if your sense of adventure – and wallet – can handle it. The green prawns (£12.50) are spicy and succulent, the crevettes sel et poivre crispy, the king prawns zingy and Mr Chow's trademark Peking duck (£28 per person) is a showy dish served from a special cart that just wouldn't work with a post-1970s name like, say, Beijing Duck. Mr Chow is a fun throwback, especially if someone else is paying.

Open: daily 12.30pm-3pm, 7pm-midnight; reservations essential; licensed

starter: £5.25-£8.50
main: £10.50-£25
dessert: £6
Set lunch £9.50

AE DC JCB MC V; SW

O Fado

Portuguese

☎ 020 7589 3002
49-50 Beauchamp Place SW3

Map 6 B1
Tube: Knightsbridge
Entertainment: guitarists Tues-Sat
Smoking throughout

London's oldest Portuguese restaurant, O Fado is a charming and popular retreat with rustic lanterns, pink tablecloths and tiled pictures of Portuguese landscapes. The lengthy menu offers a range of dishes to tempt the palate. Fish is a speciality here and is served in a variety of styles. Our starter of spicy prawns with olive oil, white wine and garlic (£6.50) was a pleasant combination, albeit a little oily, and hinted at the flavour of things to come. The mixed shellfish with rice (£25) continued to tempt the taste buds, with tasty and succulent prawns, crab and other crustaceous delights. Leave enough room for the rice pudding (£2.80), a rich and creamy dessert which is well worth the wait. O Fado enjoys the patronage of a mixed clientele, including Portuguese – what better recommendation to come along and enjoy fine cuisine at affordable prices.

starter: £2.60-£6.50
main: £7.20-£14.95
dessert: £2.80-£3.50
AE JCB MC V; SW

Open: Mon-Sun noon-3pm, 6.30pm-1am, Sun 7pm-midnight; reservations advisable; licensed

Pizza on the Park

Italian

☎ 020 7235 5273
11 Knightsbridge SW1

Map 6 A3
Tube: Hyde Park Corner
Wheelchair access
Entertainment: jazz nightly 9.15pm-11.15pm (cover charge £10-£20), jazz trio Sun lunch, string quartet Sun evening
Nonsmoking tables available
Courtyard tables

If flexing your credit card on Knightsbridge gives you an appetite, then head for Pizza on the Park. Popular for its nightly jazz, it's also busy by day with a mix of families, couples and business-types enjoying pizza and pasta dishes. Wood-panelled walls give a stylish and unusual feel in the spacious dining room and the service is efficient and unhurried. Whet your appetite with dishes from buttery garlic bread (£1.95) to decadent smoked scotch wild salmon (£9.85). The stars are the crisp-based pizzas – the 'American hot', with pepperoni and green peppers (£7.75) and the caper, anchovy and olive-topped napoletana (£7.10) were tasty but the toppings were a bit thin. A range of other dishes is available, including a crisp and light salade niçoise (£7.95) and cannelloni (£7.25). The chocolate fudge cake (£4.25) and other sweet goodies are tempting, but if your belly's full you can come back later for cake and coffee.

starter: £1.95-£9.85
main: £5.80-£9.10
dessert: £3.50-£4.50
AE DC JCB MC V; SW

Open: Mon-Sat 8.15am-midnight, Sun 9.15am-midnight; reservations not accepted; licensed

Vong ☎ 020 7235 1010
Thai/French **Wilton Place SW1**

Ever since the latest outpost of chef Jean-Georges Vongerichten's restaurant empire opened in 1995, it has been considered one of the truly top-notch Asian eateries in town – hugely hyped and very glossy. The secret to its success? A spatially impressive, minimalist dining room; an exciting, innovative menu synthesising French and Thai ingredients and flavours; extraordinary service; brilliant culinary skills; and minute attention to detail. Following complimentary rice crackers with satay sauce, the signature 'Black Plate' starter (£13) is an almost-too-good-to-eat display of bite-sized prawn brochettes, herb-filled lobster daikon rolls, quail rubbed with Thai spices and crispy crab spring rolls with a variety of spicy dips. The blend of flavours in the succulent roast chicken with lemongrass sauce is exquisite, accompanied by green beans and sweet rice baked in a banana leaf (£14.25). The trio of exotic sorbets (£5.25) include raspberry and chilli-pepper, which has a sherbet-like kick. The indulgent, warm chocolate cake with coconut ice cream (£5.75) is justifiably renowned throughout London.

Open: Mon-Fri noon-2.30pm, Sat & Sun 11.30am-2.30pm, Mon-Sat 6pm-11.30pm, Sun 6pm-10.30pm; reservations essential; licensed

Map 6 A2

Tube: Hyde Park Corner

 Nonsmoking tables available (no cigars or pipes)

starter: £5.75-£12.50
main: £13.75-£29.75
dessert: £5.25-£7.50
Set lunch £16.50/£19.50, pre-theatre Black Plate menu £16

AE DC JCB MC V; SW

Zafferano ☎ 020 7235 5800
Italian **15 Lowndes St SW1**

Zafferano caters for a cosmopolitan, well-heeled clientele. The dining area is split into two rooms, one bare brick, the other painted white. The effect is both tasteful and functional, yet retains an intimate feel. The dishes are simply and elegantly presented, such as the succulent Scotch beef starter, garnished with rocket and truffle oil. The roast pigeon with garlic purée and black truffle is also exquisite. The menu is extensive and is accompanied by an equally sizable wine list. The desserts are wickedly rich, especially the wonderful orange and pine nut tartlette served with Cointreau ice cream. The service is attentive without being fussy. Zafferano is deservedly popular, its innovative cuisine easily surpassing most of its rivals.

Open: daily noon-2.30pm, 7pm-11pm; reservations essential; licensed

Map 6 B2

Tube: Knightsbridge

Dress code: collared shirt

 Smoking throughout

  Pavement tables

Set lunch menu £18.50-£21.50, dinner £29.50, £35.50 or £39.50

AE MC V; SW

CENTRAL SOUTH-WEST

Yas

Iranian

☎ **020 7603 9148**
7 Hammersmith Rd W14

Map 7 D1
Tube: Olympia or West Kensington

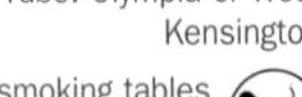

Nonsmoking tables available

Billing itself as 'London's only award-winning Iranian restaurant', Yas falls short of its own hype. It is an attractive place with a warm interior of deep orange walls and wooden floors, and a heavy doughy smell of baking bread. It's also undisputedly popular, completely full at 8pm on a midweek evening. And if the service can be slow, the black-clad young waitresses (in mini skirts, not chadors) are at least pleasant and apologetic. Starters are good, especially the kuku-ye-sabzi (£3.50), which is like a wedge of puffed-up omelette prepared with heaps of parsley, coriander and dill. Adasi (£3.50), a tomatoey red lentil soup, is also very moreish. But we found the mains did not live up to expectations. Chelo kebab-e kubideh, ordered as lamb and chicken (both £7), in which the meat is finely minced then grilled, had a hint of an aftertaste of cooking oil. Only an excellent chelo kebab-e chenjeh (£10) of diced fillet of lamb impressed. Overall, too hit and miss to be an award winner, but certainly worth a try nonetheless.

starter: £3.50
main: £6-£11
dessert: £3

AE DC JCB MC V

Open: daily noon-5am; reservations essential; licensed

Roussillon

French

☎ **020 7730 5550**
16 St Barnabas St SW1

Map 6 D3
Tube: Sloane Square
Wheelchair access
Certified organic

Smoking throughout

On a quiet side street off Pimlico Rd, Roussillon offers fine service, lovely décor and settings, and fresh English ingredients dexterously cooked à *la française*, but not à la carte. There are five starters to choose from, including melt-in-the-mouth sautéed foie gras with Jerusalem artichoke, crispy rhubarb and Williams pear. Move to 'the sea' for a delicious roasted cod with late harvest grapes, perhaps, or to 'the land' for an organic chicken cooked and served in two stages – the breast with ceps and pearl onions, the leg with fresh Kentish leaves. The seasonal degustation menu is meat and/or fish based, while the 'garden menu' is arguably the most inventive vegetarian offering available in London. On our last visit white truffle had arrived and, for a hefty supplement, we succumbed. With these incomparably flavoured funghi freshly grated into a cheesy risotto, we thought we'd died and reached nirvana.

Set lunch £13.50 or £16, set dinner £22 or £25, degustation £35 or vegetarian degustation £24
AE DC JCB MC V; SW

Open: Mon-Fri noon-2.30pm, Mon-Sat 6.30pm-10.45pm; reservations advisable; licensed

Tate Gallery Restaurant

British

☎ **020 7887 8877**
The Tate Gallery, Millbank SW1

Map 6 D6
Tube: Pimlico
Wheelchair access

Nonsmoking tables available

Whistler's famous mural *Expedition in Pursuit of Rare Meats* makes this one of London's most spectacular dining rooms. It's a delight to study the scenery and spot the odd unicorn charging across the landscape. The staff are charming and the black furniture is stylish, albeit cramped. We tried the rather dry roast pheasant (£15) but the seafood emerged as the chef's forte – try steamed sea bass (£15.75), which has a sharp bite of ginger and spring onion. The use of organic ingredients may explain why the dishes don't come cheap, but the £16.75 two-course set lunch is good value. Depending on the day, you can choose between aubergine parmigiana or English sausages served with dollops of mashed potato, accompanied by mushroom soup or game terrine. For the ultimate indulgence, top everything off with a gooey chocolate crème brûlée (£5.50). The wine list is impressive and, typically, the mineral water comes in beautifully designed bottles.

starter: £5.50-£10.50
main: £12.50-£16
dessert: £5.50-£6.50
Set lunch £16.75 or £19.50
AE DC JCB MC V; SW

Open: Mon-Sat noon-2.30pm, Sun noon-3.30pm; reservations accepted; licensed

CENTRAL SOUTH-WEST

Bibendum

Modern European

☎ **020 7581 5817**
Michelin House,
81 Fulham Rd SW3

Map 7 B5
Tube: South Kensington
Certified organic
Smoking throughout

'Bibendum' is the Michelin Man, depicted in stained glass throughout this expertly designed Conran restaurant, housed in the former Michelin Tyre Company's glorious headquarters (described as 'the most completely French of any Edwardian building in London'). The first-floor restaurant looks like a film set: the clientele are beautiful, the food is perfect and the show is run by a silent army of super-efficient staff. After wrestling with the encyclopaedic wine list, choose from sautéed scallops and shellfish ravioli (£15.50) or the piquant Bibendum terrine (£9). Having settled in, try the flavoursome steak au poivre (£19.50) or the delicately grilled John Dory on a bed of spinach and ginger salad (£23). The dessert menu will satisfy the most demanding sweet tooth, with delights such as passionfruit bavarois (£7.50) and creamed rice with lemon and rhubarb (£7). Bibendum's logo, 'Nunc est Bibendum', means 'now is the time to drink'. Cheers!

starter: £9-£21
main: £14.50-£42
dessert: £6.50-£10
Set menu lunch Mon-Fri £23, Sat & Sun £27.50
AE DC MC V; SW

Open: Mon-Fri noon-2.30pm, Sat & Sun 12.30pm-3pm, Mon-Sat 7pm-11.30pm, Sun 7pm-10.30pm; reservations essential; licensed

Cambio de Tercio

Spanish

☎ **020 7244 8970**
163 Old Brompton Rd SW5

Map 7 C2
Tube: Gloucester Rd

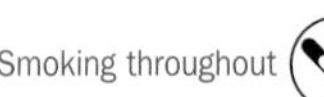
Smoking throughout

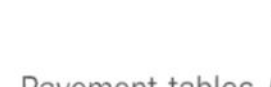
Pavement tables

If you found Cambio de Tercio in Madrid you'd be happy – that it's in South Kensington is even better. The small Victorian storefront features bullfighting paraphernalia on the vivid yellow walls, a whimsical interior that contrasts with the serious kitchen. The Jabugo ham (£14) is from a rare breed of pig highly prized by jamón fans. Other starters are far less pricey but equally noteworthy. The pulpo gallego (£7) is a fine octopus and potato salad highlighted with a touch of paprika. Calamares fritos (£5.90) is delicately deep-fried squid set off with white and black garlic oil. The rice in the arroz de hongos (£8.90) is saturated with the essence of wild mushrooms, and the fillet of pork (£12.90) continues the restaurant's fine pork pedigree. The crema de vainilla (£4.50) is a simple but smooth finish to the meal. Wines reflect the best of recent Spanish vintages. On cold nights, aim for a table in the curtained back room by the fireplace.

starter: £5.50-£8
main: £10-£16
dessert: £4.50-£6
AE MC V; SW

Open: daily noon-2.30pm, Mon-Sat 7.30pm-11.30pm, Sun 7.30pm-11pm; reservations essential; licensed

SOUTH KENSINGTON

Daquise

Polish

☎ **020 7589 6117**
20 Thurloe St SW7

Map 7 B4
Tube: South Kensington

Nonsmoking tables available

Entering Daquise is a bit like stepping into an old-fashioned, sepia-toned picture. The décor is in varying shades of brown, cream and yellow, and the only sound you can hear above the soft buzz of conversation is the creaking of the dumb waiter. It's all very Polish but awfully English at the same time – serious, even boring at first glance, but on reflection pleasantly eccentric. The service is of the brusque, no-nonsense variety and the food is solid, cold-climate fare (potato pancakes, hunters stew, meatballs) that's best appreciated after a swift winter's day walk across Hyde Park. The blinis with smoked salmon (£3.50) were satisfyingly fat and full of buckwheat flavour, but they left plenty of room for the continental sausage (£6), a chunky, mildly spicy pork sausage served with a mountain of just-caramelised fried onion and two ice-cream scoops of mashed potato. Apart from winter fuel and excellent eavesdropping possibilities, Daquise also offers an alluring range of desserts such as cheesecake, apple strudel and home-made Polish doughnuts with rose jam.

Open: daily 11.30am-11pm; reservations advisable (especially weekends); licensed & BYO (corkage £5/bottle)

starter: £2.50-£4
main: £5.50-£10.50
dessert: £2.50-£4
Set lunch £6.80
MC V; SW

The New Restaurant at the V&A

Modern British

☎ **020 7942 2506**
Victoria & Albert Museum, Cromwell Rd SW7

Map 7 A4
Tube: South Kensington
Wheelchair access

Museums aren't usually known for their fine restaurants, but the New Restaurant at the V&A runs counter to the traditional museum dining experience. Perhaps this has something to do with its history, as the V&A was the first museum in the world to provide a 'public refreshment room' in 1857. The original Victorian rooms can be admired on the ground floor, while the New Restaurant, with its blonde-wood tables, brick walls and Arts-and-Crafts-style lighting, can be found on the lower level. Our broccoli and stilton soup (£2.65) was thin, and definitely for stilton-lovers, but the chicken breast wrapped in bacon with tarragon cream sauce (£6.80) was very good, even though the sauce was virtually nonexistent. The mashed potatoes with grain mustard (£.95) defied our low expectations and had us yearning for more, and the vanilla and chocolate cheesecake (£2.95) made the perfect finish to a surprisingly good meal.

Open: daily 10am-5.30pm; reservations not accepted; licensed

starter: £2.45-£4.25
main: £5.45-£6.80
dessert: £1.95-£2.95
AE DC JCB MC V; SW

Ognisko Polskie

Polish

☎ 020 7589 4635
55 Prince's Gate, Exhibition Rd SW7

Map 7 A4
Tube: South Kensington
Dress code: collared shirt
Smoking throughout 
Balcony tables

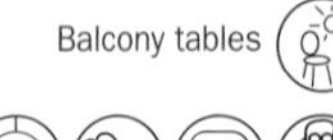

As we spun past the V&A, the cab driver informed me that 'there ain't no restaurants on Prince's Gate, love'. OK, granted. But it's not a restaurant, its more of a club for Polish gentry, the ancestors of whom hang immortalised on the walls, observing their (in our case) less aristocratic visitors. Nevertheless, the golden chandeliers, cornices and marble pillars unite with salmon walls and a soundtrack of Chopin to invite diners unconditionally to be their guest. We tried the Ukrainian beetroot soup laced with delicate creamy spirals and topped with parsley (£3) – delicious. All the Polish favourites are represented, including the ubiquitous dumplings, game and meat platters, with guinea fowl a welcome variation on the theme. The shashlik (£10.80) was a tangy skewer of lamb with smoky, roasted peppers and onions on a bed of rocket, with mangetouts, haricot verts, courgettes and leeks a veritable emerald treat on the side. Put your glad rags on because pure indulgence is fabulous once in a while.

starter: £3-£11
main: £7.20-£16
dessert: £3.50
Set lunch £8
AE DC MC V; SW

Open: daily noon-3pm, 6.30pm-11pm; reservations advisable; licensed

Pelham Street

International

☎ 020 7584 4788
93 Pelham St SW7

Map 7 B5
Tube: South Kensington
Smoking throughout

A favourite with the locals, Pelham Street offers diners a variety of interesting and colourful dishes from around the world. Thai red curry fish cakes (£5.25), Mexican lime chicken (£7.95), Italian bruschetta (£2.95) and salmon teriyaki (£11.95) are just a selection of what's available from a truly international menu. The succulent sesame noodles and Singapore-style vegetables (£9.45) are a real treat, flavoured with an aromatic hint of ginger. Portions are generous and creatively presented, and given the wide-ranging menu, staff are extremely knowledgeable and helpful. Pelham Street's refreshingly bright interior and comfortable selection of contemporary furniture make it the ideal choice for business or pleasure.

starter: £1.95-£5.25
main: £5.75-£16.95
dessert: £3.95-£4.75
AE DC MC V; SW

Open: Mon-Fri noon-3pm, 5.30pm-11pm, Sat noon-11pm; reservations accepted; licensed

SOUTH KENSINGTON

Texas Lone Star Saloon
Tex-Mex

☎ 020 7370 5625
154 Gloucester Rd SW7

Bring all the family, a hearty appetite and a sense of fun to the lively Western-style Lone Star, London's oldest and most popular Tex-Mex saloon where everything comes in Texan-sized portions. Try the bowls of nachos piled mountain-high (£3.90), a monster slab of spare ribs (£8.95) or the whopping 12oz steaks (£11.95) – a must for meat-lovers. Even the frozen fruit margaritas come by the jugful (£14.50) and the beers by the bucket (£14.40). The spicy three-bean Mexican soup set the tastebuds tingling, but didn't score highly on presentation. The succulent beef and chicken enchiladas served with colourful lashings of sour cream, refried beans and a sweet-sour jalapeño and coriander lime jelly more than compensated. The giant stuffed moose hanging on the wall beside us eagerly eyed our meal throughout, but the left-overs came home with us in true American style – in a doggy bag.

Open: daily noon-11.30pm; reservations accepted (only for groups of 12 or more); licensed

Map 7 B3

Tube: Gloucester Road

Entertainment: live music Thurs, Sun & Tues or Wed evenings

 Smoking throughout

starter: £2.60-£8.45
main: £6.25-£13.95
dessert: £2.50-£3.75

AE MC V; SW

VICTORIA

Jenny Lo's Teahouse
Chinese

☎ 020 7259 0399
14 Eccleston St SW1

Despite its name, Jenny Lo's Teahouse is a noodle bar where patrons sit communally and tuck in to some fast Chinese food with a difference. Jenny's late father, the famous Chinese chef Ken Lo, once operated his cookery school from this site. Now it's a restaurant with a vibrant interior, cheery staff and a menu so healthy it's almost therapeutic. Loyal customers come here for dishes like gong bao chicken with pine nuts (£6.95), Sichuan aubergine (£5.50) or one of the five types of noodles on offer. Chilli beef soup hofun (£6.95) is a mammoth bowl of marinated beef, flat ribbon noodles, Chinese mushrooms and an enthusiastic dose of chilli and coriander. Crispy 'seaweed' (£2.25), actually made from greens, is a sugary melt-in-the-mouth accompaniment. Those still in need of a tonic should order a cup of 'long life' or 'cleansing' tea. Takeaway and home-delivery services are available.

Open: Mon-Fri 11.30am-3pm, Sat noon-3pm, Mon-Sat 6pm-10pm; reservations not accepted; licensed

Map 6 C4

Tube: Victoria

 Smoking throughout

 Pavement tables

starter: £2-£4.50
main: £5-£7.50
dessert: £2.95

cash and cheque only

VICTORIA

Map 6 B6
Tube: St James's Park
Nonsmoking tables available

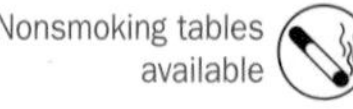

Quilon
South Indian

☎ 020 7821 1899
Crowne Plaza Hotel, 41 Buckingham Gate SW1

Quilon is run by the Taj Hotel Group, which places great emphasis on superior restaurants in its five-star resorts throughout India. This glamorous site, which previously housed a Michelin-starred French restaurant, now specialises in cuisine from the southern Indian state of Kerala, predominantly seafood, vegetables and coconut. Quilon is no ordinary Indian restaurant – it's dining out in style, with frescoed and mirrored walls, and remarkable, well-spiced dishes such as the excellent char-grilled scallops (£7.25). The powerfully flavoured crab calicut (£14.50) is dry roasted with peppercorns, chilli, turmeric, coriander and lime juice. Guinea fowl salan (£12.50) has a curry sauce combining tomato, yoghurt and coconut, and the lemon rice (£2.50) with whole spices is good enough to eat on its own.

starter: £4-£8
main: £9-£22
dessert: £2.50-£3.50
Set lunch £12.50 or £15.95
AE DC JCB MC V; SW

Open: Mon-Fri noon-2.30pm, Mon-Sat 6pm-11pm; reservations advisable; licensed

WEST KENSINGTON

Map 7 D2
Tube: Earl's Court
Smoking throughout

Mohsen
Iranian

☎ 020 7602 9888
152 Warwick Rd W14

Out on the wilderness end of Warwick Rd, opposite a giant Homebase superstore, Mohsen doesn't enjoy the best of locations. But with a sterling reputation among London's Iranian community, it's always full, with a steady stream of devotees pulling up outside to collect their pre-ordered takeaways. This is a modest, family-run affair, very reminiscent of a typical Iranian diner with an almost wholly kebab menu – lamb or chicken, chicken or lamb. But the meat is beautiful, served up with a large mound of fluffy basmati and a grilled tomato. Kebab-e makhsoos (£7.90) includes one fillet kebab and one mince – the two basic ways of presenting the meat. Order starters like sabzi (£2.30) – fresh parsley, tarragon and mint with fetta – and masto mousir (yoghurt with chopped shallots, £1.60) as accompaniments. Hot wholemeal bread sprinkled with sesame seeds comes direct from the clay oven. We could be content eating food like this every day for the rest of our lives.

starter: £1.50-£2.50
main: £5.90-£8.50
dessert: £1.80-£2
cash and cheque only

Open: daily noon-midnight; reservations advisable; BYO (no corkage)

Bayswater

Holland Park

Kensal Rise

WEST

Kensington

Ladbroke Grove

Lancaster Gate

Maida Vale

Notting Hill

Westbourne Grove

Westbourne Park

Map 10 - Notting Hill & Kensington

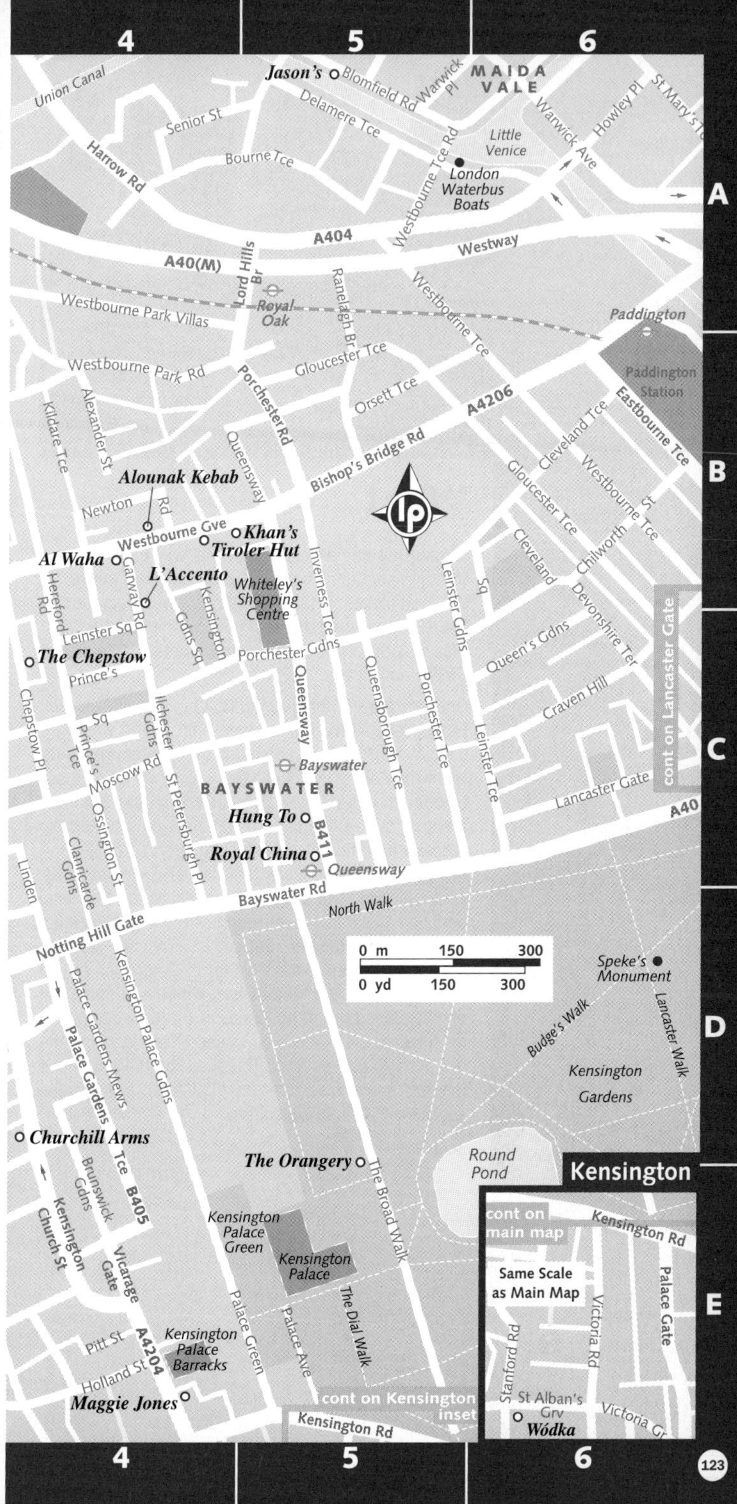

4
5
6
A
B
C
D
E
MAIDA VALE
Jason's
Blomfield Rd
Warwick Pl
Union Canal
Delamere Tce
Senior St
Little Venice
Harrow Rd
Bourne Tce
Westbourne Tce Rd
London Waterbus Boats
Warwick Ave
Howley Pl
St Mary's Tce
A404
A40(M)
Westway
Lord Hills Br
Royal Oak
Westbourne Park Villas
Ranelagh Br
Westbourne Tce
Paddington
Paddington Station
Gloucester Tce
Westbourne Park Rd
Porchester Rd
Orsett Tce
A4206
Eastbourne Tce
Kildare Tce
Alexander St
Queensway
Bishop's Bridge Rd
Cleveland Tce
Westbourne St
Gloucester Tce
Alounak Kebab
Newton Rd
Westbourne Gve
Khan's
Tiroler Hut
Chilworth St
Westbourne Tce
Cleveland Sq
Al Waha
Garway Rd
L'Accento
Whiteley's Shopping Centre
Inverness Tce
Leinster Gdns
Devonshire Ter
Hereford Rd
Kensington Gdns Sq
Leinster Sq
Queen's Gdns
cont on Lancaster Gate
The Chepstow
Porchester Gdns
Prince's Sq
Queensway
Queensborough Tce
Porchester Tce
Craven Hill
Chepstow Pl
Ilchester Gdns
Leinster Tce
Prince's Tce
Moscow Rd
St Petersburgh Pl
Bayswater
BAYSWATER
Lancaster Gate
A40
Hung To
B411
Ossington St
Clanricarde Gdns
Royal China
Queensway
Linden
Bayswater Rd
North Walk
Notting Hill Gate
0 m 150 300
0 yd 150 300
Speke's Monument
Kensington Palace Gdns
Palace Gardens Mews
Palace Gardens Tce
Budge's Walk
Lancaster Walk
Kensington Gardens
Churchill Arms
Round Pond
The Orangery
The Broad Walk
Kensington
Brunswick Gdns
B405
cont on main map
Kensington Rd
Kensington Church St
Kensington Palace Green
Kensington Palace
Same Scale as Main Map
Vicarage Gate
Palace Gate
The Dial Walk
Victoria Rd
Pitt St
A4204
Kensington Palace Barracks
Palace Green
Palace Ave
Stanford Rd
Holland St
St Alban's Grv
Victoria Gr
Maggie Jones
cont on Kensington inset
Kensington Rd
Wódka

BEST

Al Waha

- Raising Lebanese food to an art form

Bali Sugar

- A luscious mélange of cuisines

Offshore

- Sublime Mauritian-style seafood

West

Notting Hill was already well on its way to its present trendy incarnation before the eponymous movie hit the multiplexes. A focus of Caribbean immigration in the 1950s, Notting Hill is home to a multicultural mix that may or may not survive the current onslaught of BMWs and Saabs.

One restaurant that sums up this medley is Bali Sugar, a delightful place where east meets west in a delicious mix. You can also find an array of good eats and wares along Portobello Rd, which has much more to offer than its hugely popular Friday and Saturday antique and junk market. Organic bakers, ethnic grocers and felafel makers are just some of the purveyors of treats along this hilly and winding road. Look behind many of the pubs for gardens with picnic benches that offer ideal respite from the bargaining masses on summer Saturdays. Try the Earl of Lonsdale, the aptly named Sun in Splendour or you might pop into the Market Bar, where you can soak up the Bohemian atmosphere in the downstairs bar or have some excellent, cheap Thai food in the restaurant above. The Thursday organic produce market showcases the best of this fast-growing segment of British agriculture.

Hung To

Chinese

☎ 020 7727 5753
51 Queensway W2

Map 10 C5
Tube: Queensway

 Smoking throughout

Frills are sparse but taste is plenty in this David among Goliaths on the Queensway Chinese restaurant beat. The food does all the talking here. With classroom ceilings and stockpiled soft drinks, clearly no décor expense is dared, but the hard-working dumbwaiter soon proves where the priorities lie. The menu is not for the calorie conscious, but with aromas this good, who cares? From the impressive and cheap selection, the chicken and duck congee starter (£4) is tasty, although the fried king prawns (£7.10) seemed disappointingly bland for the price. If we have to be picky (and we do!), go for the succulent and tangy char siu pork (£4.90) or the chicken in black bean sauce (£4.90); both are well accompanied by the special fried rice (£3.90). Forget the spartan surroundings – cuisine triumphs over feng shui, as the reassuringly sizable Chinese clientele would agree.

Open: daily 11am-11pm; reservations not accepted; BYO (corkage £2/bottle, 50p/beer)

starter: £1.50-£2.10
main: £4-£7.10
Set menu £9.50-£10.50
cash and cheques only

L'Accento

Italian

☎ 020 7243 2201
16 Garway Rd W2

Map 10 B4
Tube: Bayswater

 Smoking throughout

 Garden tables

L'Accento attracts a well-heeled, well-groomed crowd largely drawn from the affluent neighbourhood. Lively but not loud, simply furnished with white walls and well-spaced tables that allow for discreet conversation, it's equally suitable as a venue for a business lunch, romantic tête à tête or dinner with your parents. The menu is limited to five or six options per course but all are enticing. The pumpkin ravioli (£6) with sage and melted butter was succulent though the portion disappointingly small. After such a memorable combination of sweetness and delicacy, the main courses – lamb shank in a red wine and shallot sauce (£12) and fillet of beef with a rucola and dolce latte sauce (£14) – seemed a little heavy, but you couldn't fault the preparation. A third course of chocolate cake with crème pâtissière (£4) was pure greed but well worth the extra effort. L'Accento sets very high culinary standards for itself, and the service is correspondingly slick.

Open: Mon-Sat 12.30pm-2.30pm, 6.30pm-11.15pm, Sun 6.30pm-10.30pm; reservations advisable; licensed

starter: £4.50-£8
main: £12-£14
dessert: £4-£12.50
AE JCB MC V; SW

Map 10 C5
Tube: Queensway

Smoking throughout 

Royal China
Chinese

☎ 020 7221 2535
13 Queensway W2

At 16 pages, a read through the menu at Royal China should qualify one for some minor academic achievement in Chinese cookery. Fortunately they have a talented bar here and you can relax amidst the opulent black and gold décor and get on with your reading. Although the menu won't surprise, the food will definitely please – the kitchen has a well-deserved reputation. Or you can avoid reading altogether and go for the set house dinner (£25 per person), which includes well-executed versions of typical starters like prawn balls, spicy smoked chicken and Vietnamese pancake rolls. Mains feature a moist and spicy Sichuan duck as well as fiery chicken in black bean sauce. Service is efficient but gruff. If Royal China gets crowded at night, it gets mobbed on weekend days for top-notch dim sum. There are no carts but there is a special menu. Get there before 11am on Sunday if you don't want to suffer the chaotic queues.

starter: £3-£5
main: £6-£16
dessert: £3
Set menu £25-£32
AE JCB MC V; SW

Open: Mon-Fri noon-11pm, Sat noon-11.30pm, Sun 11am-10pm; reservations advisable; licensed

Map 10 B4
Tube: Bayswater or
Entertainment: live music, Austrian yodelling, cow bell show

Smoking throughout 

Tiroler Hut
Austrian

☎ 020 7727 3981
27 Westbourne Grove W2

The Tiroler Hut is easily the most fun Austrian restaurant outside of the homeland. The restaurant is in a warren of low-ceilinged rooms, entered through a narrow door and down a steep staircase. Try to get a table as close to the displayed assortment of cow bells as possible. Most of the starters are purely functional, although the champignons Tiroler art (£5.50) is nicely garlicky. The goulash soup (£3.50) is the best starter option and is redolent with paprika. The mains are mostly – as expected – pork and there's really no reason not to opt for the huge and tender wiener schnitzel (£9.60) with fried potatoes – this is really an Austrian theme park, after all. Entertainment is provided by the delightful owner, Joseph Friedman, who works the aforementioned cow bells and other instruments in a boisterous show that encourages audience participation and only inspires even more boisterous behaviour in the lager-fuelled diners. Come with a crowd and expect to make friends.

starter: £3.50-£5.50
main: £8.90-£15.50
dessert: £3.20-£3.50
AE DC MC V; SW

Open: Tues-Sun 6.30pm-12.30am; reservations advisable (essential weekends); licensed

Julie's Wine Bar

International

☎ **020 7727 7985**
135-137 Portland Rd W11

Map 10 D1
Tube: Holland Park

 Smoking throughout

 Pavement tables

Julie's is a chatty and relaxed meeting place away from the hub of Notting Hill, popular with the locals and seemingly spacious with its white walls and high ceilings. The lunch menu has a choice of more than 20 dishes, with sushi and prosciutto sitting comfortably next to sausages and mash. Standard dishes are spiced up with unusual additions: the duck and chicken liver pâté (£3.95) comes with onion marmalade, and the smoked salmon (£5.95) is accompanied by sweet sake and ginger. There is a good selection of vegetarian dishes – the roast pumpkin and sage tart (£7.95) was the most inviting when we dined. The more expensive dishes are still reasonable, such as olive oil poached swordfish with oven-dried tomatoes and black olives (£11.95). The portions are ample and just right for lunch.

Open: Mon- Fri 12.30pm-2.45pm, 7.30pm- 11.15pm, Sun 12.30pm-3pm, 7.30pm-10.15pm; reservations advisable; licensed

starter: £3.75-£11.95
main: £7.95-£12.95
dessert: £4.95
Set menu £27 or £34

AE DC MC V; SW

Offshore

Mauritian

☎ **020 7221 6090**
148 Holland Park Ave W11

Map 10 E1
Tube: Holland Park

 Nonsmoking tables available

Conch shells, turquoise glass, a three-foot suspended swordfish and miniature crystal sea lions – yes, you could say that Offshore has a marine theme. Fishy details aside, the décor manages to be subtle and stylish, and the menu is as attractive as the meals themselves. We ate to the gentle sounds of glasses clinking, people chattering and mobile phones occasionally pinging. Our senses were primed by the gratis appetiser of crispy fishcake with a tangy chilli sauce, the perfect messenger for the red emperor (£19.50), seasoned to perfection and served with succulent scallops and tender green spinach. A tomato herb relish and zesty lime rice accompanied the red snapper à la Creole (£16) and the melting aubergine fondue proved magical (£4). For the sweet toothed, choose from a lattice banana tart with pistachio and ginger topping, passionfruit and mango mousse or, our favourite, roast baby pineapple with swirls of cinnamon toffee sauce and vanilla ice cream (all £5). Dive into Offshore for an exceptional experience.

Open: Mon-Sat noon-3pm, Mon-Fri 6.30pm-11.30pm; reservations advisable; licensed

starter: £6-£13
main: £12.50-£22
dessert: £4.50-£6.50
Gastronomic set menu £30-£40

AE MC V; SW

WEST

HOLLAND PARK

Tootsies
American

☎ 020 7229 8567
120 Holland Park Ave W11

Map 10 D1
Tube: Holland Park

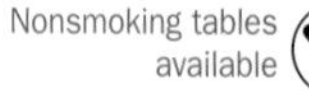
Nonsmoking tables available

Pavement tables

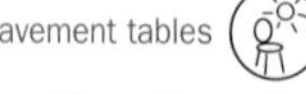

Tootsies is ever popular, serving American-style fodder to the local neighbourhood. The clientele is mixed – Sunday is a family day with waitresses handing out crayons to keep the children occupied. The restaurant uses free-range eggs, and vegetarians will be delighted to find meat-free sausages and burgers on offer. If you can't decide how to start, then try it all – the selection plate of appetisers (£7.95) is for two to share, and includes crispy, deep-fried onion rings with sweet chilli dipping sauce, herb-coated mozzarella sticks, potato skins with sour cream, and chicken satay sticks. The signature dish, the 5oz hamburger (£6), comes with fries and a choice of five toppings. Mesquite barbecue sauce gives the meat a sweet, smoky flavour. The warm chicken salad (£6.95) is packed with spinach leaves and bacon, and it eventually got the better of us – thankfully, the helpful staff are only too happy to pack leftovers into a doggy bag.

starter: £2.75-£7.95
main: £4.50-£9.25
dessert: £2.25-£3.50
AE MC V; SW

Open: Sun-Thurs 9am-11pm, Fri & Sat 9am-11.30pm; reservations not accepted; licensed

WEST

Wiz
International

☎ 020 7229 1500
123a Clarendon Rd W11

Map 10 C1
Tube: Holland Park or Ladbroke Grove
Certified organic
Smoking throughout
Rooftop terrace tables

Indian? Chinese? French? If you're unsure where to eat, TV celebrity chef Anthony Worrall Thompson will solve your dilemma with a vast selection of dishes from around the world. The tapas menu is split into various geographical zones, each with several dishes. Choose the country you like and order a selection, or be more daring and surf the world. The Asian vegetable salad with green chilli dressing (£4.25) comes crisp and piquant, the Mediterranean lamb and sweet tomato tajine (£5.95) is rich and spicy, and the delicate fragrance and colours of the Italy-inspired seared tuna looks almost too good to eat. Bread and olives come free, there's a savvy wine list and desserts (£4) range from delicate prosecco mousse to solid and wholesome bread-and-butter pudding. During winter, the cosy, relaxed dining area is welcoming with its comfy cushions in spicy colours, but Wiz really comes into its own in summer for alfresco dining.

starter: £3.45-£10.45
main: £3.45-£10.45
dessert: £4-£4.65
Set lunch £10-£25
AE JCB MC V; SW

Open: daily noon-3pm, Sun-Thurs 6.30pm-11pm, Fri & Sat 6.30pm-midnight; reservations accepted (advisable weekends); licensed

KENSAL RISE

William IV
Modern European

☎ 020 8969 5944
786 Harrow Rd NW10

If there is anything surprising about the Harrow Rd it has to be William IV. It is an oasis in a culinary desert. Weekends see young families and local trendsetters heading to this gastropub to unwind on the huge leather sofas and enjoy the European cuisine. Sunday lunch is quite an occasion here, and at £12 for two courses or £15 for three, it's great value. The Thai chicken salad comes with vermicelli noodles and chilli – the ideal refreshing dish before a traditional roast. Our lamb arrived pink, as we happen to like it; however, it would've been nicer to have been asked for our preference. The meat was beautifully succulent but the accompanying seasonal vegetables were slightly cold. The amiable staff provide fast service even at the busiest times. After lunch you can retire to the bar, relax and enjoy a bottle of crisp pinot grigio (£15.35).

Open: restaurant Mon-Fri 1pm-3pm, 6pm-10.30pm, Sat & Sun noon-4pm, Sat 7pm-11pm, Sun 7pm-10pm, bar Mon-Thurs noon-11pm, Fri & Sat 11am-midnight, Sun noon-10.30pm; reservations advisable (weekends); licensed

Map 10 A1
Rail: Kensal Rise
Wheelchair access
Certified organic

 Smoking throughout

 Courtyard tables

starter: £3.50-£6
main: £6.50-£13
dessert: £4-£5
Set lunch £7,
Sun £12 or £15

AE DC MC V; SW

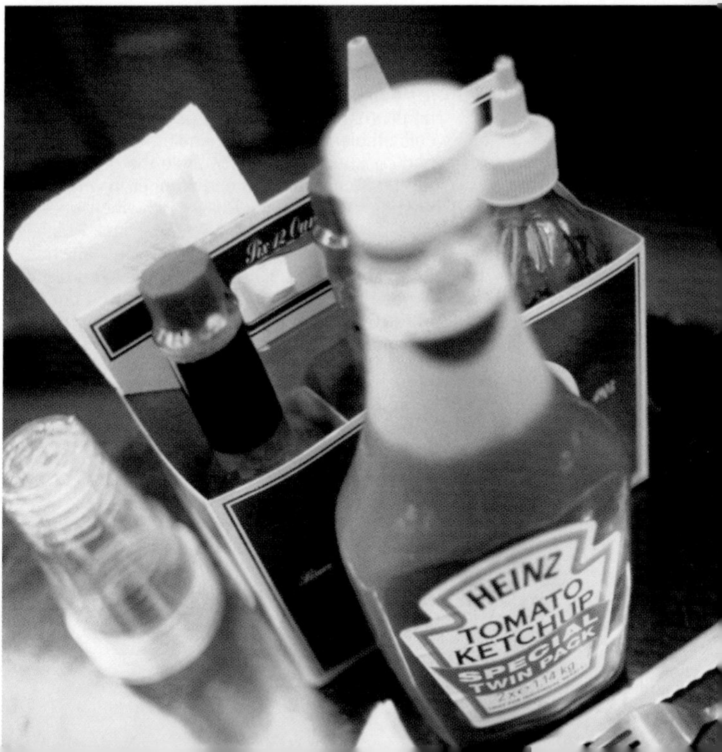

KENSINGTON

Maggie Jones's

British

☎ 020 7937 6462
6 Old Court Place, Kensington Church St W8

Map 10 E4
Tube: High Street Kensington
Smoking throughout

This place *is* a grandmother's kitchen – there's Victorian memorabilia everywhere – but the clientele is definitely up-to-date; we dined alongside media types, tourists and even a toff, his girlfriend and their transsexual sidekick. The set dinner menu has a choice of seven dishes per course, but the starter that stands out is the house speciality, Maggie's tart, cased in perfect pastry. The creamed fish pie is made from a traditional recipe with boiled eggs and plenty of fish. The roast guinea fowl (£12.50) is a classic favourite, and diners who like to experiment will love the rabbit and mustard casserole (£14.75). There's a good choice of puddings (£4), and with over 55 wine varieties to choose from you'll be sure to find one to your liking. The lunch menus have lighter portions and less variety, but you can still expect to eat well.

starter: £3.50-£6.85
main: £5.50-£18
dessert: £2.80-£4
AE DC MC V; SW

Open: daily 12.30pm-2.15pm, 6.30pm-11pm; reservations advisable; licensed

Wódka

Polish/Eastern European

☎ 020 7937 6513
12 St Alban's Grove W8

Map 10 E6
Tube: High Street Kensington
Smoking throughout

You'll find several healthy-sounding fish options on the menu at Wódka, but this friendly local restaurant remains a temple to a cuisine largely unreconstructed by dietary science. The Cracow-chic ambience is unmistakable: Polish vodka and cocktails (from £5.50) rule the drinks list, the staff chat away to one another in what sounds like authentic Polish and, when we visited, there was even a cheerful Jack Russell roaming the dining room. Staff are equally helpful in English, though the robust flavours of cheese and leek dumplings tossed with chunks of fatty bacon and wild mushrooms need no explanation – nor, perhaps, quite so much oil. The kasza salad is tossed with eye-watering doses of fresh mint and shallots (£2.50), but the fishcakes alone make a visit to Wódka essential: two plump pucks of juicy shredded fish seasoned with dill and perched in a deliciously salty leek and cream sauce (£10.50). Try the unctuous white chocolate cheesecake (£4.50), then book yourself in for that cholesterol test while you still can.

starter: £3.90-£11.50
main: £10.50-£13.50
dessert: £3.90-£4.90
AE DC MC V; SW

Open: Mon-Fri noon-2.30pm, Mon-Sat 7pm-11.15pm; reservations advisable; licensed & BYO (corkage £5/bottle)

LADBROKE GROVE

Brasserie du Marché aux Puces
French

☎ 020 8968 5828
349 Portobello Rd W10

Map 10 A1
Tube: Ladbroke Grove

Smoking throughout

Pavement tables

Brasserie du Marché aux Puces is a very pleasant surprise in over-run (and often over-priced) Notting Hill. Part of the appeal is its location on a quieter stretch of Portobello Rd, a few blocks away from the antique and curio market. On a sunny day you can grab an outside table, order a decent bottle of wine (starting from £10) and tuck into solid fare at reasonable prices. Our Sunday lunch menu offered roast pork with country potatoes and green beans, roast cod fillet with ratatouille, and a generous charcuterie plate that included salami, duck pâté, smoked ham and chorizo with a rocket salad; all three dishes cost under £10. The restaurant graciously welcomes children, but in true French style the kids are expected to behave and order from the adult menu.

Open: daily 11am-4pm, 7pm-11.30pm; reservations advisable; licensed

starter: £3.85-£8.25
main: £8.25-£13.95
dessert: £5
Set menu £9.50 or £12.50

AE DC JCB MC V; SW

Coffee Culture

The days of a grim cup of weak and tasteless coffee in London are gone. Scores of outlets sell steaming cups of coffee in myriad permutations and sizes. Many of the purveyors are chains, and competition is fierce for prime high-traffic locations. Other quality coffee bars can be found in bookstores like Borders, Books Etc and Waterstone's, allowing you to ponder your pages over a frothy brew. Even train stations and other places once known for squalid java have decent coffee outlets.

Here are the major players in London's coffee wars, where you have your choice of taking your beverage with you or remaining on the premises while you sip and possibly dip into a newspaper:

Aroma has stylish locations that belie their corporate ownership by McDonald's. The coffee comes in big, primary-coloured cups and you get a little chocolate on the side.

Coffee Republic has huge easy chairs at many of its outlets as well as baked goods and cold sandwiches.

Costa Coffee adds a menu of fresh soups, bakery items and hot and cold sandwiches at many of its locations. This is the choice for people who want more sustenance than just a hot drink.

Starbucks continues its global assault and London is a major front for the ubiquitous American chain. Stores tend to be large with a variety of seating, which makes them good for a long stay.

LANCASTER GATE

Map 10 E2

Tube: Lancaster Gate or Paddington

Smoking throughout 

Terrace tables 

Bistro Daniel

French

☎ 020 7262 6073
26 Sussex Place W2

Bare wooden tables, rush-seated chairs and corn-coloured walls set the rustic tone for this basement bistro where couples devour simple Gallic dishes by candlelight. The daily soups (£3.50) are wholesome and fresh but if you'd like a quintessentially French starter, opt for the vol-au-vent of snails (£5.30), a puff pastry box of delights oozing an oily, garlicky, parsley sauce. The coulibiac of delicate salmon and leafy spinach (£7.95) was balanced with a rich béchamel sauce. Expect to pay extra for bread (£1.50) and vegetables (£1.95). Les desserts are as calorific as you'd expect, but if you must, have the chocolate cake with crème anglais (£3.95). The charming French staff are chatty and knowledgeable, and wish you a bon appétit at each course. Amandier, the sister restaurant upstairs, offers more upmarket cuisine with prices to match.

starter: £3.50-£6.50
main: £7.50-£11.80
dessert: £3.95-£5.60
Set lunch £9.95 or £12.95
AE DC JCB MC V; SW

Open: Mon-Fri noon-2.30pm, Mon-Sat 7pm-10.45pm; reservations advisable (especially Fri & Sat evenings); licensed

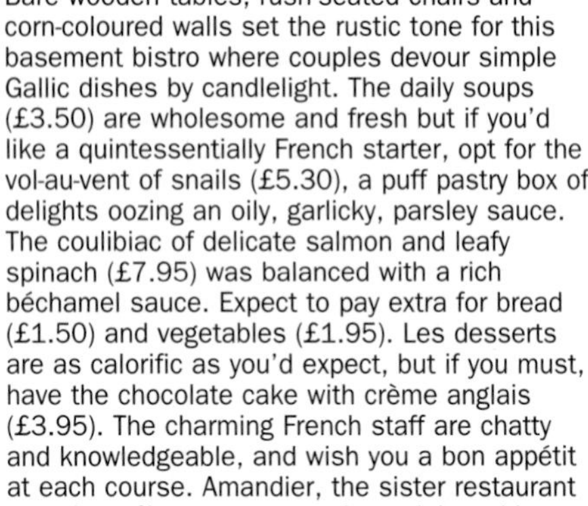

MAIDA VALE

Jason's

French, Mauritian & Creole seafood

☎ 020 7286 6752
Jason's Wharf, opposite 60 Blomfield Rd W9

Like a glass of Guinness drunk in Dublin, location often makes the experience, and summer dining on a canalside terrace is a bit of heaven. Sitting in Jason's smallish dining room in winter is a wholly different experience, of course. That's not to say the food isn't good, though how the denizens of the large display case stay fresh without an occasional big chill is anyone's guess. For starters we chose yabbies (£7.50), small freshwater Australian crustaceans in a sauce redolent of chilli and anise, and a soup de poissons (£6.95), groaning with mussels, prawns and cuttlefish done to individual perfection. Mains are 'novelty' items: capitan (£15.25), a type of grouper in a Creole sauce that tasted both piquant and palm-sugar sweet, and vacqua des îles (£15.25), a firm Mauritian fish cooked with tomato, chilli, ginger, lemongrass and a bit too much pepper. Service here is flawless and very knowledgeable – essential with such a complicated menu.

Open: daily breakfast 9.30am-11.30am (summer only), 12.30pm-3pm, Mon-Sat 6.30pm-10.30pm; reservations essential (dinner); licensed

Map 10 A5
Tube: Warwick Avenue
Wheelchair access

 Smoking throughout

 Terrace tables

starter: £6.75-£12.50
main: £15.25-£30
dessert: £4.25-£5.95
Set lunch £13.95, set dinner £21.95, chef's platter £35/person (min 2 people), menu gastronomique £36/person (min 2 people)

AE DC JCB MC V; SW

WEST

NOTTING HILL

Beach Blanket Babylon

Modern European

☎ 020 7229 2907
45 Ledbury Rd W11

The interior at Beach Blanket Babylon makes it unique, with columns and alcoves a predominant feature and candles enhancing the overall effect. The extensive modern European menu offers some interesting choices. Sautéed wild mushrooms with garlic and rosemary on toasted brioche (£7.75) worked well with the sweet-and-sour dish of quail, pickled ginger, mango and beansprouts (£6.75). Main courses are similarly successful. Chicken breast stuffed with goat's cheese and wrapped in Parma ham on a barley risotto with cherry tomatoes (£12.50) was a delight, as was the layered aubergine with cheese and pesto (£11.50). There is a wonderful choice of desserts, the pick of which is a cinnamon and chocolate bavarois with honey anglaise (£5.50). Well worth a visit!

Open: Mon-Fri noon-3pm, Sat & Sun noon-4pm, Thurs-Sat 7pm-11.30pm, Sun-Wed 7pm-10.30pm; reservations advisable; licensed

Map 10 C3
Tube: Notting Hill Gate

 Smoking throughout

 Patio tables

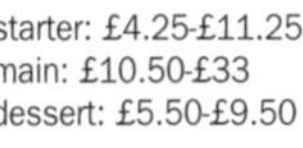
starter: £4.25-£11.25
main: £10.50-£33
dessert: £5.50-£9.50

AE DC MC V; SW

The Chepstow

Modern European

☎ 020 7229 0323
39 Chepstow Place W2

Map 10 C4
Tube: Notting Hill Gate

Smoking throughout 

Pavement tables 

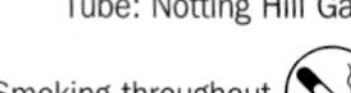

Nestled among period terrace housing, The Chepstow restaurant and bar is a popular haunt for local residents wanting a quiet drink or a meal well above usual pub standards. The front bar area is a casual, laid-back affair adorned with modern art, giving no hint of the sophisticated modern European menu available in the restaurant. Our starter of game terrine with fig chutney (£5.25) was a generous serve of chunky pieces of meat, with the fruity compote providing an interesting contrast. Next came pan-fried chicken breast (£11) served on a bed of fondant potatoes and wild mushroom ravioli. The dish was delicious, though we found the garlic sauce a little overpowering. Wrapped stuffed loin of lamb (£13.95) was perfectly paired with a redcurrant and rosemary jus which brilliantly enhanced the meat's flavour. Service here is friendly although a little slow – but then quality takes time.

starter: £4.50-£7.25
main: £8.50-£15.50
dessert: £4.50-£5
Weekday set lunch menu £12.95
(£5 min) DC MC V; SW

Open: restaurant Mon-Sat noon-3pm, 7pm-10.30pm, Sun 1pm-4pm, 7pm-10pm, bar Mon-Sat noon-11pm, Sun noon-10.30pm; reservations advisable; licensed

Churchill Arms

Thai

☎ 020 7792 1246
119 Kensington Church St W8

Map 10 D4
Tube: Notting Hill Gate

Smoking throughout 

Pub grub doesn't get much better than this for the price. In true Thai fashion, the menu gets down to basics by dispensing with starters and desserts (unless you count apple pie). There's the usual mix'n'match offerings of chilli and soya stir-fries, and red, green or jungle curries – all of which can be ordered with pork, beef, chicken or prawns. While this means there's an impressive 100-odd permutations on offer, the reality is that dishes tend to blur into that generic sameness of meals cooked from the same pot. Serves are large and Churchill's popularity guarantees freshness, but the down side is the occasional lack of attention to detail. It can all be a bit alarming when your table 'slot' is strictly for one and a half hours (only one hour for couples) – but where else in London are you able to eat restaurant-standard food while enjoying a pint in an indoor beer 'garden'?

main: £5.25-£5.50
dessert: £2.50
AE DC MC V; SW

Open: Mon-Sat noon-2.30pm, 6pm-9.30pm, Sunday noon-2.30pm; reservations advisable (essential for dinner); licensed

Churchill Arms

Mandola

Sudanese

☎ 020 7229 4734
139-141 Westbourne Grove W11

When most people think of Sudan they don't necessarily think of food. You won't be taken on a gastronomic tour at Mandola, but you can expect simple and authentic food served in a cosy atmosphere. Lighting is provided solely by ruby red candles placed on mahogany tables casually arranged in two connecting rooms – it's a bit like being at a large dinner party. Gold paper moons hang in the window and terracotta urns are dotted about. With a BYO policy and a wine shop next door, Mandola is great for big parties. The mixed salad bar (£7.95 for two) is not to be missed, comprising a selection of felafel, baked aubergine, sesame dip, spiced yoghurt, fetta and tomato salad and mixed vegetables, accompanied by oven-baked pita. A word of caution: treat the house 'chilli' with the respect it deserves!

Open: Mon 6pm-11pm, Tues-Sun noon-11pm; reservations advisable; BYO (corkage £1/bottle)

Map 10 B3

Tube: Notting Hill Gate

Smoking throughout

starter: £3.50-£4.50
main: £5.25-£8.50

cash and cheque only

Pharmacy Restaurant & Bar

Map 10 B1
Tube: Ladbroke Grove

Smoking throughout 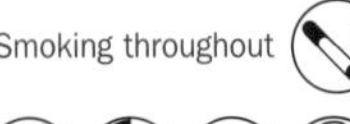

The Market Thai

Thai

☎ **020 7460 8320**
Level 1, The Market Bar, 240 Portobello Rd W11

Giant candles preside over a dining room kitted out with heavy wrought-iron furnishings in the Market Bar's upstairs den. The staff seem proud of their quest to bring reasonably priced Thai food to an otherwise trendy, expensive area, and service is pleasantly attentive. The set menu won't save you much, as the dishes are all around a fiver, but it's a good choice if you're new to the cuisine. A daintily arranged Market Thai selection of finger foods accompanies the attention-demanding, spicy tom yum gai (£3.95), a hot and sour chicken soup. The main course of kai ma muang (stir-fried chicken with cashew nuts, £4.95) and preaw wan moo (sweet and sour pork, £4.75) is prepared with a light and careful touch, but nonetheless proves more than filling. The clientele includes a healthy mix of couples and friendly gangs of bright young things.

starter: £3.25-£4.50
main: £4.25-£7.50
dessert: £2-£3.50
Set menu £13.95/ person (min 2 people)
AE MC V; SW

Open: daily noon-3pm, Mon-Sat 6pm-10.30pm, Sun 6pm-10pm; reservations accepted; licensed

Osteria Basilico ☎ **020 7727 9372**
Italian **29 Kensington Park Rd W11**

Osteria Basilico combines a rustic setting with a friendly and relaxed atmosphere which, given its trendy location, must be applauded. Classy but not pretentious, the Osteria's popularity and reputation are well deserved. And the food's great too. Traditional Italian ingredients are thrown together with such finesse that the spinach and peppers salad (£6) looked almost too good to eat. At £4.80, the antipasti buffet also makes a fine beginning. A worthy choice to follow is the house pizza (£6.80), but choosing anything is quite a decision given the range of pastas, fish, meat and specials on offer. Desserts typically include tiramisù (£3) and home-made ice cream (£3). For pure indulgence, however, the panna cotta (£3.50) is highly recommended. If you're after value for money and personable service, you're unquestionably in the right place at Osteria Basilico, and we defy anyone with a big appetite to leave unsatisfied.

Open: Mon-Fri 12.30pm-3.30pm, 6.30pm-11pm, Sat 12.30pm-4pm, 6.30pm-11pm, Sun 12.30pm-3.15pm, 6.30pm-10.30pm; reservations essential; licensed

Map 10 B2

Tube: Ladbroke Grove

 Smoking throughout (no cigars)

 Pavement tables

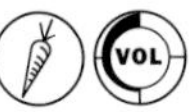 

starter: £3.80-£6.80
main: £5.80-£14.50
dessert: £3-£3.50

AE MC V; SW

WEST

Pharmacy Restaurant & Bar ☎ **020 7221 2442**
150 Notting Hill Gate W11
Modern European

When pop culture collides with nouvelle cuisine the results can be messy, but at Pharmacy the correct dose of irony has been prescribed. The downstairs bar is a chemist-shop-on-acid; the upstairs restaurant, where Damien Hirst's colourful butterflies flutter across the walls, is The Avengers circa Emma Peel. Cast your eyes to the table and you might catch a technicolour starter, such as the refreshing blood orange, fennel and olive salad (£7.50). Mains, including chunky rounds of suckling pig (£16.50) and a liberal serving of lamb on lentils (£16.50), are more down-to-earth, yet still come with artistic swirls of piquant sauces. A whole roast pigeon (£19.50) was beautifully tender, but we risked the disdain of the haughty waiters by using our fingers to ply the meat from the bones. Classic desserts, like lemon tart and chocolate pud, are dandy; persevere with the super flaky apple crisp – it all comes right in the end.

Open: daily 12.30pm-3pm, Mon-Sat 7pm-10.30pm, Sun 7pm-10pm, bar Mon-Sat noon-3pm, Mon-Thurs 6pm-1am, Fri & Sat 6pm-2am, Sun 11.15am-3pm, 6pm-10.30pm; reservations essential; licensed

Map 10 D3

Tube: Notting Hill Gate

Certified organic

 Smoking throughout

starter: £5-£13
main: £11.50-£22.50
dessert: £5.50
Set menu £15.50-£17.50

AE DC JCB MC V

Map 10 B4
Tube: Bayswater or Queensway

Smoking throughout 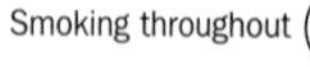

Alounak Kebab

Iranian

☎ 020 7229 0416
44 Westbourne Grove W2

You don't go to Pizza Express to sample Italian cuisine: you go for pizza. Likewise, you don't go to Alounak Kebab to sample Iranian cuisine: you go for kebab. The menu has about 12 variations on the theme, with just one non-kebab dish of the day. Specials like tomatoey khoresht (lamb stew, £5.90) can be good, but we like our Iranian kebabs too much to stray. Basic choices are lamb or chicken, minced or fillet. All the meat is beautifully marinated in orange or lemon juice and served with a grilled tomato and a huge mound of sumac-spiced rice – to which we suggest adding a knob of butter and dollops of masto mousir or masto khiar (yoghurt with shallots or cucumber, both £2.20). Large disks of flat bread come straight from a clay oven, which serves as a nice Persian touch in an interior that otherwise owes much to the pizza chain school of design. It does at least make for a breezy and informal atmosphere, complemented by very pleasant service. *Also Alounak, 10 Russell Gardens, Olympia W14 ☎ 7229 4158.*

starter: £2.20-£2.70
main: £4.20-£8.50
dessert: £2.20-£3
MC V

Open: daily noon-11.30pm; reservations not accepted; BYO (no corkage)

Map 10 B4
Tube: Bayswater or Queensway

Smoking throughout 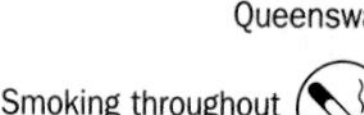

Pavement table 

Al Waha

Lebanese

☎ 020 7229 0806
75 Westbourne Grove W2

Serving excellent food in elegant, modern surroundings, Al Waha gets our vote as the best Lebanese restaurant in London. In true Levantine style, fill the table with a selection of mezze and leisurely pick and dip. The more than 50 starters range from humble hummus (£2.75) and labna (£3) to the more exotic frog's legs provençale and grilled quail (£6). Each dish is an artful blend of subtle flavourings, textures and fragrances. Even better are some of Al Waha's specials: fattah (chunks of tender lamb with a hint of rosewater, toasted bread pieces, chickpeas and pine kernels in a yoghurty sauce, £8.50) and kharouf mahshi (lamb on a bed of rice mixed with lentils, pistachios, almonds and pine kernels, £8.50). Order to share, and perhaps accompany with a glass of arak* (£3). Exquisite dining by any standards – not just those of the Middle East.

starter: £2.75-£6.50
main: £8-£14
dessert: £3
Set menu £18/person (min 2 people)
AE DC MC V; SW

Open: daily noon-11pm; reservations advisable (especially Fri & Sat evening); licensed

WESTBOURNE GROVE

Khan's

Indian

☎ 020 7727 5420
13-15 Westbourne Grove W2

At Khan's there's little time to spend at the bar admiring the décor (the palm-frond effect on the ceiling is a favourite) before being seated, as the eager staff ensure a quick turnover. For those not au fait with Indian cuisine the dishes are helpfully, if a little unglamorously, described on the extensive menu. There's plenty of alternatives to the traditional curry, with tandoori dishes a speciality. The sag prawns (£4.20) are gently spiced but just getting close to the chef's recommendation, chicken jalfrezi (£3.70), can be enough to make your eyes water. The combination of flawed acoustics and the proximity of the tables means Khan's is not the place to whisper sweet nothings; it is, however, the place to go for a buzzing atmosphere and cheap but tasty food.

Open: Mon-Thurs noon-3pm, 6pm-midnight, Fri-Sun noon-midnight; reservations accepted; unlicensed

Map 10 B4
Tube: Bayswater

Nonsmoking tables available

starter: 50p-£2.75
main: £2.75-£7.25
dessert: £1.50-£2.50
AE DC JCB MC V; SW

Pharmacy Restaurant & Bar (p 137)

Map 10 B2
Tube: Ladbroke Grove

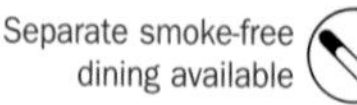
Separate smoke-free dining available

Garden tables

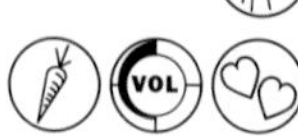

Bali Sugar

International

☎ 020 7221 4477
33a All Saints Rd W11

The name Bali Sugar doesn't do this exquisite little near-Notting Hill restaurant justice. Images of some typical Asian joint serving up piles of so-so nasi goreng are far from reality as chef Claudio Aprile melds Asian and Latin cooking in a way that could almost put some life back into the overused moniker 'fusion'. The char-grilled squid starter (£7.90) with black bean salsa and Thai dressing is a mélange of fresh flavours and spices which perfectly captures the ethos of the place. The grilled chorizo salad (£8.50) shows the potential of a dish that is so often just a pile of mixed greens. Mains include crispy salmon (£15.90) that comes perched on a beautiful arrangement of sweet potato tempura and cucumber kimchi. The wine list reflects the eclectic menu, but is also well balanced between a diverse range of producers. The décor is spare but elegant and serves as the perfect backdrop to the food and your companions.

starter: £5.50-£9.50
main: £12.50-£18.80
dessert: £5.50-£6.50
Set lunch £16.50
AE DC MC V; SW

Open: daily 12.30pm-2.30pm, 6.30pm-11pm; reservations advisable; licensed

Archway

Belsize Park

Camden

NORTH & NORTH-WEST

Chalk Farm

Crouch End

Golders Green

Green Lanes

Hampstead

Highgate

Kentish Town

Primrose Hill

St Johns's Wood

South Hampstead

Tufnell Park

Map 11 - Camden

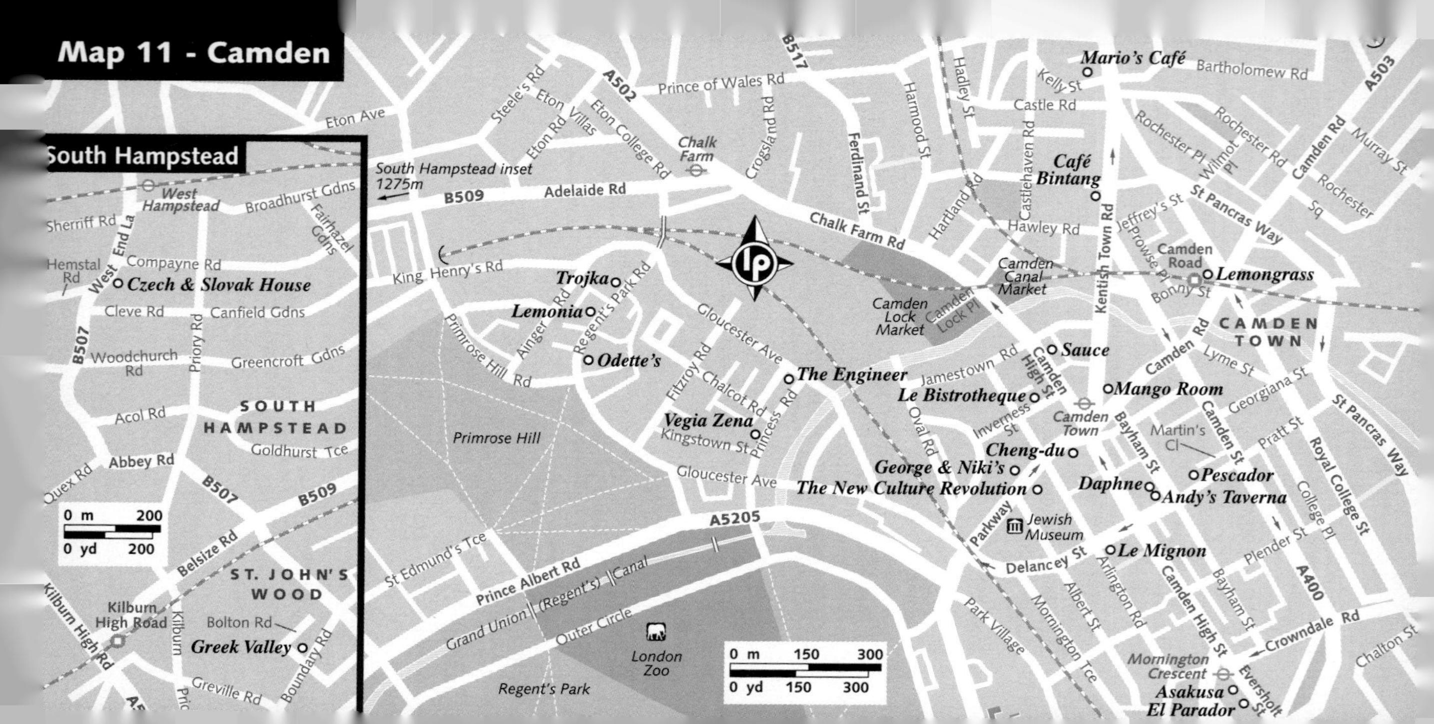

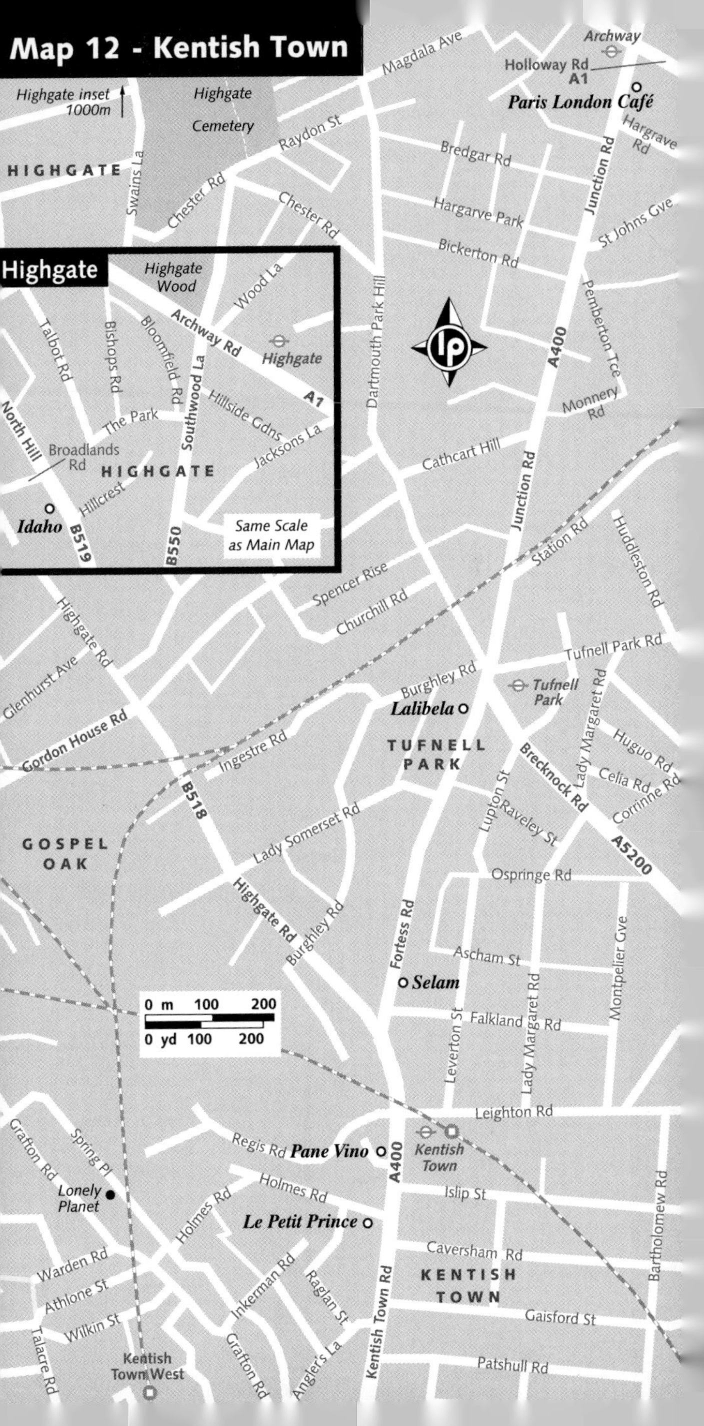
Map 12 - Kentish Town
Highgate inset 1000m
Highgate Cemetery
HIGHGATE
Swains La
Chester Rd
Raydon St
Magdala Ave
Archway
Holloway Rd
A1
Paris London Café
Hargrave Rd
Bredgar Rd
Junction Rd
Hargarve Park
St Johns Gve
Bickerton Rd
Highgate
Highgate Wood
Wood La
Archway Rd
Highgate
A1
Talbot Rd
Bishops Rd
Bloomfield Rd
Southwood La
Hillside Gdns
The Park
Jacksons La
North Hill
Broadlands Rd
HIGHGATE
Hillcrest
Idaho
B519
B550
Same Scale as Main Map
Dartmouth Park Hill
A400
Pemberton Tce
Monnery Rd
Cathcart Hill
Junction Rd
Station Rd
Huddleston Rd
Spencer Rise
Churchill Rd
Highgate Rd
Glenhurst Ave
Tufnell Park Rd
Burghley Rd
Tufnell Park
Lalibela
Gordon House Rd
Ingestre Rd
TUFNELL PARK
Lady Margaret Rd
Huguo Rd
Celia Rd
Corinne Rd
Brecknock Rd
Lupton St
Raveley St
A5200
B518
GOSPEL OAK
Lady Somerset Rd
Ospringe Rd
Highgate Rd
Burghley Rd
Fortess Rd
Ascham St
Montpelier Gve
Selam
0 m 100 200
0 yd 100 200
Leverton St
Falkland Rd
Lady Margaret Rd
Leighton Rd
Kentish Town
Regis Rd
Pane Vino
A400
Grafton Rd
Spring Pl
Holmes Rd
Islip St
Lonely Planet
Holmes Rd
Le Petit Prince
Caversham Rd
Bartholomew Rd
Warden Rd
Inkerman Rd
Raglan St
KENTISH TOWN
Athlone St
Wilkin St
Kentish Town Rd
Gaisford St
Talacre Rd
Kentish Town West
Grafton Rd
Angler's La
Patshull Rd

Map 13 - Crouch End & Around

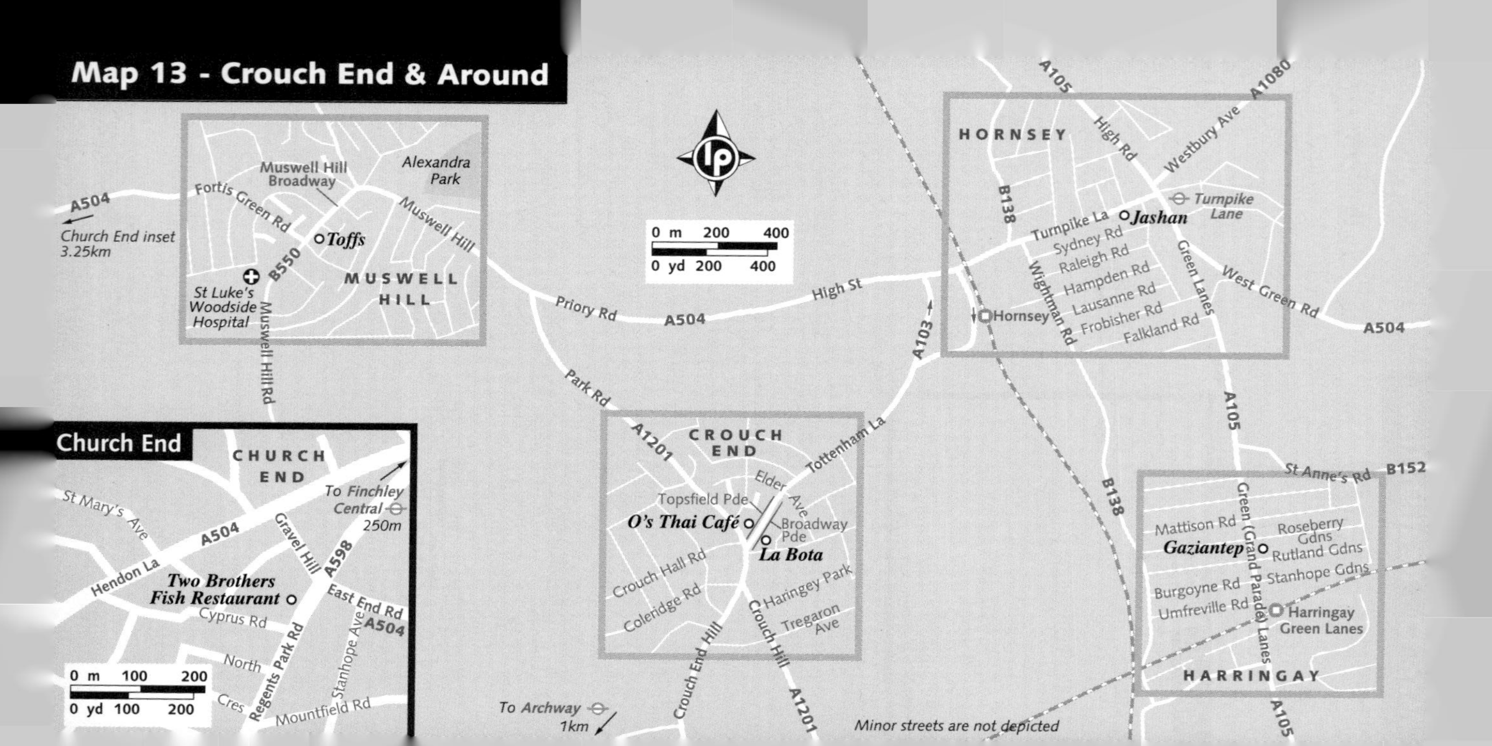

TODAY'S SPECIAL
SUNDAY ROAST
Chicken OR Beef
£4.95

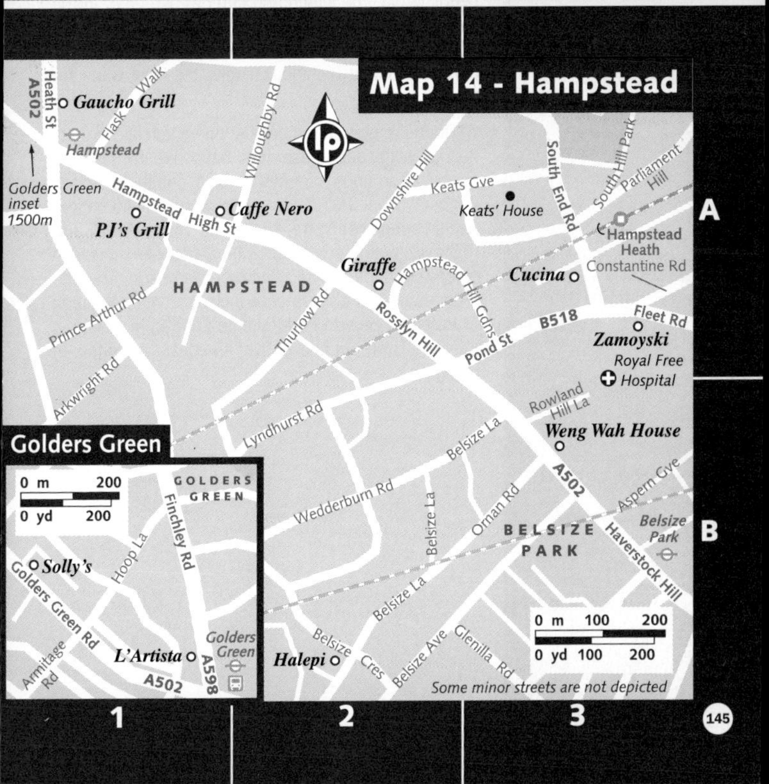

Map 14 - Hampstead

A502 Heath St
Gaucho Grill
Flask Walk
Hampstead
Golders Green inset 1500m
Hampstead High St
PJ's Grill
Caffe Nero
Willoughby Rd
Downshire Hill
Keats Gve
Keats' House
South End Rd
South Hill Park
Parliament Hill
Hampstead Heath
Constantine Rd
Giraffe
Hampstead Hill Gdns
Cucina
HAMPSTEAD
Prince Arthur Rd
Thurlow Rd
Rosslyn Hill
Pond St
B518
Fleet Rd
Zamoyski
Royal Free Hospital
Arkwright Rd
Lyndhurst Rd
Rowland Hill La
Weng Wah House
Belsize La
A502
Wedderburn Rd
Ornan Rd
Aspern Gve
BELSIZE PARK
Belsize Park
Haverstock Hill
Belsize Cres
Belsize Ave
Glenilla Rd
Halepi
0 m 100 200
0 yd 100 200
Some minor streets are not depicted

Golders Green

0 m 200
0 yd 200
GOLDERS GREEN
Finchley Rd
Hoop La
Solly's
Golders Green Rd
Armitage Rd
L'Artista
A502
A598
Golders Green

A B 1 2 3

BEST

- **Asakusa**
  The Japanese experience: sushi bar, extensive menu and basement karaoke
- **The Engineer**
  Relaxing environs, skilled modern British cooking
- **Giraffe**
  An easy-going eatery with divine desserts
- **Halepi**
  Inspired Greek on charming Belsize Lane

North & North-West

The areas north and west of Central London are a diverse lot. From the noble streets of St John's Wood and the Jewish delicatessens of Golders Green to the bargain-priced shops of Kentish Town, almost every aspect of London's diverse population and culture can be found. Many visitors – whether from south of the river, across the channel or over 'the pond', head first to Camden Town with its many shops and stalls peddling old-time kitsch and cutting-edge gear. In the side streets throughout this region can be found scores of small cafes, ethnic eateries and smart little places boasting ambitious cooks but long waits for tables.

When the temperatures get just one notch above cold, near-do-wells and those that have already made it spend afternoons outside at chic coffee spots on Regent's Park Rd in leafy Primrose Hill. Much the same scene can be found in Hampstead and Highgate, although a recent influx of faux French chain cafes has homogenised some of the charm. The fine eateries in this diverse area include upmarket Greek at Halepi in Belsize Park, simple Eritrean at Selam in Kentish Town and inventive American at Idaho in Highgate.

Paris London Café
French

☎ **020 7561 0330**
5 Junction Rd N19

Map 12 A3
Tube: Archway

 Smoking throughout

In how many places in London can you have a full five-course French meal for £16? Not many and maybe only one, the Paris London Cafe. Right across from the Archway tube, this ever-expanding example of that French institution the 'bistro' packs 'em in most nights. The five-course meal includes fish soup, grilled sardines, beef bourguignon, a selection of cheeses and a choice of desserts. À la carte choices feature classics like frog's legs (£4.95 as a starter), salade niçoise (£3.25) and Dijon rabbit (£6.95). Tables are tight in the smallish dining area but the staff are clearly having fun bringing a bit of continental charm to scruffy North London. Wine choices are broad and start cheap at £8. They also do great lunch sandwiches for under £2, and their popular breakfast delivery service brings the best of the continent (croissant, coffee, etc) and a newspaper to local homes for under £6 – perfect for the morning after that British institution, the pub.

Open: Mon-Sat 8am-11pm, Sun 8am-10.30pm; reservations advisable (Fri & Sat); licensed

starter: £2.25-£5.75
main: £5.95-£12.95
dessert: £2.25-£3.75
Set menu £9.95-£15.95

cash or cheque only

Map 14 B2
Tube: Belsize Park or Swiss Cottage
Entertainment: live music Fri & Sat
Smoking throughout

Halepi
Greek

☎ 020 7431 5855
48-50 Belsize Lane NW3

This Belsize Park sibling of the Queensway original is definitely the preferred choice of the two, and not just for its charming setting on narrow Belsize Lane. The usual mobs of chattering customers mean that you'll barely notice the stark, Ikea-simple interior. The kitchen clearly takes itself seriously, as reflected on the menu that features not just regular calamari (£5) but also baby calamari (£6). The avgolemono (£3.50) is an inspired rendition of the all-too-often pedestrian soup of rice in a lemony chicken broth. Hearty roasts and casseroles dominate the mains. The kolokassi (£9.75) is a shepherd's dream of stewed pork and stuffed cabbage. Since most nights you'll need to book to get in, you might also want to opt for special advance order dishes like suckling pig or milk-fed goat (price varies). Sides include steamed fresh asparagus (£5) with just the right amount of crunch. Service bustles but is effective, and the wine list reflects the padded wallets of the locals.

starter: £2.75-£5
main: £7.75-£16
dessert: £2.50-£3.50
Set menu, £15 or £24
AE DC JCB MC V; SW

Open: Wed-Fri noon-3pm, Mon-Fri 6pm-midnight, Sat noon-11pm, Sun noon-10.30pm; reservations advisable (essential weekends); licensed

---

Map 14 B3
Tube: Belsize Park
Entertainment: karaoke Fri & Sat 8pm
Smoking throughout

Weng Wah House
Chinese

☎ 020 7794 5123
240 Haverstock Hill NW3

This always busy, two-storey Chinese restaurant is nestled just south of the Hampstead stretch of Haverstock Hill. The fish tanks along the walls reveal that it specialises in fresh seafood, though meat lovers will be tempted by the crispy aromatic duck, which can be ordered whole (£24) or as part of a mixed dish. Diners are spoiled for choice: on the night we visited there were no fewer than five different set meals, and 25 vegetable dishes such as Chinese greens in oyster sauce and sea-spice aubergines (both £4). The three-course special set meal included starter selections of spring rolls, prawn toast and crispy seaweed, followed by pancakes with shredded duck, chicken with cashew nuts and beef slices with asparagus. We polished off the complimentary fresh orange slices, and left with satisfied appetites and happy wallets.

starter: £4-£6
main: £5.80-£24
dessert: £4
Set menu £16.50-£18
MC V; SW

Open: Mon-Fri 12.30pm-2.45pm, 6pm-11.30pm, Sat 12.30pm-midnight, Sun 12.30pm-11pm; reservations advisable; licensed

Andy's Taverna

Greek

☎ **020 7485 9718**
81a Bayham St NW1

Map 11 C5
Tube: Camden Town

 Smoking throughout

 Patio tables

At first glance Andy's Taverna looks like just another standard London Greek place: slightly tatty décor and tourist prints on the walls. The arrival of the menu does little to change the perceptions: there are all the usuals, from taramasalata (£2.45) to souvlaki (£7.25). The snappy service, however, keeps one from dwelling too long on any potential negatives. Once the order is placed, thoughts of the surroundings fade and attention happily focuses on the food. Andy's mixed dip (£3.85) of tarama, hummus and tzatziki was a winner – our tzatziki aficionado declared hers the 'best ever'. For mains, the vegetable kebabs (£6.95) were nicely grilled and seasoned. The mixed grill special (£8.25) yielded a generous selection of charcoaled meats including some excellent garlicky Greek sausage. The dessert special for £3.50 per person brought a platter of fresh fruit and Greek pastry – a great finish. Service was smiling, and after our minicab didn't show up, an employee drove us home. Andy's is a great place to go with a group for food and fun.

Open: Mon-Fri noon-3pm, daily 6pm-midnight; reservations advisable (weekends); licensed

starter: £2.45-£3.85
main: £6.95-£12.50
dessert: £2.50-£3.50
Set lunch £6.50,
set dinner £9.95

AE DC MC V

Asakusa

Japanese

☎ **020 7388 8533**
265 Eversholt St NW1

Map 11 C5
Tube: Camden Town or Mornington Crescent

 Smoking throughout

Smoky and packed with Japanese, Asakusa is a restaurant to make old Japan-hands' hearts leap. The down-at-heel mock-Tudor décor suggests that Michael Caine may have snacked on a bacon sarnie here in the 1960s, but it's also curiously reminiscent of many an *izakaya* – a kind of Japanese pub where you also eat – and has a decent sushi bar tucked away at the back. The extensive menu covers all the bases, including noodles, tempura and yakitori, at eminently reasonable prices, and service is tip-top. Set meals are particularly good value: the Asakusa A course (£18) included eight different dishes plus a large flask of sake. We particularly liked the appetisers of hijiki (tasty strands of black seaweed) and shredded radish and tofu, the summery dish of vinegared slices of seafood and the breadcrumb-covered mackerel. And if you're in the mood to party, having downed your sake, there's karaoke in the basement private room.

Open: Mon-Fri 6pm-11.30pm, Sat 6pm-11pm; reservations advisable (especially weekends); licensed

starter: £1.10-£4.20
main: £5.20-£9.80
dessert: £1.60-£3.30
Set menu £15 or £18

AE DC JCB MC V; SW

Map 11 A4
Tube: Camden Town

Smoking throughout

Pavement tables

Café Bintang

South-East Asian

☎ 020 7813 3393
93 Kentish Town Rd NW1

Camden's cosy Café Bintang offers diners a flavoursome taste of the East right in the heart of North London. And it's not just the food; rattan walls, candlelight and cold Tiger Beers all help to create the illusion that you are miles away. Choosing from the selection of South-East Asian cuisine can be difficult, but a safe bet is the iken ulek (£5.50) – a whole fish simmering in a banana leaf, mildly spiced with just the right blend of lemongrass, garlic, herbs and the occasional bite of chilli. Or you could try ayam narikal (£4.50), succulent chicken with basil, coriander, creamy coconut and, of course, the ubiquitous lemongrass. Add a bowl of rice at £1 and you have a tasty, filling meal. With very healthy portions at such reasonable prices, Café Bintang is easily a favourite with the wallet as well.

starter: £1-£4.50
main: £2.50-£24.50
dessert: £2
Set lunch £5
MC V; SW

Open: Mon-Thurs 5.30pm-midnight, Fri & Sat 5.30pm-12.30am, Sun noon-11pm; reservations advisable; licensed & BYO (corkage £2/bottle)

Map 11 B4
Tube: Camden Town

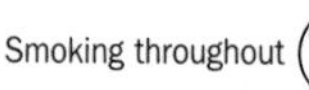

Cheng-Du

Chinese

☎ 020 7485 8058
9 Parkway NW1

Cheng-Du's smart, modern appearance makes it a good choice for a special occasion, but you can also pick dishes from the extensive menu to make a meal that won't break the bank. Service is discreet and attentive, and the air is filled with the beautiful scent of lemongrass (and, unfortunately, cigarette smoke). There's a range of goodies to whet the appetite, like crispy fried won ton puffs (£3.40) and meaty sesame prawn fingers (£4.80). General Tseng's chicken (£5.40) is rich and succulent but unfortunately not 'hot', as described on the menu. The fresh squid in garlicky black bean sauce (£6.80), teamed with Cheng-Du special fried noodles (£4.20) and fluffy egg fried rice (£2.30), is the most tender we've ever tasted. The fish selection is impressive, including whole steamed sea bass with red dates, black fungi and golden lilies (£12 per lb) which is filleted at the table. The well-chilled house wine makes a good accompaniment and is reasonably priced at £9.75.

starter: £2-£4.80
main: £5-£12
dessert: £3
Set menu £20
MC V; SW

Open: daily noon-2.30pm, 6pm-11.30pm; reservations advisable; licensed

Daphne **☎ 020 7267 7322**
Greek **83 Bayham St NW1**

Map 11 B5
Tube: Camden Town

 Nonsmoking tables available

 Roof terrace tables

Ordering the mezze platter is usually a safe and fun option at most London Cypriot-run Greek places. You get lots of little plates with tasty treats that demand sampling and sharing around the table. This tradition is certainly upheld at Daphne, but here you might want to forgo the meze (£10.75 with meat, £15.50 with fish) and explore the long list of interesting items from the menu, or the even more enticing line-up of daily specials. The warm starter of chickpeas infused with spices (£4.50) is a nice contrast to the usual hummus. The salmon (£12.50) with aubergines and potatoes is flavoured with fresh dill and cooked to that fleeting level of crispy moistness that evades many chefs. Meze habitués will still be cheered by the offerings here. The smoked fish was silky and the dolmades among the best we've had. The décor is Greek simple and in summer there's great deck dining outside.

Open: Mon-Sat noon-2.30pm, 6pm-11.30pm; reservations advisable; licensed

starter: £2.40-£3.75
main: £6.50-£12.50
dessert: £2.15-£3
Set lunch £5.75, meat meze £10.75/ person or fish meze £15.50/person

MC V; SW

El Parador **☎ 020 7387 2789**
Spanish **245 Eversholt St NW1**

Map 11 C5
Tube: Camden Town or Mornington Crescent

 Smoking throughout

 Garden tables

In winter, El Parador is just another convivial restaurant serving a wide selection of Spanish tapas, but in summer it moves into that elusive category of London eateries where you can dine alfresco. On a balmy night, after a glass or two of Spanish wine, shielded from the sound of the traffic and with a table full of tapas before you, you begin to feel you're somewhere much further south. Our favourite dishes include the roast fennel (£3.70), the fleshy and lime-doused grilled swordfish (£4.50) and the tender grilled marinated lamb (£4.20). Book well ahead if you're hoping to grab a seat in the garden – open from around 1 May to the onset of colder weather, usually sometime in September.

Open: Mon-Fri noon-3pm, Mon-Thurs 6pm-11pm, Fri & Sat 6pm-11.30pm, Sun 7pm-10.30pm; reservations accepted (for groups of 3 or more); licensed

main: £2.90-£4.80
dessert: £3-£4

MC V; SW

On Your Plate **Chinese**

London has plenty of Chinese restaurants – almost every high street will have two or three cheap or medium-priced eateries. Although these aren't the 'chop-suey houses' of the 1960s and 70s, the cooking is so adapted to English tastes that most of the food is as 'Chinese' as french fries are genuinely French.

For authentic Chinese food, go to the place where the Chinese go – Chinatown. During the 1950s, the area in and around Gerrard St was extremely run down and rents were cheap: Chinatown was born. Originally staff lived in dingy rooms above the restaurants and accommodation accounted for a large part of their wages – which probably explains the legendary rudeness of Chinatown waiters. Some diners still judge the authenticity of a restaurant by how bad tempered its waiters are. Soho's Chinatown is roughly bound by Leicester Square, Charing Cross Rd, Wardour St and Shaftesbury Ave. The area around Queensway in Bayswater is also becoming a centre for Chinese restaurants.

Most of the genuine Chinese food in Chinatown is Hong Kong Cantonese. This can roughly be split into 'banquet cuisine' (highly flavoured, often with rich sauces), which most Chinese people would eat only occasionally, and 'yum cha'. Yum cha literally means 'drink tea', and is an opportunity for families and friends to get together for a good gossip. A yum cha meal is made up of several dishes, including steamed or deep-fried filled dumplings (dim sum), noodle dishes and soups. In some restaurants, waiters push around trolleys with plates piled high with dim sum: simply point at whatever takes your fancy. The gastronomically adventurous might like to try braised duck or chicken feet, or tripe. For a good traditional selection, try the **Golden Dragon** (for its loh mai kai) or **Harbour City** (for its duck tongue in black bean sauce). Starting at under £2 per dish, two people could eat their fill for under £20 – a bargain for central London.

Traditionally dim sum is an afternoon meal served between 11am and 5pm; ordering it outside these hours is considered rude. But if you can't live without dim sum at 9pm, some restaurants *will* accommodate you. Expect the quality of the food to be poorer, however, and you may hear an array of Cantonese swear words, too.

Most of the chefs who prepare dim sum are trained in Hong Kong and are highly skilled. They can command astronomical salaries and, just like star footballers, transfers (often between Hong Kong and London) are big news in the trade.

Evening Chinatown dining provides a plethora of sumptuous Cantonese food. Lisle St's **New Diamond** cooks up sauces comparable to anything you'll find in Hong Kong or Singapore. But you need to balance these dishes with the cleaner tastes of steamed fish, stir-fried vegetables, such as choi sam, and clear soups. For standout seafood try the **Golden Harvest** on Lisle St, but be prepared to pay at least three or four times as much as you would for yum cha.

Simon Heng

Simon Heng has spent much of his adolescence in a variety of Chinese kitchens, as his father worked in the restaurant trade for over 20 years. He has managed to eat his way around much of Europe and parts of South-East Asia, blagging his way into many kitchens to learn the tricks of the trade.

George & Niki's
Traditional English

☎ **020 7485 7432**
38 Parkway NW1

Map 11 B4
Tube: Camden Town

 Smoking throughout

 Courtyard tables

You're tired and hungry, and you just want some good solid food with no pretensions. This long-running family institution catering to locals and hung-over partygoers could be just what the doctor ordered. The food at George & Niki's is filling but not refined, and definitely secondary to the atmosphere. It's best on rainy weekends after a hard night on the town, when you can relax in the cosy dining and enjoy the deliciously hearty special set breakfast (£5) with a reassuringly strong coffee (90p) while soaking up the Camden gossip. Though the restaurant specialises in fry-ups, you can opt for (marginally) healthier dishes like poached salmon (£6.95), but that's about as adventurous as the menu gets – basically, don't expect to find anything here your mum wouldn't cook. One thing to be sure of: you won't leave hungry after a meal at George & Niki's.

Open: Mon-Fri noon-midnight, Sat & Sun 11am-midnight; reservations accepted; licensed

starter: £1.95-£4.15
main: £4-£13.75
dessert: £2-£2.15
Set breakfast £5

(5% handling charge) MC V; SW

Le Mignon
Lebanese

☎ **020 7387 0600**
9a Delancey St NW1

Map 11 C4
Tube: Camden Town

 Smoking throughout

 Pavement tables

This cosy restaurant off Camden High St is becoming a regular haunt for Camdenites in the know. Owner/chef Hussein Dekmak took over the space in February 1998, keeping the French name and warm Mediterranean décor but drastically changing the menu to his native Lebanese cuisine. Mains such as farrouge moussahab (grilled chicken, £7.80) and stuffed lamb (£8) are enticing, but a meal of meze dishes is definitely the authentic way to go. You can't beat the golden felafel served with tahini (£3.25), the spicy fattoush (mixed vegetable salad, £2.90), the aromatic hummus snoubar (with pine nuts; £4.50), any of the sambouseks (stuffed pastries, £3.25) and the garlic-sauced fawaneh (chicken wings, £4.50). Try one of the imported Chateau Kefraya wines, finish with some sugary baklava and a glass of arak, and you won't be disappointed.

Open: Tues-Sun noon-11.30pm; reservations advisable (especially Fri & Sat evening); licensed

starter: £2.50-£4.50
main: £6.50-£11
dessert: £2.50

MC V; SW

Lemongrass

South-East Asian

☎ **020 7284 1116**
243 Royal College St NW1

Map 11 B5
Tube: Camden Town, rail: Camden Rd

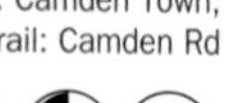

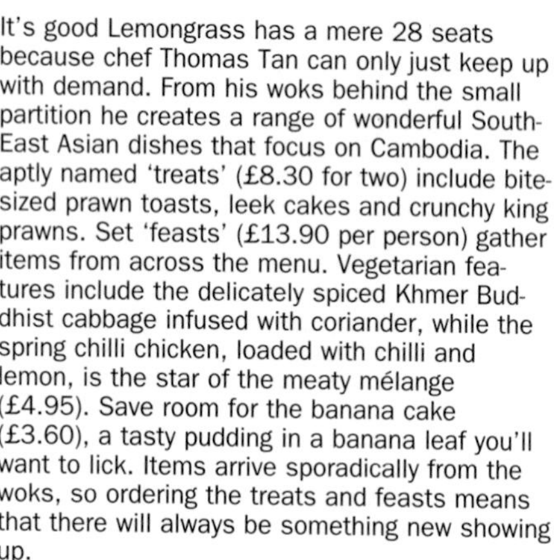

It's good Lemongrass has a mere 28 seats because chef Thomas Tan can only just keep up with demand. From his woks behind the small partition he creates a range of wonderful South-East Asian dishes that focus on Cambodia. The aptly named 'treats' (£8.30 for two) include bite-sized prawn toasts, leek cakes and crunchy king prawns. Set 'feasts' (£13.90 per person) gather items from across the menu. Vegetarian features include the delicately spiced Khmer Buddhist cabbage infused with coriander, while the spring chilli chicken, loaded with chilli and lemon, is the star of the meaty mélange (£4.95). Save room for the banana cake (£3.60), a tasty pudding in a banana leaf you'll want to lick. Items arrive sporadically from the woks, so ordering the treats and feasts means that there will always be something new showing up.

starter: £2.60-£3.90
main: £4.80-£6.90
dessert: £3-£3.90
Set menu £13.90 or £15.90
MC V; SW

Open: Wed-Fri 12.30pm-2.30pm, Mon-Sat 6.30pm-10.30pm; reservations advisable (especially weekends); licensed

Mango Room

Caribbean

☎ **020 7482 5065**
10 Kentish Town Rd NW1

Map 11 B4
Tube: Camden Town
Wheelchair access
Smoking throughout

Like transubstantiation and the allure of Cliff Richard, Caribbean cuisine had always been a mystery to us so we turned to this shrine of 'traditional and modern Caribbean cuisine' for enlightenment. We found the latter in the fluffy crab and potato balls (£3.70) with their hint of coriander but not in the salt cod fritters (£3.80), which were mini-sponges for the oil they were fried in. The rich goat curry (£7.80) was redolent of cumin, pimento and fresh coriander, and the platter of half a dozen cooked vegetables (£8.50), including akee, was generous. But the banana and mango brûlée (£3.50) was disappointing – a cup of viscous pudding topped with a cold disk of burnt sugar. The young staff at the warm-toned Mango Room made us feel welcome, as did the impressive cocktail list.

starter: £3-£4.75
main: £7-£10.50
dessert: £3.50-£4
set menu £18-£22
MC V; SW

Open: daily noon-3pm, 6pm-midnight; reservations advisable(especially weekends); licensed

CAMDEN

The New Culture Revolution

Chinese

☎ 020 7267 2700
43 Parkway NW1

Map 11 B4
Tube: Camden Town

Nonsmoking tables available

A short walk from Camden Tube station brings you to this small and simple restaurant whose refreshing, untypical Chinese menu has now been expanded to include more seafood and duck selections. Service is casual yet fast, and dishes are MSG, peanut and genetically modified-ingredient free. Main meals are filling, but if you have the appetite the gui tei (pan-fried dumplings; £5.60) make an excellent starter. The marinated beef slices (£3) were a little dry on the night we dined, so for tender beef slices in a sea of noodles, spices and vegetables try the si chuan chilli beef lo mein (£5.60). The chow mein standards (ask for chilli sauce for extra kapow) include chicken, pork, beef, prawn (£5.50) and vegetarian (£4.80). If you haven't had too much complimentary jasmine tea, enjoy a gusto original (£2.20), a herbal drink of Chinese herbs, fruit juices and guarana. You'll hit Camden on a healthy, natural high.

Open: Mon-Thurs noon-3.30pm, 5.30pm-11pm, Fri noon-11pm, Sat & Sun 1pm-11pm; reservations advisable (especially weekends); licensed

starter: £1.80-£6
main: £4.60-£9.50

AE MC V; SW

Pescador

Portuguese

☎ 020 7482 7008
33 Pratt St NW1

Map 11 B5
Tube: Camden Town

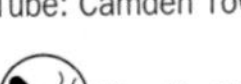

Smoking throughout

Pavement tables

Pescador is a simple neighbourhood Portuguese place that makes for a good and inexpensive night out. All the classics enjoyed by generations of travellers to the Iberian nation are here: pork with clams (£8.50) has tender meat with small, fresh clams in a rich, garlicky broth; grilled salt cod (£7.90) deftly captures the national staple; and clams cooked in white wine are seasoned with coriander, garlic and peppers (£7). Starters are equally simple and cheap – the salt cod fishcakes and grilled sardines are both £2.50 and are good renditions of the kinds of dishes that Portuguese fishermen have eaten for generations. You'll find these same dishes on the menus at small, family-run restaurants all over Portugal, places just like Pescador. Service is congenial and by your second visit you're like one of the, well, you guessed it. Desserts include another standard – smooth crème caramel (£2). Appropriately, there's a long line of vintage ports behind the bar for after-dinner libations.

Open: Tues-Sat noon-3pm, 6pm-11.30pm, Sun 1pm-10pm; reservations advisable (especially weekends); licensed

starter: £3
main: £8
dessert: £2
Sunday set lunch £10

MC V; SW

Map 11 B4
Tube: Camden Town
Certified organic

Smoking throughout 

Sauce

British

☎ 020 7482 0777
214 Camden High St NW1

Marketing itself as a 'barorganicdiner', Sauce has a young, trendy feel to it but don't let that put you off. An organic oasis in the hubbub of Camden, this eatery not only offers hearty meals, it also encourages you to relax and read the papers while sipping on a smoothie. Menu options are appetising, interesting and nutritious, instantly thwarting any ideas that organic food is boring. A spicy crème fraiche gave a kick to our perfectly constructed corn fritter with sautéed spinach and squash (£4.75). Served with fat fries, crunchy coleslaw and tomato relish, the veggie burger (£6.50) that followed was milder but no less tasty and easily washed down with the intriguingly named organic 'Freedom' beer. The service at Sauce is thoughtful and attentive, the atmosphere relaxed. Be good to your mind, body and soul – return to the Sauce!

starter: £2.75-£4.95
main: £5.95-£11
dessert: £2.95-£3.50
MC, V; SW

Open: Mon-Sat noon-11pm, Sun noon-4.30pm; reservations advisable; licensed

Lemonia
Greek

☎ **020 7586 7454**
89 Regent's Park Rd NW1

Map 11 B2
Tube: Chalk Farm, bus: 31
Wheelchair access

 Smoking throughout (no pipes or cigars)

 Pavement tables

Lemonia is a model of a popular Greek restaurant. The outside is classy with cute tiles of lemons; inside, the walls are uncluttered, the wood natural and there's lots of light from the huge windows overlooking the heart of classy Primrose Hill. The menu holds no surprises. From the hummus (£2.80) to the dolmades (£3.40) to the souvlaki (lamb, £7.40), all the dishes familiar to anyone whose been to a Cypriot restaurant in London are here. But in this case the location and above-average quality of the food combine to ensure that Lemonia is jammed every night. Just about every table opts for meze (£13.50 per person), which manages to go one better than many other local mezzes and often leaves diners trying to distract their mates so they can nab the last bit of calamari. Service is minimal since most of the waiters merely have to spin out the array of meze plates. Wines include the more interesting Greek/Cypriot offerings.

Open: Sun-Fri noon-3pm, Mon-Sat 6pm-11.30pm; reservations accepted; licensed

starter: £2.75-£4.75
main: £8-£13.50
dessert: £2.50-£3
Set menu £13.50

MC V; SW

Trojka
Russian/ Eastern European

☎ **020 7483 3765**
101 Regent's Park Rd NW1

Map 11 B3
Tube: Chalk Farm
Entertainment: Russian music Fri & Sat 8pm-10pm (£1/person cover)

 Nonsmoking tables available

 Pavement tables

Although Trojka bills itself as a Russian tearoom, its menu embraces a whole swathe of eastern and central Europe right down to Vienna (schnitzel, of course). The Poles are well represented by a hunters' stew (£6) heavy with sauerkraut and smoked sausage, while Hungary is done credit by a rich gypsy latke (£6.50) – chunks of beef in a red wine sauce served with potato pancakes and smetana. We usually can't resist the pelmeni (£6) – little doughy packets stuffed with meat and smothered in butter and smetana. There are lighter dishes, especially on the lunchtime menu, plus plenty for vegetarians. And the restaurant itself is anything but stodgy, with large windows, light wooden floors and bright walls. The one let down is in the limited choice of vodkas; there are only two or three bottles on the shelf, and the one that looks most intriguing – a golden liquid with suspended herbs – turns out to be olive oil. No matter, the Ukrainian 'zhiguli' beer goes down just fine.

Open: daily 9am-10.30pm; reservations accepted; licensed & BYO (corkage £3/bottle wine, £1.50 beer, £10 spirits)

starter: £2.50-£3.70
main: £5.50-£8.50
dessert: £3-£3.50
Set lunch £6.95

AE DC MC V; SW

Map 13 A4
Tube: Turnpike Lane

Smoking throughout

Jashan

Indian

☎ 020 8340 9880
19 Turnpike Lane N8

If for some reason you don't arrive at Jashan hungry, a read of the menu will change that. A glossy work of art, each page presents a list of dishes over sumptuous photos that would do any Soho food stylist proud. And for once the dishes actually live up to the pictorial promise. The hara bhara kebab (£2.75) are little fried cakes of vegetables with a creamy cottage cheese sauce. Bhape chingre (£7.95) is a zingy concoction of prawns cooked in fresh mustard, then served dry on a bed of fragrant rice. Aaj ki dhal (£2.95) has a luxurious smoothness from the lentils, butter and fresh spices. Bharwan paratha (£2.25) is typical of the freshly made Indian breads, this one filled with lightly seasoned minced vegetables. You can order by the pictures or you can ask for advice from the ingratiating staff, but be sure to stress that you'd like some of the chef's spicy favourites so you'll avoid getting the good but common fare.

starter: £2.75-£3.50
main: £5.95-£7.95
dessert: £2.95

AE DC MC V; SW

Open: Tues-Sun 6pm-11pm; reservations advisable; licensed

Map 13 C3
Rail: Archway

Smoking throughout

La Bota

Spanish

☎ 020 8340 3082
31 Broadway Pde
(Tottenham Lane) N8

The shoe-scuffed floor is testament to the stream of diners who have enjoyed La Bota's offerings for nigh on eight years – not to mention the miles covered by waiting staff who've jovially delivered endless plates of tapas treats. The walls are brightened by Picasso and Miró prints (as you might expect), but you'll probably be too busy admiring the colourful creations in front of you to take much notice. Try bright green beans in onion, tomato and chilli sauce (£1.80), succulent fried aubergine (£1.75) or marinated fresh, white anchovies – plump and tantalisingly lined up on the plate ready for the plucking (£2.95). Or perhaps you'd prefer a delicious chicken and prawn paella (£3.25)? La Bota excels in generous portions of fresh fish, but the squeamish should be warned that it's sometimes served with shell, eyes and innards intact. You can also order mains such as bistec a la madrilena (sirloin steak with mushroom and wine sauce, £9.80) or whole fish dishes (£6.25-£10.75), but they're not half the fun.

tapas: £1.75-£5.50
main: £5.95-£10.75
dessert: £2.50

AE JCB MC V; SW

Open: Mon-Fri noon-2.30pm, Sat noon-3pm, Sun noon-3.30pm, daily 6pm-11.30pm; reservations advisable; licensed

O's Thai Café — *Thai*

☎ 020 8348 6898
10 Topsfield Pde N8

Map 13 C3

Tube: Hornsey

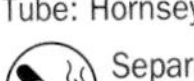
Separate smoke-free dining available

Book far ahead for this light, airy and delicious Thai cafe in 'buzzing' Crouch End. Somchai Kantanavich – otherwise known as 'O' – serves up foods from his homeland that you don't often find on the run-of-the-mill London Thai menu; mussels red curry (£6.50) is just one example. Standards like chicken green curry (£5.95) surprise with their freshness and bold yet balanced flavours. A starter platter for two (£7.95) contains many familiar items such as spring rolls and prawn toast, but this presentation should be used as homework for other, less-skilful chefs in town. There are several beers on tap, including the excellent Belgian Leffe, a tasty alternative to the hackneyed Singha and Tiger you usually face when eating Thai. The crowd is young and stylish, like the place itself. On most nights it fairly rocks with energy which is given an extra punch from booming speakers.

Open: Tues-Sun noon-3pm, Mon-Sat 6.30pm-11pm, Sun 6.30pm-10.30pm; reservations advisable (evening); licensed

starter: £2.95-£4.95
main: £5.50-£13.50
dessert: £1.95-£2.50
Set menu £13.95

MC V; SW

L'Artista

Italian

☎ **020 8458 1775**
917 Finchley Rd NW11

Map 14 B1
Tube: Golders Green

Smoking throughout

Terrace tables

We could smell the garlic from well up the road. Underneath the arches, L'Artista was full of folk chatting over the rumble of the rickety trains overhead. Generous starters included polenta crostini with various toppings (£4.60) and a plateful of mussels which were juicy and plump by London standards (£3.90). The saltimbocca (£7.20), tender veal with plenty of salty parma ham, was served with our choice of light and fresh zucchini fritti (£1.40). The ample portion of rigatoni all'amatriciana (£4.80) was good, but immediately upstaged by L'Artista's 'special', a tomatoey garlicky pizza replete with pocketfuls of fresh rocket on a crisp base (£5.90). We washed this down with a bottle of Orvieto Secco Classico, which at £10.70 went down nicely. A couple of scoops of Italian ice cream (£2.60) and the world's frothiest cappuccino later (£1), and we were undone.

starter: £3.10-£5.90
main: £6.60-£11.80
dessert: £2.60-£3.50
MC V; SW

Open: daily noon-midnight; reservations not accepted; licensed

Solly's

Jewish

☎ **020 8455 0004**
148a Golders Green Rd NW11

Map 14 B1
Tube: Golders Green

Separate smoke-free dining available

Pavement tables

Set among the many fine bagel bakeries and delicatessens at the south-eastern end of the Golders Green Rd commercial strip, Solly's bills itself as 'The Taste from Jerusalem'. That's too modest – it should be 'The Excellent Taste from Jerusalem'. The kitchen is up front and everything is on display, a major inducement since the sliced vegetables, salads and pickled items in view are all picture perfect. There are three options for dining: takeaway, the counter along the kitchen (where you'll get the most interesting view) or at the simple but tablecloth-covered tables at the rear. The hummus (£3) is garlicky and smooth, and for an extra £1.50 it comes with a pile of fresh, warm pita. A shawarma cut from the usual rotating stack of lamb filled a huge pita and required two hands to handle (£4). It was worth the effort as the meat was tender, well spiced and had some good crunchy brown bits. The dining room upstairs has a longer menu, slightly higher prices and more attentive service.

starter: £3-£3.50
main: £9.25-£15
dessert: £3.50
Set menu £19 -£22
MC V; SW

Open: Sun-Thurs 11.30am-11.30pm, Fri 11.30am-3am, Sat from one hour after Sabbath to midnight; reservations advisable; licensed

GREEN LANES

Gaziantep ☎ **020 8802 5498**
Turkish **52 Grand Pde N4**

Map 13 C5

Tube: Manor House, Turnpike Lane, rail: Harringay Green Lanes

 Smoking throughout

Green Lanes is a busy avenue in N4 which runs all the way from Turnpike Lane to Dalston and Kingsland. Its northern end cuts through a lively Turkish neighbourhood where Gaziantep is just one of several restaurants, but arguably the best. Though the official closing time is 2am, it's not unusual for staff to continue serving to 4am on weekends. Most of the dishes are prepared on the charcoal-fired grill set up right in the middle of things on the restaurant floor. The chef will whip you up a yaprak doner, the classic sliced lamb dish (£5.50), or a shish kebab (£6.50), both served with flat bread, rice and salad. Side orders include vine leaves and koc yumurtasi, a Turkish pizza with minced meat. Prices are cheap across the board – a bottle of wine costs just £7.50 – and in the unlikely event that you have room for dessert, there's rice pudding or baklava for £2.

Open: daily 11am-2am; reservations advisable; licensed

starter: £2-£4.50
main: £5.50-£8
dessert: £2
AE MC V; SW

Map 14 A1
Tube/Rail: Hampstead

Smoking throughout

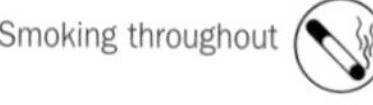

Pavement tables

starter: £2.50-£5
main: £3.50-£8
dessert: £1.50-£4.50
cash or SW only

Caffè Nero

Italian

☎ 020 7431 5958
1 Hampstead High St NW3

Caffé Nero is a reliable coffeehouse chain with 12 London outlets, including this comfortable Hampstead High St branch. The deep, strong espresso served up at all outlets has been widely and justifiably praised – and the consistent quality is no small achievement in this day of homogenised coffee factories. What's more, Caffè Nero also serves up decent sandwiches (£3.50 for parma ham with mozzarella and rocket) and first-class pizzas (all around £6), certifying its status as an all-day budget choice. Desserts are reasonably priced and include the kind of selections usually found only in Italy, such as toasted pannetone* laced with honey. Service at lunch and Sunday brunch tends to be erratic in some branches, so relax and crack open a book while you wait. *Also at 43 Frith St, Soho, W1 ☎ 7434 3887, 62 Brewer St, Soho W1 ☎ 7437 1497 and 29 Southampton St, Covent Garden W1 ☎ 7240 3433.*

Open: Mon-Fri 7am-11pm, Sat & Sun 8am-11pm; reservations not accepted; unlicensed

Map 14 A3
Tube: Hampstead, rail: Hampstead Heath

Smoking throughout

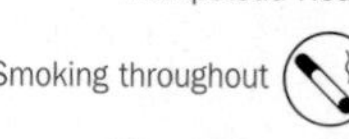

starter: £3.95-£6.50
main: £10.50-£14.95
dessert: £5
Set menu dinner £16.95
AE MC V; SW

Cucina

International

☎ 020 7435 7814
45a South End Rd NW3

It's entertaining simply reading Cucina's menu to find the country that hasn't lent an item to its brilliantly cosmopolitan selection of dishes. There's a colourfully presented starter to everyone's taste, but we were tempted by the mouthwatering egg, vermicelli, mango, vegetable and peanut roll in hot and sweet sauce (£5.50). The confit of duck with baked ginger plums and sesame-fried courgettes (£12.95) is also a success, the perfect mix of fruity and savoury. Though we were unsure about the warm chocolate and beetroot cake (£5), it turned out to be delicious, the beetroot playing down the richness of the chocolate. While the well-heeled Hampstead clientele chatter in pleasant but unimaginative surroundings – tangerine walls and asymmetric furniture – what really stands out is the exceptionally friendly and cheerful staff, who behave as if it is their only joy to fulfil difficult requests.

Open: daily noon-2.30pm, Mon-Thurs 7pm-10.30pm, Fri & Sat 7pm-11pm; reservations advisable (especially evenings); licensed

Gaucho Grill
Argentinian

☎ 020 7431 8222
64 Heath St NW3

Map 14 A1
Tube: Hampstead
Wheelchair access

 Smoking throughout

 Courtyard tables

For a really good steak, it has to be Argentinian beef. So where better to head for than Hampstead's Gaucho Grill? The stylish interior combines industrial fittings with cowhide furnishings, and the open-plan kitchen provides a focal point for this busy eatery. In the evenings the dimmed lighting and Latin background music give the restaurant a romantic, laid-back feel. Of course, to dine at Gaucho it does help to have a hankering for meat. Start with matambre (£4.25) – a typical Argentinian dish of grilled beef à la meatloaf with an egg centre, spiced with a good kick of chimichurri* Argentinian-style salsa. When it comes to the main course there are only four choices: rump, sirloin, fillet or rib-eye. The 300g sirloin (£13) is a sensational piece of meat cooked exactly to specification, with a generous portion of hand-cut chips on the side (£2). Service is efficient and knowledgeable, with any obscure dishes well explained.

Open: Mon-Fri noon-3pm, 5pm-midnight, Sat noon-midnight, Sun noon-10.30pm; reservations advisable; licensed

starter: £4.25-£7
main: £7.50-£17.50
dessert: £4.25-£4.75
AE DC JCB MC V; SW

Giraffe
International

☎ 020 7435 0343
46 Rosslyn Hill NW3

Map 14 A2
Tube: Hampstead

 Pavement tables

Much like its animal namesake, Giraffe stands out from the crowd in Hampstead's busy strip of chain restaurants and shops. The cafe has an eclectic menu, from tabouli to salmon fish cakes, at reasonable prices. Eating is a communal affair on long blond-wood tables with benches, unless you're lucky enough to grab one of the pavement tables. Open all day, Giraffe offers vegetarian and standard full breakfasts (£4.25) and stacked banana and blueberry pancakes (£4.25). For lunch or dinner there's interesting meals like Moroccan chicken with saffron mashed potato (£7.95) and wok-fired noodles with spring vegetables (£5.95). The desserts are head and shoulders above ordinary cafes, with both the blueberry and vanilla-bean cheesecake and the Toblerone and mascarpone trifle (each £3.50) deserving praise. The cafe's motto is 'Be happy', and Giraffe certainly succeeds in making its diners just that.

Open: Mon-Fri 8am-11.30pm, Sat & Sun 9am-11pm; reservations not accepted; licensed

starter: £3.95-£5.95
main: £5.95-£8.95
dessert: £2.95-£3.50
MC V; SW

The Breakfast Brigade

Nursing a hangover? Craving a fry-up? Or just looking for a cheap meal and a convivial spot to read the paper? Then what you need is a good local cafe, caff or greasy spoon. By popular demand, traditional English breakfast fare has so far survived the relentless invasion of croissants, bagels and Starbucks coffee – breakfast is one of Britain's few culinary specialities. Most of the places listed below offer an all-day, traditional English breakfast. For between £3 and £5, you'll be served eggs (fried, poached or scrambled) with sausages and bacon and then any number of extras, which may include mushrooms, tomatoes, baked beans, chips, black pudding, bubble and squeak, toast or fried bread plus a steaming mug of tea or coffee.

Mario's Cafe 6 Kelly St, Kentish Town NW1 ☎ 020 7284 2066
Open: Mon-Fri 7.30am-5pm, Sat 8.30am-5pm (Map 11 A4)
Loyal locals and others in the know flock to this friendly cafe, which is also muse to indie pop band St Etienne. All the cooked breakfast staples plus toasted ciabatta sandwiches, pasta dishes and an excellent parmigiana (aubergine, tomato and mozzarella bake) are just a few of the choices on the menu. The food is caff fare at its best, prepared by Mario's Italian mum, who keeps a low profile in the kitchen while her son takes good care of the punters.

Bar Estrela 111-115 South Lambeth Rd, Stockwell SW8 ☎ 020 7793 1051
Open: daily 8am-midnight (Map 23 A1)
Come to the Estrela any time of day on a Saturday or Sunday and you'll find it packed with Portuguese locals. The service is slow, the telly loud and the cafe slightly cold in winter but the coffee is superb, and a bifana sandwich – fried pork in a bap – followed by a nata or custard tart makes an unbeatable breakfast. (See review on p 249.)

Da Marco 417 the Strand WC2 ☎ 020 7836 0654
Open: Mon-Sun 7am-8.30pm (Map 4 E1)
Close to the Adelphi Theatre and easily missed with its discreet sign and narrow entrance, Da Marco is a rare find – an old-fashioned, family-run cafe hidden among the brash, modern upstarts which dominate the Strand. The interior is surprisingly large, with rows of padded seats stretching deep into the recessed panelled room. The extensive menu offers all the usual combinations of egg, bacon, sausage, tomato and beans plus omelettes, salads, sandwiches, pasta dishes and more.

Cafe on the Common 2 Rookery Rd, Clapham Common SW4
☎ 020 7498 0770
Open: daily 10am-6pm (Map 22 B5)
Spot the pale blue concrete pavilion on Clapham Common and chances are you'll have found the cafe. Everything on the menu, including the cooked breakfast, is vegetarian and there's a good range of vegan fare as well. Select plantain chips, muesli yoghurt, a fresh salad or slice of cake, and settle down in the snug interior decked out in red drapes or at one of the patio tables.

Fosby's 23 Chapel Market, Islington NW1 ☎ 020 7837 9187
Open: daily 6.30am-4pm, Sat 6.30am-5pm (Map 15 E2)
Fosby's is a handy local if you want to take a break from shopping in Chapel Market and sit back and watch the crowds. The friendly owners serve good-value English breakfast fare alongside Philippine and Chinese options such as chicken noodle soup and chow mein.

Chez Monique 7 Little Turnstile, Holborn WC1 ☎ 020 7405 1337
Open: Mon-Fri 6am-3pm, Sat 6.30am-11am (Map 4 C2)
Cheap and cheerful central caff with orange formica tables, speedy service and above average fry-ups. There's all the usual breakfast fare plus baked potatoes, grilled meats and a big selection of sandwiches and puddings.

Le Bistrotheque 4 Inverness St, Camden NW1 ☎ 020 7428 0546
Open: daily 9am-midnight (Map 11 B4)
Le Bistrotheque serves a choice of around six set breakfasts between 9am and 5pm, ranging from continental to poached egg florentine and full English – the latter comes with tasty Cumberland sausage. More cafe than caff in the comfort stakes, this is an ideal place to escape the chaos of Camden. And if you come between 4.30pm and 5pm on a weekday, you can combine breakfast with a happy hour cocktail.

The Troubadour 265 Old Brompton Rd, Earl's Court SW7 ☎ 020 7370 1434
Open: daily 9am-midnight (Map 7 C1)
With multicoloured coffee pots in the window, wooden floors and dozens of battered old musical instruments hanging from the ceiling, the Troubadour is one of London's most charming cafes. Come here any time of day for breakfast and if you stay long enough you can switch from coffee to hair of the dog. Head downstairs to the club and enjoy live music, poetry or comedy depending on the night.

E Pellicci 332 Bethnal Green Rd, Bethnal Green E2 ☎ 020 7739 4873
Open: Mon-Sat 6.30am-5pm (Map 17 A6)
Established 90 years ago and still in the same family, E Pellicci is in a league of its own. Trad English breakfast foods – the scrambled eggs especially – are taken to new heights by these affable Italo-Eastenders. And it's not just the food – the nonstop banter and cosy, wood-panelled interior alone are worth the trek across town. If you live in east London, you don't need to be told.

Anna Sutton

PJ's Grill

Modern European

☎ 020 7435 3608
82 Hampstead High St NW3

Map 14 A1
Tube: Hampstead

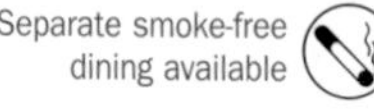
Separate smoke-free dining available

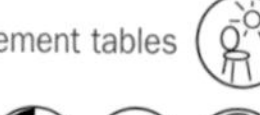
Pavement tables

Formerly Café des Arts, PJ's has been recently refurbished to attract more than its established Hampstead clientele. Retaining the wood panelling and fireplace it now includes a bar and upstairs private room. Slick service complements the creatively assembled and well-presented meals. Asian-style duck and coriander spring rolls with plum sauce (£5.45) and baked field mushrooms with goat's cheese and balsamic (£5.50), chosen from the diverse range of starters, opened affairs. Mains of honey-roast duck with bubble and squeak (£12.95) and grilled salmon fillet with lemon and chive beurre blanc (£10.95) didn't disappoint. The dessert menu includes standards such as crème brûlée (£4.50) although the addition of lemon and elderberry honey lifted it beyond the ordinary. Several dishes weren't available on the night we dined but we were happy with the substitutes. The adequate wine list includes half bottles at fair prices. Treat yourself to an enjoyable lunch or dinner in this restaurant that makes an obvious effort to please.

starter: £3.95-£6.95
main: £7.95-£12.95
dessert: £4.25-£4.75
Set lunch £6.95
AE DC MC V; SW

Open: Mon-Sat noon-11.30pm, Sun 11.30am -11pm; reservations advisable (especially Fri & Sat evening & Sun lunch); licensed

---

Zamoyski

Eastern European/Slavic

☎ 020 7794 4792
85 Fleet Rd NW3

Map 14 A3
Tube: Belsize Park; rail: Hampstead Heath
Wheelchair access

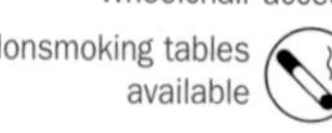
Nonsmoking tables available

Ever had an inexplicable craving for egg-flavoured vodka? No? You surprise me. In this diminutive hideaway, Eastern Europe is authentically explored with Slavic staff, bare brick walls, candlelight and terracotta floor tiles, but Western Europe is represented by suited sorts, pseudo-designer platters and quirky vodka flavours. Inaugurate the experience with klops (£3.95). Never was onomatopoeia so misguided – the delicious meatloaf arrives with a crimson side serving of swikla (beetroot and horseradish relish). Try placki po wegiersku (£8.25), tender lamb goulash served with a crispy onion and potato pancake, red sauerkraut and juicy vegetables. If you're not a linguistic type, we're sure your pronunciation of the dishes will improve immeasurably after you tuck into the barrels of bisongrass vodka from the bar. Smacznego (enjoy your meal)!

starter: £2.20
main: £6.50-£9.50
desert: £2.95
Set menu £6.95
AE MC V; SW

Open: Mon-Fri 5.30pm-11pm, Sun 5.30pm-10.30pm; reservations advisable; licensed

Idaho ☎ **020 8341 6633**
American **13 North Hill N6**

A band of windows provides a view of the white interior contrasting with the uniform brown exterior, evoking the image that Idaho is one big baked potato. It's a fitting visual metaphor for a restaurant named after America's main spud-producing state. The menu draws on ingredients and cuisines from around the US and its neighbours. Wild mushroom broth (£6) gives the tongue a tingle thanks to Mexican seasonings. Braised beef (£13) is perked up with chorizo sausage and smoothed out with pumpkin. Thick, char-grilled tuna steak is accented with a complex smoked tomato salsa. Despite the name, potatoes are a minor component of the menu, appearing as mash and the ubiquitous chips (£2), albeit here with smoked paprika mayonnaise. Banana pudding paired with caramel ice cream (£5) is typical of the rich and delightful desserts. Service is relaxed yet professional. The long wine list spans the globe and there's a large patio for al fresco dining with lots of overhead heaters to lengthen the season.

Open: daily noon-3pm, 6.30-11.30pm; reservations advisable; licensed

Map 12 B1

Tube: Highgate

Wheelchair access

Entertainment: jazz pianist some evenings

 Smoking throughout

 Terrace tables

starter: £4-£7
main: £9-£16
dessert: £5

AE MC V; SW

Map 12 E2
Tube: Kentish Town

Smoking throughout

Le Petit Prince

French/Moroccan

☎ 020 7267 3789
5 Holmes Rd NW5

Tucked just off bustling Kentish Town Rd, this 20-year-old North London institution is a dinner-only hole in the wall serving simple French-Moroccan fare at extremely fair prices. Essentially, this is a couscous house – you order lamb brochette, spicy merguez sausages or chicken and you're entitled to as much of the grainy stuff as you can eat, all for about £7. Non-meat eaters will be satisfied with the mixed root-vegetable couscous laced with hot harissa* sauce (£6.95). Starters have a more Gallic influence, such as salade de Roquefort or a garlicky hot plate of escargot. Le Petit Prince might not be worth a trip across town, but it is a real break from the rampant mediocrity found along nearby Camden High St.

starter: £1.90-£4
main: £7-£10
dessert: £2.20-£2.90
cash only

Open: Tues-Fri 12.30pm-2.30pm, daily 7pm-10.30pm; reservations accepted; licensed

Map 12 E2
Tube: Kentish Town

Smoking throughout

Pane Vino

Italian

☎ 020 7267 3879
323 Kentish Town Rd NW5

At first sight, Pane Vino is your typical Italian restaurant – checked tablecloths, 'subtle' lighting and a modest array of pizza and pasta dishes at reasonable prices. But prepare to be pleasantly surprised. Our garlic and tomato bread (£3.50) may have been rather ordinary, but it was followed by deliciously different main courses. The penne alla siciliana (£6.80) had just enough chilli to complement the rich aubergine and black olives without masking their distinctly fresh taste, while the pizzas were large, flavoursome and cooked with care. The ambience did nothing to mar our enjoyment, as Pane Vino buzzed gently all night to soft candlelight and the sound of happy chatter. It's cosy but not crowded, the service relaxed yet attentive. Stick with tradition in this enticing Italian restaurant, and you can't go wrong.

starter: £2.60-£5.80
main: £5.80-£14.50
dessert: £3.40-£3.60
AE MC V; SW

Open: Mon-Sat noon-3pm, 6pm-11.30pm, Sun 6pm-10.30pm; reservations advisable; licensed

KENTISH TOWN

Selam
Eritrean

☎ **020 7284 3947**
12 Fortress Rd NW5

Map 12 D2
Tube: Kentish Town

 Smoking throughout

 Pavement tables

Eritrean cuisine? We had to double-check the map to locate Africa's newest country just north of Ethiopia, with which it has much in common – including a cuisine. We shared tender chunks of lamb cooked in a red chilli sauce and spices (zigni, £6), chicken legs and hard-boiled eggs in a denser sauce redolent of sun-dried tomatoes (derho, £6), a mild dish of marinated minced lamb served with a cottage cheese (kitfo, £7.50) and a mild 'ratatouille' (alicha, £5.50). Everything is served in the traditional way on a platter-sized piece of injera. The special Jebena Eritrean coffee is expensive at £5, but that's the table price and everyone gets a couple of small cups – a more than sufficient amount of this extra-strong brew.

Open: daily 5pm-midnight; reservations advisable (weekends); licensed

main: £5-£10
dessert: £2.75

DC MC V; SW

PRIMROSE HILL

The Engineer
Modern British

☎ **020 7722 0950**
65 Gloucester Ave NW1

Map 11 B3
Tube: Chalk Farm
Wheelchair access
Certified organic

 Smoking throughout

 Courtyard tables

Many a Sunday afternoon has been whiled away at the Engineer. In winter the candle-lit bar is the perfect snug to glug away on red wine, while in summer the garden is positively blooming with trendy 20- and 30-somethings primed on Pimms. You can eat in the bar, restaurant and garden, but as it's a popular haunt it pays to book for the restaurant. The downstairs dining room is fresh and white, making first-daters and regulars alike feel comfortable and relaxed. The menu offers the modern British staples of mash and mixed leaves in predictable abundance but changes regularly and offers a balanced choice. The lamb chump is a regular favourite, always cooked rare and with a wonderful rosemary Madeira jus (£15). If the day's fish is salmon you're onto a winner (£15) – poached and very simply garnished it's light enough to leave room for an indulgent chocolate cake with berries and cream.

Open: Mon-Sat 9am-3pm, Mon-Fri 7pm-10.30pm, Sat 7pm-11pm, Sun 9am-3.30pm, 7pm-10pm; reservations advisable (especially Fri & Sat evening); licensed

starter: £3.75-£6.95
main: £8.75-£16.50
dessert: £4.50-£6.50

MC V; SW

PRIMROSE HILL

Map 11 B2
Tube: Chalk Farm

Odette's
Modern European

☎ 020 7586 5486
130 Regent's Park Rd NW1

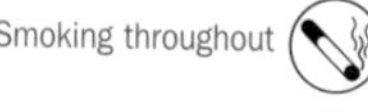
Smoking throughout

Pavement tables

Although it's called a 'wine bar', Odette's is really the best restaurant in trendy Primrose Hill. The romantic upstairs dining room is lined with mirrors, and no doubt has been the scene for more than one marriage proposal. There's a refined, continental menu on offer, and simple starters like oysters or a warm asparagus salad can be paired with heartier mains like roast Gressingham duck or rump of lamb on a goat's cheese cream. Predictably, the wine list is spectacular, with hard-to-find selections like Chinon and Vorvrays from the Loire available at reasonable prices; the house wine is good value, too (£10.50/bottle). If Odette's has a flaw, it's the standard selection of puddings: there's nothing exactly exciting about crème caramel or chocolate mousse, though both are well prepared. A lower-priced menu is available in the wine cellar, offering lighter fare like grilled steak for around £10.

starter: £6-£12
main: £10-£17.50
dessert: £4.75
Set lunch £10
AE DC MC V ; SW

Open: Mon-Sat 12.30pm-2.30pm, 7pm-10.30pm, Sun noon-2.30pm; reservations essential; licensed

Map 11 B3
Tube: Chalk Farm

Vegia Zena
Italian

☎ 020 7483 0192
17 Princess Rd NW1

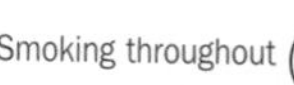
Smoking throughout

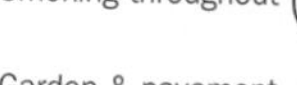
Garden & pavement tables

Vegia Zena is a little neighbourhood Italian place that has aspirations of something grander. However, you wouldn't know this from the simple and small rose-coloured ground-floor dining room, which is naturally lit by day and warmly illuminated at night. (Avoid the dreary basement room.) The restaurant's ambitions focus on the food and service, which is as it should be. Trenette with pesto, potatoes and green beans (£6.65) combines al dente pasta with very fresh and flavourful vegetables; the garlic and parmesan cheese providing the pesto with just the right kick. A roasted guinea fowl (£12) came with a well-balanced wild mushroom polenta that did a good job of complimenting the distinct flavour of the fowl. Wine choices are many, with good descriptions of the several chiantis on offer. Although Vegia Zena is a good choice for an intimate dinner, it's also fine for lunch owing to its excellent-value set menu that includes two courses and a glass of wine for £7.45.

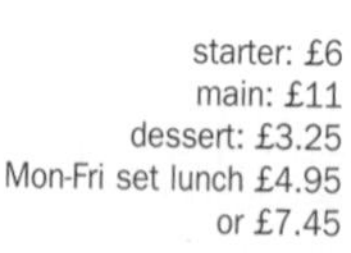
starter: £6
main: £11
dessert: £3.25
Mon-Fri set lunch £4.95
or £7.45
AE DC JCB MC V; SW

Open: Mon-Sat noon-3pm, 7pm-11pm, Sun noon-11pm; reservations advisable (especially Fri & Sat); licensed

ST JOHN'S WOOD

Greek Valley
Greek

☎ **020 7624 3217**
130 Boundary Rd W8

Map 11 C1
Tube: Swiss Cottage

Smoking throughout

Pavement tables

You'll be hard-pressed to get a table at this secluded Greek find at the weekend, with its friendly staff, Mediterranean décor and food that will have even the most parochial expatriates making favourable comparisons to their own mothers' cooking. We ordered mixed dips (£6.50), grilled haloumi (£3), spanakopita (fetta and spinach pastry, £2.50) and very tender, fried calamari (£3.50). Unusually, rice accompanies most of the mains, with two exceptions – kleftiko (tender lamb on the bone, £6.95) and the excellent moussaka (£6.95). The gharithes yiouvetsi (prawns in tomato sauce with fetta, £9.50) are rich and tasty. Wash it all down with herby retsina from the large wine list. Then, finish with baklava (£2.50) and Greek coffee and ask the owner for a coffee-ground reading. *Also, a branch of Greek Valley, Cafe 100, 100 Boundary Rd, St John's Wood NW8 ☎ 7372 2042.*

Open: Mon-Sat 6pm-midnight; reservations advisable (especially Fri & Sat evenings); licensed

starter: £2.50-£3.50
main: £6.50-£10.95
dessert: £2-£2.50
Set meze £15/person (min 2 people)

MC, V; SW

SOUTH HAMPSTEAD

Czech and Slovak House
Czech/Slovak

☎ **020 7372 5251**
74 West End Lane NW6

Map 11 B1
Tube/rail: West Hampstead

Smoking throughout

Pavement tables

Entering this restaurant is like stepping out of South Hampstead and into a turn-of-the-century Czech spa-town hotel. Potted palms and gold-painted plasterwork frame a strange assortment of old photos: Vaclav Havel, Winston Churchill and a young Queen Elizabeth. The motherly waiting staff serve the elderly East European regulars specialities to remind them of home. Starters include topinky (garlic bread with pâté; £2.10) and deliciously sharp rollmop (£2.20), wrapped around pickled cucumber, smothered with onion and draped with sour cream to take away the bite. Meaty mains include goulash (£7.70), wiener schnitzel (£8.10) or meat loaf (£6.20) – served with dumplings and sauerkraut. The cinnamon-rich apple strudel (£1.40) is delicious, if you can find the room. Of course, you can't drink wine with rumbustious food like this, so try the beer (there is only one, an excellent fruity Czech import).

Open: Sat & Sun noon-3pm, Tues-Sun 6pm-10pm; reservations advisable (especially Sat & Sun); licensed

starter: £1.50-£4
main: £6.20-£8.70
dessert: £1.10-£3.50

cash and cheques only

Map 12 C3
Tube: Tufnell Park

Smoking throughout

Lalibela
Ethiopian

☎ 020 7284 0600
137 Fortess Rd NW5

If you want to experience hearty, communal-style Ethiopian dining, then Lalibela is the place to go. Low chairs surround glass-topped wicker tables, and dishes are spooned on top of a plate of injera (a sourdough flat bread) and eaten without cutlery. There's no distinction between starters and mains, as all dishes are served at the same time. Dishes typically feature lamb, cod or chicken cooked in a lentil or tomato sauce; for example, alicha doro wot is chicken in a mild tomato sauce with hard-boiled egg. A mixed selection of dishes costs £11 for two. The service is gracious, but very slow, so be prepared to be patient. The traditional finish to a Lalibela meal is the 'coffee ritual' – a strong brew boiled at your table.

starter: £4.50-£7
main: £6-£9.50
dessert: £4
AE DC MC V; SW

Open: Mon-Fri 6pm-midnight, Sat & Sun 12.30pm-midnight; reservations advisable; licensed

NORTH-EAST

Barnsbury

Clerkenwell

Farringdon

Highbury

Holloway

Islington

King's Cross

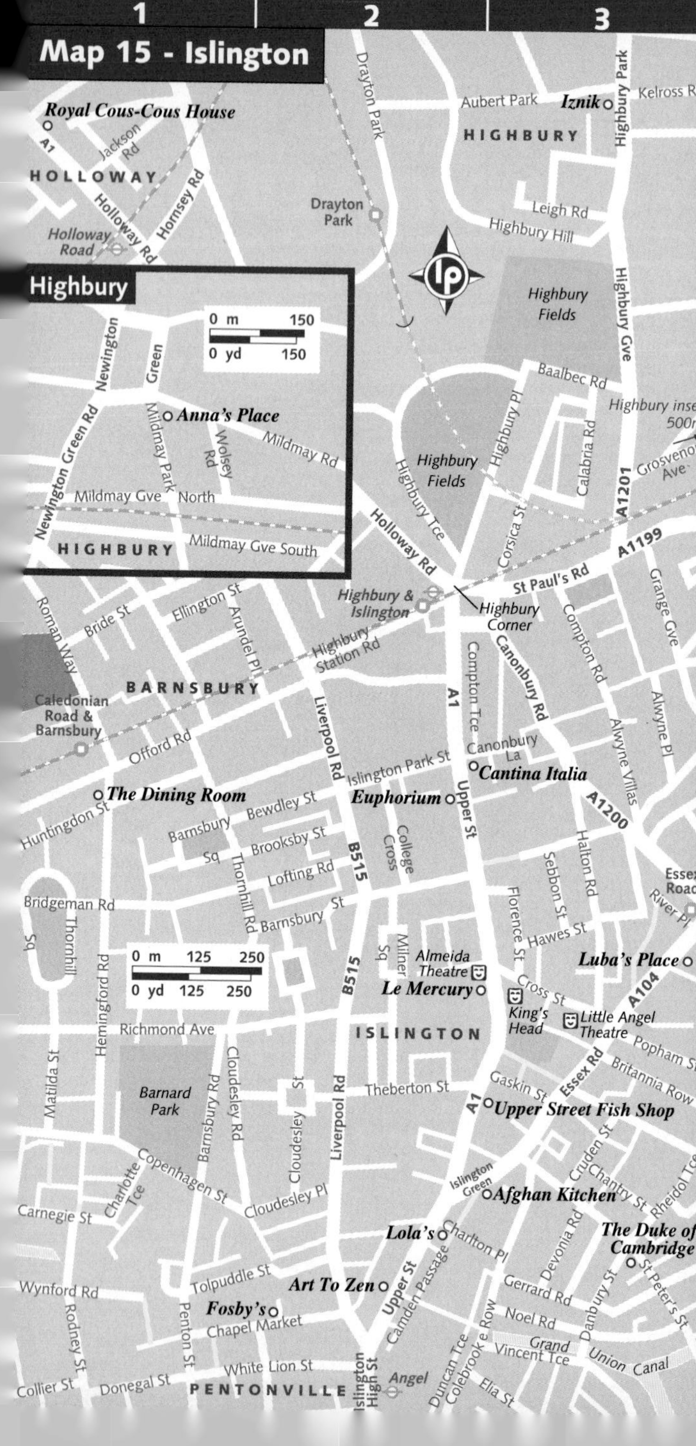

1
2
3
Map 15 - Islington
Royal Cous-Cous House
Iznik
HIGHBURY
HOLLOWAY
Drayton Park
Holloway Road
Highbury
Highbury Fields
Anna's Place
HIGHBURY
Highbury inset 500m
Highbury & Islington
Highbury Corner
BARNSBURY
Caledonian Road & Barnsbury
Cantina Italia
The Dining Room
Euphorium
Essex Road
Luba's Place
Almeida Theatre
Le Mercury
King's Head
Little Angel Theatre
ISLINGTON
Barnard Park
Upper Street Fish Shop
Afghan Kitchen
The Duke of Cambridge
Lola's
Art To Zen
Fosby's
Angel
PENTONVILLE
Union Canal

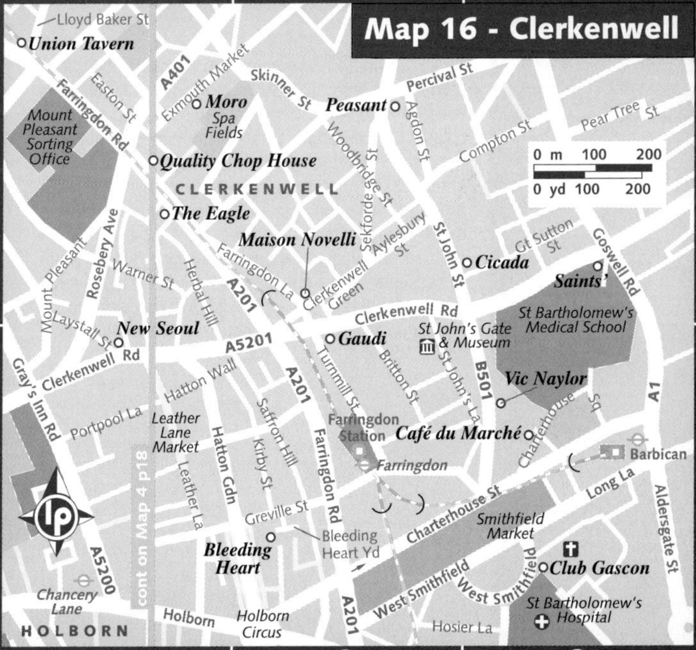

Map 16 - Clerkenwell

BEST

- **Euphorium**
  Comfort food with a twist
- **Iznik**
  Hearty Turkish food, magical milieu
- **Moro**
  Spanish, Portuguese and North African flavours skilfully intertwined
- **The Union Tavern**
  Good-value gastropub fare
- **Upper Street Fish Shop**
  Classic fish & chips

North-East

Islington is the place where you wanted to corner the market on property 20 years ago. Discovered by legions of 'New Labourites' – Tony Blair among them – property values have soared and the streets are now lined with Saabs and BMWs, parked along pavements trod by brie-toting swells rushing home with their copies of the *Guardian*. Upper St is an unending succession of trendy restaurants and bars where the beverage of choice comes in a wine rather than a pint glass. George Orwell, who lived here when *Animal Farm* was published, would hardly recognise the place.

Stoke Newington by comparison is less trendy, less storied and less hilly. Stoke Newington Church St is lined with fun little eateries and this is a fine place for classic London ethnic treats from curries to kebabs. However, all through these neighbourhoods are enclaves of poverty, overlooked by economic progress. Islington may be the spot where the elite meet to eat, but it's also the place where they get their car stereos stolen. In the evening, you may not want to stray far from Upper St. And in Kings Cross, which steadfastly resists all efforts to clean up its mangy environs, you may not want to wander day or night.

BARNSBURY

The Dining Room
Modern European

☎ 020 7609 3009
169 Hemingford Rd N1

Map 15 C1

Tube/rail: Highbury & Islington, rail: Caledonian Rd & Barnsbury

Certified organic

Nonsmoking tables available

The Dining Room is as close to a Parisian *restaurant du quartier* as we've found in London, with well-prepared, simple yet imaginative dishes at very affordable prices. Seating just 22 diners in the front room of a terraced house, with a large shop-like window, low lighting and deep blue walls, this charming place might just as well be called the Living Room. Portions are unusually generous: after enjoying a large plate of complimentary bread and olives, the delightful pappardelle with hare sauce (£5) and salt cod cakes (£4) bound with a titch too much egg white, we soldiered on, slowly battling through sea bass on spinach and caramelised fennel (£10) and enough braised pork, white beans and pumpkin to feed a battalion (our four-legged friend at home slept contentedly that night). We managed to polish off a dish of plums and quince stewed in red wine (£3.50) but were finally defeated by the variously flavoured organic ice cream.

Open: Tues-Sat noon-2.30pm, 7pm-11.30pm, Sun 1pm-4pm; reservations advisable; licensed

starter: £3.20-£5
main: £6.75-£12
dessert: £3.50-£4.50

cash and cheques (with a card only)

CLERKENWELL

Bleeding Heart Bistro
French

☎ 020 7242 8238
Bleeding Heart Yard, Hatton Garden (off Greville St near Farringdon Rd) EC1

Map 16 B2

Tube/rail: Farringdon/Chancery Lane

Dress code: collared shirt

Smoking throughout

Courtyard tables

The courtyard may be named after a particularly gruesome Elizabethan murder, but the Bleeding Heart Bistro is one of the city's most romantic outdoor dining venues – in the warmer months at least. The square is secluded, the ground underfoot is cobblestoned and the delicious food is light French. The kitchen is best known for its country salad with bacon, and salmon fish cakes. Standard meat fare is also expertly handled, with juicy lamb burgers available at lunch. If you want to make a night of it, you can repair to the nearby Bleeding Heart Tavern or simply stay put in the wine bar on the restaurant's ground floor, where you can quaff selections from the reasonably priced wine list (most bottles are in the £10-£15 range).

Open: Mon-Fri noon-3pm, 6pm-11pm; reservations essential; licensed

starter: £4-£5.95
main: £6.95-£12.50
dessert: £3.95
Set menu £16.95

AE DC MC V; SW

Map 16 A3

Tube/rail: Farringdon/Angel

Nonsmoking tables available

Pavement tables

Cicada

Pan-Asian

☎ 020 7608 1550

132-136 St John St EC1

This pioneer of the flourishing restaurant scene in Clerkenwell (which *fashionistas* dub 'the new Soho') presents an excellently balanced range of authentic pan-Asian dishes – Japanese, Thai, Vietnamese, Sri Lankan. The restaurant is laid out like a stylish diner, with an adjacent lively bar area. Tables of 10+ can order set menus and be served oriental banqueting style. As a table of two, we used a mix 'n' match approach, ordering salmon sashimi with ginger and wasabi (£6), crispy tempura vegetable clusters (£4.50) and succulent gyoza dumplings (£4.75). The bamboo-wrapped cod (£8.75) was cleverly accented by soy, sake and honey, while the portion of prawn phat thai (£7.95) was so generous that the few king prawns were swamped by noodles. Our Asiatic gastro-tour culminated in poached nashi pears (£5.50) and chocolate and lemongrass brûlée (£4.50). All that was needed was the sound of chirping cicadas to make us forego long-haul travel to the Far East forever.

starter: £4.50-£6
main: £7.50-£10
dessert: £4.50-£6
Set menu £18 or £22 (for groups of 10 or more)
AE DC JCB MC V; SW

Open: Mon-Fri noon-3pm, Mon-Sat 6pm-11pm; reservations advisable (essential on weekends); licensed

---

Map 16 B3

Tube/rail: Barbican or Farringdon

Smoking throughout

Club Gascon

South-Western French

☎ 020 7253 5853

57 West Smithfield EC1

The concept at Club Gascon – starter-sized portions (only) of south-west French cuisine – is inventive and the food itself very good. Dishes are as diverse as carpaccio of magret with cauliflower 'milk' flavoured with truffle and sea urchin (£7), warm tatin of duck foie gras (£8), plump grilled scallops in a caviar cream (£9) and joue de bœuf in orange sauce (£7.50), with very few complaints (the duck foie gras was decidedly more than 'half-cooked'). Few complaints about the food, that is ... for it must be said that the service at this flavour-of-the-month establishment is among the worst we've encountered. From a 'punishing' wait for our table, having had the temerity to arrive with one less person than the number booked, to the frenetic and unknowledgeable staff, we almost felt unwelcome at times. It didn't all end in tears, as we had memories of the food to savour but – sacré bleu! – an evening at Club Gascon can be a crying shame.

main: £3.50-£24
dessert: £4
Degustation £30 or £50
JCB MC V; SW

Open: Mon-Fri noon-1.45pm, 7pm-9.45pm, Sat 7pm-10.30pm; reservations essential; licensed

The Eagle ☎ **020 7837 1353**
Mediterranean **159 Farringdon Rd EC1**

Map 16 A1
Tube/rail: Farringdon

 Smoking throughout

 Pavement tables

There's a relaxed, good-humoured vibe at this jolly gastro-pub, patronised by Clerkenwell trendies and *Guardian* journalists (the paper's offices are just a few steps away along Farringdon Rd). Order at the bar from the daily changing blackboard menu, then grab a seat where you can. There's no truck with pretentious starters here, though a basket of fresh bread is squeezed onto the tiny tables amid the mishmash of crockery and heavy, old-fashioned cutlery. We chose the red mullet (£9) and bean and yellow-pepper risotto (£7) from the hearty Mediterranean-inspired selection. The fish looked wonderful but was slightly tasteless, though its accompanying tomato-soaked Tuscan bread was very good. The risotto, meanwhile, had a tangy taste and creamy texture. There are no desserts, other than a tiny Portuguese tart (£1) served with your espresso (£1), but you'll leave with a sweet taste in your mouth nonetheless.

Open: Mon-Fri 12.30pm-2.30pm, Sat & Sun 12.30pm-3.30pm, Mon-Sat 6.30pm-10.30pm; reservations not accepted; licensed

main: £5.50-£11.50
dessert: £1

cash or cheques only

Map 16 B2
Tube/rail: Farringdon
Nonsmoking tables available

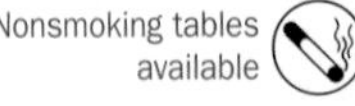

Gaudi

Spanish

☎ 020 7608 3220
63 Clerkenwell Rd EC1

Serve good food and they will come. It's a maxim they've got down at Gaudi and you'd best book well ahead if you want to sample their fine, sophisticated Spanish cuisine. The fantastically twisting iron and colourful tiles inside owe their inspiration to the restaurant's namesake. However, maybe it should be called Jiménez since the real appeal is provided by Nacho Jiménez, the inventive Castilian chef. Typical of his efforts is the alcachofas con jamon (£10), which seamlessly melds baby artichokes with Spanish ham and truffles. The gazpacho (£10) is a sensation of fresh flavours and is accompanied by lobster. The mains are equally stellar, such as the roast duck with a foie gras stuffing and a surprising sauce redolent with spices that include sesame and cinnamon (£14.50). Desserts change regularly, and the manchego cheese mousse is divine. Service is smooth and knowledgeable – a help with the unusual menu – and the wine list would do the Spanish wine board proud.

starter: £8-£13
main: £14-£19
dessert: £5
Set lunch £15
AE DC JCB MC V

Open: Mon-Fri noon-3pm, 7pm-11pm; reservations advisable (essential Fri); licensed

---

Map 16 A2
Tube/rail: Farringdon
Smoking thoughout

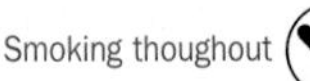

Maison Novelli

Modern French

☎ 020 7251 6606
29 Clerkenwell Green EC1

A jewel in fashionable Clerkenwell's crown, Maison Novelli is the place to impress business clients or commemorate a special occasion – you can rely on exquisitely presented modern French cuisine, against the backdrop of polished wooden floors, elegant furniture and impeccable service. Home-smoked salmon with a poached quail's egg topped with caviar (£8.50) is an audacious suggestion of what is to follow. Pea soup cappuccino with cured foie gras scented with bay leaf (£4.50) is a very light starter. The pavé of sea bass roasted with thyme flower is moist and succulent, with aromatic soft aubergine, chorizo, sweet olives, sun-dried tomato and truffle oil (£23). The fillet of beef with mild mushroom risotto is cleverly contrasted by the parmesan crackling (£21). The fine-spun sugar on the crème brûlée (£4.95) is a worthy contender for the Turner prize, and coffees come with dainty petits fours. If you want to sample food from the same kitchen for less, visit their brasserie on the premises.

starter: £4.50-£12
main: £13.50-£28
dessert: £4.95
AE DC JCB MC V; SW

Open: Mon-Fri noon-3pm, Mon-Sat 6pm-11pm; reservations advisable; licensed

CLERKENWELL

Moro

Spanish

☎ 020 7833 8336
34-36 Exmouth Market EC1

Map 16 A1
Tube/rail: Farringdon
Wheelchair access

Smoking throughout

Pavement tables

We were attracted by the unlikely sound of Moro's 'Moorish' cuisine, which turned out to be a successful blend of Spanish, Portuguese and North African flavours. The crab brik (£6.50), a crispy packet deep-fried with cumin and piquant harissa, was redolent of a North African bazaar, while the pickled anchovies served with a bland pumpkin purée (£5) evoked those tart little fish served in Spanish bars. The main fish dishes were excellent: charcoal-grilled monkfish with pomegranate molasses (£13.50) and wood-roasted red mullet (£12.50), whose slightly oily taste was cut by sharp Seville orange. For puddings, the Málaga raison ice cream with Pedro Xímenez sherry (£4) and pistachio yoghurt cake (£4) were both first-rate, though the latter was overly zested. The upbeat staff are always ready to help (with words like cecina, membrillo and manti on the menu, you'll need it), but the sterile décor in such a large open space makes conversation difficult at times.

Open: Mon-Fri 12.30pm-2.30pm, 7pm-10.30pm; reservations advisable; licensed

starter: £4.50-£6.50
main: £9.50-£13.50
dessert: £4

AE DC MC V; SW

New Seoul Restaurant

Korean

☎ 020 7278 8674
164 Clerkenwell Rd EC1

Map 16 B1
Tube/rail: Farringdon

Smoking throughout

True to the photos of its food in the window, this neighbourhood restaurant offers unpretentious dining, friendly service and good Korean food at reasonable prices. The New Seoul's vast menu can be intimidating at first, particularly for Korean neophytes, but things are made easier by the three set menus, including one that is vegetarian. Our eight-course set menu kicked off with kimchi – pickled sliced cabbage with chilli powder, spring onion and garlic – which did a good job of both jump-starting the meal and clearing our sinuses. The spring onion pancake with seafood was delicious and laden with crab and shrimp, so much so that when the waitress brought the sizzling bulgogi* (sliced beef marinated in sesame oil) we were feeling quite satisfied, and still had three courses to go.

Open: Mon-Fri noon-3pm, 6pm-10.30pm; reservations advisable (especially lunch); licensed

starter: £4.50-£7
main: £5-£7.50
Set menu £14-£18/person
(min 2 people)

AE DC JCB MC V; SW

CLERKENWELL

Map 16 A2
Tube/rail: Angel or Farringdon

Smoking throughout 

Pavement tables 

The Peasant

Modern Italian

☎ 020 7336 7726
240 St John St EC1

The Peasant has stayed close to its public house origins, albeit only in décor, retaining the original mahogany counter and servery, open fireplace and mosaic flooring. Young 20-somethings are drawn to the Peasant by its Belgian beers and Mediterranean meze menu, including hummus, dolmades, fetta with capers, aubergine stewed in tomato (all £2.20), squid with lime and chilli, Spanish meatballs (both £3.50) and a platter selection for £10, served fresh and fast. The calamari and cod fritters are accompanied by a mayonnaise which lacks much of the coriander, coconut and chilli that is promised (£4.80), but the sautéed chicken liver and lardon bruschetta is spot on (£4.50). Baked salmon with fennel and curly kale (£9.50) is crispy-topped but not overdone, and the lamb stewed with winter vegetables (£9.80) served in a decent-sized soup dish is peasant-like, but contains superior meat. Meals are best eaten in the atmospheric and lively bar area, rather than the austere restaurant upstairs.

starter: £3.80-£5.50
main: £8-£10
dessert: £4.20-£4.50
AE DC MC V; SW

Open: Mon-Fri 12.30pm-3pm, Mon-Sat 6.30pm-11pm; reservations accepted; licensed

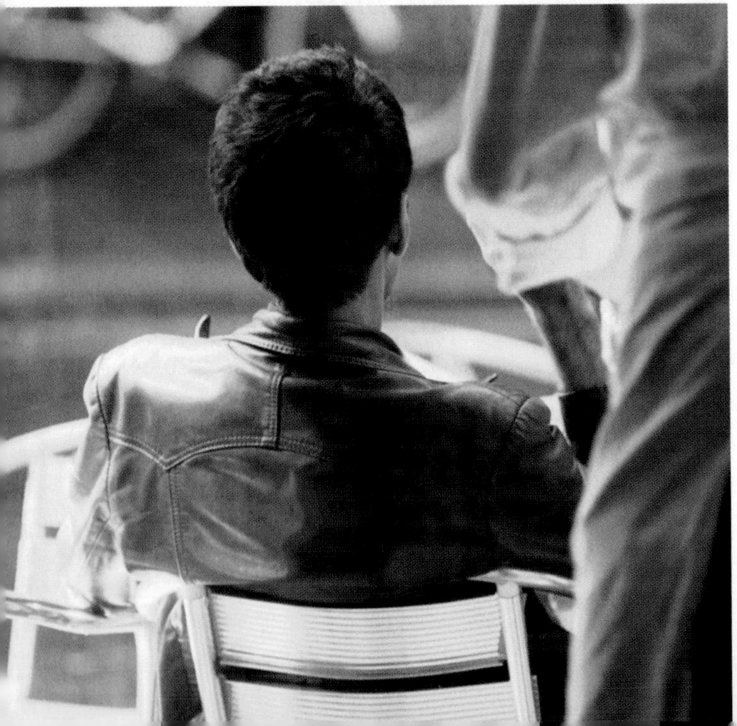

Quality Chop House ☎ 020 7837 5093
British **92-94 Farringdon Rd EC1**

Map 16 A1
Tube/rail: Farringdon

 Nonsmoking tables available

When the Victorian-era Quality Chop House recently expanded into the building next door, the extension was dubbed the 'Quality Fish House' – a symbol of trends in modern British cooking. By any name, this upmarket workman's cafe is one of London's top media hangouts (in fact, the restaurant serves as a virtual canteen for the *Guardian* newspaper, which is located across the street). The menu (identical in both rooms) offers a winning mixture of old and new – red meat perennials like rump steak and grilled sausages co-exist with a raw bar and daily seafood specials (brill and new potatoes or haddock with lentils). Unusually for this business-oriented part of town, the QCH is open for Sunday brunch – more than a few hangovers have been fed by a big plate of eggs benedict or beef hash. Those who haven't overindulged will appreciate the wine list, with house bottles starting at around £11.

Open: Mon-Fri noon-3pm, Mon-Sat 6.30pm-11.30pm, Sun noon-4pm, 7pm-11.30pm; reservations essential; licensed

starter: £4.50-£7
main: £11.50-£16
dessert: £5
MC V; SW

Saints' ☎ 020 7490 4199
International **1 Clerkenwell Rd EC1**

Map 16 A3
Tube: Farringdon

 Smoking throughout

Saints' is housed in what used to be a bank, one of the first in London to be changed to an eaterie. It offers the upwardly mobile masses good food at budget prices, and is especially popular at lunchtime. Smoked salmon and scrambled eggs (£4.75) or cereal with fruit, honey and Greek yoghurt (£3) are excellent ways to start the day. At lunch, the home-made pea and potato soup (£2.50) is flavoursome and thick, and mains range from classic English dishes to Sri Lankan fish cakes and a vegan cashew-nut casserole. The beef and ale pie (£5.75) is full of chunky steak and mushrooms, topped with golden brown pastry and served with mounds of chips and salad. For dessert there's a basic selection of puddings, ice cream and staples like apple pie and custard (£2.75).

Open: Mon-Fri 8am-6pm; reservations accepted; licensed

starter: £1-£4.75
main: £5.75
dessert: £2.75
cash only

Map 16 B3
Tube/rail: Farringdon
Dress code: collared shirt
Entertainment: jazz from 8pm

Smoking throughout

Le Café du Marché

French

☎ 020 7608 1609
22 Charterhouse Square, Charterhouse Mews EC1

Tucked away in an alley near the Smithfield meat market, the hip Le Café du Marché is well worth seeking out for a business lunch, a romantic tryst or to complete a night out at the Barbican Centre just across the way. Indeed, with its exposed brick walls, bustling open kitchen and jazz combo on the first floor, it's the perfect place to while away those cold winter hours. Vegetarians are offered several choices on the daily menu, but the restaurant is justifiably proud of its delicious porterhouse steak and game dishes such as roast pigeon and quail. Crème caramel and chocolate mousse, accompanied by a drop from the wine list (starting at £10 a bottle), continue the no-nonsense theme.

Set menu £24.45
MC V; SW

Open: Mon-Fri noon-2.30pm, Mon-Sat 6pm-10pm; reservations essential; licensed

Map 16 B3
Tube/rail: Farringdon

Smoking throughout

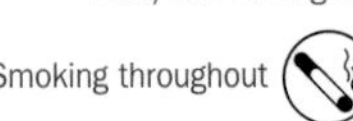

Vic Naylor

Modern British

☎ 020 7608 2181
38-40 St John St EC1

Vic Naylor led the renaissance of Clerkenwell/Farringdon in the 1980s, and the exposed brick walls now almost give it a historical look. But there's nothing historical about the atmosphere, which heaves with 20-somethings from the City. The lively bar action spills into the dining room through the evening, so don't be surprised if plans for an assignation are negotiated right over your shoulder. Depending on your mood, this can count as entertainment or annoyance. Somehow the staff fjord the sea of bodies and deliver good, simple modern British fare. The changing menu leans toward simple meat and fish, which is good given the often diminished cognitive powers of the crowd. The large roast pork fillet (£8.50) is flavoured with fennel and served with creamy mashed potato and garlic. A char-grilled sirloin steak (£14) was cooked as ordered and got a nice punch from sun-dried tomato relish. The passionfruit tart (£4) has plenty of passion and a great flaky crust. The wine list is long, with many good choices by the glass.

starter: £5-£7.50
main: £8-£15
dessert: £4
AE MC V; SW

Open: Mon-Fri noon-midnight, Sat noon-5pm, 7pm-midnight; reservations advisable; licensed

Anna's Place

Swedish

☎ 020 7249 9379
90 Mildmay Park N1

Map 15 B1

Tube/rail: Highbury & Islington, then bus 30 or, 277

 Smoking throughout

One of London's few Swedish restaurants, this well-established neighbourhood favourite is still going strong after 25 years. Home-cured Scandinavian fish is the speciality here, particularly the delicious home-cured herrings (£5.90) and gravlax with dill-mustard sauce (£5.95). Fresh fish, such as grilled fillet of trout with mashed potato (£11.10), is also well executed. On the down side, some of the non-fish dishes can be bland – the couple of mouthfuls of bean stew wrapped in a cabbage leaf were instantly forgettable, apart from the Scandinavian price tag (£9.80). Despite the high-rise block opposite, Anna's retains a charming, cottagey feel, complete with pine boards on the floor and brightly painted walls covered with Swedish folk art. There's no music – perhaps the temptation to play ABBA songs would be too great – but chat from a diverse base of regulars keeps the atmosphere lively, and the all-Swedish staff are unfailingly delightful.

Open: Mon-Sat 7pm-11pm, Sat noon-2pm; reservations advisable (especially weekends); licensed

starter: £4.90-£7.85
main: £9.90-£14.80
dessert: £4.15-£4.65
Set menu Mon-Thurs £10

cash or cheque only

Iznik

Turkish

☎ 020 7354 5697
19 Highbury Park N5

Map 15 A3

Tube/rail: Highbury & Islington

 Smoking throughout

For down-to-earth Turkish food in magical surroundings, Iznik is well worth a trip to the edge of Highbury. Relaxed, friendly and always busy, the restaurant is filled with gorgeous Turkish artefacts, including dozens of colourful glass lanterns winking above the tables. The menu offers a wide selection of Turkish favourites, and with a long list of scrumptious starters it takes some mulling over. The house speciality is the dozen or so lamb dishes, such as the excellent lamb and herb-filled filo parcels (£3.50). There's no separate charge for vegetables and so on as most dishes come with rice and a simple salad, but it's worth splashing out for a dish of puréed broad-bean salad dressed with dill and mint (£2.95). Desserts include baklava, of course, but there's also semolina cake drenched in syrup and thick cream, and perfectly poached pears stuffed with pistachios and served with chocolate sauce and cream (all £3).

Open: daily 10am-4pm, 6.30pm-midnight; reservations advisable; licensed

starter: £2.95-£3.95
main: £7.25-£9.50
dessert: £3

MC V; SW

Map 15 A1
Tube: Holloway Road

Smoking throughout 

starter: £1.80-£3.50
main: £5.50-£7.95
dessert: £1.90-£2.50
Set menu £15/person (min 10 people)
JCB MC V; SW

Royal Cous-Cous House

North African

☎ 020 7700 2188
316 Holloway Rd N7

Despite the fact that the ceiling started to leak halfway through our meal, the Royal Cous-Cous House is well worth a visit for some fine North African cuisine. Appropriately bleary Moroccan music greeted us and colourful garments and pictures adorned the walls, giving the restaurant a warm and welcoming atmosphere. Smoked peppers (£1.80) and brochette salad (£3.50) were good indications of the spices to come. The chicken in the Agadir tajine (£6.50) literally fell off the bone and the vegetables were plentiful and filling. Unfortunately the Marrakech couscous (£5.95) was made too sweet by a surfeit of raisins, but we still managed to sample the Moroccan pâtisseries (£2.20), an acquired taste and very sweet. The evening was warmed by a Syrah Cabernet (£9.49) and service that was pleasant and friendly – and very apologetic about the ceiling.

Open: daily 5pm-11pm; reservations advisable (essential noon-3pm); licensed & BYO (corkage £1/bottle)

Afghan Kitchen

Afghan

☎ **020 7359 8019**
35 Islington Green N1

Map 15 E3
Tube: Angel

 Smoking throughout

Catering for lunch on the run or a quick bite in the evening before you head across Islington Green to catch a movie, Afghan Kitchen offers traditional home cooking in a recently refurbished, trendy setting. Expect to share a table and don't come if you don't like yoghurt. The short menu has no starters and only one dessert, so order a mix of meat and vegetarian dishes, basmati rice (£2) and bread (£2), and dig in. The mint flavours of the lavand-e-murgh (chicken in yoghurt, £5) are calmed by yoghurt, and the dish of kidney beans, chickpeas and potatoes, cooked in yoghurt, is complemented by pepper spices. For a top up of zing, order a plate of mixed pickles (£2). In spite of the quick service and diner turnover, you can linger over the solitary dessert of baklava (£1), while sipping a cardamom-flavoured green tea.

Open: Tues-Sat noon-3.30pm, 5.30pm-midnight; reservations advisable (especially evenings); licensed

main: £4.50-£5
dessert: £1

cash or cheque only

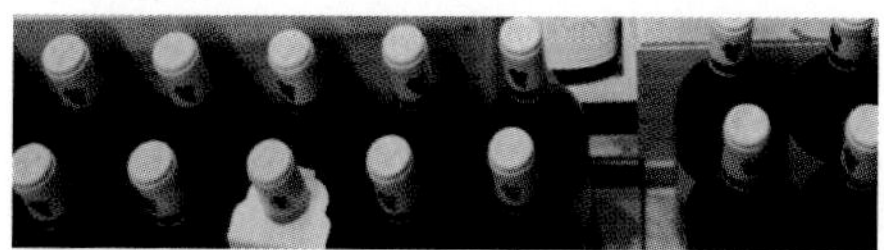

Art to Zen

Modern European

☎ **020 7226 5300**
27 Upper St N1

Map 15 E2
Tube: Angel
Entertainment: live classical music on the first Mon of every month

 Smoking throughout

 Pavement tables

With modern art on the walls for sale and a Japanese chef in the kitchen, our contemplation of zen and concluding enlightenment was that a restaurant in London can serve good food at remarkably cheap prices. During Sunday lunch the fully occupied room refills during the course of a meal. Go for the home-made vegetable and spinach soups, delicious spiced red shrimps with ginger and garlic (£2.90), served in their shells, or a thick and tender slice of roast lamb with crunchy roast potatoes and tonkatsu* pork cutlets (£5.50). The set desserts are lemon or hot chocolate pancakes. Throw in a bottle of Lindemans shiraz (£9.50), and the bill for five comes to an amazing £42.80.

Open: Mon-Sat 10.30am-11.30pm, Sun 10.30am-10.30pm; reservations accepted; licensed

starter: £2.45-£3.50
main: £4.50-£7.50
dessert: £2-£3.50
Set lunch £5.95 or £9.95

(£5 min) MC V; SW

Map 15 C2

Tube/rail: Highbury & Islington

Smoking throughout

Cantina Italia

Italian

☎ 020 7226 9791

19 Canonbury Lane N1

You can love your flat, but what really makes the neighbourhood? A good pub? Probably. A good market? Sure. But having a great local place to get a meal when the thought of your kitchen turns your feet to stone is essential. Cantina Italia, an unprepossessing joint off hopping Upper St, fits the bill just fine. There's good food and no frills on two levels, the no-nonsense point carried through right down to the sturdy but comfy chairs. A long list of thin and crispy pizzas for around £6 leads the left side of the menu. The sauce has just the right hint of fresh tomato. The more serious right side has a fine char-grilled filetto alla griglia (£14.90), although just because it's beef doesn't mean they have to go overboard for the locals by including a portion of chips. The fresh gnocchi (£5.80) is warming and comes bathed in a zesty tomato basil sauce. The affable service delivers and the wine list has many numbers that won't strain a mid-week budget.

starter: £5-£8
main: £5-£7.50
dessert: £3

MC V; SW

Open: Tues-Sun noon-3pm, Sun-Thurs 6.30pm-11pm, Fri & Sat 6.30pm-11.30pm; reservations advisable (especially weekends); licensed

---

Map 15 E3

Tube: Angel

Certified organic

Non smoking tables available

Pavement tables

The Duke of Cambridge

International

☎ 020 7359 3066

30 St Peter's St N1

London's 'first organic gastropub' doesn't have an extensive menu, aiming for quality rather than quantity. And a rustic type of quality it is too: unpolished wooden chairs and tables, unadorned walls, tin bowls for the bread and simple but very effective dishes such as cod with peppers, green beans and potatoes (£10.50). Our peppers and green beans were cooked just enough to bring out all the flavours without masking that of the fish, though the slightly crunchy potatoes added a whole new dimension to the textures on the palate. Dessert was a pear (£4) dripping in rich mulled wine with the creamy zing of crème fraîche. Super-friendly, highly efficient staff ensured we had everything we wanted, while leaving us to enjoy the meal. Indeed, with its lack of music and basic décor, the Duke of Cambridge concentrates on providing good food and leaves it up to you to create your own ambience.

starter: £4-£6
main: £7.50-£14
dessert: £4-£4.50

AE MC V; SW

Open: Mon 5pm-11pm, Tues-Sun noon-3.30pm, Tues-Sat 6.30pm-10.30pm, Sun 6.30pm-10pm; reservations accepted; licensed

ChainChainChain...

In high-traffic, high-rent areas such as the West End, Soho and Knightsbridge, it may seem like the only places to eat are part of chains. It's a sorry development, driven by the high costs of establishing new restaurants in places where expenses are high. It's much easier for a corporation to endlessly replicate a concept with food and drink that can be easily prepared by semi-skilled staff than it is to run high-quality, unique restaurants with individual chefs, menus, concepts etc.

With the proliferation of chains in London, there may be times that you've no choice but to try one. Here's a rundown of some of the better options:

Lunch

Pret a Manger is a massive chain of sandwich outlets that provide wonderfully fresh sandwiches in innovative variations: the chicken caesar (£2.39) exudes parmesan; the 'more than mozzarella' comes with basil and pine nuts (£2.35). The coffees (99p) are made to order. Pret deserves credit for lifting the standards of the London takeaway lunch.

Soup Opera has a range of freshly made soups that changes daily and can include interesting recipes like Tuscan bean and smoked haddock chowder.

Brasseries

Café Flo, Café Rouge and **Dôme** all try to replicate casual French brasseries. The menus are heavy with salads, omelettes, steaks and frites, frites and more frites. All three are usually bright and airy, but something else they share, as we've found in several visits, is slow service, possibly because the owners sit in corporate offices far away. (In fact, Café Flo and Dôme are both owned by the huge Whitbread group.) Expect to pay between £15 and £20 per person, including drinks.

Italian

Pizza Express is a quirky chain that individualises its outlets with smart but eclectic décor. Individual pizzas (about £6) come in a panoply of flavours and are usually quite good. Some locations even have regular live jazz.

Café Pasta and **Spaghetti House** are considered the pick of the formula Italian joints. Both have dishes on the menu that go a few steps beyond spaghetti bolognese. Expect to pay around £15 per person with drinks.

Theme

Belgo (see the review for Belgo Centraal, p 27) gives each one of its locations a unique name, but the buckets of fresh mussels, frites with mayonnaise and many tasty Belgian beers are the same at each location.

Pubs

All Bar One apes the best of the modern local pubs in London's residential neighbourhoods: light and airy, big tables with comfortable chairs, decent beers and large plates of vaguely modern European food. Of course, the places don't capture the individual charm of the best of the locals.

Hogshead is notable solely for its excellent range of hard-to-find beers from some of Britain's best and smallest breweries. However, the food is much less interesting.

Ryan Ver Berkmoes

Map 15 C2
Tube: Highbury & Islington
Wheelchair access
Smoking throughout 
Garden tables 

Euphorium
Modern British

☎ 020 7704 6909
203 Upper St N1

Despite its hyperbolic name, Euphorium serves British comfort food with a modern spin, a twist reflected in the décor's hardwood floors, teal and tangerine-coloured walls. We return regularly for the smoked haddock and leek chowder (£5.95), and have been tempted at least once by the artichoke and goat's cheese galette (£6.95), but the chef's predilection for mixing poached egg with offal such as lamb sweetbreads and spinach (£7.45) confuses both us and the texture of the dish. For mains, try the roast chicken with butternut chilli (£11.95) or even a generous starter like the bowl of mussels in a spicy (read Thai-inspired – very British nowadays) broth. The attractive, friendly staff always offer a warm welcome and provide some of the most seamless service in recent memory. Come to think of it, we often feel somewhat euphoric upon leaving Euphorium.

starter: £4.95-£7.95
main: £7.25-£15.50
dessert: £5
Set lunch £12.50
AE MC V; SW

Open: Mon-Sat noon-2.30pm, 6pm-11pm, Sun noon-3.30pm; reservations advisable; licensed

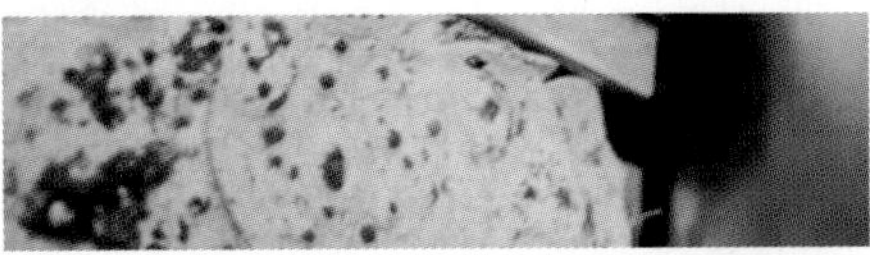

Map 15 D3
Tube/rail: Angel or Highbury & Islington
Smoking throughout 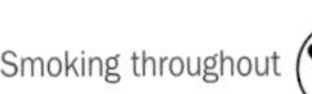

Le Mercury
French

☎ 020 7354 4088
140a Upper St N1

Le Mercury is one of the more romantic corners of fashionable Upper St, with candles, plenty of gilt mirrors and tables for two positioned beneath reproductions of glorious old masterpieces. Starters (all £2.85) include ever-popular mussels with wine and shallots, garlic mushrooms (two large succulent discs that almost ruin you for what's to come) or choux de crab – profiteroles with crab meat and hollandaise sauce. Mains (all £5.85) are along the lines of pork medallions with cream of mushroom sauce, poached salmon mousse with avocado salsa or perhaps a well-executed dish of fish cakes – two large balls with crispy thin skin served with fresh herb sauce. Desserts (all £2.75) are a bit of a hit-and-miss affair, but Sunday lunch by the upstairs fire is one meal not to be missed.

starter: £2.85
main: £5.85
dessert: £2.75
Set lunch £5.95
DC JCB MC V; SW

Open: Mon-Sat 11am-1am, Sun noon-midnight; reservations advisable (essential weekends); licensed

Lola's

Modern European

☎ 020 7359 1932
The Mall Building, Camden Passage, 359 Upper St N1

Looking for somewhere romantic to dine? Take only your best friend and climb the stairs to foodie heaven, where you'll discover an elegant and airy dining room, well-spaced tables and attentive yet unobtrusive service, along with the tender tinkle of piano and lights that dim just at the right moment. The menu changes according to what's in season, and flavourful dishes reflect quality ingredients prepared in an accomplished and unpretentious style. A choice of eight starters offers various lip-smacking favourites – pine nuts and parmesan, goat's cheese, roast peppers and caesar salad (£4.75), and a potato pancake with smoked salmon, caviar and chives (£7). Try the butternut squash risotto with rocket and parmesan (£10.75), lamb with chickpea mash (£12.75) or monkfish with fennel coleslaw and gremolata (£13) as a main. Desserts tend to be fruity à la sorbet (£5), but also include a perfect raspberry and almond tart (£5.75). A fine selection of cheeses (£5.25) and wines are further proof that Lola's attention to detail is hard to fault.

Open: Mon-Fri noon-2.30pm, Mon-Sat 6pm-11pm, Sat & Sun noon-3pm, Sun 7pm-10pm; reservations advisable (especially weekends); licensed

Map 15 E2

Tube: Angel

Entertainment: pianist nightly, jazz duo Sun noon-3pm

 Smoking throughout

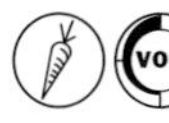

starter: £5-£8
main: £10-£16
dessert: £4-£6

AE DC MC V; SW

Luba's Place

Russian

☎ 020 7704 2775
164 Essex Rd N1

A bistro opposite a bingo hall may not sound too impressive, but good food and a great night out are guaranteed at Luba's. The 75 varieties of vodka at £1.75 a shot certainly help, as does the Russian violinist playing a medley of Abba hits. Start with a shot of Russian vodka served with a plateful of pickled herring (£3.35) or a sweet, sharp bowl of borscht (£2.55). Main courses are always tasty and hearty, though our tender turkey goulash (£5.45) had been zapped way too high, and the vegetables were soggy. But the good news for blini lovers is that you can have them for every course, with everything from spinach and buckwheat to honey and lemon. Mismatched crockery and furniture add to the charm, with cast-off office chairs called back into service alongside 1960s dining chairs – and not a hint of retro chic intended.

Open: Mon-Sat 6pm-midnight; reservations advisable (especially weekends); licensed

Map 15 D3

Tube: Angel, then bus 38, 56 or 73

Entertainment: Russian saxophone, guitar or violin Wed-Sat 8pm-11pm

 Smoking throughout

starter: £2.55-£6.25
main: £4.45-£7.95
dessert: £2.10

MC V; SW

ISLINGTON

Map 15 D3
Tube: Angel
Nonsmoking tables available

Upper Street Fish Shop

British/fish & chips

☎ 020 7359 1401
324 Upper St N1

The crowded dining room and the frequent line at the takeaway counter speak for themselves at the Upper Street Fish Shop. This popular Islington eatery has been serving up some of the best fish and chips in London since it opened in 1982. The surroundings are simple, with straw placemats atop blue gingham tablecloths, and the service is fast. At peak times, dining can be a communal affair with groups sharing the larger of the 11 tables. The 10 varieties of fish, including cod (£8.50), plaice (£9), salmon (£9) and halibut (£10), can be fried, grilled or poached. Fried fish is cooked according to a recipe used by owner Alan Conway's family for three generations. If you're not a fish fan, this may not be the restaurant for you, since chicken (£6) is the only non-fish item on the menu. But if you do love fish and yearn for some traditional British fare, this is the place to go.

starter: £2.50-£6.50
main: £6-£12
dessert: £3
cash only

Open: Tue-Fri noon-2.15pm, Sat noon-3pm, Mon-Thurs 6pm-10.15pm, Fri & Sat 5:30pm-10.15pm; reservations not accepted; BYO (no corkage)

KING'S CROSS

Map 16 A1
Tube/rail: King's Cross
Smoking throughout

The Union Tavern

British

☎ 020 7278 0111
52 Lloyd Baker St WC1

This wonderful old pub, with its ornate wooden bar and coved high ceiling, shares half its space with an open kitchen offering an interesting, if limited, 'gastropub' menu. A typical starter is grilled polenta with parma ham and mixed salad for £4.50. The daily specials are all under £11, and lighter fare such as hamburgers, steak sandwiches, and fish and chips are available every day. The Union offers several real ales on tap (£2.25 for a pint of Old Speckled Hen) and has an interesting wine list, with selections from France, Australia, the USA, Chile, Spain and even Mexico (bottles range from £10 to £15.50). The Union's King's Cross location ensures that its dining room attracts a large number of exhausted tourists, most of whom clear out well before closing time.

starter: £2.50-£6
main: £6.95-£12
dessert: £4
AE MC V; SW

Open: daily noon-3pm, 6pm-10pm; reservations advisable; licensed

Aldgate

Bethnal Green

Brick Lane

EAST

City

Dalston

Haggerston

Shoreditch

Spitalfields

Stoke Newington

Tower Hill

Whitechapel

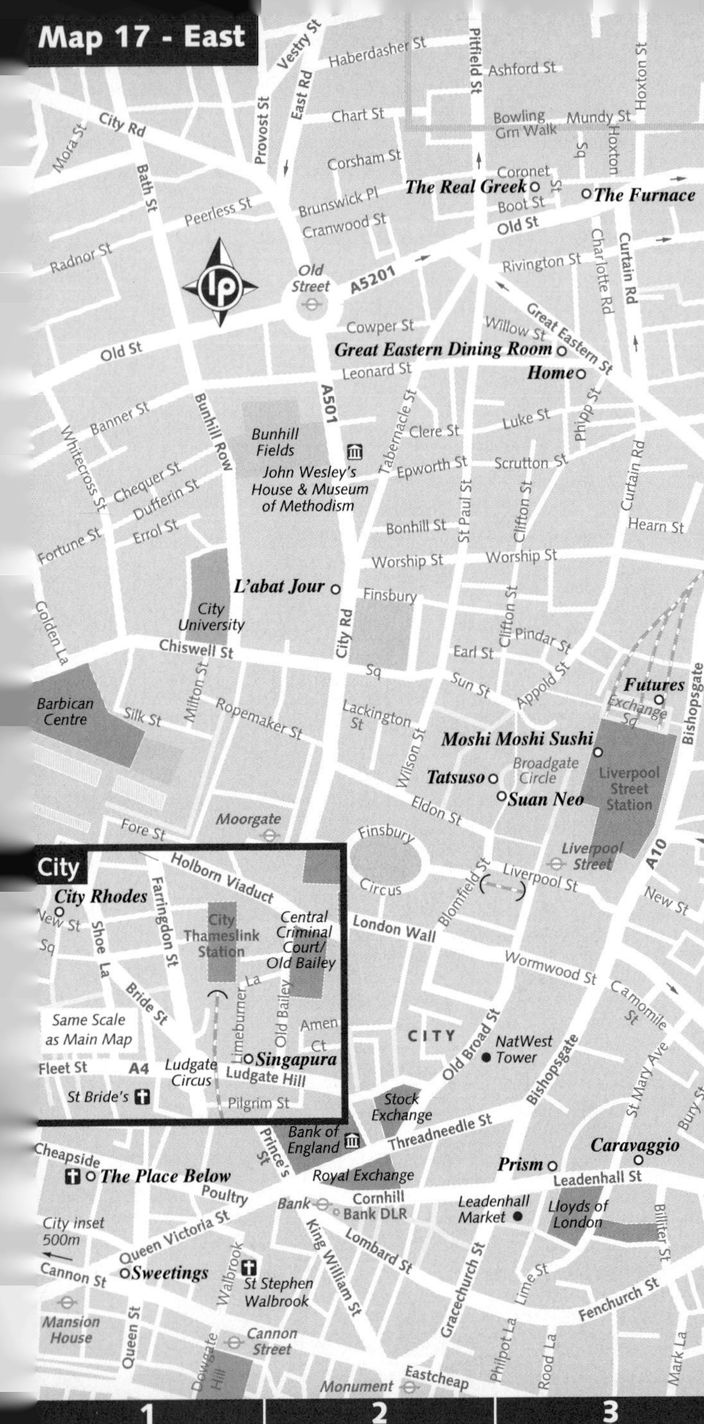

Map 17 - East
Vestry St
Haberdasher St
Pitfield St
Ashford St
Hoxton St
East Rd
Provost St
Chart St
Bowling Grn Walk
Mundy St
Hoxton Sq
City Rd
Mora St
Bath St
Corsham St
Coronet St
The Real Greek
The Furnace
Brunswick Pl
Boot St
Peerless St
Cranwood St
Old St
Charlotte Rd
Curtain Rd
Radnor St
Rivington St
Old Street
A5201
Great Eastern St
Cowper St
Willow St
Old St
Great Eastern Dining Room
Home
Leonard St
A501
Bunhill Row
Banner St
Tabernacle St
Phipp St
Clere St
Luke St
Bunhill Fields
John Wesley's House & Museum of Methodism
Epworth St
Scrutton St
Whitecross St
Chequer St
Dufferin St
St Paul St
Clifton St
Curtain Rd
Errol St
Bonhill St
Hearn St
Fortune St
Worship St
Worship St
L'abat Jour
Finsbury Sq
Golden La
City University
City Rd
Clifton St
Pindar St
Chiswell St
Earl St
Appold St
Milton St
Sun St
Futures
Exchange Sq
Bishopsgate
Barbican Centre
Silk St
Ropemaker St
Lackington St
Wilson St
Moshi Moshi Sushi
Broadgate Circle
Tatsuso
Suan Neo
Liverpool Street Station
Eldon St
Fore St
Moorgate
Finsbury Circus
Liverpool Street
A10
Liverpool St
Blomfield St
New St
London Wall
Wormwood St
Camomile St
CITY
Old Broad St
NatWest Tower
St Mary Ave
Bishopsgate
Bury St
Stock Exchange
Threadneedle St
Bank of England
Caravaggio
Prism
Royal Exchange
Leadenhall St
Cheapside
The Place Below
Poultry
Prince's St
Bank
Cornhill
Bank DLR
Leadenhall Market
Lloyds of London
Billiter St
City inset 500m
Queen Victoria St
Lombard St
King William St
Cannon St
Sweetings
Walbrook
St Stephen Walbrook
Gracechurch St
Lime St
Fenchurch St
Mansion House
Queen St
Dowgate Hill
Cannon Street
Philpot La
Rood La
Mark La
Monument
Eastcheap
City
City Rhodes
New St Sq
Shoe La
Farringdon St
Holborn Viaduct
City Thameslink Station
Central Criminal Court/ Old Bailey
Bride St
Limeburner La
Old Bailey
Same Scale as Main Map
Amen Ct
Fleet St
A4
Ludgate Circus
Singapura
Ludgate Hill
St Bride's
Pilgrim St
1
2
3

Viet Hoa
Waterson St
Kingsland Rd
Columbia Rd
Quilter St
B118
cont on Map 18 p196
Hackney Rd
Austin St
Virginia Rd
Barnet Gve
Vallance Rd
BETHNAL GREEN
0 m 150 300
0 yd 150 300
Calvert Ave
Arnold Circus
Swanfield St
Brick La
A1209
E Pellicci
Voss St
Derbyshire St
Boundary Street
Club Row
A10
Old Nichol St
Bethnal Green Rd
B108
Redchurch St
Brick Lane Beigel Bakery
B136
Shoreditch High St
Sclater St
Brick La
SHOREDITCH
Shoreditch
Whitechapel
A1202
Quaker St
Headlam St
Cambridge Heath Rd
Cleveland Way
Elder St
Commercial St
Grey Eagle St
Spital St
Sweet Chilli
Folgate St
Le Taj
Woodseer St
(side road)
Mile End Rd
Lamb St
Hanbury St
Mesón Los Barriles
B134
Princelet St
A11
Same Scale as Main Map
Steward St
Spitalfields Market
Arkansas Café
Fournier St
Brushfield St
Brick Lane Market
Heneage St
Whitechapel inset 350m
Artillery La
Bengal Trader
White's Row
Fashion St
Brick La
Chicksand St
Davenant St
SPITALFIELDS
A11
Old Montague St
Barcelona Tapas Bar
Bell La
New Tayyab
Wentworth St
Osborn St
Whitechapel Rd
Cobb St
Commercial St
Whitechapel Art Gallery
Fieldgate St
Middlesex St
Adler St
Greenfield Rd
Settles St
Petticoat Lane Market
Goulston St
Old Castle St
Aldgate East
WHITECHAPEL
Whitechapel High St
Parco's
St Botolph St
Fenchurch Street Station
Minories
Tower Hill
Houndsditch
Aldgate
Tower Gateway DLR
Aldgate High St
Braham St
cont on main map
Duke's Pl
Alie St
Tower Hill
Shorter St
Mansell St
Leman St
Tower Hill
Mansell St
E Tenter St
East Smithfield
Jewry St
Minories
Mark St
Vine St
Haydon St
Tower of London
Prescot St
Tower Bridge Approach
St Katharine's Way
Café Spice Namaste
Quayside
Fenchurch Street Station
Goodmans Yd
Chamber St
Tower Gateway DLR
Same Scale as Main Map
cont on Tower Hill

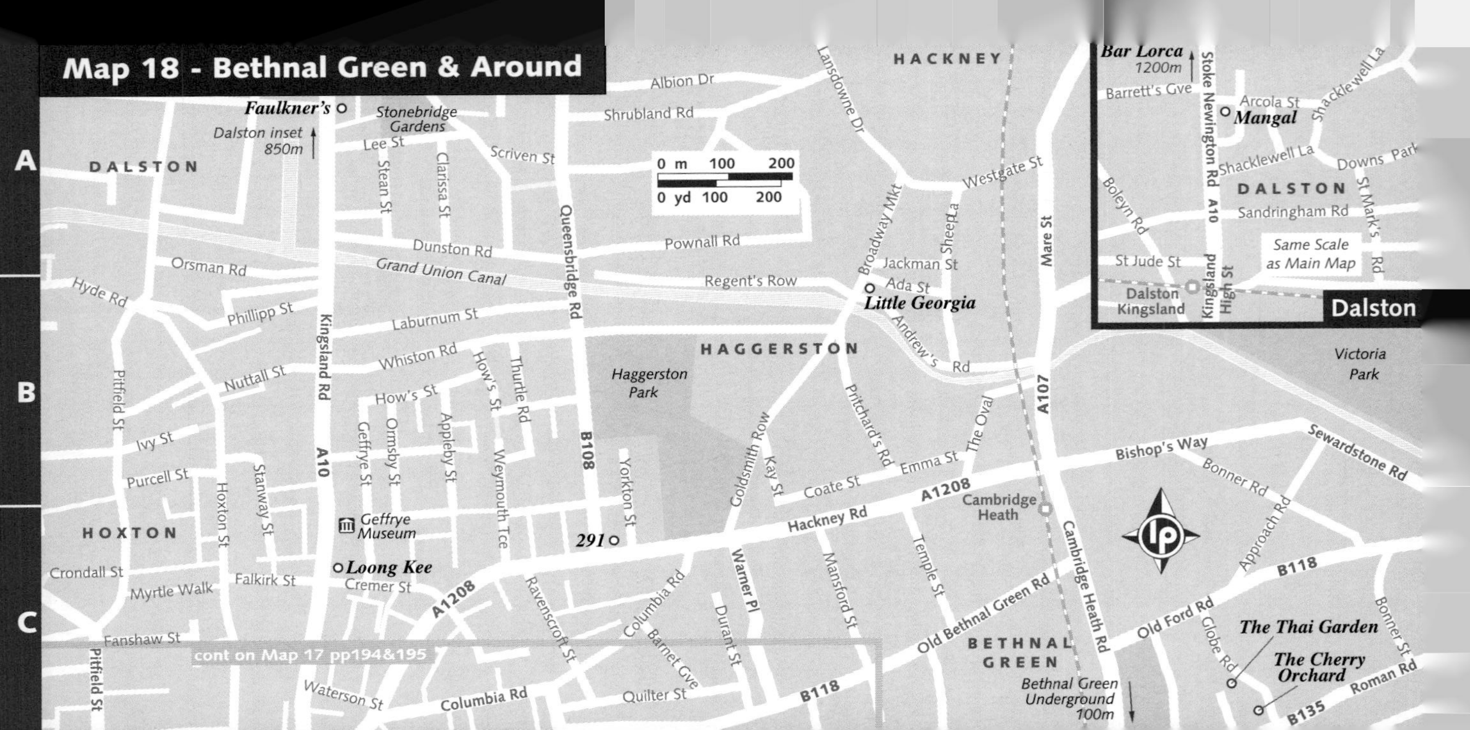

Map 18 - Bethnal Green & Around
A
B
C
DALSTON
HOXTON
HAGGERSTON
HACKNEY
BETHNAL GREEN
Faulkner's
Dalston inset 850m
Little Georgia
Loong Kee
291
Geffrye Museum
The Thai Garden
The Cherry Orchard
Bethnal Green Underground 100m
cont on Map 17 pp194&195
0 m 100 200
0 yd 100 200
Haggerston Park
Victoria Park
Cambridge Heath
Dalston Kingsland
Same Scale as Main Map
Dalston
Bar Lorca 1200m
Mangal
Albion Dr
Shrubland Rd
Stonebridge Gardens
Lee St
Scriven St
Stean St
Clarissa St
Queensbridge Rd
Dunston Rd
Grand Union Canal
Pownall Rd
Regent's Row
Orsman Rd
Hyde Rd
Phillipp St
Kingsland Rd
Laburnum St
Whiston Rd
Nuttall St
How's St
Thurtle Rd
Pitfield St
Ivy St
Purcell St
Hoxton St
Stanway St
A10
Geffrye St
Ormsby St
Appleby St
Weymouth Tce
B108
Yorkton St
Crondall St
Myrtle Walk
Falkirk St
Cremer St
A1208
Ravenscroft St
Columbia Rd
Barnet Gve
Durant St
Warner Pl
Mansford St
Temple St
Fanshaw St
Waterson St
Quilter St
B118
Hackney Rd
Goldsmith Row
Kay St
Coate St
Emma St
Pritchard's Rd
The Oval
Andrew's Rd
Ada St
Jackman St
Sheep La
Broadway Mkt
Westgate St
Lansdowne Dr
Mare St
A107
Bishop's Way
Cambridge Heath Rd
Old Bethnal Green Rd
Old Ford Rd
Bonner Rd
Approach Rd
Sewardstone Rd
Globe Rd
Bonner St
Roman Rd
B135
Barrett's Gve
Stoke Newington Rd
Arcola St
Shacklewell La
Downs Park
Sandringham Rd
St Mark's Rd
Boleyn Rd
St Jude St
Kingsland High St

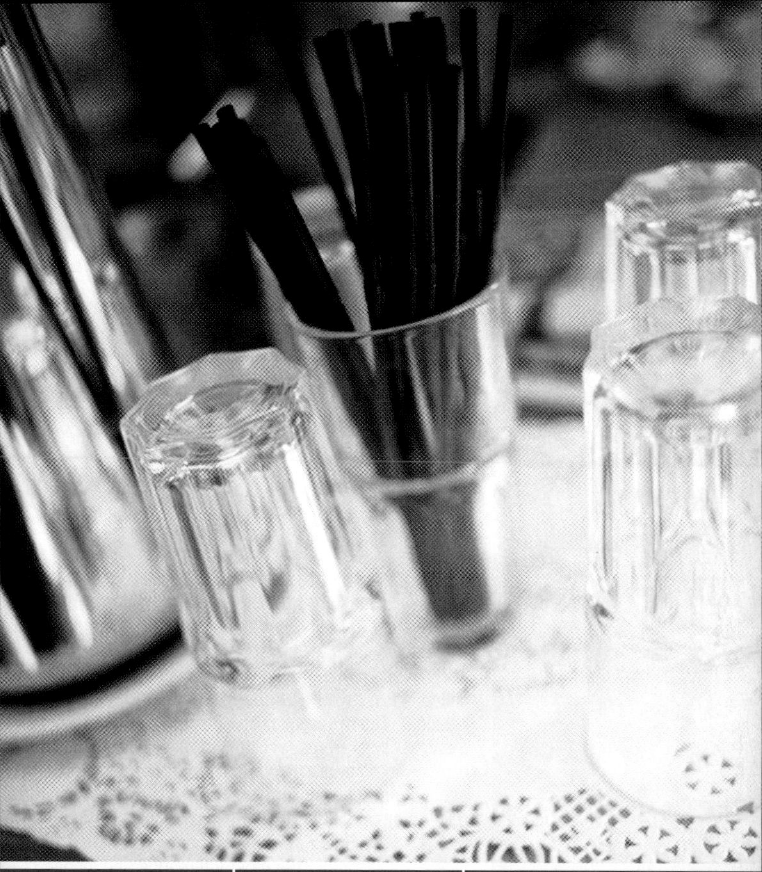

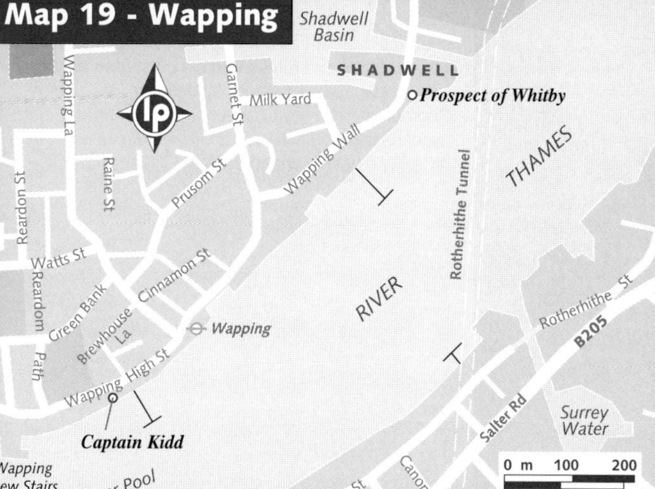

Map 19 - Wapping
Shadwell Basin
SHADWELL
Prospect of Whitby
Milk Yard
Garnet St
Wapping La
Raine St
Prusom St
Wapping Wall
Reardon St
Watts St
Reardom Path
Green Bank
Cinnamon St
Brewhouse La
Wapping
Wapping High St
Captain Kidd
Wapping New Stairs
Lower Pool
RIVER
THAMES
Rotherhithe Tunnel
Rotherhithe St
B205
Salter Rd
Surrey Water
Canon Beck Rd
Rotherhithe St
0 m 100 200
0 yd 100 200
A
B
1
2
3

BEST

- **Café Spice Namaste** Sensational South Indian
- **City Rhodes** Puts modern British cooking back on the gourmet map
- **Little Georgia** Must-try Georgian/ Russian cuisine
- **The Real Greek** Nothing like Greek you've eaten before

East

Even if Hoxton needed verification of its cutting-edge status – it doesn't – it couldn't do much better than having artist Damien Hirst's dealer set up shop there. At galleries around this former grouping of derelict warehouses can be found the works of numerous so-called YBAs (young British artists). The English National Opera has a studio here and various theatres and arthouse cinemas attract crowds at night, who venture out not just from the many local, pricey lofts but from farther afield as well. The focal point of all this creativity is Hoxton Square, just north of Old St. It's fitting that this is the home of the Real Greek, easily one of the most interesting and innovative spots for casual dining in London.

The activity isn't just confined to Hoxton. About a mile south, design-mogul Terence Conran has taken the shabby old Great Eastern Hotel across from Liverpool Street Station and turned it into a must-have address for people who judge a hostelry by its status. Shoreditch is not far behind Hoxton in its ascendancy and Brick Lane is now known as much for its galleries as its cheap curries.

Barcelona Tapas Bar

Spanish

☎ 020 7247 7014
1a Bell Lane E1

Map 17 D4

Tube: Liverpool Street

 Smoking throughout

A Brick Lane back street is a surprising place to find some of the best tapas in London, but Barcelona Tapas Bar provides just that. As you descend the dingy stairs, the restaurant's tacky façade gives way to a mock Gaudi and Formica-enhanced interior that is truly Spanish in feel. The place doesn't seem to attract ex-pat Spaniards though – most of the clientele is from the City. The main focus here is drinking, but though the wine is relatively expensive the food is exceptional value, with over 60 choices on the menu. All the classics are here, including paella (£10.95), richly flavoured chorizo (£2.95) and enormous mussels (£2.95). Barcelona's other branches are nearby in Middlesex St and in Dulwich; they may be larger and more airy, but the Bell Lane restaurant is the original and most authentic.

Open: Mon-Fri 11am-11pm; reservations accepted; licensed

starter: £2.95-£6.95
main: £10.95
dessert: £2.95-£4.50

AE DC JCB MC V; SW

Parco's Restaurant and Brasserie

Modern Italian

☎ 020 7488 2817
Aldgate Barrs,
Marsh Centre,
1 Whitechapel High St E1

Map 17 D5

Tube: Aldgate or Aldgate East

Dress code: collared shirt

 Smoking throughout

Parco's is one of the City's most originally designed restaurants. The brasserie is dominated by three 50-foot trees growing up towards the glass-domed roof, while the restaurant is set on a mezzanine level among the tree tops, reached by a spiral staircase from the reception area. Our starter of garlicky king scallops were plump and juicy, and accompanied by warm pasta tossed in olive oil, basil and fresh tomato (£7.95). The salad of fresh crab, avocado and smoked salmon (£7.75) was as fresh as the menu promised, and came with plenty of crab meat. The pot-roasted pigeon and pheasant (£12.95) is the signature dish of Parco's head chef, Gennaro Grella, and comes with braised winter vegetables in a red wine sauce served with cheese polenta. The meat was tender and succulent, with a strong gamey flavour. Parco's is a lively lunchtime venue, both in the brasserie and restaurant, but is unfortunately not open for dinner.

Open: Mon-Fri noon-3pm; reservations advisable; licensed

starter:
brasserie: £3.75-£6.50,
restaurant: £3.95-£8.95
main:
brasserie: £7.25-£10.95,
restaurant: £8.95-£16.50
dessert:
brasserie: £3.50-£4,
restaurant: £3.95-£4.95

AE DC MC V; SW

The Cherry Orchard

Modern British vegetarian

☎ 020 7980 6678
241-247 Globe Rd E2

Map 18 C5
Tube: Bethnal Green

Courtyard tables 

At the Cherry Orchard the lunchtime crowds regularly spill out onto the street as hungry workers and locals queue up for a serving of delicious vegetarian fare such as vol-au-vent with mushrooms, cauliflower and cashew cream sauce (£4.25) or quiche served with a delicious salad – perhaps cracked wheat, olives, spring onions, sun-dried tomato and a touch of chilli (£3.95). There's usually a soup of the day (we tried a tasty spinach and coconut £1.60), but if it's afternoon tea time, go for something sweet like the hearty flapjacks (£1) or chocolate cake (£1.25). Wash it all down with a refillable coffee (it's percolated, but only 90p), home-made lemonade (£1.10) or a pure juice (80p). The food is fabulous and the garden courtyard is equally so – a peaceful oasis in the inner city. Indoors there's plenty of room too, with earthy wooden chairs and tables, and original artwork decorating the walls.

starter: £1.60-£3
main: £3.95-£4.25
dessert: £1-£2.25
MC V; SW

Open: Mon 11am-3pm, Tues-Fri 11am-7pm; reservations accepted; BYO (corkage £1/bottle)

The Thai Garden

Thai

☎ 020 7981 5748
249 Globe Rd E2

Map 18 C5
Tube: Bethnal Green

Smoking throughout

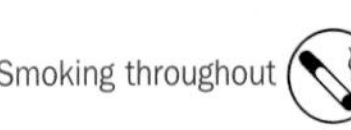

Box-sized from the outside and intimate within, the quaintly decorated Thai Garden attracts a relaxed and slightly bohemian clientele. Immediately, the kra tong thong curried vegetable starter (£4) rivals the ornate numbering on the door for delicate presentation. But as with the hed tord mushrooms (£4), the taste is not as fancy as the aesthetics. Do not be too hasty in your judgements, however, as the Thai chef and her English husband save the fullest flavours for the main courses. The preaw wahn (£4.50) with fried vegetables (including cucumbers – what will they think of next?) is satisfying in its slightly syrupy sweet and sour sauce. Alternatively, try the keaw wahn goong (£6), succulent prawns and fig-like Thai aubergines prepared in coconut milk and bathed in a rich green curry sauce. Waste not, want not as they say, and with such overflowing sauces we recommend at least one rice platter to soak it all up. With no MSG used in the cooking, you can do this with a clear conscience.

starter: £3.50-£5.50
main: £4.50-£6.95
dessert: £2.50
Set menu £12-£21
DC MC V

Open: Mon-Fri noon-3pm, Mon-Sun 6pm-10.45pm; reservations accepted (reservations advisable Thurs-Sat); licensed

291

Modern European

☎ 020 7613 5675
291 Hackney Rd E2

291 is in a converted church off Hackney Rd. The nave hosts modern art shows and off the lobby is a bustling bar filled with loud jazz and locals drinking cappuccino and reading the Sunday newspapers. The small restaurant is tucked upstairs in a dormered space that feels like a chapel or meeting room. Starters include a tangy borscht (£4.25) laced with vodka, traditional Ukrainian potato cake and a filling toasted brioche with chorizo and bacon (£4.95). The salmon (£11.25) seems a bit overwrought, presented with a 'quenelle of tagliatelle verde and finely latticed vegetables' topped with caviar Romanov. The braised duck leg bourguignon (£10.95) is a creative take on the classic, served with cranberries and shallots. Round things off with the deliciously rich white and dark chocolate pistachio mousse. Lunch is a good deal at £12.50 for two courses and £16.50 for three. The staff had a few kinks to iron out when we were there, but they cheerfully dealt with the glitches.

Open: Mon-Wed 6pm-midnight, Thurs & Fri 5pm-2am, Sat 10am-2am, Sun 10am-6pm; reservations advisable; licensed

Map 18 C3

Tube: Bethnal Green or Liverpool St, then bus 48

Wheelchair access

Entertainment: Fri & Sat night live music and DJ, Sun 1pm-5pm live jazz

 Smoking throughout

 Garden tables

starter: £4-£5
main: £8-£12
dessert: £4

DC MC V; SW

Map 17 B5
Tube: Shoreditch

Brick Lane Beigel Bakery

Jewish

☎ **020 7729 0616**
159 Brick Lane E1

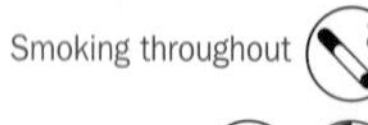
Smoking throughout

Down the other end of Brick Lane, away from the curry houses that lure most to this area, sits the Brick Lane Beigel Bakery, an East End landmark. You'll spot the queue of eager bagel-biters from a distance – it stretches out into the street at most times. But don't worry, service at this takeaway is lightning quick and anyway, when you're paying 95p for a delicious (albeit diminutive) smoked salmon and cream cheese bagel, and 12p for plain ones, you can't whinge. While you're there, stock up on the excellent long-lasting bread – the rye (40p for a small loaf) is divine toasted with cheese. You can gobble down a five-minute meal here if you want, or try the brownie-like chocolate cake (50p) with thick, crunchy icing, but there's no seating, just a bar along one wall. A rare treat for Londoners, this place is open round-the-clock. We only wish our appetite for late-night munchies could be sated as easily as it is for the lucky residents of Spitalfields.

starter: 12p-£1
main: 60p-£2.10
dessert: 50p-85p
cash only

Open: daily 24 hours; reservations not accepted; unlicensed

Brick Lane Beigel Bakery

Fancy a Curry?

London's favourite dish is not a banger or a burger or even a kebab – it's chicken tikka masala, the ubiquitous 'Indian' dish that has only recently begun appearing on menus back in India.

It all began in the mid-1960s when the sauce-happy Brits demanded that their chicken tikka should come swimming in sauce, rather than being presented simply as grilled bits of chicken. No one can say definitively which Indian cook should take credit for the innovation, but the addition of curry-spiced cream of tomato soup (Heinz was the popular choice as a base) resulted in the creation of chicken tikka masala.

The rest, as they say, is history. During the 1970s curry houses spread from London to the Midlands as thousands were opened. Today, chicken tikka masala routinely ranks as the most popular dish among Brits. No one knows how much is consumed in London every day, but one company that makes ready meals for London's supermarkets produces 10 tonnes of the reddish concoction daily.

Ryan Ver Berkmoes

Le Taj
Bangladeshi/Indian

☎ 020 7247 4210
134 Brick Lane E1

Map 17 C5
Tube: Aldgate East

Smoking throughout

Everything associated with Brick Lane venues – good-value meals and packed tables – holds true for Le Taj. Yet with its understated décor and gentle lighting, this is Brick Lane with a softer, more subtle focus that extends to the food. The balti murgh jalfrezi (£3.95) is a pleasantly piquant dish which has a chilli warning on the menu, despite being relatively cool. Meals without chilli warnings such as the chingri arr mushrooms (£3.75) are mild to the point of meekness, but this is all part of the delicate approach. The aloo chat (£1.85), potato slices in a spicy sauce, has more zip to it, while the shami lamb kebab (£1.85) whets the appetite without spoiling it. Subtle surroundings and cuisine notwithstanding, the overbearing service gives little respite. However, this is unlikely to mar a discreetly satisfying meal.

Open: daily noon-2.30pm, 5.30pm-midnight; reservations accepted (except Friday); BYO (no corkage)

starter: £1.60-£3.60
main: £3.20-£8.50
Set menu £7.50

AE MC V; SW

Map 17 C4
Tube: Liverpool St

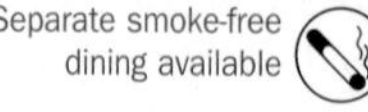
Separate smoke-free dining available

Terrace tables

Arkansas Café

American BBQ

☎ 020 7377 6999
Unit 12, Old Spitalfields Market (107B Commercial St) E1

The test of any cuisine served far from its origins is whether locals with the same roots will eat it. Thus the number of barbecue-sauce-smeared American expats chowing down at Arkansas Café is really recommendation enough. Bubba Helberg has created an American barbecue outpost in the pigeon-filled wilds of Spitalfields Market which is better than you'll find in most cities back in the US. The menu is short and to the point: lots of meat grilled to perfection and slathered with his own-recipe barbecue sauce (another good sign since no self-respecting barbecue chef would ever use anyone else's recipe). The char-grilled US rib-eye steak (£12.25) was cooked right to the medium we'd requested. The beef burger (£3.95) is one of the best in London, especially with the optional – but think mandatory – cheddar cheese (50p). However, Bubba really delivers with his classic BBQ platter of ribs, chicken and sausage (£10.50). With the addition of a little sunshine, you could almost think you're in the American south.

main: £3.40-£12.25
dessert: £2.25
MC V; SW

Open: Mon-Fri noon-2.30pm, Sun noon-4pm; reservations advisable; licensed

---

Map 17 E3
Tube: Bank
Wheelchair access
Dress code: collared shirt

Smoking throughout

Caravaggio

Italian

☎ 020 7626 6206
107-112 Leadenhall St EC3

Caravaggio is a cleverly designed split-level venue that captures the available natural light to transform yet another of the City's former banks into a bright and spacious restaurant. Lunchtimes are always busy, overloading the kitchen and making service a little slow, so be prepared to wait. The starter of sea scallops with beetroot and herb mayonnaise (£8.50) was well worth waiting for, as was the sfoglia calda ai funghi (£7.80), a warm puff-pastry case filled with flavoursome wild mushrooms, asparagus and a rich cheese sauce. The roast fillet of pork (£14), served with spiced apples, celeriac and garlic spinach, was a little too pink, and sent back to the kitchen; it swiftly returned, cooked through and tender. Make a date with Caravaggio in the evening, when City restaurants are generally quiet.

starter: £6-£9
main: £12.50-£17.50
dessert: £5.50
Set dinner £23.50 or £28
AE DC JCB MC V; SW

Open: Mon-Fri 11.45am-3pm, 6.30pm-10pm; reservations advisable; licensed

City Rhodes

Modern British

☎ **020 7583 1313**
1 New Street Square EC4

Map 17 D1
Tube: Blackfriars or Chancery Lane

 Smoking throughout (no pipes or cigars)

Gary Rhodes and the excellent reputation of modern British cooking are inseparable. Indeed, this spikey-haired TV celebrity chef has brought flair and imagination to traditional English fare, making it light, delicate and sophisticated. Our pressed tomato cake with peppered goat's cheese (£8.50) was a perfect combination, accompanied by a crisp Alsatian Pinot blanc (bottle £25, glass £5). The roast loin of lamb on a bed of leeks with caramelised onion gravy of lingering sweetness (£24) epitomised Gary's concept of modern comfort food. The spacious, minimalist dining room, in soothing shades of grey with gentle mauve lighting, provided the perfect backdrop for such dazzling culinary creations. Sadly, we were too full to try the famous Rhodes bread and butter pudding (£7.50), although we did manage to squeeze in several delectable baby chocolate sponge cakes with coffee (£2.50). Be prepared for an unconventional menu (great for fans of foie gras, veal, pig) and exorbitantly priced vegetables (£3 a portion), but otherwise an undeniably impressive dining experience.

Open: Mon-Fri noon-2.30pm, 6pm-9pm; reservations advisable (especially lunchtime); licensed

starter: £7.50-£16.80
main: £16-£24
dessert: £7.50
AE DC JCB MC V; SW

Futures

Modern British vegetarian

☎ **020 7638 6341**
2 Exchange Square EC2

Map 17 C3
Tube/rail: Liverpool Street
Wheelchair access

 No smoking 11.30am-3pm

 Terrace tables

This all-glass structure in the ultra-modern confines of Exchange Square hosts a crowd of fast-forking suits and a small army of brusquely efficient serving staff. The big surprise is that Futures is all vegetarian – and in an area where half a roast pig and a glass of port is still the normal lunchtime fare, this is futuristic indeed. You won't find cutting-edge vegetarian cuisine here, but it's unquestionably fresh and fast – we were in and out in 40 minutes. The short, sharp menu majors on simple classics – baby corn, carrots and sugar snaps with a tangy champagne and coconut sauce (£7.35) was simple and delightful, though the creamy risotto (also £7.35) was disappointingly bland. Futures is just the job for a swift business lunch or first thing in the morning, when there are fresh juices and pastries or a full breakfast (£5.20); in the evenings it transforms into a bar.

Open: Mon-Fri 7.30am-10pm (breakfast 7.30am-10.30am); reservations advisable; licensed

starter: £3.20-£4.95
main: £5.20-£7.35
dessert: £3.90
Set menu £8-£10.50
AE JCB MC V; SW

L'abat Jour
Italian

☎ **020 7588 5489**
14 City Rd EC1

Map 17 C2
Tube: Moorgate

Smoking throughout

Pavement tables

Although L'abat Jour is a French name, the proprietor Joseph Verona is from Madrid and the cuisine is Italian. This large, rustic-style restaurant has an extremely friendly atmosphere, so often missing from City restaurants, and the food is traditional Italian, not new wave designer. The meatballs and spaghetti (£6.50) merged tender meat with 'al dente' spaghetti smothered in a rich meat and tomato sauce. The excellent-quality grilled rib-eye (£9.95) oozed flavour and side orders of new potatoes and deep-fried crispy mushrooms (both £3.75) were bounteous enough for two. Desserts chosen from the trolley (£3.50) include the obligatory tiramisù and Italian chocolate ice cream with chocolate chips and thick, creamy caramel sauce. For faster lunchtime service, there's a small brasserie section with a cheaper choice of pastas, steaks and salads.

starter: £3.50-£6.50
main: £6.50-£14.50
dessert: £3.50-£3.75
AE DC JCB MC V; SW

Open: Mon-Fri noon-3pm; reservations accepted; licensed

Mesón Los Barriles
Spanish

☎ **020 7375 3136**
8a Lamb St,
Spitalfields Market E1

Map 17 C4
Tube: Liverpool St

Smoking throughout
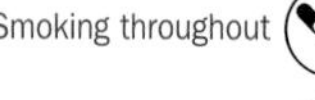
Conservatory tables

This lively Spanish tapas bar/restaurant in Spitalfields Market is one of just a few places to welcome night-time diners around Liverpool St. Spanish food often tastes of little more than garlic, salt and olive oil, and Los Barriles doesn't often stray from that trinity; its albóndigas* (£3.90), tortilla española (£3.20) and champiñones al ajillo (mushrooms with garlic, £3.90) taste the same as they do in Spanish restaurants from Segovia to Seattle. But it does offer a wide choice of fresh fish and other seafood – gambas a la plancha (£6.90), a delightfully light swordfish (£12.50), almejas* a la marinara (£6.90) and so on. Overall it's a satisfying feed and the all-Spanish staff are charming and helpful – though the dishes do come fast and furious. Avoid Friday night as the restaurant is closed on Saturday (and there's nothing more tired than food at a restaurant on the eve of closing day).

starter: £2-£4.90
main: £5-£17.50
dessert: £2.80-£4
AE JCB MC V; SW

Open: Mon-Fri 11am-11pm, Sun noon-4pm; reservations advisable (not accepted 1pm-6pm); licensed

Moshi Moshi Sushi

Japanese

☎ 020 7247 3227
Unit 24, Upper level, Liverpool St Station EC2

Map 17 C3
Tube/rail: Liverpool St

Hurrying home to Essex? Need to discuss City business while grabbing a quick lunchtime bite? Then head to the upper level of Liverpool St Station and into glass-encased Moshi Moshi Sushi. Choose from a seat at London's first kaiten or a table overlooking the train platforms. It's easy to order: just hook a plate you like the look of from the conveyor belt – the price depends on the plate's decoration (£1.20 to £2.90) – stack 'em up, and when you leave the staff will count them and present you with the bill. All the usual suspects are there, including cucumber maki (£1.20), prawn nigiri sushi (£2) and tuna sashimi (£2.50), plus a few unusual ones too, such as rice ball desserts (£2.50). There's a cover charge (50p) but no service charge and tips aren't allowed. Check out the inside information on eating techniques subtly stuck around the counter. If you've ever wanted to try this style of cuisine, this is the place to start. Perfect dining for one person or for many.

Open: Mon-Fri 11.30am-9pm; reservations not accepted; licensed

main: £1.20-£2.90
dessert: £2.50
Set menu £4.90-£11.50
(£8 min) MC V; SW

The Place Below

Modern British vegetarian

☎ 020 7329 0789
St Mary le Bow Church, Cheapside EC2

Map 17 E1
Tube: Bank or St Paul's

 Courtyard tables

The Place Below is housed in a Norman crypt underneath the St Mary le Bow Church. Appropriately, kitchen staff in white frocks serve up their offerings from an altar-sized display bench, while true believers in their wholesome vegetarian fare eagerly queue for their daily fix. The menu changes daily but follows a reliable formula: there's generally an imaginative soup (£2.70) – try the tomato, saffron and almond – a hot dish (£6.50), perhaps an aubergine and almond filo pie, or pasta with broccoli and plum tomatoes in pesto cream sauce, or a three mushroom casserole with haricot beans, tomato and basmati rice. The other standards are a freshly made quiche (£6), a salad that's a meal in itself (£7) and some truly yummy desserts (£3) – maybe a pear and pecan tart and fresh fruit salad. A raspberry and banana smoothie is recommended, and coffee lovers will love the do-it-yourself coffee maker, which grinds fresh beans each time you refill your unlimited cup.

Open: Mon-Fri 7.30am-2.30pm; reservations not accepted; unlicensed

starter: £2.70
main: £6-£7
dessert: £1.10-£3
MC V; SW

Map 17 E3
Tube: Bank
Wheelchair access
Smoking throughout

Prism

Modern British

☎ 020 7256 3888
147 Leadenhall St EC3

Prism, in the heart of London's financial district, seems to have been created for those looking to close a deal but who don't want to be distracted by overly creative food. Housed in a former Bank of New York building, the restaurant's stark marble interior reflects the serious business that's conducted at most of the tables. The restaurant clearly caters to the City crowd, offering an extensive 14-page wine list complete with index, a selection of post-dinner cigars, and attentive service. Prices are high, with starters beginning at £6.50 for serviceable sweet potato soup. Fish dishes feature heavily in the main course selections. The halibut chunk with Lyonnaise potatoes and béarnaise sauce (£15.50) and sea bass with fennel and rocket purée (£16) are both good, but not necessarily memorable. Prism is an excellent choice for those with an excellent expense account.

starter: £6.50-£14
main: £10-£16.50
dessert: £6-£7
AE DC MC V; SW

Open: Mon-Fri 11.30am-3pm, 6pm-10pm; reservations esssential; licensed

Map 17 E6
Tube: Tower Hill
Wheelchair access
Smoking throughout
Terrace tables

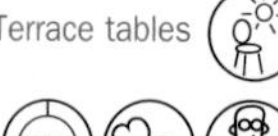

Quayside

Modern British

☎ 020 7481 0972
World Trade Centre,
1 St Katharine's Way E1

Set alongside the marina, adjacent to Tower Bridge and the Tower of London, the Quayside restaurant attracts smarter-dressed tourists and business suits. At night the lights from the yachts and barges moored alongside the restaurant's terrace are reminders of that last holiday in the Med. This is not exactly a buzzy restaurant, but it's certainly romantic. The menu is eclectic, with a choice from modern European and Pacific Rim dishes, as well as some old English standbys. Catfish, lobster, scallops and prawns made up the risotto of bouillabaisse with baby fennel (£5.25), but there wasn't exactly a full catch. The main course redeemed the situation with Blairmore Scottish fillet of beef (£16.95) accompanied with garlic purée and a beetroot sauce. The tarte tatin with coffee ice cream (£4.95) seemed an impossible proposal, but we were glad a persuasive and charming waiter melted our resistance. The Quayside is expensive, but the view alone makes it worthwhile.

starter: £3.95-£7.50
main: £10.95-£17.50
dessert: £4.95
AE DC JCB MC V; SW

Open: Mon-Sat noon-2.30pm, 6pm-11pm; reservations advisable; licensed

Singapura

South-East Asian

☎ 020 7329 1133
1-2 Limeburner Lane EC4

Singapura is a buzzy lunchtime favourite and a quieter dinner destination, close to St Paul's and Fleet St in an area not known for its modern restaurants. The traditional Indonesian outfits worn by the staff add authenticity to this large, comfortable and stylish South-East Asian restaurant. A complimentary dish of prawn crackers with spicy sauce is served as you peruse the difficult-to-choose-from dozen starters. Siput, a dish of stir-fried mussels with lemongrass, lime leaves, ginger and chilli in sherry sauce (£5.95), assaults the taste buds with flavours, and few Thai fishcakes (£5.75) offered in London are as good as these, served with spices and lime leaves. The itek sio, braised magret duck in soya sauce flavoured with galangal and star anise (£11), is a feature of the main courses, as is the ayam goreng, crispy chicken marinated in sesame oil and soy sauce (£7.50). With rice dishes at £3 and vegetables £4.95, Singapura is a little pricey but well worth the little extra.

Open: Mon-Fri 11.30am-10pm; reservations advisable (lunch); licensed

Map 17 D1
Tube: St Paul's
Wheechair access
Dress code: collared shirt

 Smoking throughout

starter: £3.95-£7.50
main: £7.50-£10.95
dessert: £4.50
Set menu £15.50, £18 or £22.50/person feast (min 2 people)
AE JCB MC V; SW

Suan Neo

South-East Asian

☎ 020 7256 5045
31 Broadgate Circle EC2

It's posh, closes early and is very expensive – an unusual trio in this city of cheap Thai nosheries above corner pubs – but Suan Neo extends beyond the borders of Thailand into Malaysia for laksa (£14.50) and to Singapore for fried noodles with prawns and choi sum (£9.50/£11.50). The décor is clean and fresh too – bleached wood floors, spring flowers on the table and ultra-comfortable chestnut-coloured leather chairs. We opted for the 'bouillabaisse', a flavourful but tame coconut broth studded with shellfish and monkfish (£16), a dry Laotian duck salad with herbs and roasted rice (£8.50) and a large dish of the Singapore noodles and overcooked okra in sambal sauce. As for the service, well, this is the City – the land of expensive lunches and liquid dinners. The staff seemed sorry to see us arrive (at 8.30pm) and happy when we left an hour later.

Open: Mon-Fri noon-3pm, 6pm-9.30pm; reservations essential (lunchtime); licensed

Map 17 C3
Tube: Liverpool St

 Smoking throughout

starter: £6-£8.50
main: £11.50-£18.50
dessert: £6
Set menu £25-£33/person (min 2 people), £35/person (min 4 people)
AE DC JCB MC V; SW

Sweetings

Fish

☎ 020 7248 3062
39 Queen Victoria St EC4

Map 17 E1
Tube: Mansion House
Smoking throughout

Step back a decade, or even a century or two, at this city fish house set in an 1880s fishmonger. Idiosyncrasies abound: seating is mostly on stools but the wine list is pretty serious. The menu looks pre-war but the service provided by the young staff is friendly and enthusiastic. There are no descriptions of the food and none are needed. Potted shrimps (£5) ooze butter, the smoked Scotch salmon (£8.50) is an excellent cut that almost melts in the mouth and prawn cocktail (£8.50) has just the right kick of horseradish. Dover sole (£19.50) is a nostalgic version of this once ubiquitous dish and grilled halibut (£17) is both moist and flaky. The mostly male clientele take boyish glee from desserts like spotted dick, jam rolls and bread pudding (all £3). One quibble is the number of cigar smokers – select your seat with caution so you don't choke. And try to arrive before the 1pm rush.

starter: £4.50-£12.50
main: £8-£21
dessert: £3
cash or cheque only

Open: Mon-Fri 11.30am-3pm; reservations not accepted; licensed

Tatsuso

Japanese

☎ 020 7638 5863
32 Broadgate Circle EC2

Map 17 C3
Tube/rail: Liverpool St
Dress code: collared shirt
Certified organic
Smoking throughout

A favourite with the business crowd, Tatsuso offers expensive but high-quality versions of two very different kinds of Japanese cuisine. Upstairs it's teppanyaki, the chefs staging cookery performances as they fry up beef, lobster and the like on steel griddles inches from diners' plates. Downstairs there's the less theatrical traditional dining room, where kimono-robed waitresses proffer warm, scented hot towels and cups of green tea. It's possible to sit at the counter watching the sushi chefs, but if you have a small party, go the whole hog and book one of the private tatami mat rooms and enjoy your meal in appropriate surroundings. The Tekago set lunch (£38) includes fine sashimi and tempura, plus seven other dishes, but the highlights were the melt-in-the-mouth deep-fried fig appetiser and the savoury egg custard – as good as we've ever had. Note that there's an added service charge of 13%.

starter: £3.50-£9.80
main: £15-£35
Set lunch £28-£43
or £41-£80
AE DC JCB MC V; SW

Open: Mon-Fri 11.30am-2.30pm, 6pm-9.45pm; reservations advisable; licensed

Faulkner's
Fish

☎ 020 7249 5661
424-426 Kingsland Rd E8

Map 18 A2
Rail: Dalston Kingsland

Nonsmoking tables available

Faulkner's has built up a reputation over many years as a good-quality fish and chip shop. The restaurant has a simple layout of two connecting dining rooms with creamy-coloured walls and the ubiquitous fish tank. Even on particularly busy evenings, the service is swift and friendly. The starters are not overly exciting but our prawn cocktail (£3.25) had stacks of fresh, plump prawns on crispy lettuce with creamy mayonnaise. Our plaice fillet (£7.25) was huge and perfectly fried, with a thin, light crispy batter and not a single bone. The haddock (£7.75) was equally good, with moist, flaky flesh. All main dishes have golden fries included in the price, but try the side orders of coleslaw (95p) and sweet and sour gherkin (70p) which are big enough to share. Children are welcome at Faulkner's, and they have their own menu: a choice of scampi, chicken nuggets or a small piece of cod, all with chips, a soft drink and ice cream (£3.25).

Open: Mon-Fri noon-2pm, 5pm-10pm, Sat noon-10pm, Sun noon-9pm; reservations not accepted; licensed

starter: £1.20-£3.95
main: £3.95-£12.50
dessert: £1.50-£2.50
MC V; SW

Mangal
Turkish

☎ 020 7275 8981
10 Arcola St E8

Map 18 A5
Rail: Dalston Kingsland

Smoking throughout

This hole-in-the-wall restaurant in less-than-salubrious Dalston has been preparing the same dishes year in, year out for aeons, and it continues to draw in the crowds. And why not? Using the freshest ingredients, the tong-wielding cook turns out superb charcoal-grilled lamb and chicken kebabs, from adana and doner to shish (£6), perfectly grilled lamb chops and plump little quails that retain a wonderful smoky flavour. Salads (£2.50-£3) are generous; we particularly like the tomato salad chopped so finely it resembles steak tartare. Mangal is BYO (an off-licence is conveniently located round the corner) though nonalcoholic drinks include a delicious yoghurt-based drink called ayran and mint tea, poured from great heights by the friendly waiter. For dessert there's baklava (£2) and other sweeter-than-sweet honey and nut concoctions. Best of all, you'll see change from a tenner.

Open: daily noon-midnight; reservations accepted; BYO (no corkage)

starter: £2.50-£4
main: £4-£8.50
dessert: £2
cash only

HAGGERSTON

Little Georgia

Georgian/Russian

☎ 020 7249 9070
2 Broadway Market E8

Map 18 B3
Tube: Bethnal Green
Entertainment: occasional pianist
Smoking throughout
Pavement tables

Set in a spacious room with windows on two sides, wooden floors and Georgian folk costumes on the walls, Little Georgia is immediately inviting. And the restaurant's appeal increases as the food starts to arrive. Unable to choose from the wide selection of starters, we opted for the mixed vegetarian meze (£12.50). We used bread to scoop up fresh-flavoured pastes made of various combinations of crushed walnuts, herbs and spices with leek, beetroot, spinach and aubergine. Part of the pleasure of eating here is the novelty of almost everything on the menu. We continued with satsivi chicken (£8.50), in a strongly flavoured garlic and walnut sauce, and chakinzuli (£8.50), an aromatic lamb stew prepared with abundant fresh coriander. With eight Georgian wines to choose from – at around £12 a bottle – it seemed churlish to drink anything else. We quaffed balanchine, higher in alcohol content than most European wines but eminently drinkable. The service was charming and relaxed yet we were never kept waiting.

starter: £3.80-£4
main: £7.50-£9
dessert: £2.50
MC V; SW

Open: Tues-Sat 6.30pm-midnight, Sun 1pm-4pm; reservations advisable (especially weekends); licensed

Mesón Los Barriles (p 206)

The Furnace

Mediterranean

☎ **020 7613 0598**
1 Rufus St N1

Map 17 A3
Tube: Old Street

 Smoking throughout

Furnace, a new venture off Hoxton Square, plans to expand into a small London chain, and with a bit of luck the formula will be successful. Minimalist Mediterranean cuisine is delivered with aplomb by the disarmingly professional, mostly Italian staff. A stark décor is softened by dim designer lighting, and both the tableware and the toilets have stimulating ergonomics. A well-chosen wine list adds further appeal. We think the pizza is the safest bet on the menu; that's fortunate, as it constitutes the lion's share of what's on offer here. Ours was a delectable carciofini* con pancetta (£6.75) with a perfect base. The vegetarian pasta (£6.75) wasn't too inspiring but pasta dishes change daily, so something more interesting is bound to come along. Starters (both £4.55) were more consistent: succulent, fresh slices of pork for the antipasto prosciutto e salame, and impressively delicate flavouring in the mozzarella di bufala. The delizie (£3.60), an unmissable sponge cake full of rich contrasting textures and temptingly elusive scents of almond and cream, is an absolutely lovely dish.

Open: Mon-Fri noon-3pm, 6pm-11pm, Sat 6pm-11pm; reservations accepted; licensed

starter: £2.50-£5.50
main: £5.50-£8.50
dessert: £3.60-£3.80
MC V; SW

Great Eastern Dining Room

Modern Italian

☎ **020 7613 4545**
54-56 Great Eastern St EC2

Map 17 B3
Tube: Old Street

 Smoking throughout

Sinking into a squishy brown sofa with a glass of wine at the Great Eastern Dining Room is a just reward after a hard day at the office. The staff are as trendy as the punters but the atmosphere is easy and relaxed. The dining room is nicely lit and the dark brown wooden walls give the room an ocean-liner air. Bread sticks and olive oil start the proceedings, soaked up by some very good house red (£9.50). The linguine primavera (£7.50) tastes fresh but definitely needs a good flirt with the seasonings. The roast halibut is crowned with a zealous tapenade and pesto sauce (£10), making it altogether a better choice than the whole grilled seabream cooked in lemon and fennel (£10) – although a generous-sized fish, the dish needs a bit more lemon and fennel to warrant its title. A unanimous decision voted the olive mash (£2.50) comfort-food king.

Open: Mon-Fri noon-3pm, Mon-Sat 6.30pm-11pm; reservations advisable; licensed

starter: £4.50-£7.50
main: £8-£10
dessert: £4.50-£5.50
AE DC JCB MC V; SW

Map 17 B3
Tube: Old Street

Smoking throughout

Home
Modern British

☎ 020 7684 8618
100-106 Leonard St EC2

Home has been a Shoreditch hideaway for a while now, but the dining experience has been greatly improved with the opening of the bright, airy storefront restaurant upstairs. The funky basement bar with its ripped sofas is still there, but now diners no longer have to huddle behind a curtain in the corner. Instead, they can relax in colourful leather chairs in front of giant windows. The food is reliable and leans toward gastropub. Start with courgette and chilli fritters with guacamole (£4.50) at lunch or a goat's cheese and onion tart (£5.50) in the evening. Pappardelle with field mushrooms, sweet shallots and sage (£8) and the char-grilled yellow fin tuna (£13) for dinner are both well done with colourful presentations. Desserts vary, but Neal's Yard cheese is always on offer (£4). Hopefully the expanded upstairs will prevent an experience like ours, when we were hustled from our table without prior warning.

starter: £3-£7
main: £7-£14
dessert: £4
AE MC V; SW

Open: Mon-Sat noon-3pm, 7pm-11pm; reservations advisable (especially weekends); licensed

Map 18 C2
Tube/rail: Old Street

Smoking throughout

Loong Kee
Vietnamese

☎ 020 7729 8344
134g Kingsland Rd E2

It's a much smaller and entirely more modest affair than the better-known Viet Hoa just a few doors down the road, but if it's authenticity you're after, the number of Vietnamese and South-East Asian faces among the satisfied diners has to be the ultimate recommendation. Dishes are a couple of pounds cheaper here, and are served up in a cosy room featuring plastic gingham tablecloths and a TV. Loong Kee's trump card has to be its steamed spring rolls with prawn or pork (£3 small or £5 large) – it claims to be the only place in London to grind its own rice to make the delicious pastry for these freshly steamed rolls. Other dishes from the extensive menu include a Vietnamese salad of finely shredded coriander, carrot and cabbage (£3.50), and pork cooked 10 different ways (£3.50-£4).

starter: £1.20-£3.50
main: £2-£7
dessert: £1.50-£2
cash or cheque only

Open: Wed-Mon noon-3pm, 5pm-10pm; reservations advisable; BYO (no corkage)

The Real Greek

Greek

☎ 020 7739 8212
15 Hoxton Market N1

Map 17 A3
Tube: Old Street

Smoking throughout

The name alone might lead diners to think they're in for the usual Greek-Cypriot fare. They're not. The restaurant's huge windows looking out over restored Hoxton Market reveal a simple yet elegant interior with a partially open kitchen at the side. Great openers include combinations such as mellow, barbecued squid paired with a lighter-than-air deep-fried fillet of salted cod on a bed of potato and garlic cream and roasted beets (£6.35). A bowl of warm lentils hinted of rosemary and came with a delicate anchovy pâté on warm bread. (Speaking of bread, there's not a pita in sight; rather, diners are offered a selection of hearty whole-grain breads throughout the meal.) Among the main courses – which cover various meats and seafoods – a tender, juicy lamb and spicy sausage combo served with cannellini beans was well balanced (£14.50). An ice-cream terrine (£4.90) for dessert set off a war of spoons around the table. Service was quick and cheery, and the staff were happy to explain the list of good but lesser-known Greek wines.

Open: Mon-Sat noon-3pm, 5.30pm-10.30pm; reservations essential; licensed & BYO (corkage £10/bottle)

starter: £6-£7
main: £14.50-£15
dessert: £5
Set lunch £10

AE MC V; SW

Viet Hoa Café

Vietnamese

☎ 020 7729 8293
70-72 Kingsland Rd E2

Map 17 A4
Tube: Old Street

Smoking throughout

Shoreditch may sit just a stone's throw away from the City, but Viet Hoa is a throwback to the time when the neighbourhood was all warehouses and massage parlours – the austere dining room has all the charm of a school canteen. The restaurant serves filling, honest fare with two courses totalling all of £10. A typical option is rice vermicelli and mini spring rolls with a choice of pork, chicken or prawns for an incredible £3.95. At this price, splashing out means choosing the 'drunken fish' (poached in white wine) for £6.50 or stir-fried seafood (£7). Those used to healthier cuisine are forewarned: the fried paper-wrapped prawns (£3.50) and spring rolls (£2.50) are dripping with oil. Vegetarians are offered a choice, as long as that choice is tofu (featured in at least nine starters). Viet Hoa remains one of the top budget choices in this part of town.

Open: Tues-Sun noon-3.30pm, 5.30pm-11pm; reservations accepted; licensed

starter: £2.50-£4.50
main: £3-£7
Set lunch £3.95

cash or SW

SPITALFIELDS

Map 17 C4
Tube: Liverpool St
Wheelchair access
Nonsmoking tables available

Bengal Trader
Indian

☎ 020 7375 0072
1 Parliament Court, 44 Artillery Lane E1

City high rollers escape to the Bengal Trader after a day's dealings, but this is more than just a wide-boy refuge. Those willing to pay that little extra will find a curry house with impeccably attentive service spiced with a seamlessly chic interior design. The savoury Goan mochmochay bindi (£2.95) is a crisp starter, but beware of stray chillis lurking among the okra. A mint yoghurt accompaniment offsets the slight dryness of the tandoori murgh momolee chicken tikka (£3.50), while the saag bhaji (£2.95) is a perfect side dish. The Chef's Specialities main courses provide the highlights. Although the loknai gosht (£7.50) lamb chunks were not as tender as hoped, the richly textured tomato and onion sauce lent this dish a vivid taste. Even more alluring is the creamily smooth chicken murgh hyderbadi (£9.50), deftly balanced by a lively cashew nut paste. Such finesse should not be the exclusive reserve of Square Mile suits.

starter: £2.95-£6.50
main: £4.95-£11.50
dessert: £2-£4
Bar menu £7.95 or £10.95
AE DC JCB MC V; SW

Open: Mon-Fri 11am-3pm, 6pm-midnight; reservations accepted; licensed

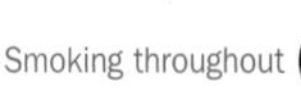

STOKE NEWINGTON

Map 18 A5
Rail: Stoke Newington, bus 73 Tube: Finsbury Park, bus 106
Wheelchair access
Smoking throughout

Bar Lorca
Spanish

☎ 020 7275 8659
175 Stoke Newington High St N16

Bar Lorca may look like a traditional pub, but it's actually an exciting, loud and lively Spanish bar and restaurant. There's some form of entertainment almost every night, from salsa classes to pure funk. While the bar is open all day for coffee, pastries, beers and cocktails (£7), the candlelit restaurant has an excellent tapas menu, closest to the real thing outside of Espa¤a. The tapas dishes may at first seem expensive, but portions are sizable and even the tortilla (£3.50) was more than enough for two. All the usual suspects are here: spicy chorizo (£3.70), moreish albondigas (£4.20), grilled spicy langostinos* (£5.50) and, at weekends, paella. Oh, and plenty of Spanish waiters.

starter: £2.50-£6.50
main:£5-£8
dessert: £2.50-£3.50
Set lunch £4.90 or set dinner £12.80-£16 (groups of 4 or more)
AE MC V; SW

Open: Mon-Thurs noon-1am, Fri & Sat noon-2am, Sun noon-midnight; reservations advisable; licensed

TOWER HILL

Café Spice Namaste
South Indian

☎ **020 7488 9242**
16 Prescot St E1

The cuisine served in this old courthouse building is Goan and Keralan, and both service and atmosphere are as bright as the 'carnival'-coloured walls. Check out the specials menu while nibbling on pappadams served with four types of chutney (60p per person). Favourite dishes include frango piri-piri (£7.75), a fiery-hot chicken tikka marinated in red masala, and the muglai maas (£10.25), lamb in a nut-based sauce. Vindaloo de porco (£9.75) is the real 'vindaloo' – made with pork, red masala, garlic and palm vinegar. Vegetarian side dishes (also available as main courses) include rajmah aur maa (£3.25/£6.50), a smoky-tasting bean dish, and bhindi (okra) cooked with fennel and cumin (£3.80/£6.25). The wine list is international, even offering several types of Indian vintages, but our drink of choice with Indian food is beer – either Kingfisher (£2.95) or Cobra (£4.25).

Open: Mon-Fri noon-3pm, 6.15pm-10.30pm, Sat 6.30pm-10pm; reservations advisable; licensed

Map 17 E5

Tube: Tower Hill, DLR: Tower Gateway

Smoking throughout

starter: £3.25-£7
main: £5.25-£14.50
dessert: £3-£3.50

AE DC MC V; SW

WHITECHAPEL

New Tayyab
Indian/Pakistani

☎ **020 7247 9543**
83 Fieldgate St E1

New Tayyab serves up some of the most authentic northern Indian and Pakistani food this side of the Punjab. Choose perfectly spiced sheekh kebabs (70p), lamb chops (£2.50 for four) or one of several rich karahi* dishes such as quail (£4) or chicken (£3.50), add a vegetable and one of several dhals, and you'll eat for less than £10. There are also nightly specials to choose from – lamb on a fluffy pilau (£3.50) or biryani. New Tayyab's main clientele is Muslim and the restaurant is strictly BYO; should you forget to bring a bottle, drown your sorrows in the wonderful lassi, which comes sweet, salty or flavoured with fresh mango or banana (£1.20-£2).

Open: daily 5pm-midnight; reservations not accepted; BYO (no corkage)

Map 17 D6

Tube: Whitechapel

Smoking throughout

Pavement tables

starter: 70p-£2
main: £2.50-£4
dessert: £2

cash only

Sweet Chilli

Thai

☎ 020 7702 7977
63-67 Mile End Rd E1

Map 17 C6
Tube: Whitechapel

Smoking throughout

The dado rails, yuka plants and origami do little to ornament this otherwise spartan eatery, and the triple-barred electric heaters reinforce Sweet Chilli's cafeteria air. If the ambience isn't to your liking, spice up your visit by trying the melt-in-the-mouth chicken (£5.50) with cashews, straw mushrooms and chillies that bite back. Alternatively, choose the old Thai standard kang phed dang (£6.50), an aromatic mélange of coconut, ginger and gentle spices in a red curry. Veto the unyielding noodles and request rice instead. Wash it all down with a Tiger beer, and enjoy the impeccable service. While not exactly a rare find, Sweet Chilli hits the spot.

starter: £3.95-£9.95
main: £5.50-£7.95
dessert: £2.50
Set menu £15-£20
AE JCB MC V

Open: Mon-Sat 6pm-11pm, Sun 6pm-10.30pm; reservations advisable; licensed

Bermondsey

Elephant & Castle

SOUTH-EAST

Greenwich

Kennington

London Bridge

South Bank

Southwark

Tower Bridge

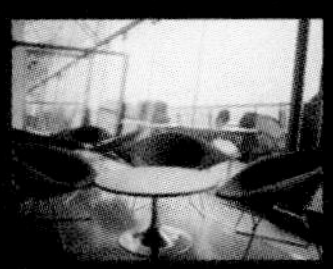

Waterloo

Map 20 - Southwark & Tower Bridge

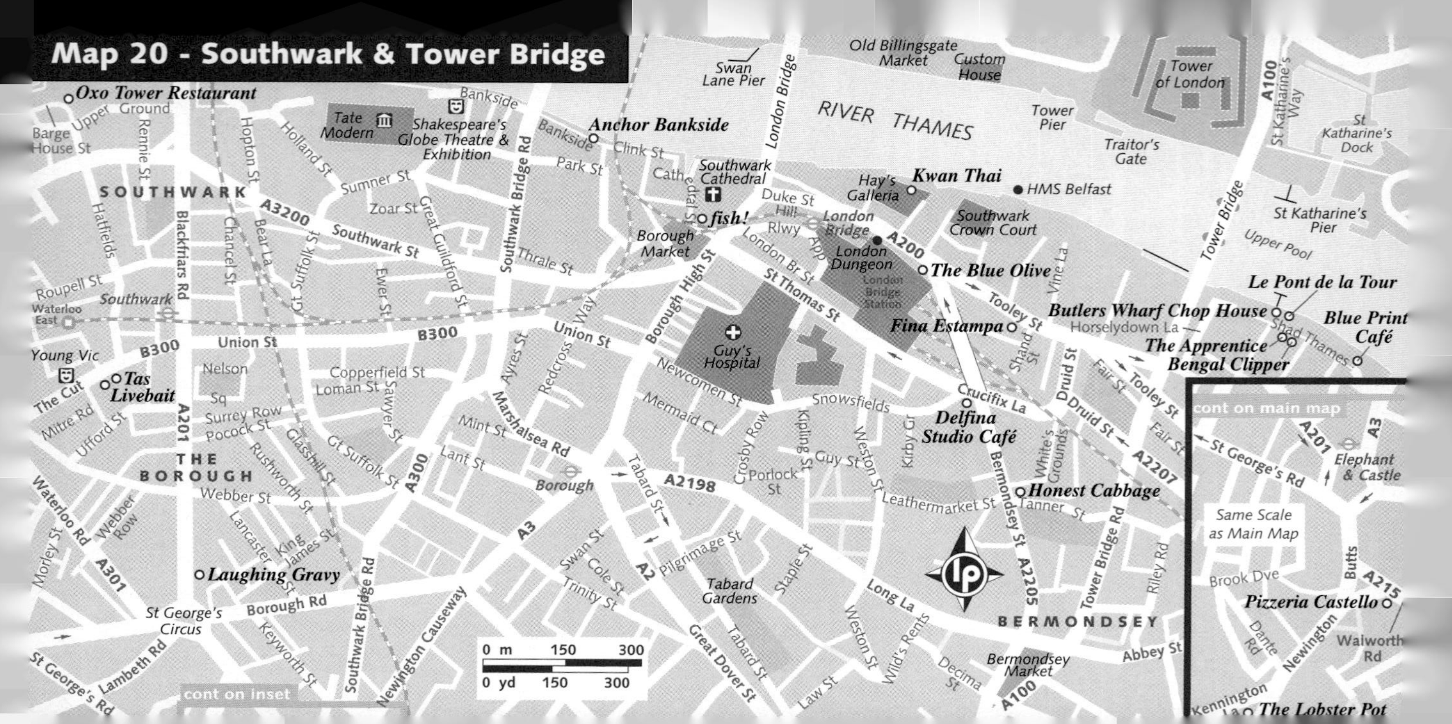

BAKERY · FOODSTORE · MERCHANT

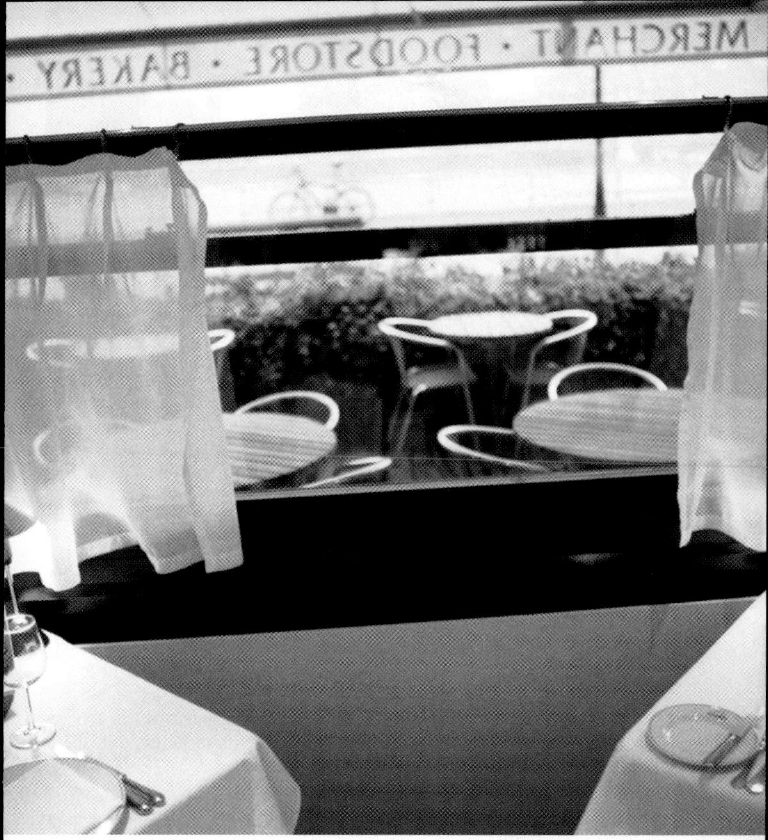

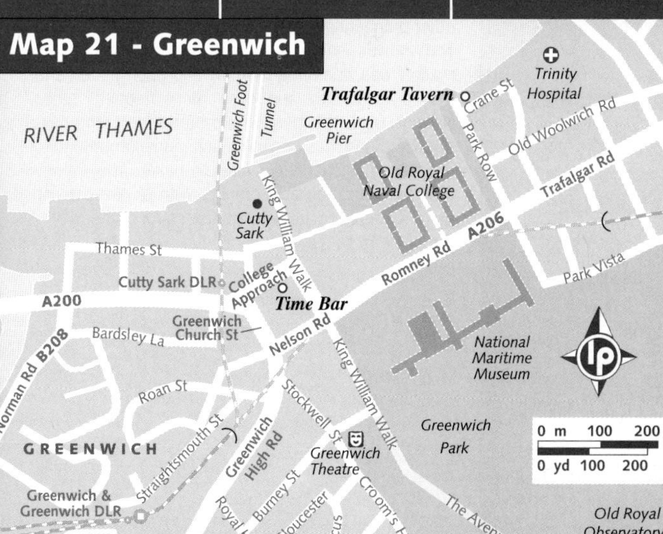

Map 21 - Greenwich
RIVER THAMES
Greenwich Foot Tunnel
Trafalgar Tavern
Greenwich Pier
Crane St
Trinity Hospital
Old Woolwich Rd
Park Row
Old Royal Naval College
Trafalgar Rd
King William Walk
Cutty Sark
A206
Thames St
Romney Rd
Park Vista
Cutty Sark DLR
College Approach
Time Bar
A200
Greenwich Church St
Bardsley La
Nelson Rd
King William Walk
National Maritime Museum
Norman Rd B208
Roan St
Stockwell St
Straightsmouth St
Greenwich High Rd
Greenwich Park
GREENWICH
Greenwich Theatre
0 m 100 200
0 yd 100 200
Burney St
Croom's Hill
Greenwich & Greenwich DLR
Royal Hill
Gloucester Circus
The Avenue
Old Royal Observatory
A206
A
B
1
2
3

BEST

- **Butlers Wharf Chop House**
  First-rate British with a view
- **Delfina Studio Café**
  A successful gallery/eatery combination
- **Tas**
  Tops for untraditional Turkish

Butlers Wharf Chop House (p 230)

South-East

Long derided by snooty Londoners living across the Thames, the gritty South Bank has been in the ascendant for years. Now with the new Tate Modern filling the cavernous Bankside Power Station and the seductive Millennium Bridge luring pedestrians right to the gallery's door, the South Bank has more than arrived, it's there. Its history as the roughest part of London is now part, not just of its character, but of its fascination.

Borough Market, under the train tracks just west of London Bridge Station and under 10 minutes by foot from the Tate, was home to a smattering of surviving vegetable traders when Neal's Yard Dairy decided to organise thrice-yearly sales of their cheese, as well as other pioneering British purveyors of organic produce. The crowds came and soon the speciality foods market was operating monthly and shortly thereafter moved to weekly and even more frequent sales. Nearby, fish!, the trendy home for simple and ultra-fresh seafood, has opened a fish market and Konditor & Cook, the legendary Waterloo bakers, have come east to open their first branch. With all the development, Londoners are finding that 'south of the river' is the place to be.

Delfina Studio Café

Modern European

☎ 020 7357 0244
50 Bermondsey St SE1

Map 20 B4
Tube/rail: London Bridge

 Smoking throughout

The Delfina Studio Café showcases both art and the art of food. The restaurant, housed in a converted chocolate factory, displays works by members of its charitable trust, and the same lucky artists can lunch at Delfina for £1. But it is the food that takes centre stage. Our cauliflower soup sprinkled with pecorino, parsley and pine nuts (£3.75) was creamy and warm, with just the right hint of cheese, and the juicy slow-roasted shank of lamb rubbed with tarragon and mustard (£13.25) fell off the bone. The chocolate tart with cardamom ice cream (£4.25) was sublime, the crisp pastry filled with smooth chocolate. It's such a shame that Delfina is only open for lunch on weekdays, as the restaurant is hired for private parties for the balance of the time.

Open: Mon-Fri 10am-5pm (lunch noon-3pm); reservations advisable; licensed

starter: £3.75-£5.75
main: £9.95-£13.95
dessert: £4.25

AE DC JCB MC V; SW

Honest Cabbage

Modern British

☎ 020 7234 0080
99 Bermondsey St SE1

Map 20 B4
Tube/rail: London Bridge
Wheelchair access

 Smoking throughout

 Pavement tables

True to its name, the Honest Cabbage serves up good, honest food. The portions are generous, the ingredients are fresh and the atmosphere is Bohemian. The menu, which changes daily, is posted on a series of blackboards on the restaurant's main wall. With a choice of 10 main dishes, you're bound to find something that appeals. Our choices ranged from carrot and wild rice soup (£3) to pan-fried monkfish with star anise and sweet chilli (£12). The pasta for the day, spinach and ricotta ravioli with a wild mushroom cream sauce (£4 small, £7 large), was fresh and delightful; the fresh meat offering of ostrich sausages in red wine jus (£9) was inventive and interesting. The restaurant is just a few blocks from London's legendary Bermondsey flea market, and those lucky enough to stumble upon it will feel they have found a treasure indeed.

Open: Mon-Fri noon-3pm, Sat & Sun noon-4pm, Mon-Wed 6.30pm-10pm, Thurs-Sat 6.30pm-11pm; reservations advisable; licensed

starter: £3-£4
main: £5-£12
dessert: £4

DC MC V; SW

SOUTH-EAST

Pizzeria Castello

Italian

☎ **020 7703 2556**
20 Walworth Rd SE1

Map 20 C5
Tube/rail: Elephant & Castle
Wheelchair access

Smoking throughout

Pizzeria Castello is where South Londoners come to eat thick, crusty, filling pizzas in a relaxed but lively atmosphere. There are pasta dishes, and meat or shellfish 'house specials' too, but it's the 23 different pizzas which ensure packed tables every night. Choices range from alla Genovese (grilled courgettes, pepper, aubergine, mozzarella and pesto, £5.80) to alla rucola (rocket salad, dolcelatte cheese and parma ham, £6.50) to the gooey but gorgeous quattro formaggi (mozzarella, gruyère, cheddar and fontina, £4.90). There's also an extensive range of Italian wine, which are cheaper here than elsewhere in London. Because it is such good value and so welcoming, Pizzeria Castello attracts a varied crowd, from families and groups of friends to couples on a date. The only drawback is the warren of unsavoury underpasses you have to negotiate on foot in order to get here.

starter: £2.50-£3.60
main: £4.20-£9.20
dessert: £2.80
AE DC MC V; SW

Open: Mon-Thurs noon-11pm, Fri noon-11.30pm, Sat 5pm-11.30pm; reservations advisable; licensed

Oxo Tower Restaurant (p 227)

GREENWICH

Time Bar Gallery Restaurant
Modern European

☎ 020 8305 9767
7a College Approach SE10

Housed in an old music hall (circa 1831), this light and spacious bar/restaurant displays a stylish mix of original features along with modern furniture and artwork. Bringing a welcome West End buzz to Greenwich, it's a great drinking hang-out – but climb the stairs to the mezzanine restaurant and you won't be disappointed. The delicious array of starters includes deep-fried, poached duck egg with herb salad (£5.95) and roasted pumpkin and leek soup (£4.50). The tempting main courses feature perfectly cooked char-grilled calf's liver and pancetta with mustard mash (£12.95) and a roast cod with wild mushroom tagliatelle and salsa verde (£13.95). The desserts vary from a fairly standard selection of English farmhouse cheeses with chutney to the more off-beat beignet* of cracked black pepper ice cream with raspberry coulis. Go easy on the drinks though – it's a long trek down three staircases to the basement toilets.

Open: Mon-Sat noon-3pm, Sun noon-6pm, daily 7pm-midnight; reservations advisable (especially weekends); licensed

Map 21 A2

Rail: Greenwich, DLR: Cutty Sark

Entertainment: jazz Tues, Wed & Sun evenings, DJ's Fri & Sat evenings

Smoking throughout

starter: £4.50-£8.50
main: £12.50-£16.95
dessert: £4.50-£5.50
Set lunch £14.50 & £18.50 or set dinner £18.50 &S £23.50

AE MC V; SW

KENNINGTON

The Lobster Pot
French/seafood

☎ 020 7582 5556
3 Kennington Lane, (cnr Kennington Park Rd) SE11

Why did French owner/chef Hervé choose a bleak junction in South London for his nautically themed restaurant? Perhaps the grim surroundings account for the effort he has put into creating such a charming interior. The wood-panelled room looks like the cabin of a small boat, complete with fishing nets hanging from the ceilings and portholes that open on to fish-filled aquaria. With the slow but attentive waiters dressed in snug matelot tops, the maritime theme veers towards high camp. From the seafood-dominated menu we tried the marinated salmon (£7.50), grilled garlic prawns (£8.50) and bouillabaisse (£16.50) – all well prepared with strong, clear flavours. But don't expect any exciting twists – the accent is firmly on the hearty and traditional. Desserts – try a crêpe filled with crème brûlée (£4.50) – are exquisite. Save the Lobster Pot for an evening when you have time to linger.

Open: Tues-Sat noon-2.30pm, 7pm-11pm; reservations essential; licensed

Map 20 C5

Tube: Kennington

Smoking throughout

starter: £6.50-£26.50
main: £16.50-£25.50
dessert: £4.50-£6.50
Special lunch menu £15.50 or menu gastronomique £22.50

AE DC JCB MC V; SW

Map 20 B4
Tube/rail: London Bridge
Smoking throughout

The Blue Olive

Italian

☎ 020 7407 6001
56-58 Tooley St SE1

With the downstairs bar creating the ideal background murmur and a myriad of small lights creating a relaxing mood, the 'New York Italian' Blue Olive makes the most of its spacious, open-plan setting. To the sound of sweet soul music, we deliberated over the tempting à la carte menu but eventually chose the good-value, three-course set meal. Swordfish gave an unusual but very tasty twist to the fresh tomato bruschetta to start and was followed with a well-braised shoulder of lamb. Accompanied by a creamy parmesan mash and a red wine jus, it was filling and perhaps slightly too rich, but it worked. Last up was a huge bowl of great chocolate ice cream. Not the best place for calorie counters perhaps, but a little of what you like does you good, and this we definitely liked.

starter: £3.95-£6.75
main: £9.95-£13.25
dessert: £4.50
Set menu £10 or £12.50
AE DC JCB MC V; SW

Open: Mon-Fri noon-3pm, Mon-Sat 6pm-11.45pm; reservations advisable; licensed

---

Map 20 B4
Tube: London Bridge
Entertainment: Peruvian guitar music once a month

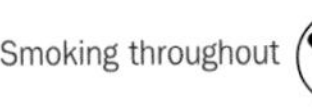

Smoking throughout

Fina Estampa

Peruvian

☎ 020 7403 1342
150 Tooley St SE1

Just past the London Dungeons you'll find another curiosity, the Peruvian restaurant Fina Estampa, whose elegant dining room is exquisitely decorated with South American artefacts and striking photographs. Most dishes feature rice or potatoes – staples of the Peruvian diet – teamed with more exotic ingredients. Start with the ocopa (£6.95), a piquant peanut and walnut sauce served over cold new potatoes with garlic prawns. Chicken seco (£10.95) is a fusion of subtle flavours – tender chicken, fresh coriander sauce and sweet garden peas, served with a generous portion of fragrant parsley basmati rice. To spark things up, spoon on some home-made salsa criolla made with red onions and peppers. The carapulca* (£10.95) is a pork and chicken dish featuring the secret ingredient of the Inca table – dried potatoes, which are added to a spicy sauce of chilli, cumin, stock, onions and garlic. The fried yucca* accompaniment makes this a truly intriguing main course. Fina Estampa's staff are warm, knowledgeable and well deserving of the 10% service charge.

starter: £4.95-£9.50
main: £7.95-£14.95
dessert: £3.50
AE DC JCB MC V; SW

Open: Mon-Fri noon-2.30pm, Mon-Sat 6.30pm-10.30pm; reservations advisable (especially Fri & Sat); licensed

Kwan Thai

Thai

☎ 020 7403 7373
The Riverfront, Hay's Galleria, Tooley St SE1

Thai cuisine may have been the flavour of the last few years, but Kwan Thai's mixed seafood starter (£24 for three) made out like Chinese yum cha: minced prawn and sesame on toast, whole prawns in spring-roll casings and battered calamari. Do what the Thais do and skip the finger food, unless of course you go for the tom yum soup (£6). Kwan Thai's strengths lie in its seafood-based main dishes like squid salad (£9) and spicy mixed seafood (£14). The gang panang is a creamy red curry served with generous portions of beef, chicken (£8) or prawns (£11). Or maybe you'll go for the modestly titled stir-fried aubergine with sweet basil and fresh Thai chilli (£6) – a dish that melts tenderly, sweetly and saucily. Even the phat thai (£8.50) is a cut above your corner takeaway's – as it should be in such swanky surrounds.

Open: Mon-Fri 11.30am-3pm, Mon-Sat 6pm-10pm; reservations advisable; licensed

Map 20 A4

Tube: London Bridge

 Nonsmoking tables available

 Riverside tables

starter: £4-£7.50
main: £8-£14
dessert: £3-£5
Set menu £20 or £28

AE DC JCB MC V; SW

SOUTH-EAST

Oxo Tower Restaurant

Modern European

☎ 020 7803 3888
Oxo Tower Wharf, Barge House St SE1

The red Oxo emblem stands out along the Thames like a beacon, a stunning venue which boasts some of London's best views. To get a taste of the Oxo's vibrant atmosphere, relax in the bar with a pre-dinner drink amid the City types and romantic couples. A window seat here is like gold dust: St. Paul's, the Royal Opera House and Victoria Embankment provide a stunning backdrop. The smoked salmon, gravlax and horseradish terrine (£11.50) makes an awesome opener, the accompanying tangy pickled cucumber and deep-fried oysters adding a little refinement. Roast pigeon (£19.50) is robust in flavour and beautifully pink and tender. The accompanying pumpkin ravioli and fondant potato should alleviate the need for side orders, and is perfect for soaking up the juices. The banana and chocolate bread-and-butter pudding with banana ice cream (£6.50) is unmissable. The service is faultless, heightening this wonderful dining experience.

Open: Mon-Fri noon-3pm, Mon-Sat 6pm-11pm, Sun noon-3.30pm, 6.30pm-10.30pm; reservations advisable; licensed

Map 20 A1

Tube: Waterloo

Wheelchair access

Dress code: collared shirt

Entertainment: pianist in the bar daily

  Smoking throughout

 Balcony tables

starter: £8-£14
main: £13-£27
dessert: £6.50
Sunday lunch £27.50

AE DC JCB MC V; SW

SOUTHWARK

fish!

Seafood

☎ 020 7234 3333
Cathedral St, Borough Market SE1

Map 20 A3
Tube: London Bridge
Wheelchair access

Smoking throughout 

Terrace tables 

The response to the opening of fish! in a glassed-in pavilion overlooking Borough Market was as unrestrained as its logo's punctuation. But was the brouhaha deserved? We'd say yes, with the simple proviso that what you're getting is fresher-than-fresh fish and seafood, simply prepared. There are the classic starters and simple main courses: dressed crab (£6.50/£10.50), served with a plump crescent of roe; devilled whitebait (£4.80/£8.90) that doesn't stick together as one greasy 'brick'; and smoked haddock with a cheddar rarebit (£5.95). For major mains, it's what's 'just in' (10 out of 22 choices that night): swordfish, cod, skate, squid etc either steamed or grilled and served with one of five side sauces. The service is smart and well informed; we were advised that the swordfish (£11.50) went best with the salsa and the delicate scallops (£14.50) with the olive oil dressing – and they did!

starter: £3.95-£6.50
main: £8.50-£16.95
dessert: £3.95
AE DC MC V; SW

Open: Mon-Sat 11.30am-3pm, 5.30pm-10.30pm; reservations advisable; licensed

---

Laughing Gravy

International

☎ 020 7721 7055
154 Blackfriars Rd SE1

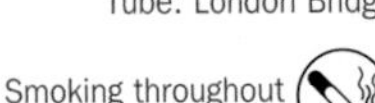

Map 20 C1
Tube: London Bridge

Smoking throughout 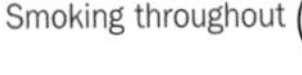

Pavement tables 

Named after the pet dog in a Laurel and Hardy movie, the Laughing Gravy is a small wine bar and restaurant situated in the backwater south of Blackfriars Bridge. Informal by day, in the evening the restaurant is transformed by candlelight and background music, making it the ideal place for a romantic night out. The international menu is somewhat limited but the daily specials add to the choices. Our starters of deep-fried camembert (£4.75), served with potted red currants, and seared scallops (£5.95) accompanied by crispy spinach and saffron yoghurt were tasty and imaginative. Making a pork chop more interesting is not easy, but the chef managed it by serving the meat perched on top of anchovy potato gratin and thyme sauce, surrounded by marinated aubergine pequillo peppers which gave the dish a slightly aniseed flavour. The Grand Marnier bread and butter pudding with Galliano custard (£4.75) was just gorgeous – light and fluffy and surrounded by fresh strawberries.

starter: £4.50-£6.25
main: £10.25-£14.95
dessert: £4.75
AE DC MC V; SW

Open: Mon-Fri noon-10.30pm, Sat 6.30pm-11pm; reservations advisable; licensed

The Apprentice

Modern European

☎ 020 7234 0254
Cardamom Building, 31 Shad Thames, Butlers Wharf SE1

The Apprentice sits in the shadow of several Conran restaurants in Butlers Wharf but in some respects it outshines its better-known neighbours. The restaurant serves as a training ground for students attending the Butlers Wharf Chefs School, and consequently the highly stylised dishes are just as impressive but less expensive than those served at the restaurants where the chefs will ultimately work. Meals are ordered from the set menus only, with six or more choices available for each course. Our saffron gnocchi was a feast in itself, with baked field mushrooms and garlic butter, and the roast pork fillet served with a vegetable gratin and pea purée tasted even better than it looked – which was extraordinary. With prompt, earnest and friendly service, the Apprentice is the place for culinary gamblers to take a gastronomical chance.

Open: Mon-Fri noon-1.45 pm, 6.15pm-8.45pm; reservations advisable; licensed

Map 20 B5
Tube/rail: London Bridge
Wheelchair access

Nonsmoking tables available

Set lunch £10.50 & £13.50 or set dinner £15.50 & £18.50

AE DC MC V; SW

Bengal Clipper

Indian

☎ 020 7357 9001
11-12 Cardomom Building, 31 Shad Thames, Butlers Wharf SE1

This stylish Indian restaurant is in one of London's trendiest dining areas, close to the riverside warehouses which once housed the spices delivered by clippers from all over the world, including Bengal. Designed to give the feel of ocean-liner dining, the spacious room has comfortable seating, crisp white linen and music from a grand piano adding to the buzzy atmosphere. The diners are a mixture of trendy locals, tourists and expense-account city slickers. The Goan speciality roti chingri (£3.95) is homemade bread fried in ghee and served with a heap of prawns, arousing the senses with its excellent use of spices. Rajahstani gosht (£8.50) is fairly spicy lamb stewed with tamarind and yoghurt to melt in the mouth. The stuffed chicken masala (£10.95) combines potatoes, onion and flaked almonds, cooked in yoghurt and served in a medium-hot sauce. Desserts, ice creams and sorbets, are a bit of a let down, and not as enticing as the rest of Bengal Clipper's fare.

Open: daily noon-3pm, 6pm-11pm; reservations advisable; licensed

Map 20 B5
Tube/rail: London Bridge or Tower Hill
Entertainment: pianist in the evening

Smoking throughout

starter: £3.15-£6.95
main: £8.50-£13.95
dessert: £2.25-£4.95
Set menu £10 or £28

AE DC MC V; SW

SOUTH-EAST

Blue Print Café

Modern European

☎ 020 7378 7031
Design Museum, 28 Shad Thames, Butlers Wharf SE1

Map 20 B5
Tube/rail: London Bridge

Smoking throughout  

The views of Tower Bridge and the River Thames from the Blue Print Café are unbeatable. Indeed, diners may be so busy looking at the bridge that they fail to notice the restaurant's utilitarian interior, the white walls adorned only with black and white photographs. They may also fail to notice that although the views are large, portions are small. Our chicken and cep terrine (£6.50) was a light starter, despite the lovely whole pieces of chicken layered between the mushrooms, and the tart of portobello mushrooms, parsley and parmesan (£12) was like a puff-pastry pizza, and not very filling. Feast your eyes on the view and try not to notice the fact that you may still be hungry at meal's end.

starter: £5-£7.50
main: £12-£16
dessert: £5-£6.50
AE DC JCB MC V; SW

Open: daily noon-3pm, Mon-Sat 6pm-11pm; reservations advisable (especially Fri & Sat evenings); licensed

Butlers Wharf Chop House

British

☎ 020 7403 3403
Butlers Wharf Building, 36e Shad Thames SE1

Map 20 B5
Tube: Tower Hill, tube/rail: London Bridge

Smoking throughout  

Terrace tables 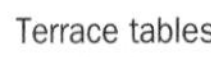 

Reminiscent of a cricket pavilion or boathouse, this light-flooded, wood-lined restaurant is situated under the south-east rampart of Tower Bridge, and is part of Conran's 'Gastrodome' complex. We entered the Chop House to the sound of sizzling beef and the aroma of home-made sausages for a memorable Sunday lunch. A choice of five types of bread eased us into the afternoon, warmed by potato pancake with smoked eel (£8.50) as an inventive starter. The menu's two mandatory roasts were delectably tender: roast rump of lamb (£17), accompanied by delicately minted parsley potatoes, and juicy roast beef (£17), served with a massive gravy-topped Yorkshire pudding. There was also an excellent selection of fresh fish to choose from as a variation to the traditional Sunday lunch. We finished with desserts well worth crossing town for – beautifully presented bread and butter pudding and mouthwatering mocha fudge and walnut tart. There's no doubt about it: this chophouse is a first-class standard bearer for British cuisine.

starter: £4.95-£10
main: £12-£28
dessert: £4.75-£6
Set menu £19.75 or £23.95
AE DC JCB MC V; SW

Open: Mon-Fri noon-3pm, Mon-Sat 6pm-11pm, Sun noon-3pm; reservations advisable (especially summer); licensed

Le Pont de la Tour

Modern European

☎ 020 7403 8403
Butlers Wharf Building, 36d Shad Thames SE1

Established by Sir Terence Conran in 1991, Le Pont de la Tour is situated on the River Thames with a great view of Tower Bridge. The interior is styled to resemble a 1930s Norwegian cruise liner, and service is attentive without being intrusive. Roast rack of lamb with vine tomatoes, rosemary and balsamic vinegar (£19) is served pink and very tender. The poached fillet of veal (£18.50) was equally well prepared. Choosing from the dessert list is agonising, as there are so many wicked sweets to choose from. We were fully justified in thinking the hot chocolate fondant with mint ice cream (£8.50) sounded too good to resist. The menu has something to tempt almost everyone, although you have to ask for the weekly changing vegetarian menu. The pre- and post-theatre set menu is available from 6pm to 6.45pm and 10.30pm to 11pm. Of all of the restaurants in the Conran group, this is certainly a favourite.

Open: Sun-Fri noon-11pm, Sat 6pm-11pm; reservations essential; licensed

Map 20 B5

Tube: Tower Hill, tube/rail: London Bridge

Entertainment: pianist evenings and Sun lunch

Smoking throughout

Terrace tables

starter: £7-£22
main: £12.50-£22
dessert: £6.50-£8.50
Set lunch £28.50 or pre- & post-theatre menu £19.50

AE DC JCB MC V; SW

SOUTH-EAST

Manic Organic

Organic produce is all the rage in London. Sainsbury's, the leading supermarket chain, now reports that close to 25% of its fruit and vegetable sales are now from its organic range. The Prince of Wales is just one among scores of people with profiles big and small who boast of their preference for pesticide-free foods.

Restaurateurs have been quick to seize upon this popular trend and the word 'organic' is now gracing more and more menus. However, all good intentions aside, what exactly makes for genuine organic food is not always clear. The Soil Association is the largest of five non-profit organisations allowed by the government to certify that food is genuinely organic. The others are the Bio-dynamic Agriculture Association, the Organic Farmers & Growers Ltd, the Organic Food Federation and the Scottish Organic Producers' Association.

All five can certify that restaurants are able to bill themselves as 'organic'. However, the requirements are so rigorous that for this book only 15 places were able to be labelled certified organic. Many other places can claim that various ingredients used in their food are organic, but without certification, those claims are just that: claims.

Celebrity chef Anthony Worrall Thompson discovered the perils of trying to run a true organic restaurant in 1999. His Bistrorganic closed after he was unable to get a guaranteed supply of organic ingredients. If the bugs ravage a crop, he found, menu-planning becomes impossible.

Map 20 B1
Tube: Waterloo
Wheelchair access
Smoking throughout 
Pavement tables 

starter: £4.95-£8.95
main: £12.75-£24
dessert: £4.50
Set lunch £12.50 or Livebait platter £42.50 (for 2 people)
AE DC JCB MC V; SW

Livebait

Fish

☎ 020 7928 7211
41-43 The Cut SE1

Livebait in Waterloo is the first link in this ever-expanding 'chain' of fish restaurants, done up in floor-to-ceiling green and white tiles in an attempt to look more proletarian than it really is. It seems to have taken a page from the menu of its strongest competitor, Fish! (see p 228). Livebait offers a 'catch of the day' selection of fish and shellfish, char-grilled or pan-roasted, served with one of four sauces. Our whitebait (£4.95) clung together like old mates who couldn't let go, and the cherrystone clams (£7.50 a half-dozen) had bits of broken shell clinging to the firm, sweet flesh. The black bream (£15.75) was obviously fresh, though left in the grill a titch too long, but the scallops (£9.95) were perfect – plump and coral, sweet and creamy. Service here is relaxed – some might even say lethargic – but the staff are young and hip, and know the game.

Open: Mon-Sat noon-3pm, 5.30pm-11.30pm; reservations advisable (essential at dinner); licensed

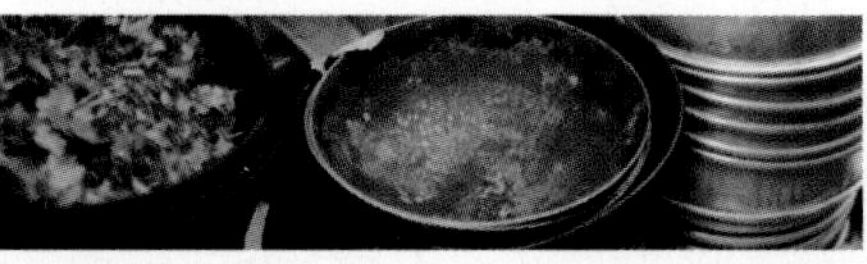

Map 20 B1
Tube: Waterloo
Wheelchair access
Entertainment: guitarist nightly
Nonsmoking tables available 
Pavement tables 
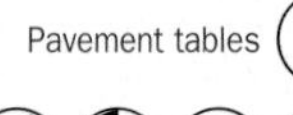

starter: £2.45-£3.45
main: £4.45-£14.45
dessert: £2.25-£3.25
Set menu £6.45-£17.45
AE JCB MC V; SW

Tas

Turkish

☎ 020 7928 1444
33 The Cut SE1

At Tas the surroundings are plush, the menu is reasonably priced and the appetite is soon whetted by fluffy Turkish bread with pâté while a guitarist strums melodies which could warm a cold Waterloo winter. The sucuk izgara (garlic sausages, £3.25) are hearty and the domatesli pilaf (£1.95) is well presented. But the impressive choban kavurma lamb casserole (£6,95) almost defies description – tender lamb infused with coriander and a bazaar of various other spices. Just as succulent but not as exotic was the tavuk shish chicken (£6.95). All were sweetly succeeded by the rich kazandibi dessert (£2.25). And the bad bits? Well, our table was slightly wobbly. Satisfied? We certainly were.

Open: Mon-Sat noon-11.30pm, Sun noon-10.30pm; reservations advisable (Thurs-Sat); licensed

Balham

SOUTH & OUTER SOUTH

Battersea

Brixton

Camberwell

Clapham

Dulwich

Stockwell

Tooting

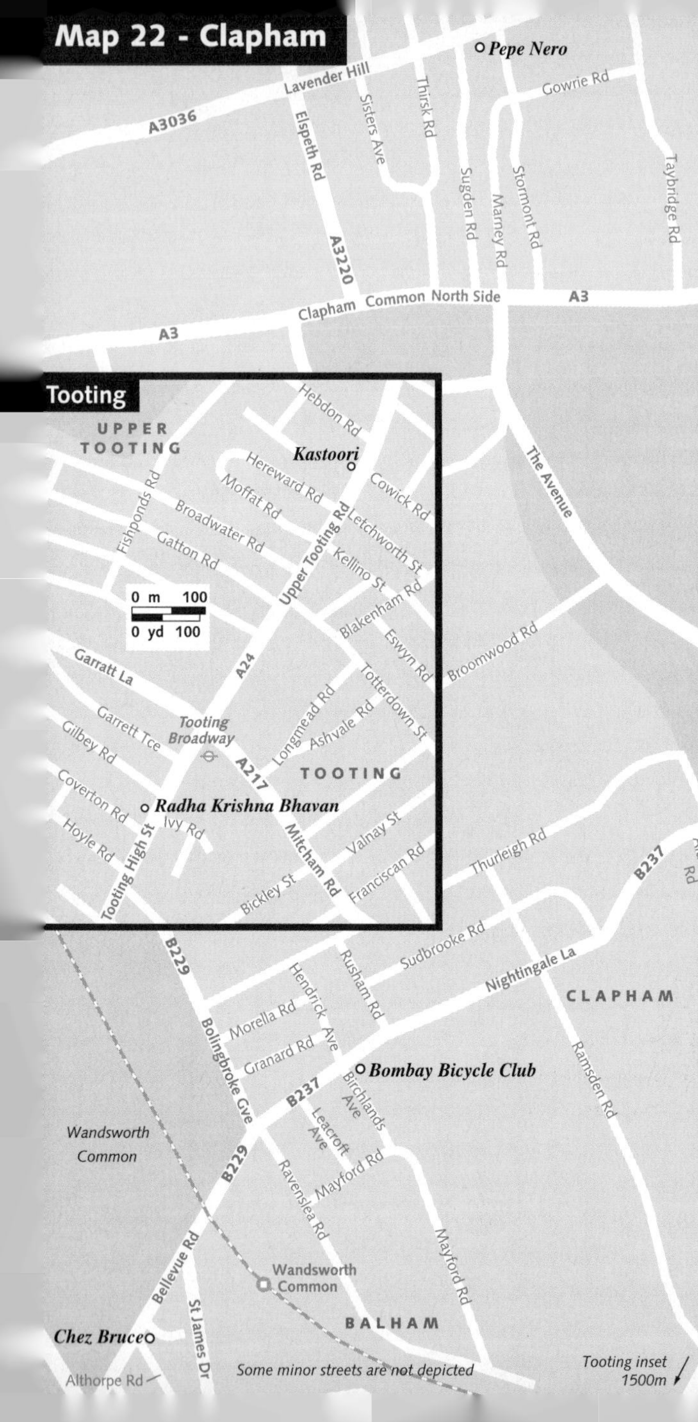

Map 22 - Clapham
Pepe Nero
Lavender Hill
A3036
Gowrie Rd
Elspeth Rd
Sisters Ave
Thirsk Rd
Sugden Rd
Marney Rd
Stormont Rd
Taybridge Rd
A3220
Clapham Common North Side
A3
A3
Tooting
UPPER TOOTING
Hebdon Rd
Kastoori
Hereward Rd
Moffat Rd
Cowick Rd
The Avenue
Fishponds Rd
Broadwater Rd
Gatton Rd
Upper Tooting Rd
Letchworth St
Kellino St
Blakenham Rd
0 m 100
0 yd 100
Garratt La
A24
Eswyn Rd
Broomwood Rd
Garrett Tce
Tooting Broadway
Gilbey Rd
Longmead Rd
Ashvale Rd
Totterdown St
A217
TOOTING
Coverton Rd
Radha Krishna Bhavan
Ivy Rd
Hoyle Rd
Mitcham Rd
Valnay St
Tooting High St
Bickley St
Franciscan Rd
Thurleigh Rd
B237
Alderbrook Rd
B229
Sudbrooke Rd
Rusham Rd
Hendrick Ave
Nightingale La
CLAPHAM
Morella Rd
Granard Rd
Bolingbroke Gve
Bombay Bicycle Club
B237
Birchlands Ave
Leacroft Ave
Ramsden Rd
Wandsworth Common
B229
Mayford Rd
Ravenslea Rd
Bellevue Rd
Mayford Rd
Wandsworth Common
St James Dr
BALHAM
Chez Bruce
Althorpe Rd
Some minor streets are not depicted
Tooting inset 1500m

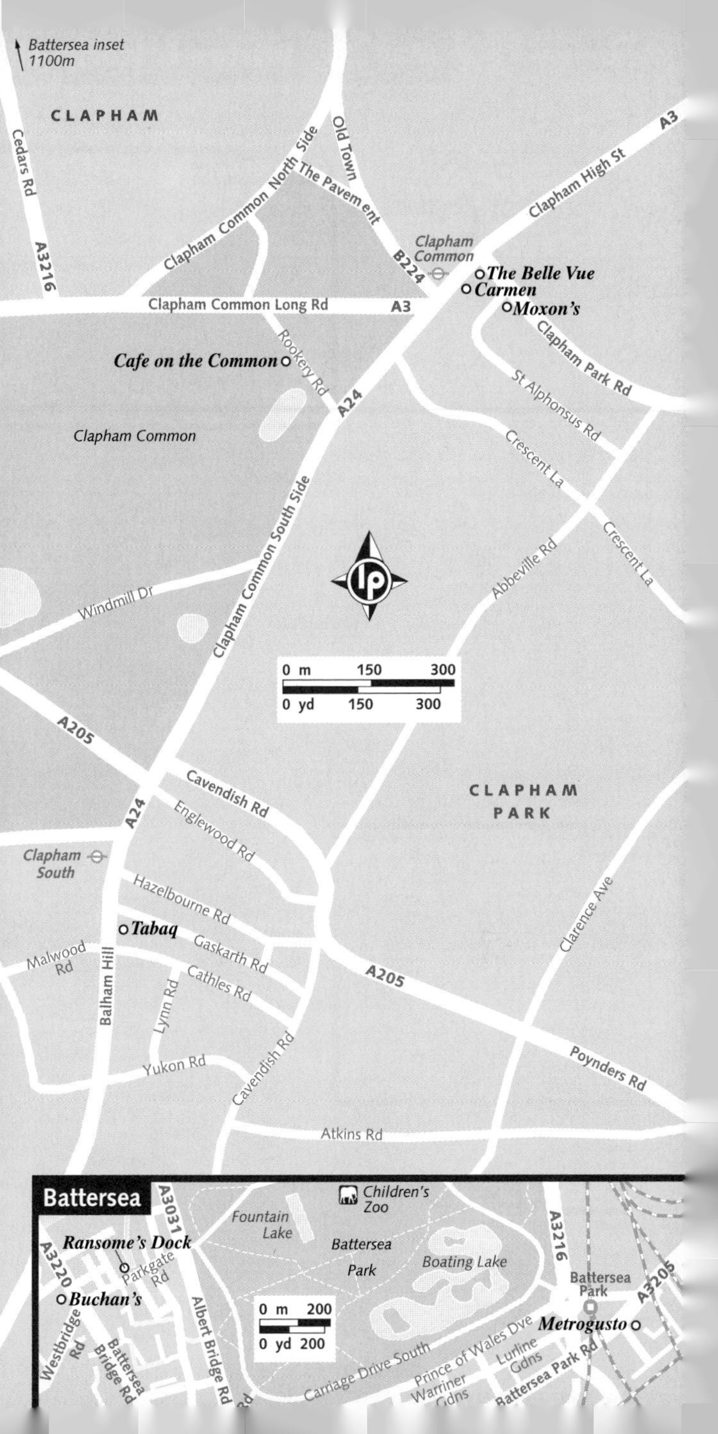

Battersea inset 1100m
CLAPHAM
Cedars Rd
A3216
Clapham Common North Side
Old Town
The Pavement
Clapham High St
A3
Clapham Common
B224
The Belle Vue
Carmen
Moxon's
Clapham Common Long Rd
A3
Clapham Park Rd
Cafe on the Common
Rookery Rd
A24
St Alphonsus Rd
Clapham Common
Crescent La
Clapham Common South Side
Crescent La
Abbeville Rd
Windmill Dr
0 m 150 300
0 yd 150 300
A205
CLAPHAM PARK
Cavendish Rd
A24
Englewood Rd
Clapham South
Hazelbourne Rd
Tabaq
Gaskarth Rd
Clarence Ave
Malwood Rd
Balham Hill
Cathles Rd
A205
Lynn Rd
Cavendish Rd
Yukon Rd
Poynders Rd
Atkins Rd
Battersea
A3031
Children's Zoo
Fountain Lake
Ransome's Dock
A3220
Parkgate Rd
Battersea Park
Boating Lake
A3216
Battersea Park
A3205
Buchan's
0 m 200
0 yd 200
Metrogusto
Westbridge Rd
Battersea Bridge Rd
Albert Bridge Rd
Carriage Drive South
Prince of Wales Dve
Warriner Gdns
Lurline Gdns
Battersea Park Rd

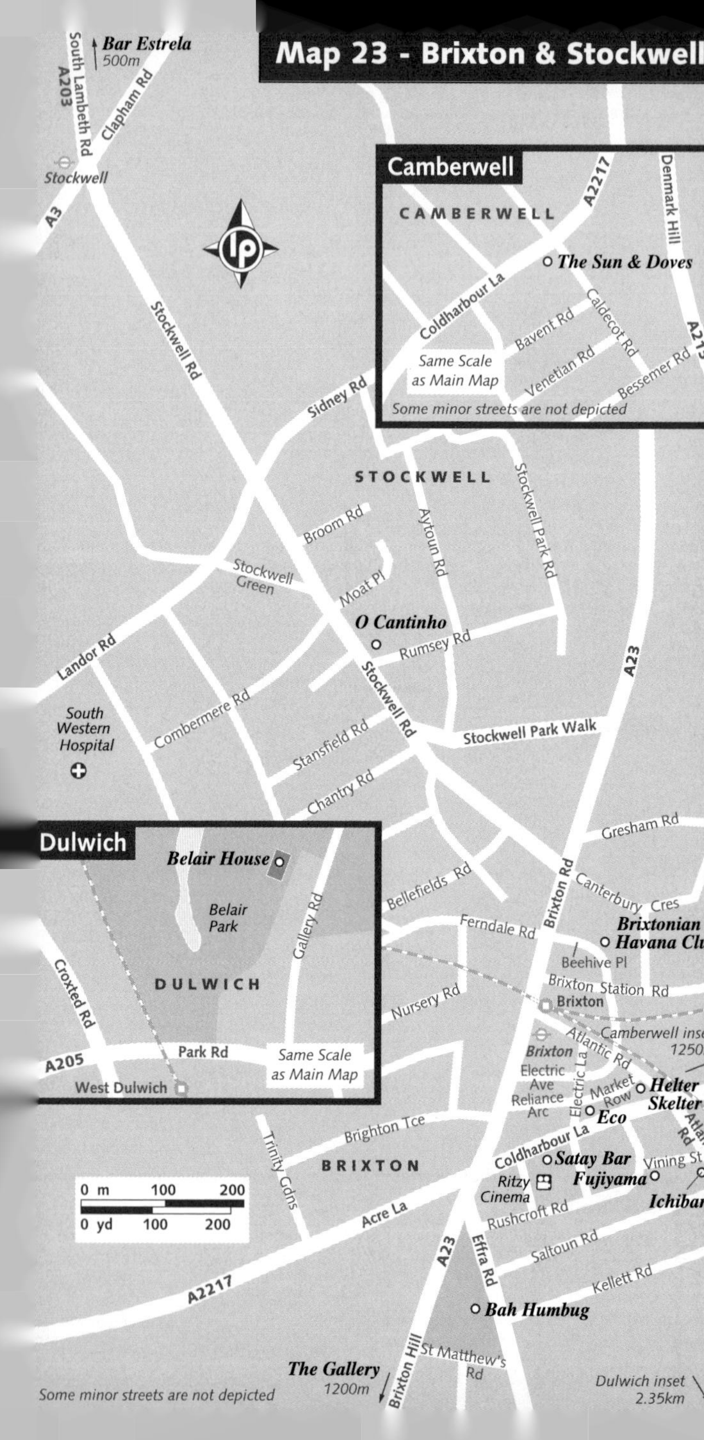

Map 23 - Brixton & Stockwell
Bar Estrela
500m
South Lambeth Rd
A203
Clapham Rd
Stockwell
A3
Stockwell Rd
Camberwell
CAMBERWELL
A2217
Denmark Hill
The Sun & Doves
Coldharbour La
Caldecot Rd
Bavent Rd
A215
Same Scale as Main Map
Venetian Rd
Bessemer Rd
Some minor streets are not depicted
Sidney Rd
STOCKWELL
Stockwell Park Rd
Aytoun Rd
Broom Rd
Stockwell Green
Moat Pl
O Cantinho
Rumsey Rd
Landor Rd
A23
South Western Hospital
Combermere Rd
Stansfield Rd
Stockwell Rd
Stockwell Park Walk
Chantry Rd
Dulwich
Belair House
Belair Park
Gallery Rd
DULWICH
Croxted Rd
Park Rd
A205
Same Scale as Main Map
West Dulwich
Gresham Rd
Bellefields Rd
Brixton Rd
Canterbury Cres
Ferndale Rd
Brixtonian Havana Club
Beehive Pl
Brixton Station Rd
Nursery Rd
Brixton
Camberwell inset 1250m
Atlantic Rd
Brixton
Electric Ave
Reliance Arc
Electric La
Market Row
Helter Skelter
Eco
Brighton Tce
Trinity Gdns
BRIXTON
Coldharbour La
Satay Bar
Atlantic Rd
Vining St
Fujiyama
Ritzy Cinema
Ichiban
0 m 100 200
0 yd 100 200
Acre La
Rushcroft Rd
Saltoun Rd
A23
Effra Rd
Kellett Rd
A2217
Bah Humbug
Brixton Hill
St Matthew's Rd
The Gallery
1200m
Some minor streets are not depicted
Dulwich inset 2.35km

BEST

- **Metrogusto**
  Authentic Italian – from pizza to pecorino ice cream
- **Moxon's**
  A favourite of fish lovers and locals in the know
- **Ransome's Dock**
  Mouthwatering modern European

South & Outer South

Long-time Londoners often think of riots when they think of Brixton, but for more recent arrivals, those with young minds or tourists, memories of the racial problems of the 1980s are nonexistent. Instead, Brixton is the place to go for a vibrant mix of second-hand shops, just-graduated designers peddling their first wares, bars in odd locations and a range of ethnic and not-easily-classified eateries with everything from plantains and goat on the menu, to DJs spinning disks in the corner. For innovative food from across Europe, try Helter Skelter, and for authentic Indonesian amidst the street hubbub, visit Satay Bar.

The Brixton tube and rail stations are a centre of the shopping, browsing and eating action, which fans out along Atlantic, Brixton and Brixton Station Rds, as well as the promisingly named Electric Avenue and Coldharbour Lane. Little first-floor galleries can be found throughout the area, often with discreet cards above the bell you ring to get buzzed in. Bookstores such as Index Bookcentre carry progressive and liberal literature of the kind never to be found at a High St Borders. But the best browsing occurs just walking the streets.

In contrast to Brixton is staid Clapham, just north-west. The much quoted 'home to Britain's busiest railway junction' is also home to Clapham Common, a 205-acre patch of green set among the ceaseless rows of middle-class housing. A commuter area since Victorian times, its residents are happy with reliable and tasty places, such as Moxon's, for dinner after a long day toiling north of the Thames. Dulwich, south-east of Brixton, is another middle-class row house belt that, despite its rather unfortunate name, boasts the Dulwich Picture Gallery, a fine museum which received a new wing in 2000.

BALHAM

Chez Bruce — ☎ **020 8672 0114**
Modern British
2 Bellevue Rd SW17

Map 22 E1
Train: Wandsworth Common
Smoking throughout

If you want proof that fine dining in London needn't cost the earth nor involve an inquisition by the style police, then head south of the Thames to Chez Bruce. The interior of this charming Wandsworth Common-facing restaurant is a curious but relaxed mix of fake Spanish farmhouse with modern art and closely packed tables. The prix fixe menus include three courses and change regularly to take advantage of the season's best produce. Start with the foie gras and chicken liver parfait with toasted brioche – heaven on a plate. The hunk of roast turbot on a broad bean and pea risotto is worth the additional £5 charge, while the whole Tuscan pigeon yields just enough slightly gamey meat to compliment the accompanying lentils, artichokes and balsamic sauce. Desserts are equally colourful, in particular the Sauternes crème caramel festively surrounded by slices of strawberry and kiwi fruit. With friendly service to boot, you could hardly wish for more.

Set lunch £21.50 or set dinner £27.50
AE DC JCB MC V; SW

Open: Mon-Fri noon-2pm, Sat 12.30pm-2.30pm, Sun 12.30pm-3pm, Mon-Sat 7pm-10.30pm; reservations essential (evenings & weekends); licensed

BATTERSEA

Buchan's — ☎ **020 7228 0888**
Modern Scottish/ British
62-64 Battersea Bridge Rd SW11

Map 22 E4
Tube: Sloane Square, then bus 19
Smoking throughout

Buchan's takes pride in sourcing most of its meat and fish from Scotland, and offers authentic haggis, neeps* and tatties* with a wee dram of whisky for £4.95 or £8.95. The front is casual, so for a touch of elegance choose the fine-dining area at the back. This room has crisp white linen tablecloths and seems a bit more kasbah than Caledonia with its woven rugs hanging from the walls. The tartare of thick, smoked salmon (£4.95) had a fleshy texture contrasted by the creamy tartare sauce. We couldn't resist the robust char-grilled T-bone steak (£16.50), well matched with pungent stilton butter and accompanied by peppery watercress. The not-so-Scottish pudding of pistachio ice cream (£4.45) was wonderfully nutty and cooled our taste buds in a flavoursome fashion.

starter: £4.95-£6
main: £9.50-£16.50
dessert: £4.45
Set lunch Mon-Sat £9.50
AE DC JCB MC V; SW

reservations advisable; licensed & BYO (corkage wine £7/bottle, champagne £10/bottle)

Metrogusto

Italian

☎ 020 7720 0204
153 Battersea Park Rd SW8

Map 22 E6

Rail: Battersea Park

 Nonsmoking tables available

Metrogusto opened in summer 1999, and quickly built up a loyal following for its authentic Italian cuisine. The converted pub, with elongated lampshades dangling from the high ceiling and primitivist art hanging on the walls, attracts a youngish, casual crowd. The calamari starter (£6.50) is delicious – tender, and steeped in a reduced onion/sultana sauce – though we were less impressed by the watery polenta alla carbonara (£6). Tasty pizzas (around £7) are sizable, with generous toppings and a light, crispy base. Most other mains are on the small size, but they are creatively conceived and presented. Lamb with garlic and spinach (£12.50) includes a whole bulb of roasted garlic, with the cloves bursting out of their skins. Duck (pinkish, and perfectly cooked) sat on a pasta parcel of orange-infused broccoli. Desserts include a delectable pear and almond tart, served with a strange yet memorable pecorino ice cream (£4). We'll be back for more.

Open: Mon-Sat noon-3pm, 6.30pm-11pm, Sun noon-4pm; reservations advisable (Thurs-Sat); licensed

starter: £5-£7
main: £6.50-£12.50
dessert: £3.75-£5.50

JCB MC V; SW

Ransome's Dock

Modern European

☎ 020 7223 1611
35-37 Parkgate Rd SW11

Map 22 E4

Tube: Sloane Square or South Kensington, then bus 49

 Smoking throughout

 Terrace tables

Diners flock to this restaurant, not because it's trendy or on the dock of a bay (actually a narrow inlet of the Thames) but for the food – fresh and thoughtfully prepared. Crab cakes with lamb's lettuce and Romanesco sauce (£6.25), and smoked Norfolk eel – not the least bit muddy-tasting – served with little buckwheat pancakes and crème fraîche (£7.50) had us rewriting our next dinner party menu. For mains we went for solid British fare: noisette of English lamb with roast root vegetables (£15), done to pink perfection, and melt-in-the-mouth calf's liver with pancetta and field mushrooms (£13.50). The hot prune and armagnac soufflé (£5.75) is light, fluffy and studded with jewels of brandy-soaked fruit, and the baked banana with rum, orange, cream and cardamom (£5.25) is so rich, so dark, so sweet that if we believed in the 'heating' and 'cooling' properties of food, we would have set ourselves alight. The wine list is an oenophile's delight – among the best in London.

Open: Mon-Sat noon-11pm, Sun noon-3.30pm; reservations advisable; licensed

starter: £4-£8.75
main: £10.50-£16.95
dessert: £4-£5.75
Set lunch £12.50

AE DC JCB MC V; SW

Map 23 E2
Tube/rail: Brixton

Smoking throughout 

Pavement tables 

Bah Humbug

International

☎ 020 7738 3184
The Crypt, St Matthew's Church Peace Garden SW2

Set in a church crypt, Bah Humbug buzzes each night and relaxes in style during the day at the weekend. Huge lounging sofas beckon on entry, tables of all shapes and sizes are moulded into the crypt's nooks and crannies, and the occasional bronze hangs on the wall, all adding to the individuality of the place. We went for the chilled-out option of Sunday brunch, or 'mood food'. The Totus Porcus (£10.70) vegetarian organic fry up was pure indulgence, as was the aptly named Sybaryte (£14.50). It kicked off with a truly fruity smoothie, swiftly followed by fluffy scrambled eggs with slivers of smoked salmon, and wild and oyster mushrooms. Then came maple syrup pancakes with a fresh lemon to give a tang to the sweet. Oh, and not forgetting the glass of champagnoise. A brunch perfect for the hungry and the hung over.

starter: £3.80-£5.90
main: £8.10-£14
dessert: £2.10-£4.10
DC MC JCB V; SW

Open: Mon-Fri 5pm-midnight, Sat 11am-midnight, Sun 11am-11pm; reservations advisable (essential on weekends); licensed

---

Map 23 D3
Tube/rail: Brixton
Entertainment: Gospel music Sun afternoon, jazz Wed evenings

Smoking throughout (no cigars or pipes) 

Courtyard tables 

The Brixtonian Havana Club

Caribbean

☎ 020 7924 9262
11a Beehive Place SW9

Despite its less than salubrious location beside the grubby Brixton Recreation Centre, the Havana Club is a lively bar/restaurant offering an eclectic, adventurous menu ('Black British') and just the right gloss of tongue-in-cheek glamour (starched white tablecloths against a background of concrete and red leatherette). Though much of the menu has a Caribbean flavour, French, British and African influences are also evident. The spicy-hot roast pepper and ginger soup (£5.50) is perfect for mid-winter, but unfortunately the same can't be said of the lobster and green mango salad (£5.50) – it tasted like crab had stepped in to fill the lobster's shoes, but it wasn't up to the job. The mains, however, restored our faith: the baked ham, infused with cloves and served with sweet sorrel sauce (£12), is sensational, while the chicken breast stuffed with spinach and dates with a yellow pepper sauce (£12) is a successful combination of more subtle textures and flavours. By the time the coconut tart with rum cream (£5.50) had been and gone, the lobster had long been forgotten.

starter: £4-£5.50
main: £10-12.50
dessert: £4.50-£5.50
MC V

Open: Mon-Wed noon-midnight, Thurs-Sat noon-2am, Sun noon-11pm; reservations essential; licensed

Eco

Italian/Pizza

☎ 020 7738 3021
4 Market Row,
Electric Lane SW9

Map 23 D3
Tube/rail: Brixton

Smoking throughout

Pavement tables

Tucked in between market stalls selling balloons, fresh fish and frilly underwear, Eco caters to a predominantly local crowd. Stallholders, shoppers and others in the know willingly stand in line for a table – though not for long, as a quick turnaround ensures you're usually seated within 10 minutes. The menu ranges from salads (£5.40-£7.20) to oven-baked dishes such as melanzane al forno (£3.90) and focaccia or pizza bread sandwiches (£5.20-£5.90) – but skip all these and plump for the pizza (£4.50-£7.50). We tried the fiorentina: the spinach was tender, the egg just right and the base thin and crispy without being overdone. The service was brisk and efficient rather than attentive, but then Eco isn't the sort of place that encourages lingering; it's only open during market hours and doesn't serve alcohol unless you bring your own. Eco's enduring appeal lies in the consistently delicious pizza, reasonable prices and bustling market location.

Open: Mon & Tues, Thurs-Sat 8.30am-5pm; reservations accepted (except Sat); BYO (no corkage)

starter: £1.90-£4.90
main: £4.80-£7.50
dessert: £3.20-£3.50
MC V DC; SW

Fujiyama

Japanese

☎ 020 7737 2369
5-7 Vining St SW9

Map 23 E3
Tube/rail: Brixton
Entertainment: jazz Sun & Mon 8pm-11pm

Separate smoke-free dining available

One of Brixton's best-kept secrets, Fujiyama is an intimate canteen-style Japanese noodle bar. The décor is much more congenial and cocoon-like than its central London counterparts, with a deep-red colour scheme and bench seating. The main offerings on the menu are ramen (£4.95-£5.95) and fried noodle dishes (£4.50-£5.50). Ginger, lemongrass, chilli and spring onions figure prominently, lending a hot yet fresh flavour. The karai beef ramen with chillies and coriander was the perfect antidote to a cold night, and we also loved the prawn gyoza (£3.90) – deep-fried prawn dumplings served with a tangy dip. For quality, quantity and price, Fujiyama can't be faulted.

Open: Mon-Thurs noon-11pm, Fri & Sat noon-midnight, Sun noon-11pm; reservations advisable (especially Fri & Sat); licensed

starter: £2.95-£3.95
main: £4.50-£6.95
Bento lunchboxes £6.50-£6.95
JCB MC V; SW

The Gallery

Portuguese

☎ **020 8671 8311**
256a Brixton Hill SW2

Map 23 E2
Tube/rail: Brixton

Smoking throughout 

Dispel your reservations about The Gallery's uninspiring location and your persistence will be rewarded with a taste of real Portugal, strangely marooned in south-west London. Behind the takeaway disguise (go through the door by the counter) is a Portuguese restaurant in a sunny Atlantic villa style. With bona fide Portuguese ownership and colourful wall paintings of Madeira seas, you wonder if the food can match the ambience. To a large extent it does, but be adventurous when choosing your meal, as gastronomic satisfaction favours the brave here. More ordinary sounding dishes such as lamb cutlets (£9) are more ordinary tasting, but platters that hint at the exotic like the Portuguese grilled sausages (£2.50) or the Old Goa chicken curry (£9) will not disappoint. Main dishes are escudo-friendly and generously portioned at around a tenner, although for the flush the house specialities go up to £32. As a finale, the sweet memory of the Molotov dessert (an egg and syrup-based pudding, £2) will linger long after you step back from Portugal to Brixton Hill.

starter: £2-£8.50
main: £9-£32
dessert: £2-£4
DC MC V; SW

Open: Mon-Fri 7pm-10.30pm, Sat & Sun 1pm-10.30pm; reservations advisable (especially Thurs-Sun); licensed

Helter Skelter

International

☎ **020 7274 8600**
50 Atlantic Rd SW9

Map 23 D3
Tube/rail: Brixton

Smoking throughout 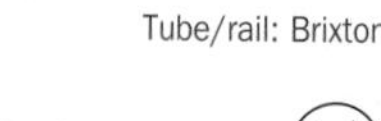

Having picked your way through the aftermath of Brixton's colourful Atlantic Rd market, it's a welcome relief to enter Helter Skelter's simple premises and immerse yourself in its innovative and imaginative menu. The richly flavoured tender sirloin steak (£12.50) contrasts with the sweet potato rösti and bitter fresh spinach on which it is beautifully presented. Continuing Helter Skelter's refreshing combination of ingredients, the seared yellow-fin tuna (£12.80) is tangy and light on a bed of salad and green beans. The dishes are substantial, but an extra serve of potato or rice (£1.95) won't go astray. The extensive international wine list (£12-£35/bottle), dessert wines and spirits are highly tempting, especially as the only nonalcoholic drinks available are water and elderflower pressé.

starter: £4-£6.20
main: £9.80-£12.80
dessert: £4.80
AE DC MC V; SW

Open: Mon-Thurs 7pm-11pm, Fri & Sat 7pm-11.30pm, Sun 6pm-10.30pm; reservations advisable (especially Fri & Sat evenings); licensed

Ichiban

Japanese

☎ 020 7738 7006
58a Atlantic Rd SW9

Map 23 E3
Tube/rail: Brixton

 Smoking throughout

This friendly, family-run Japanese restaurant is unpretentious, with a relaxed and casual atmosphere. The aromas emanating from the open kitchen entice you to be adventurous when choosing from the large menu, which includes over 25 sushi dishes. The delicious spring rolls are only £1.50 and the skewered chicken tashy yakitori (£3.60) is a taste sensation. Mains are equally generous and reasonably priced. Tori teriyaki (£5.80) is a delicious sizzling-hot platter of tender glazed chicken on a bed of beansprouts, and the yaki soba noodles (£5) combines a variety of textures with a rich sauce. The only alcohol served is the imported Asahi beer (£2.50), which makes a refreshing accompaniment to your inexpensive meal.

Open: Mon-Sat 11.30am-10.30pm; reservations not accepted; licensed

starter: £1.50-£3.60
main: £4.80-£9.90
cash and cheque only

Satay Bar

Indonesian

☎ 020 7326 5001
447-450 Coldharbour Lane SW9

Map 23 E3
Tube/rail: Brixton
Wheelchair access

 Pavement tables

Favoured by a young, trendy crowd, the Satay Bar is bustling and congenial, even on week nights. Decorated with constantly changing artwork, it's alive with funky music and the animated shouts of the waiters. There's an extensive cocktail list (£3.95, £12 per jug) and a good range of international bottled beers. The choice of dishes is extensive, good value and unpronounceable! The chicken satay (£5.95) is slightly hotter than most, with a delicious rich sauce, while the duck with peach in a mild rice wine sauce (bebek hijau, £5.95) offers an interesting combination of flavours. The hot and spicy prawns (sambai udang, £6.25) are tender and tasty, and to soak up the plethora of sauces there's boiled coconut rice (£1.95) or noodles, which are a meal in themselves (hence the price, £4.45). If you can cope with another taste sensation, green pancakes (£2.95) make a great way to finish.

Open: Mon-Fri noon-3pm, Mon-Thurs 6pm-11pm, Fri 6pm-2am, Sat noon-3am, Sun 1pm-10.30pm; reservations advisable (especially weekends); licensed

starter: £3.95-£8.95
main: £3.95-£7.75
dessert: £2.95-£3.95
Set menu £11.95/person (min 2 people)
AE MC V; SW

CAMBERWELL

Map 23 A3
Tube: Brixton, then bus 35, 45 or 345, rail: Denmark Hill

Nonsmoking tables available 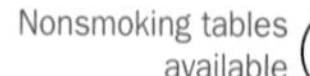 

Courtyard tables 

The Sun and Doves

International

☎ 020 7733 1525
61-63 Coldharbour Lane SE5

'Gallery, restaurant and bar' is perhaps too grand a description for this light and airy renovated old pub, although the walls do display a changing array of work by local artists. The pub attracts a young arty crowd, thanks in part to its large beer garden. There's a great selection of pub snacks, including roast garlic with bread (£2.50) and Spanish tortilla (£3), while the restaurant offers an innovative and varied menu with an international wine list (bottles start at £9.95). The piquant Thai lamb salad (£6.95) incorporates basil, peanut and pomegranate – a strange but pleasing combination of flavours. The salmon fillet (£6.95) is deliciously smoky and complemented by horseradish mash and parsley sauce, while the goat's cheese and sweet pepper tart (£7.95) is tangy and rich. With most mains available as starters, you can enjoy either a light snack or a slap-up meal.

starter: £1.50-£5.50
main: £5.25-£8.95
dessert: £3.75
AE DC MC V; SW

Mon-Fri 11am-11pm, Sat noon-11pm, Sun noon-10.30pm; reservations advisable; licensed

CLAPHAM

Map 22 A6
Tube: Clapham Common

Smoking throughout 

The Belle Vue

International

☎ 020 7498 9473
1a Clapham Common South Side SW4

When pubs carry signs reading 'tables may be required for diners', you can either bemoan the demise of the honest local, or swallow your London pride and place your order. The Belle Vue's mismatched décor (garage-sale furniture and orange-washed walls) is as strangely effective as its regularly changing imaginative menu. Potato pancakes with camembert (£4.25) and Irish soda bread are easily outshone by the bruschetta with grilled Mediterranean vegetables and mozzarella (£3.95). The subtle flavours of the smoked cod and prawn fish pie (£8.75) remained intact despite the creamy sauce. But the two-inch-thick slice of Mediterranean vegetable tart with fetta, black olives and pesto (£8.25) won the day, the caramelised roast peppers and red onions balanced by the magnificently spiced and chunky chips. And, of course, the sticky toffee pudding (£3.50) beckons the gourmands and hearty eaters among us.

starter: £3.95-£4.25
main: £7.75-£8.90
dessert: £3.50
cash only

Open: Mon-Fri 5pm-11pm, Sat noon-11pm, Sun noon-10.30pm; reservations advisable (weekends); licensed

Bombay Bicycle Club

Indian

☎ 020 8673 6217
95 Nightingale Lane SW12

Map 22 D2
Tube: Clapham South, rail: Wandsworth Common

 Smoking throughout

Forget flock wallpaper and screechy background music: Bombay Bicycle Club is an Indian restaurant with a difference. Huge vases of lilies and roses, attentive Polish waitresses and Nepalese chefs are part of a successful package that the management proudly proclaims to be '100 per cent non-authentic' Indian. Everything is freshly cooked, and regular favourites such as the spicy chicken dhansak (£8) are supplemented with daily specials. The fish samosas (£5) are exceedingly good, the filling generous and the pastry crisp and not the least greasy. Main courses tend to be small, so you'll probably want to order a couple or go for a vegetable side dish. We were most impressed with the pasanda khybari (£8), lamb in a sweet creamy sauce, which goes down very nicely with the flaky pilau rice (£3.75). The chicken murgh mangalore (£8) is much spicier, and provides the perfect excuse to indulge in a syrupy mango and papaya sorbet (£3) for dessert.

Open: Mon-Sat 7pm-midnight; reservations essential; licensed

starter: £4-£9.50
main: £8-£11.50
dessert: £3
AE DC MC V; SW

Carmen

Spanish

☎ 020 7622 6848
6 Clapham Common South Side SW4

Map 22 A6
Tube: Clapham Common

 Smoking throughout

The ochre-washed walls and typically blue-toned Hispanic tiles add credence to the authenticity of this small, friendly tapas bar. Coax the taste buds into a Mediterranean mood with spicy gazpacho (£3.95), shiny fat olives (£1.95) and chilli-tinged patatas bravas (£2.95). Vegetarians are spoiled for choice, with a range of almost 20 tapas and salad dishes to choose from, including champiñones a la crema (£3.85), mushrooms and spinach smothered in a herby béchamel. Fish fiends do almost as well, with tantalising anchovies, mussels, prawns, whitebait and cod. The calamares a la romana (£4.20), deep-fried battered squid rings, are reassuringly tender, with subtle citrus undertones. With bright, friendly service, huge jugs of sangria and tapas as tempting as you'll find this side of Seville, Carmen serves up a taste of sunny España in deepest, darkest South London.

Open: Mon-Thurs 6pm-11.30pm, Fri & Sat noon-12.30am, Sun noon-11.30pm; reservations advisable; licensed

starter: £1.25-£5.95
paella: £14.70 (2 people)
dessert: £2.95-£3.10
cash only

Map 22 B6
Tube: Clapham Common

Smoking throughout

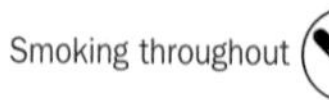

Moxon's

Fish

☎ 020 7627 2468
14 Clapham Park Rd SW4

You know you're in a fish restaurant as soon as you walk into Moxon's. The walls are adorned with tasteful fish compositions and even the restrooms provide a slice of water life, depicting fish and their vital statistics and the best time to eat them! A chilled-out atmosphere presides and the waiters are friendly and honest, suggesting the best, as opposed to the most expensive, wine on the list for the dishes ordered. And Moxon's knows its fish: the menu changes regularly according to the fish season. Already won over by the complimentary prawns, we were not at all surprised to find that the salmon with asparagus (£11.95) was delightfully tender and melt-in-the-mouth fresh, as was the equally flavoursome tuna in black-bean salsa (£12.95). The imaginatively presented roast peach with cherries (£4.50) and strawberries in Champagne gratin with ice cream (£4.50) tasted as good as they looked. Moxon's is well worth the trip to Clapham.

starter: £4.25-£7.25
main: £10.50-£14.95
dessert: £4.50
MC, V; SW

Open: Mon-Sat 6pm-11pm; reservations advisable; licensed

Map 22 A2
Rail: Clapham Junction

Smoking throughout

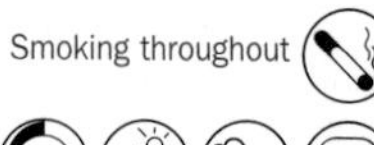

Pepe Nero

Modern Italian

☎ 020 7978 4863
133 Lavender Hill SW11

At Pepe Nero, host Antonio welcomes you like an old friend, while head chef Alberto works wonders in the kitchen. There's no à la carte menu, you just choose two courses for £13.95 or three for £15.95. Grilled scallops with layers of broad bean purée and bacon made an innovative and diversely textured starter. We then proceeded to the perfectly executed roast rack of lamb, the tender meat delicately flavoured with black truffle and served with a contrasting accompaniment of earthy lentils. Traditional fish stew comes in a heavy, earthenware dish and is piled high with octopus, prawns, clams, mussels, salmon, monkfish and tuna. The wine list features a good Italian selection, and the restaurant's rustic, bare wooden tables add to the Italian charm. It's well worth travelling across London for a meal at Pepe Nero.

Set menu £13.95 or £15.95
MC V; SW

Open: Mon-Fri noon-2.30pm, Mon-Sat 7pm-11.30pm, Sun noon-3.30pm, 6pm-10.30pm; reservations advisable (especially Fri & Sat); licensed

The Reel Deal

The British are renowned for their fish and chips but, while there is a chippie on almost every street corner in London, not all of them live up to expectations. The following are some of the best:

The Rock & Sole Plaice 47 Endell St, Covent Garden WC2
☎ 020 7836 3785 (Map 4 D1)
You can tell these guys know what they're doing (they've been in business since 1871) – crispy batter, succulent fish and fat, golden chips. Perfect. (See review on p 35.)

North Sea Fish Restaurant 7-8 Leigh St, Bloomsbury WC1
☎ 020 7387 5892 (Map 4 A1)
Very fresh fish. Ask any of the regulars, it's definitely worth the visit.

Geales 2 Farmer St, Notting Hill W8
☎ 020 7727 7528 (Map 10 D3)
Slightly reminiscent of an English tearoom, Geales is the place for your upmarket fish and chips and even your champers, if you fancy it.

Toffs 38 Muswell Hill Broadway, Muswell Hill N10
☎ 020 8883 8656 (Map 13 A1)
Unchanged since being proclaimed UK chippie of the year in 1989. Need we say more?

Golden Hind 73 Marylebone Lane, Marylebone W1
☎ 020 7486 3644 (Map 2 C4)
Simple and unassuming in both décor and food, Golden Hind is a good reminder that sometimes simple is most effective.

Seafresh Fish Restaurant 80-81 Wilton Rd, Victoria SW1
☎ 020 7828 0747 (Map 6 C5)
There had to be one somewhere ... 'ye olde worlde fishe and chippie', complete with nets hanging from the ceiling and fake fish adorning the walls.

Two Brothers Fish Restaurant 297-303 Regent's Park Rd, Finchley N3
☎ 020 8346 0469 (Map 13 C1)
Another of the classier fish restaurants, Two Brothers has a well-heeled clientele and well-turned out kosher fish and chips to match.

Upper Street Fish Shop 324 Upper St, Islington N1
☎ 020 7359 1401 (Map 15 D3)
You know it's good when you can really taste the potato and the flavour of the fish isn't masked by that of the batter, and the Upper Street has got it very good indeed. (See review on p 192.)

Brady's 513 Old York Rd, Wandsworth SW18
☎ 020 8877 9599 (Map 26 B3)
With its low ceiling, gentle lights and first-class fish, Brady's is the place for the romantic fish and chips lover.

Fryer's Delight 19 Theobald's Rd, Holborn WC1
☎ 020 7405 4114 (Map 4 B3)
Cheap and cheerful, this is your real nitty-gritty takeaway. Black cab drivers

CLAPHAM

Map 22 D4
Tube: Clapham South
Separate smoke-free dining available
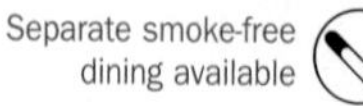

Tabaq

Indian

☎ 020 8673 7820
47 Balham Hill SW12

Tabaq takes deserved pride in its curries, and contest awards decorate the walls. (Although whether you find a huge photo of William Hague tucking into a dish inspirational depends on your political stance.) Within sight of Clapham Common, but on a slightly barren stretch of Balham Hill, the homy dining room is accented with pink tablecloths. The long menu derives from Lahore and features an array of tandoori, grilled and 'charga' dishes, a method of cooking meat with steam to maintain moistness. The gingery chicken jalfrezi (£6.50) combines chunks of boneless breast with a tomatoey sauce. Dhal gosht (£6.50) combines lamb and lentils in a hearty casserole – perfect with the peshawari naan (buttery tandoori bread with raisins and nuts, £2.75). Service is welcoming and the wine list competent.

starter: £2.45-£4.25
main: £5.50-£12.25
dessert: £2.25-£12
AE DC JCB MC V; SW

Open: Mon-Sat noon-2.45pm, 6.30pm-11.45pm; reservations advisable; licensed

DULWICH

Map 23 D2
Rail: West Dulwich
Wheelchair access
Entertainment: occasional live music
Smoking throughout

Terrace tables

Belair House

Modern European

☎ 020 8299 9788
Gallery Rd SE21

Elegant but unstuffy, Belair House serves beautifully presented food in a Georgian mansion surrounded by the green lawns of Dulwich Park. Top-quality, seasonal ingredients feature on the Euro-friendly menu. The complimentary cup of smooth, spicy gazpacho put us in the mood for starters like the cloud-light stilton parfait and poached pear salad (£5.95), and mayonnaisey lobster and truffle cocktail (£11.50). The roast fillet of salmon (£16.95) and tender duck breast drizzled with cinnamon cherry sauce (£16.95) maintain the high standards, and come with vegetable garnishes which make vegetable sides superfluous. The palette of sorbets (£5.75) – intensely flavoured scoops of blackcurrant, coconut, passionfruit and mango ices – atop an orange-infused biscuit make for a sensational finale. This might be treat territory but it's an affordable indulgence, especially if you go for one of the set menus.

starter: £5.95-£11.50
main: £15.50-£17.95
dessert: £5.75-£7
Set lunch £14.50, £17.50 or £24.95
AE DC JCB MC V; SW

Open: Mon-Sat noon-2.30pm, Mon-Thurs 7pm-10.30pm, Fri & Sat 7pm-11pm, Sun noon-3pm, 7pm-9.30pm; reservations advisable; licensed

Bar Estrela

Portuguese

☎ **020 7793 1051**
111-115 South Lambeth Rd SW8

Map 23 A1
Tube: Stockwell

 Smoking throughout

 Pavement tables

Step off the South Lambeth Rd into Bar Estrela and you are immediately transported to Portugal. On summer evenings the tables spread onto the pavement, becoming the focal point of the local Portuguese community. Everything at Bar Estrela is truly Portuguese: the waiters, the service, the clientele, the drinks and, of course, the extensive menu. The restaurant area is rather dingy, so most people opt for the bar/cafe where Portuguese TV flickers in the corner. The menu offers a wide selection of tapas and mains, and includes typical bacalhau (£8.80) accompanied by fava beans and sausage (£3.50), and porco a Alentejana (£9) with clams – an unusual yet delicious combination of flavours. Bar Estrela is well worth the trip over the river for the atmosphere alone, and to relive that Portuguese holiday.

starter: £1.20-£5
main: £4.50-£9
dessert: £1.50-£2.50

Open: daily 8am-midnight; reservations accepted; licensed

AE DC MC V; SW

O Cantinho

Portuguese

☎ **020 7924 0218**
137 Stockwell Rd SW9

Map 23 C2
Tube: Brixton or Stockwell, or bus 322, 345 or 355

Smoking throughout

O Cantinho is an institution within the local Portuguese community, with families gathering here to catch up with the news and football on satellite television. Smiling staff present you with olives and bread while you peruse the menu. Unlike the food, the décor is uninspiring – the walls are painted a gaudy pink, and dark-green tiles crawl up from the floor. On the waiter's recommendation we ordered beef a cantinho (£8), a dish served with bravado. This juicy steak doorstep, accompanied by mushrooms, ham, fried potatoes, salad and rice, could easily have fed half of Lisbon. The succulent king prawns (£5) were smothered with garlic butter and had a slight kick of piquant sauce. In contrast, the sea bass (£8) – just a grilled fish served with boiled potatoes and carrots – tasted disappointingly bland, and the vegetarian choices of pasta and omelettes were rather dull, but we still think O Cantinho provides a real taste of Portugal.

starter: £2-£6.50
main: £4.50-£9
dessert: £2-£3.50

Open: daily 11am-11pm; reservations accepted; licensed

cash only

Map 22 B2
Tube: Tooting Broadway

Smoking throughout

Kastoori

Indian/African vegetarian

☎ 020 8767 7027
188 Upper Tooting Rd SW17

Vegetarians used to being offered only one dish to choose from will be spoiled by choice in this spacious, family-run local restaurant. Start with the dahi puri (£2.50) – delicately fried discs filled with various tasty fillings – then mix and match from the variety of main courses. The vegetable, tomato and bean curries (each £4.25) can be supplemented by vegetable dishes such as aloo palak (spinach and potato in a rich sauce, £4.25) and roasted aubergine (£4.50). It's a safe bet to try the exotic daily special, whatever it may be – matoki (£4.50), an African green banana curry, is highly recommended. Shrikhand (£2.95), sweet-flavoured curd cheese, makes an excellent finish to your delicious vegetarian meal.

starter: £1.80-£2.75
main: £2.75-£7.95
MC V

Open: Wed-Sun 12.30pm-2.30pm, daily 6pm-10.30pm; reservations advisable (weekends); licensed

Map 22 C1
Tube: Tooting Broadway

Smoking throughout

Radha Krishna Bhavan

South Indian

☎ 020 8682 0969
86 Tooting High St SW17

For affordable South Indian food you can't go wrong with Radha Krishna Bhavan. While the palm-and-sunset photo murals are straight out of a holiday brochure, the cuisine is more authentic. There are many dishes you've probably never seen at your local tandoor – only some of them are described in the menu so you may need to seek guidance from the staff (they're happy to oblige). The Kerala masala dosa (£2.25) was a meal in itself – a massive crispy pancake folded over a potato curry – but the plain vadai doughnut (£1.40) was less interesting than its menu description. Vegetarian dishes predominate: curries (around £2.50) have a sauce base of coconut and yoghurt, lentils or sweet mango. Among the 'home-made specialities' we found a good chicken curry for £5.95 – the rich sauce tastes peppery and slightly sweet, and goes perfectly with the accompanying rice-based pancakes.

starter: £1.40-£2.45
main: £1.95-6.95
dessert: £1.95-2.50
Sunday Special Thali
£4.95 or £6.95
AE DC MC V; SW

Open: daily noon-3pm, Sun-Thurs 6pm-11pm, Fri & Sat 6pm-midnight; reservations advisable (Fri & Sat); licensed

Chiswick

Ealing

Earlsfield

OUTER WEST & SOUTH-WEST

Kew

Merton

Mortlake

Putney

Richmond

Wandsworth

Wembley

Wimbledon

Map 24 - Outer West

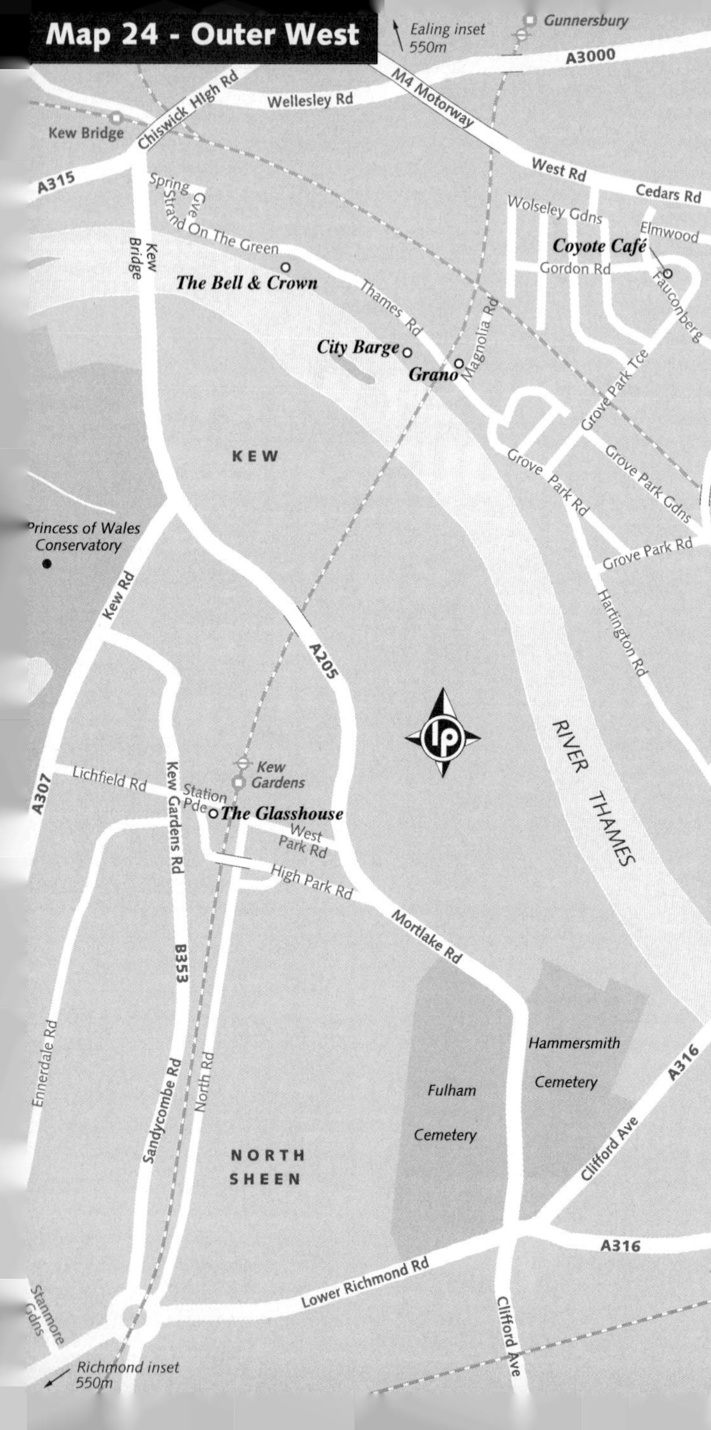

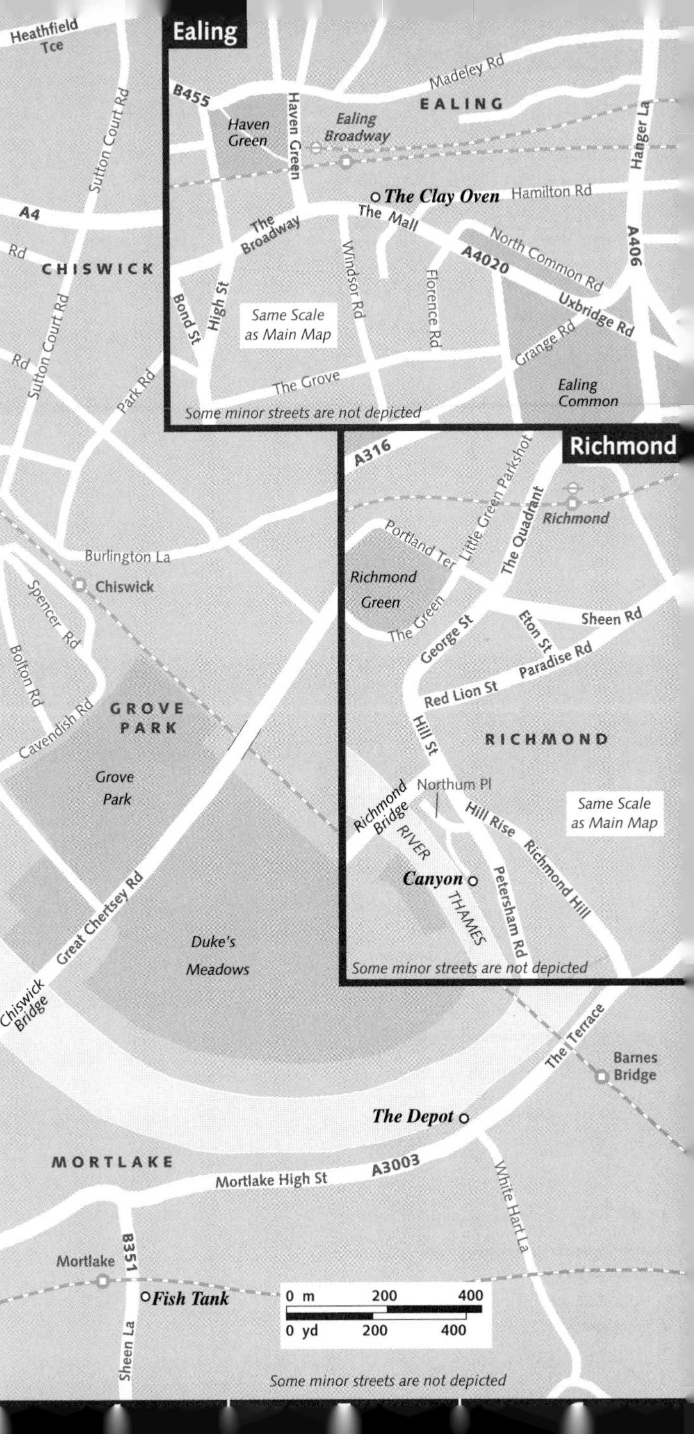
Ealing
Madeley Rd
B455
EALING
Haven Green
Haven Green
Ealing Broadway
Hanger La
The Clay Oven
Hamilton Rd
The Broadway
The Mall
North Common Rd
A406
A4020
Windsor Rd
Florence Rd
Uxbridge Rd
Bond St
High St
Same Scale as Main Map
Grange Rd
The Grove
Ealing Common
Some minor streets are not depicted
Heathfield Tce
Sutton Court Rd
A4
Rd
CHISWICK
Sutton Court Rd
Rd
Park Rd
Richmond
A316
Little Green Parkshot
The Quadrant
Richmond
Portland Ter
Richmond Green
The Green
George St
Eton St
Sheen Rd
Paradise Rd
Red Lion St
Hill St
RICHMOND
Northum Pl
Richmond Bridge
Hill Rise
Richmond Hill
Same Scale as Main Map
RIVER
THAMES
Canyon
Petersham Rd
Some minor streets are not depicted
Burlington La
Chiswick
Spencer Rd
Bolton Rd
Cavendish Rd
GROVE PARK
Grove Park
Great Chertsey Rd
Duke's Meadows
Chiswick Bridge
The Terrace
Barnes Bridge
The Depot
MORTLAKE
Mortlake High St
A3003
White Hart La
Mortlake
B351
Fish Tank
Sheen La
0 m 200 400
0 yd 200 400
Some minor streets are not depicted

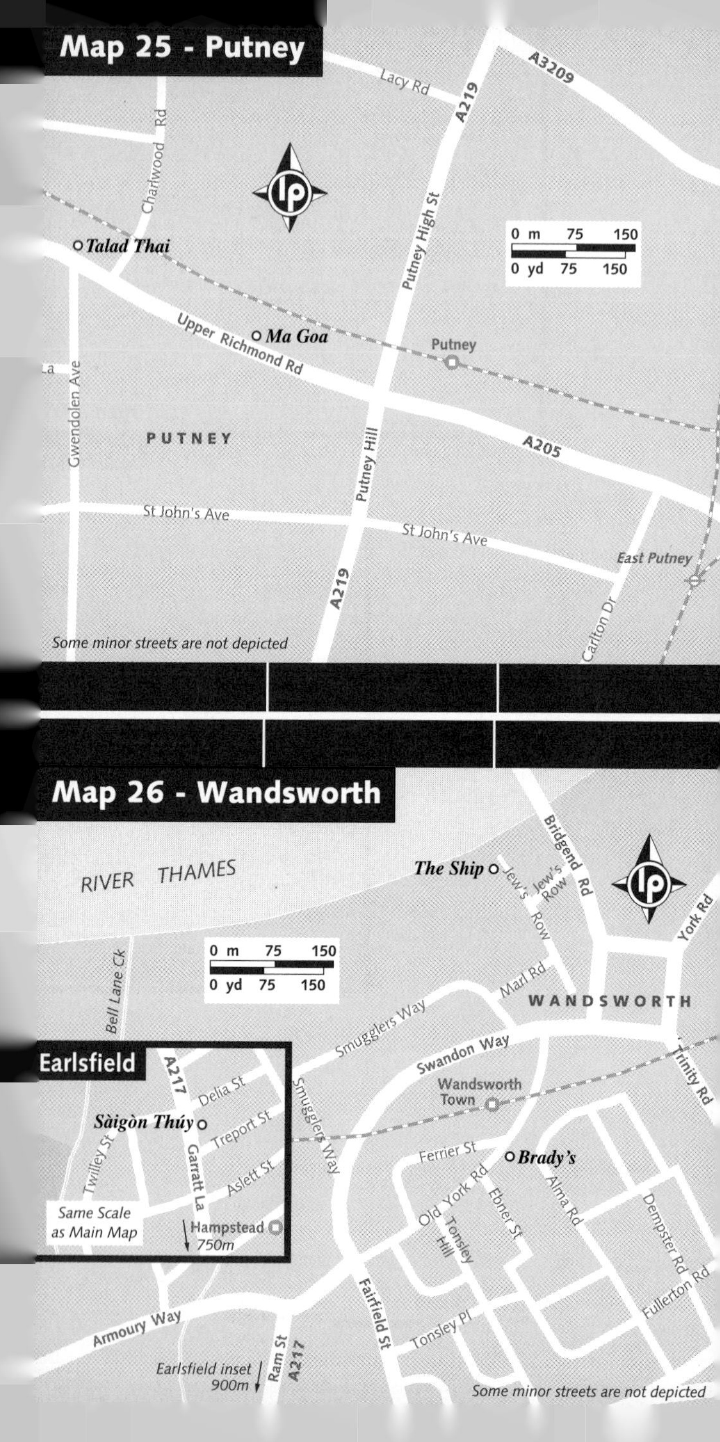

Map 25 - Putney
Lacy Rd
A3209
A219
Charlwood Rd
0 m 75 150
0 yd 75 150
Talad Thai
Putney High St
Upper Richmond Rd
Ma Goa
Putney
Gwendolen Ave
PUTNEY
Putney Hill
A205
St John's Ave
St John's Ave
East Putney
A219
Carlton Dr
Some minor streets are not depicted
Map 26 - Wandsworth
Bridgend Rd
RIVER THAMES
The Ship
Jew's Row
Jew's Row
York Rd
Bell Lane Ck
0 m 75 150
0 yd 75 150
Marl Rd
WANDSWORTH
Smugglers Way
Earlsfield
A217
Swandon Way
Trinity Rd
Delia St
Wandsworth Town
Smugglers Way
Sàigòn Thúy
Treport St
Twilley St
Garratt La
Ferrier St
Brady's
Aslett St
Old York Rd
Ebner St
Alma Rd
Dempster Rd
Same Scale as Main Map
Hampstead 750m
Tonsley Hill
Fullerton Rd
Fairfield St
Armoury Way
Tonsley Pl
Ram St
A217
Earlsfield inset 900m
Some minor streets are not depicted

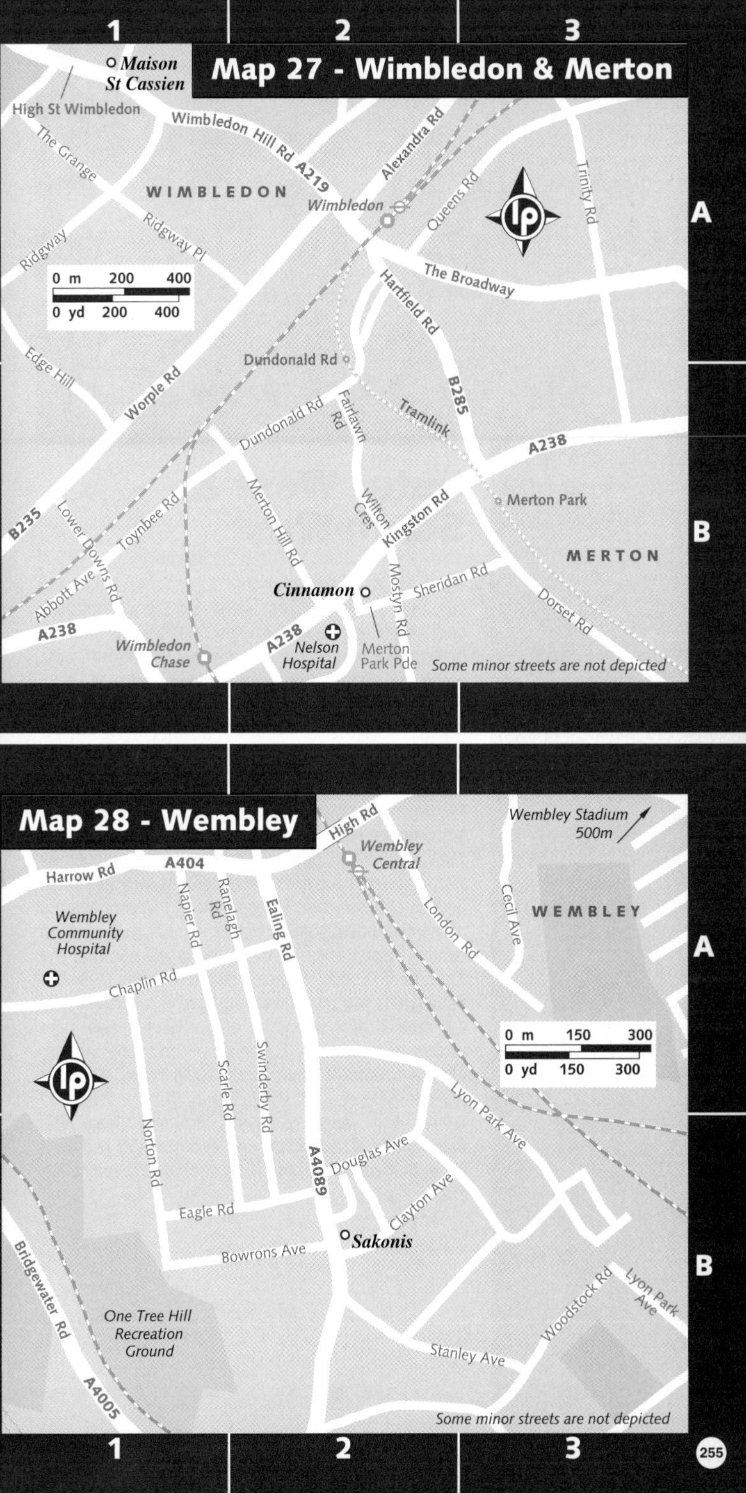
Map 27 - Wimbledon & Merton
Maison St Cassien
High St Wimbledon
Wimbledon Hill Rd
A219
The Grange
WIMBLEDON
Alexandra Rd
Wimbledon
Queens Rd
Trinity Rd
Ridgway
Ridgway Pl
The Broadway
0 m 200 400
0 yd 200 400
Hartfield Rd
Edge Hill
Dundonald Rd
Worple Rd
B285
Dundonald Rd
Fairlawn Rd
Tramlink
A238
Toynbee Rd
Merton Hill Rd
Wilton Cres
Kingston Rd
Merton Park
B235
Lower Downs Rd
MERTON
Abbott Ave
Mostyn Rd
Sheridan Rd
Cinnamon
Dorset Rd
A238
Wimbledon Chase
A238
Nelson Hospital
Merton Park Pde
Some minor streets are not depicted
Map 28 - Wembley
High Rd
Wembley Stadium 500m
Wembley Central
Harrow Rd
A404
Napier Rd
Ranelagh Rd
Ealing Rd
London Rd
Cecil Ave
WEMBLEY
Wembley Community Hospital
Chaplin Rd
0 m 150 300
0 yd 150 300
Scarle Rd
Swinderby Rd
Lyon Park Ave
Norton Rd
A4089
Douglas Ave
Clayton Ave
Eagle Rd
Sakonis
Bowrons Ave
Bridgewater Rd
Woodstock Rd
Lyon Park Ave
One Tree Hill Recreation Ground
Stanley Ave
A4005
Some minor streets are not depicted
1
2
3
A
B

BEST

- **The Depot**
  Tranquil Thames-side dining
- **Fish Tank**
  Loved by locals and worth the trip
- **The Ship**
  Generous serves of faultless organic fare

Outer West & South-West

When you're sick of the noise, fumes and soot of the city, one of the quickest ways into the country is a short tube or rail ride to Kew, not for the famous botanic gardens but rather for the path south-west along the south bank of the Thames. Here the tidal influences on the river are almost nonexistent and, rather than the wide commercial waterway of central London, the Thames is much closer to a country stream.

Midway from Kew to Hampton Court, Richmond was first populated by royalty in the 12th century. In the 19th century it became popular with prosperous Victorians and today is as bucolic as any gentrified English country town. The path along the sinewy route of the river passes grand manor houses such as 17th century Ham House, formerly the grand home to the 1st Earl of Dysart ('whipping boy' to Charles I). Before setting off, you might want to have a lunch befitting the area's royal splendour at the Glasshouse, right across from the Kew Gardens rail and tube station. After a couple of hours' walk you'll come to fabled Hampton Court, the 16th century Tudor castle and home to a range of royals including Henry VIII. Richmond's White Cross, one in a string of riverfront pubs, is ideal for whiling away a few hours, especially after a bit of a walk.

Coyote Café

Americas/Mexican

☎ 020 8742 8545
2 Fauconberg Rd W4

Map 24 A3

Tube: Chiswick Park or Tube/Rail: Gunnersbury

 Nonsmoking tables available

 Pavement tables

Most Mexican food in London should cause a protest to the highest levels at the Mexican embassy: gooey, gloppy cheese over tasteless piles of meat, beans and cardboard tortillas. Yuck. In contrast, Coyote Café is a small local that draws fans from far beyond its Chiswick environs. Granted, there are some concessions to the expectations of the masses, but you can request a real margarita instead of the fake frozen variety and the nachos (£5.95) are layered with fiery jalapeño peppers. The star of the main courses is the blackened rib-eye steak (£11.95) which radiates spice and charcoaled flavour, and has a fine chipotle sauce* infused with the smoky taste of the peppers. Chicken fajitas (£8.95) are sizzling and fresh, and the meat has a nice tangy lime marinade. Anchor Steam Beer, one of the finest beers from the US, is on tap and delightfully priced at £2.40. Service can get harried, but on temperate nights you can sit outside and mingle with the Chiswick swells.

Open: Mon-Thurs 5pm-11pm, Fri & Sat 11am-11pm, Sun 11am-10.30pm; reservations advisable; licensed

starter: £3.95-£6.95
main: £6.95-£11.95
dessert: £3.50

AE MC V; SW

Grano

Modern Italian

☎ 020 8995 0120
162 Thames Rd W4

Map 24 B2

Tube/rail: Gunnersbury, rail: Kew Bridge

Wheelchair access

 Smoking throughout

One of London's best Italian restaurants is hidden away in residential Chiswick. Affluent locals love it for its exceptional menu and impeccable service, and rightly so. Presentation is the key here, with the largely meaty dishes sculpted into mini constructions and beautifully crafted artworks such as the tender slices of beef carpaccio perched precariously on a tower of baby aubergine and crunchy lettuce. This set-menu starter is joined by the rich and substantial pumpkin tagliatelle with sausage and chestnut, an interesting combination of textures. The main courses are equally delicious and include succulent veal stuffed with smoked cheese on a bed of fresh spinach and roasted peppers, and subtly flavoured monkfish served with bitter olives and red cabbage. Grano is a real find, but beware the supplements on most dishes, as they make the set price something of a fallacy.

Open: Tues-Fri noon-3pm, Mon-Sat 7pm-10pm; reservations essential; licensed

Set menu £19 or £24

AE DC MC V; SW

EALING

The Clay Oven

North Indian

☎ 020 8840 0313
13 The Mall W5

Map 24 A5
Tube/rail: Ealing Broadway

Smoking throughout

The Clay Oven is a deservedly popular tandoori restaurant of the traditional British-Indian kind – with an extensive menu, ghazals playing in the background, carved mirrors on the walls and painted deities across the ceiling. There are few surprises on the menu, and all the usual tandoori items (from £5.50) and varieties of lamb, chicken and prawns (madras/vindaloo/doh peeazah/mughlai, etc) are there, but all are very well prepared. The onion in our chicken doh peeazah* (£5.25), for example, was not overcooked, as it often is in Indian restaurants. The naan (£1.60) is perfect and the rice (£1.95) high-quality basmati. Indian Kingfisher beer (£2.25) goes well with spicy food but a range of wines is also available. The dependable quality of the cooking, the friendly service and the reasonable prices continue to draw us back.

starter: £1.95-£4.95
main: £4.25-£11.95
dessert: £1.50-£2
(£15 min) AE DC JCB MC V; SW

Open: Sun-Thurs noon-3pm, 6pm-midnight, Fri & Sat noon-3pm, 6pm-1am; reservations advisable (especially weekends); licensed

EARLSFIELD

Sàigòn Thúy

Vietnamese

☎ 020 8871 9464
189 Garratt Lane SW18

Map 26 B1
Rail: Earlsfield

Smoking throughout

This unobtrusive, neighbourhood restaurant promises 'authentic Vietnamese food', and generally succeeds admirably. Its two smallish dining areas are filled with well-to-do diners of all ages. The pleasant back room features potentially gaudy decorations of mother-of-pearl on varnished wood, and there's a background hum of Vietnamese pop throughout. The service is friendly and polite, and the staff wear traditional dress on weekends. The restaurant offers a wide range of starters – even frog's legs, a legacy of French colonial rule in Vietnam, or you can hedge your bets with the selection at £6.80 for two. The traditional Vietnamese omelette (£3.50) was fine, but little different to its western counterpart. The special fried crystal noodle (£5.50) had an enjoyable smoky taste, and went well with the sizzling platter of tender chicken (£5.80); the subtleties of the latter's chilli, pepper and onion sauce may be lost if you ask for it too spicy (you have the choice).

starter: £2.80
main: £4.50-£6.80
dessert: £2
MC V; SW

Open: daily 6pm-11pm; reservations advisable (weekends); licensed

KEW

The Glasshouse
Modern British

☎ 020 8940 6777
14 Station Pde TW9

Map 24 C1
Tube: Kew Gardens

 Smoking throughout

The Glasshouse does indeed feature plenty of glass: two walls of floor-to-ceiling glass overlook the hum of activity around Kew train station. White walls, modern art, polished floors and recessed lighting complete the contemporary ambience of this upmarket eatery. Service is very attentive, with staff eager to explain the daily changing set menu. Though primarily modern British, dishes encompass several European traditions, with German, French, Italian and Spanish terms sprinkled amid the menu descriptions. The food is pleasingly presented – the mackerel tartare with cucumber, smoked salmon and crème fraîche is a palette of colour, and tastes as good as it looks. We found the slow-roasted pork belly fairly fatty and plain, but loved the duck magret and rump of lamb. The three-course dinner (£25) has eight or more options per course, whereas at lunch there's a choice of one (£15) or three (£21.50) courses.

Open: Mon-Sat noon-2.30pm, Sun 12.30pm-3pm, Mon-Thurs 7pm-10.30pm, Fri & Sat 6.30pm-10.30pm; reservations advisable; licensed

Set lunch £15-£21.50 or set dinner £19.50-£25

AE MC V; SW

MERTON

Cinnamon
South-East Asian

☎ 020 8540 1717
10 Merton Park Pde, Kingston Rd SW19

Map 27 B2
Tube: South Wimbledon

Recently opened Cinnamon is meeting the growing demand for quality food in South Wimbledon. The interior is crisp and modern, displaying original art for sale produced by students from the nearby art college. Cinnamon's ambitious menu represents a range of South-East Asian cuisines, and careful attention is paid to both composition and presentation. The delicately spiced tod mon pla (£5), fish and crab-cakes, filled us with anticipation for the more substantial main courses, which range from Indonesian lontong sayur (£10.50), sliced chicken with a coriander sauce, to north Indian tandoori pork escalopes (£11). The combination of mother in the kitchen and daughter running the front-of-house gives the overall service a friendly and personal feel, and both are more than happy to take the time to chat.

Open: Mon-Sat 6.30pm-midnight, Sun 10am-2.30pm; reservations advisable; licensed

starter: £4.75-£7.50
main: £9.50-£15
dessert: £5-£6.50

JCB MC V; SW

Special Order
A Glossary for All Tastes

London's diversity is preserved by individuals from a mosaic of social and cultural backgrounds. And while we might all like to devour a plate of bacon and eggs without too much deliberation, there are some of us who cannot because of religious, moral or health reasons. Here is a small list of dietary guidelines:

vegetarian: one who does not eat the flesh of animals, including fish and seafood.

lacto-ovo vegetarian: a vegetarian who eats eggs and dairy products.

vegan: a vegetarian who doesn't eat dairy products or eggs and does not buy or use any other animal products, including leather, wool, silk and, often, honey.

macrobiotic: an eating practice which uses wholefoods, locally grown vegetables, pulses, sea vegetables and complex carbohydrates to achieve health and a yin-yang balance. A macrobiotic lifestyle excludes red meat, poultry and dairy products, but allows a small amount of white-meat fish and shellfish.

Pritikin Program: guidelines for a healthy lifestyle which exclude the intake of most meat, poultry, fish, eggs, processed grains and fat. Created by Nathan Pritikin more than 20 years ago to cure his own heart disease, the diet is used to reduce the effects of health problems such as angina, arthritis, cancers, diabetes and hypertension.

kosher: prepared in accordance with Jewish dietary laws. Animals must be slaughtered by a trained kosher slaughterer, and their flesh must undergo the prescribed koshering processes. Mammals may become kosher if they are cloven hoofed and chew their cud. Kosher poultry is usually limited to chicken, duck, geese and turkey. Shellfish are not kosher, but fish which have fins and scales may be. The combination of dairy products and meat on utensils, in sinks and in the same meal is forbidden. Dairy products are kosher if they come from a kosher animal.

halal: prepared in accordance with Muslim dietary laws. Animals must be slaughtered by a Muslim who cuts the animal's jugular vein, oesophagus and respiratory tract with a stainless-steel knife (which is rinsed after each slaughter). The animal must be dead prior to skinning. Dogs, donkeys, pigs, amphibians, animals with protruding canine teeth, birds of prey and carnivores are not halal. Alcohol and blood are also prohibited.

celiac disease: a condition that is caused by glutens which destroy villi in the small intestine, and which results in the malabsorption of nutrients. Celiacs must maintain a gluten-free diet, abstaining from barley, oats, rye, wheat and products made from these grains. Prohibited products include durum, semolina, spelt, kamut, and grain alcohols such as beer, bourbon, gin and whisky.

lactose intolerance: an inability to digest the lactose (milk sugar) in dairy products. People with lactose intolerance do not produce sufficient amounts of lactase, the enzyme which digests lactose. Dairy products low in lactose, like butter, margarine, aged cheeses and yoghurt, are often tolerated by people with lactose intolerance. Those who suffer lactose intolerance must reduce their consumption of foods containing high amounts of lactose.

Courtney Centner

The Depot

Modern British

☎ **020 8878 9462**
Tideway Yard, Mortlake High St SW14

This delightful sanctuary is hidden away on the Thames' south bank between the Barnes and Chiswick bridges. If you're lucky enough to secure a table by the window you can watch the river traffic sail by while you dine. The split pea and mint soup (£3.80) is a great way to warm up if it's nippy outside, and if the sun's shining you can opt for a generous serve of avocado, tomato and emmenthal salad (£4.75). Watching the Thames flow by could well inspire a choice of fish from the broad range of main courses. The beautifully presented pan-fried red snapper is spicy with lime and chilli (£9.90), while the beer-battered plaice and thick-cut chips comes with ample helpings of tartare (£9.80). Desserts include crème au miel with winter fruits (£4.20) and chocolate bread-and-butter pudding with creamy vanilla ice cream (£4.30). The clientele at the Depot is mainly locals, and children are welcomed, creating a wonderful family atmosphere that makes it a home away from home.

Open: Mon-Sat noon-3pm, 6pm-11pm, Sun noon-10.30pm; reservations essential; licensed

Map 24 D6

Rail: Barnes Bridge or Mortlake

 Nonsmoking tables available

 Courtyard tables

starter: £3.80-£5.50
main: £7.50-£12.50
dessert: £3.60-£4.50
Set menu £9.90 or £12.50

AE DC MC V; SW

Fish Tank

Fish/Modern European

☎ **020 8878 3535**
45 Sheen Lane SW14

Yes, SW14 is a bit of a haul for most Londoners, but by the time the second course rolls around, you'll have forgotten the hassle. The chef at tiny Fish Tank clearly loves his job. Everything on the menu is painstakingly presented, and the cooking is spot-on. Our pan-fried sardines (£4.75) came sprinkled with sautéed garlic and pine nuts, a crumbly delight that dissolved marvellously on the tongue. Seared scallop salad on a bed of warm 'wilted' spinach (£10.50) followed, the fish yielding to the teeth at just the right instant. The vanilla panna cotta (£4.25) was appropriately dense, well balanced by the staccato crunch of the accompanying passionfruit. As the restaurant only occupies one small room, the service here is ever watchful, but respectful of privacy. We thoroughly enjoyed the experience of lingering over a masterful meal. The sign on the timber merchant's opposite says it all: 'where quality matters'.

Open: Mon-Sat 7pm-10pm; reservations accepted; licensed

Map 24 E4

Rail: Mortlake

 Smoking throughout

  Pavement tables

starter: £3.95-£5.95
main: £8.50-£15.95
dessert: £4-4.75

MC V; SW

Map 25 A1
Tube: East Putney or rail: Putney

Smoking throughout

Ma Goa

Goan

☎ 020 8780 1767
244 Upper Richmond Rd SW15

If you thought Indian cuisine was all tandoori chicken and pork vindaloo, this excellent little family-run restaurant will offer you something very different to savour. The cuisine of the tiny Indian state of Goa was heavily influenced by the Portuguese, its colonial masters until 1961. Starters (mostly £3.95) include some of the best-known Goan specialities: sorpotel (lamb's liver, kidney and pork in a very spicy sauce), shrimp balchao (a rich shrimp masala dish) and Goan sausage. All are delicious and absolutely authentic, but quite heavy for starters; one between two people would be fine. The sev puri (gram flour wafers with vegetable toppings) were much lighter, and the prawns 'D'Cruz' style (£8.25) were cooked to perfection with coconut, cumin, garlic and tamarind. Ma Goa's early-bird deal is popular: a free starter or dessert if you vacate your table by 8.30pm (8pm on Saturday).

starter: £2.50-£3.95
main: £6.50-£10
dessert: £3-£4

AE DC JCB MC V; SW

Open: Tues-Sat 6.30pm-11pm, Sun 12.30pm-3pm, 6pm-10pm; reservations advisable (especially weekends); licensed

Map 25 A1
Rail: Putney

Talad Thai

Thai

☎ 020 8789 8084
320 Upper Richmond Rd SW15

Talad Thai serves excellent Thai food, freshly cooked in an open kitchen in full view of the hungry throng. Décor is plain, and the small eating area features fairly cramped, long tables where diners sit alongside their fellows, making things sociable rather than uncomfortable. Every dish on the menu is £3.95, and as Talad Thai is a dessert desert you'll have to seek your sugar fix elsewhere. The starters, being smaller, aren't such good value, but we've never complained about the crisp, mini spring rolls, accompanied by sweet chilli sauce. Our favourite main is the green chicken curry – just the right mix of coconut milk, aubergines and sweat-inducing heat. The jungle curry, on the other hand, seems too fiery, even for our chilli-inured palates. The phat thai is very satisfying – the prawns and peanut flavours complementary rather than contradictory. You may have to queue for a seat at peak times, but it'll be worth the wait.

starter: £3.95
main: £3.95

cash and cheque only

Open: Mon-Sat 9am-3pm, 5.30pm-10pm, Sun 10am-8pm; reservations not accepted; licensed & BYO (corkage £1/bottle)

Canyon
American

☎ **020 8948 2944**
The Tow Path, Riverside TW10

Canyon's modern, airy environment is perfect for sampling its attractively presented American cuisine. Seating overlooks the Thames-lapped garden (landscaped to evoke Arizona – just imagine the Thames is the Colorado River). The riverside promenade provides the only access, so expect some walking or telephone ahead to be met by their electric buggy. We started with roast vegetables, a flavoursome combination of courgette, aubergine, sweet potato and bell pepper, accompanied by a tangy tomato sauce. We loved the pheasant, cooked to perfection and resting on a bed of creamy mashed potato, and fish and chips (£9) were enlivened by a chunky home-made tartare sauce. All portions are large, including our dessert of moist chocolate bourbon tart. Service, though sometimes slow, is friendly. Weekend brunches are a speciality here, and offer a wide choice from fruit salad to huevos rancheros.

Open: Mon-Fri noon-3.30pm, Sat & Sun 10.30am-4pm, Mon-Sat 7pm-11pm, Sun 5.30pm-10.30pm (breakfast Sat & Sun 11am-4pm); reservations advisable; licensed

Map 24 D6
Tube/rail: Richmond
Wheelchair access

Separate smoke-free dining available

Terrace & patio tables

starter: £5-£8
main: £9-£15
dessert: £5-£6
Set weekday lunch £14

AE MC V; SW

WANDSWORTH

The Ship

Modern British

☎ **020 8870 9667**
41 Jews Row SW18

Map 26 A3

Tube: Fulham Broadway, then bus 28 or 295, rail: Wandsworth Town

Certified organic

Smoking throughout 

Balcony & courtyard tables 

The Ship is a gem of an organic restaurant with an imaginative menu, generous portions and friendly, efficient service. We started with lamb's liver in onion sauce and red wine dressing (£4.75) and Mediterranean prawns with sweet chilli sauce (£4.95), progressing to an enormous swordfish steak with stir-fried vegetables in oyster sauce (£9.25) and loin of pork with an interesting stilton sauce and parsnip mash (£7.50). The food was faultless, our only gripe being the noise of the kitchen ventilation fans. Real ale connoisseurs should note that the Ship is owned by the local brewery, Young & Co. It's crowded at weekends, particularly in summer when there is an additional BBQ menu (£4.50-£10.50), but well worth a venture south of the river. On Bonfire Night the Ship holds one of the best fireworks displays in London.

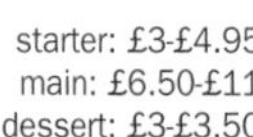

starter: £3-£4.95
main: £6.50-£11
dessert: £3-£3.50

AE DC MC V; SW

Open: Mon-Fri noon-10.30pm, Sat noon-4pm, 7pm-10.30pm, Sun noon-4pm, 7pm-10pm; reservations accepted (except Sun lunch); licensed

WEMBLEY

Sakonis
Indian/vegetarian

☎ 020 8903 9601
127-129 Ealing Rd HA0 4BP

Map 28 B2
Tube: Alperton

Classic Indian vegetarian fast food like masala dosas and idlis are served in tiled, utilitarian surroundings at this popular restaurant and juice bar. You can come just for a drink (fresh coconut water served in its shell, £2.25) and a snack such as mogo (cassava) chips (£2.75) or bhel puri, a deliciously crunchy sweet-sour pile of puffed rice, puris, potatoes, onion, garlic and tamarind chutney (£3). Main dishes include dosas (£3.50-£4.40) which are excellent – better than many we've had in India – vegetable biryani (£3.85) and Indian-style Chinese dishes such as chow mein (£5.50). Puddings include kulfi (£1.65-£2.50) and gajjar halva and ice cream (£2.50), surprisingly good despite being made from carrots. For the full subcontinental experience stop for a paan* (60p) from the paan-wallah by the door on the way out, and pick up a CD of the latest Bollywood hits from the stall next door.

Open: Sun-Thurs 11am-11pm, Fri & Sat 11am-midnight; reservations accepted; unlicensed

starter: £1.40-£3.60
main: £2.75-£6.50
dessert: 50p-£3
MC V; SW

WIMBLEDON

Maison St Cassien
Mediterranean/Lebanese

☎ 020 8944 1200
71 High St SW19

Map 27 A1
Tube/rail: Wimbledon

Smoking throughout

Patio & pavement tables

This cafe and sandwich bar in the centre of Wimbledon village is a low-key and relaxed place which attracts local office workers, shoppers and families. Vegetarian choices are emphasised, and the 10 'house specialities' are served with a crisp and copious Mediterranean salad. Elaborate sandwiches are £3.95 each, pasta of the day is £6.75. For a variety of taste treats, delve into the Lebanese selection, available in vegetarian (£7.95) and meat (£9.25) varieties. Each comes with dips, stuffed vine leaves, fatayer (a waffle-like pastry filled with spinach and herbs), salad and home-made Lebanese bread. In the meat version you'll get either delicious marinated chicken, or lamb and pine nuts within a coating of deep-fried cracked wheat. There's also a selection of naughty but nice cakes at £2.90 per slice (apparently they come from the same specialist bakery which supplies Harrods), and several options for coffee (from £1.20).

Open: daily 8am-6pm; reservations accepted; unlicensed

main: £5.75-£9.25
dessert: £2.90
MC V; SW

Glossary

These are general definitions. The interpretation and spelling of these terms in individual restaurants may differ from this list.

A

akee: *Caribbean;* red fruit with a distinctive creamy white flesh used as a vegetable in Caribbean cooking.

albóndigas: *Mexican & Spanish;* meatballs.

almeja: *Spanish;* clam.

arak: *Middle Eastern;* anis-flavoured spirit that is often imbibed at meal times.

B

baccalà: *Italian;* salt cod.

beignet: *French;* term generally used to describe fritters but which specifically refers to a sugary deep-fried French pastry similar to a doughnut.

boudin: *French;* sausage.

bulgogi: *Korean;* refers to a fiery dish of grilled beef strips and chilli, and also to the circular hot plate on which the dish is cooked at the table.

C

carapulca: *South American;* tomato-based meat stew that is a speciality of Peru.

carciofini: *Italian;* artichoke hearts.

char siu bow: *Chinese;* fluffy steamed buns filled with char siu (honey roasted pork), hoisin sauce and vegetables such as mushrooms and shallots.

chimichurri: *Argentinian;* tangy sauce of garlic, oil, cayenne pepper, vinegar and spices used to enhance meat dishes.

chipotle sauce: *Mexican;* salsa made from the chipotle, a large, plump chilli distinguished by its smoky flavour.

D

doh peeazah: *Indian;* literally means 'two onions' - a rich, substantial, braised dish which uses onions at two stages in its preparation.

E

escalope: *French/English;* very thin, boneless fillet of meat that is tenderised before cooking.

F

fuul: *Middle Eastern;* staple of stewed fava beans with many variations of added ingredients such as oil, lemon, salt, meat, eggs and onions.

G

galbi: *Korean;* chilli and soy marinated short ribs cooked on a hot plate at the dining table in a similar fashion to bulgogi.

gambas a la plancha: *Spanish;* dish of grilled prawns often served as a tapa, or starter.

gari: *Japanese;* thin slices of pickled ginger that are pink in colour, served as a compliment to many dishes.

gravlax: *Scandinavian;* thin salmon fillets dry-cured with sugar, salt and dill.

H

ha gau: *Chinese;* steamed prawn dumplings commonly eaten as dim sum.

harissa: *North African;* a paste of ground hot red chillies, garlic, cumin and olive oil.

K

kaiten-zushi: *Japanese;* establishment where sushi is served via a conveyor belt that runs along the counter where patrons sit and dine.

karahi: *Pakistan;* small metal dish with a rounded bottom used for cooking individual meals.

L

labna: *Middle Eastern;* small balls of cheese traditionally made from goat's milk yoghurt, herbs and oil.

langostino: *Spanish;* crayfish.

langoustine: *French;* crayfish.

M

mapo doufu: *Chinese;* famous Sichuan dish of bean curd, pork and chopped spring onions in a chilli sauce.

mozzarella di bufala: *Italian;* soft mozzarella cheese made from buffalo milk.

mughlai: *Indian;* regional cooking style of Northern India in which the emphasis is more on spices and less on chilli; similar to cuisines of the Middle East and Central Asia.

N

namul: *Korean;* general term referring to the seasoned vegetables served with every meal.

natto: *Japanese;* traditional staple of fermented soy beans.

neep: *Scottish;* colloquial word for turnip.

O

oden: *Japanese;* slow-cooked stew of vegetables, eggs, squid, meat balls and tofu often served with wasabi.

P

paan: *Indian;* sweet-smelling seed mixture chewed after meals to cleanse the palate and freshen the breath.

pai gwat: *Chinese;* dim sum dish of small steamed spare ribs in black bean sauce.

panettone: *Italian;* yeast-raised fruit and nut cake eaten during holiday periods, originating in Milan.

R

robatayaki: *Japanese;* literally means 'hearth-side cooking'; traditionally a rustic drinking restaurant serving a wide variety of foods grilled over charcoal.

S

siu mai: *Chinese;* delicate steamed dumplings filled with a mixture of prawn, pork and herbs.

T

tarama: *Greek;* exquisite delicacy consisting of mullet's roe that is dried and salted before eating.

tatties: *Scottish;* colloquial term for potatoes.

tonkatsu: *Japanese;* thin, deep-fried, crumbed fillets of pork commonly served with lemon and a rich barbecue sauce.

tournedos Rossini: *French;* lavish dish of a fried circular fillet of beef served with truffle and foie gras atop crisped bread.

Y

yucca: word used both as a description of a form of cactus, the strong tasting stem of which can be cooked and eaten, and as an alternative description for cassava, a carbohydrate-rich tuber found in much of Africa and Latin America.

Lonely Planet Offices

Australia
PO Box 617, Hawthorn 3122, Vic
☎ 03 9819 1877
fax 03 9819 6459
email:
out2eat@lonelyplanet.com.au
talk2us@lonelyplanet.com.au

USA
150 Linden St, Oakland,
CA 94607
☎ 510 893 8555
TOLL FREE: 800 275 8555
fax 510 893 8572
email: info@lonelyplanet.com

UK
10a Spring Place, London NW5 3BH
☎ 020 7428 4800
fax 020 7428 4828
email: go@lonelyplanet.co.uk

France
1 rue du Dahomey, 75011 Paris
☎ 01 55 25 33 00
fax 01 55 25 33 01
email: bip@lonelyplanet.fr

World Wide Web:
www.lonelyplanet.com or
AOL keyword: lp

Lonely Planet Images:
lpi@lonelyplanet.com.au

Lonely Planet Products

City Products

City Guides offer an in-depth view to over 50 cities around the globe. Featuring the top restaurants, bars and clubs as well as information on accommodation and transport, these guides are suited to long-term and business travellers and anyone who wants to know everything about a city.
They come with reliable, easy-to-use maps, cultural and historical facts and a run-down on attractions, old and new.

For the discerning short-term visitor, **Condensed** guides highlight the best a destination has to offer in a full-colour pocket-sized format designed for quick access. From top sights and walking tours to opinionated reviews of where to eat, stay, shop and have fun.

CitySync lets travellers use their PalmTM or VisorTM hand-held computers to guide them through a city's highlights with quick tips on transport, history, cultural life, major sights and shopping and entertainment options. It can also quickly search and sort hundreds of reviews of hotels, restaurants and attractions and pinpoint the place on scrollable street maps. CitySync can be downloaded from www.citysync.com

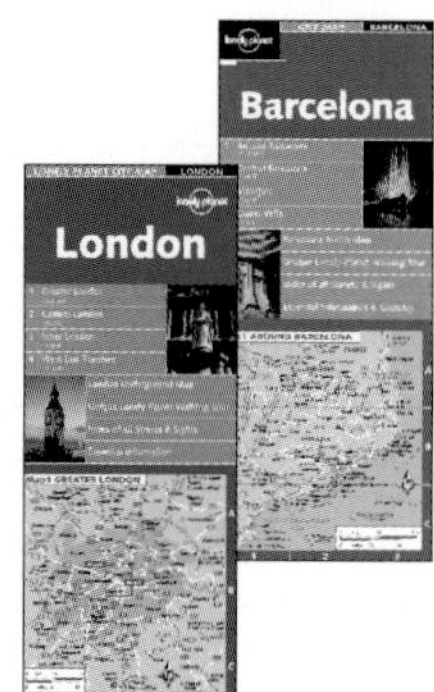

City Maps

Lonely Planet's **City Maps** feature downtown and metropolitan maps as well as transit routes and walking tours. The maps come complete with an index of streets, a listing of sights and plastic coated for extra durability.

Food Guides

For people who live to eat, drink and travel, **World Food** guides explore the culinary culture of each country. Entertaining and adventurous, each guide is packed with detail on staples and specialities, regional cuisine and local markets, as well as sumptuous recipes, comprehensive culinary dictionaries and lavish photos good enough to eat.

Travellers Network

Lonely Planet online, Lonely Planet's award-winning web site, has insider information on hundreds of destinations from Amsterdam to Zimbabwe complete with interactive maps and relevant links. The site also offers the latest travel news, recent reports from travellers on the road, guidebook upgrades, a travel links site, an online book buying option and a lively traveller's bulletin board. It can be viewed at www.lonelyplanet.com or AOL keyword: lp

Planet Talk is the quarterly print newsletter full of gossip, advice, anecdotes and author articles. It provides an antidote to the being-at-home blues and lets you plan and dream for the next trip. Contact the nearest Lonely Planet office for your free copy.

Comet, the free Lonely Planet newsletter, comes via email once a month. It's loaded with travel news, advice, dispatches from authors, travel competitions and letters from readers. To subscribe, click on the Comet subscription link on the front page of the web site.

Thanks

Thanks to Jenny McCracken who allowed us to reproduce her artwork, and to all the restaurants who kindly allowed us to take photographs for this edition:

Balans West, Bar Italia, Brick Lane Beigel Bakery, Butlers Wharf Chop House, Café Fish, The Café in the Crypt, Churchill Arms, Gay Hussar, The Ivy, Kettners, Le Pont de la Tour, Mash, Mesón Los Barriles, Mildred's, Oxo Tower Restaurant, Pharmacy Restaurant & Bar, Quo Vadis, The Rock & Sole Plaice, Soba, Sri Siam, Wagamama, World Food Cafe and Yo! Sushi.

INDEX

INDEX

INDEX

INDEX

INDEX

INDEX

INDEX

INDEX

INDEX

INDEX

INDEX

RESTAURANT NAME	PAGE NUMBER	Wheelchair access	Meet for a drink	Outdoor	Open for Breakfast	Child Friendly	Romantic
Royal Cous-Cous House, Holloway ☎ 020 7700 2188	186				●		
Rules, Covent Garden ☎ 020 7379 0258	35				●		●
Sàigòn Thúy, Wandsworth ☎ 020 8871 9464	258		●		●		●
Saints', Clerkenwell ☎ 020 7490 4199	183					●	
St Tropez, Shorts Gardens ☎ 020 7379 3355	36		●		●		
Sakonis, Wembley ☎ 020 8903 9601	265				●		
Saloon, Wembley ☎ 020 8903 9601	119						
Satay Bar, Brixton ☎ 020 7326 5001	243	●	●	●	●		
Satsuma, Soho ☎ 020 7437 8338	80	●			●		
Sauce, Camden ☎ 020 7482 0777	156		●		●		
The Savoy Grill, Strand ☎ 020 7836 4343	89						
Schnecke, Soho ☎ 020 7287 6666	81	●	●		●		
Selam, Kentish Town ☎ 020 7284 3947	169			●			
The Ship, Wandsworth ☎ 020 8870 9667	264		●	●			
Singapura, City ☎ 020 7329 1133	209	●	●				
Soba, Soho ☎ 020 7734 6400	81						
Solly's, Golders Green ☎ 020 8455 0004	160			●	●		
Sotheby's Café, Mayfair ☎ 020 7293 5077	57					●	
Spiga, Soho ☎ 020 7734 3444	82				●		
The Square, Mayfair ☎ 020 7495 7100	56	●					●
Sri Siam, Soho ☎ 020 7434 3544	83						
Stockpot, Soho ☎ 020 7287 1066	83			●	●		
Stonemason's Arms, Hammersmith ☎ 020 8748 1397	109	●	●				
Suan Neo, City ☎ 020 7256 5045	209						
Sugar Club, Soho ☎ 020 7437 7776	84						
Sugar Reef, Soho ☎ 020 7851 0800	84	●	●		●		
The Sun and Doves, Camberwell ☎ 020 7733 1525	244		●	●	●	●	

INDEX

INDEX

Notes

INDEX

By Cuisine

Fish

French

Fusion

Georgian

Goan

Greek

INDEX

By Cuisine

Greek *cont*

Japanese

Jewish

Korean

Lebanese

Mauritian

Mediterranean

Mexican

Middle Eastern

Modern British

INDEX

By Cuisine

Modern British cont

Vietnamese

Vegetarian

INDEX

By Neighbourhood

INDEX

By Neighbourhood

King's Cross

Knightsbridge

Ladbroke Grove

Lancaster Gate

Leicester Square

London Bridge

Maida Vale

Marble Arch

Marylebone

Mayfair

Merton

Mortlake

Muswell Hill

Notting Hill

Olympia

Oxford Circus

Piccadilly

Pimlico

Primrose Hill

INDEX

By Neighbourhood

Notes

Notes

Notes

Legend

○	Restaurant
	Airport
	Bus Station
	Church
	Cinema
	Golf Course
	Hospital
	Information
	Mosque
	Museum
P	Parking Area
●	Point of Interest
	Pool
	Post Office
	Synagogue
	Theatre
	Zoo

Sample	Meaning
Bank	**Underground Station**
Hornsey	**Railway** with station
Greenwich DLR	**Docklands Light Railway** with station
Dundonald Rd	**Tramlink** with station
Fulham Rd	**Motorway, Major Road**
Belgrave Rd	**Road**
Georgiana St	**Street**
Gerrard Pl	**Minor Street**
←	**One Way Street**
SOHO	**Area**
	Parks, Gardens
	Buildings
	Mall, Market
see Inset	Extents of **Inset Map, Overlap or Enlargement**

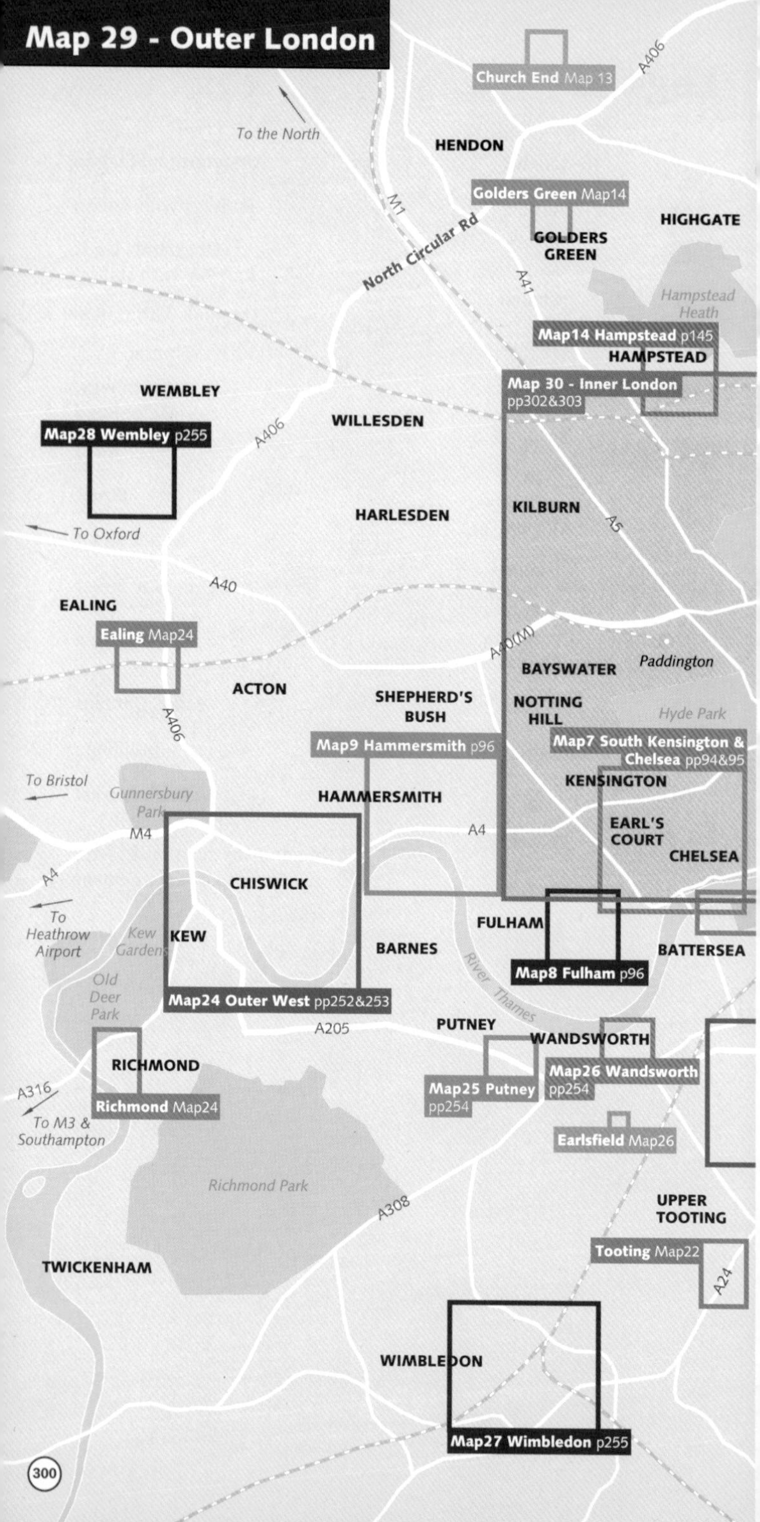

Map 29 - Outer London
Church End Map 13
A406
To the North
HENDON
M1
Golders Green Map14
HIGHGATE
North Circular Rd
GOLDERS GREEN
A41
Hampstead Heath
Map14 Hampstead p145
HAMPSTEAD
Map 30 - Inner London pp302&303
WEMBLEY
WILLESDEN
Map28 Wembley p255
A406
KILBURN
HARLESDEN
A5
To Oxford
A40
EALING
Ealing Map24
A40(M)
BAYSWATER
Paddington
ACTON
SHEPHERD'S BUSH
NOTTING HILL
Hyde Park
A406
Map9 Hammersmith p96
Map7 South Kensington & Chelsea pp94&95
To Bristol
Gunnersbury Park
HAMMERSMITH
KENSINGTON
M4
A4
EARL'S COURT
CHELSEA
A4
CHISWICK
To Heathrow Airport
FULHAM
Kew Gardens
KEW
BARNES
BATTERSEA
River Thames
Map8 Fulham p96
Old Deer Park
Map24 Outer West pp252&253
A205
PUTNEY
WANDSWORTH
RICHMOND
Map26 Wandsworth pp254
Map25 Putney pp254
A316
Richmond Map24
To M3 & Southampton
Earlsfield Map26
Richmond Park
A308
UPPER TOOTING
Tooting Map22
A24
TWICKENHAM
WIMBLEDON
Map27 Wimbledon p255

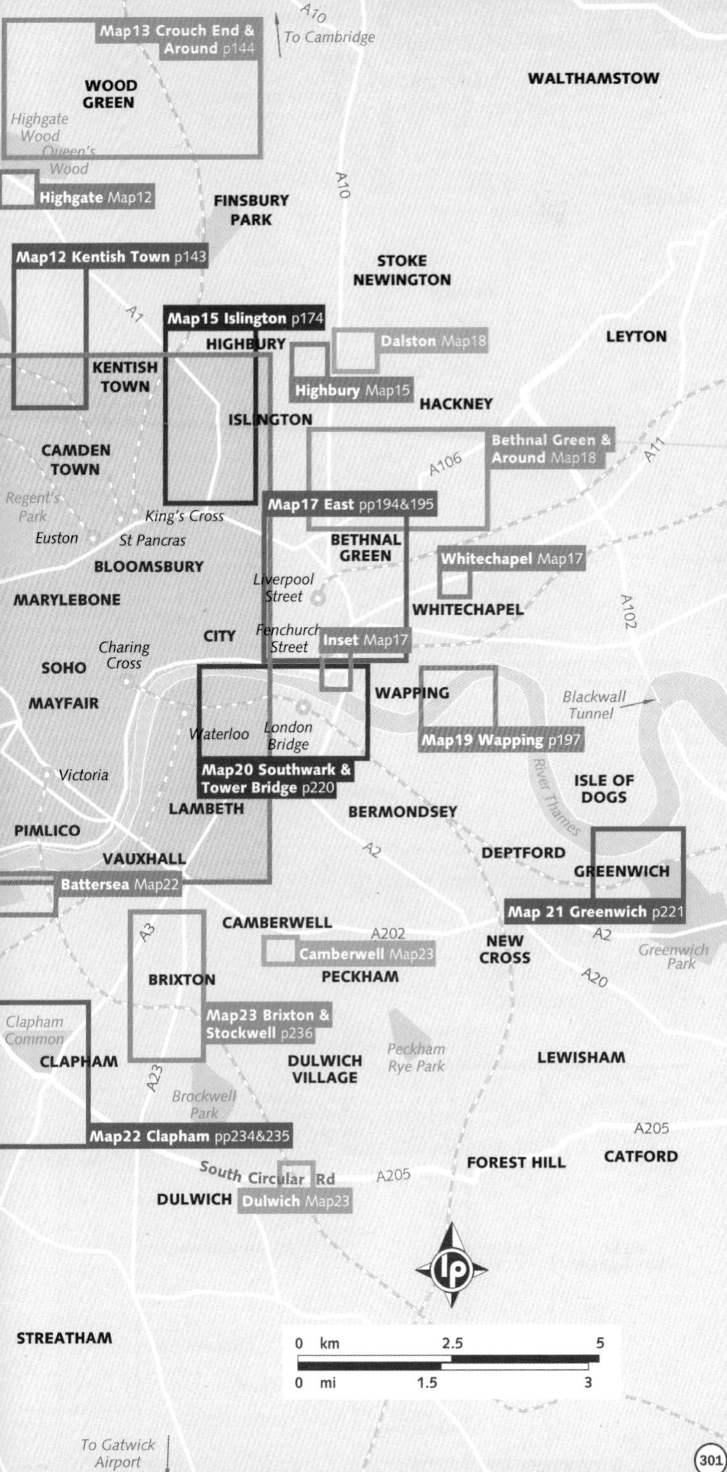
A10
To Cambridge
Map13 Crouch End & Around p144
WOOD GREEN
Highgate Wood
Queen's Wood
Highgate Map12
FINSBURY PARK
WALTHAMSTOW
A10
Map12 Kentish Town p143
STOKE NEWINGTON
A1
Map15 Islington p174
HIGHBURY
Dalston Map18
LEYTON
KENTISH TOWN
Highbury Map15
HACKNEY
ISLINGTON
CAMDEN TOWN
Bethnal Green & Around Map18
A106
A11
Regent's Park
King's Cross
Map17 East pp194&195
Euston
St Pancras
BETHNAL GREEN
BLOOMSBURY
Whitechapel Map17
Liverpool Street
MARYLEBONE
WHITECHAPEL
A102
CITY
Fenchurch Street
Inset Map17
Charing Cross
SOHO
WAPPING
MAYFAIR
Blackwall Tunnel
Waterloo
London Bridge
Map19 Wapping p197
Map20 Southwark & Tower Bridge p220
River Thames
Victoria
ISLE OF DOGS
LAMBETH
BERMONDSEY
PIMLICO
A2
DEPTFORD
VAUXHALL
GREENWICH
Battersea Map22
Map 21 Greenwich p221
CAMBERWELL
A202
A3
NEW CROSS
A2
Camberwell Map23
Greenwich Park
BRIXTON
PECKHAM
A20
Map23 Brixton & Stockwell p236
Clapham Common
CLAPHAM
DULWICH VILLAGE
Peckham Rye Park
LEWISHAM
A23
Brockwell Park
Map22 Clapham pp234&235
A205
South Circular Rd
A205
FOREST HILL
CATFORD
DULWICH
Dulwich Map23
STREATHAM
0 km 2.5 5
0 mi 1.5 3
To Gatwick Airport

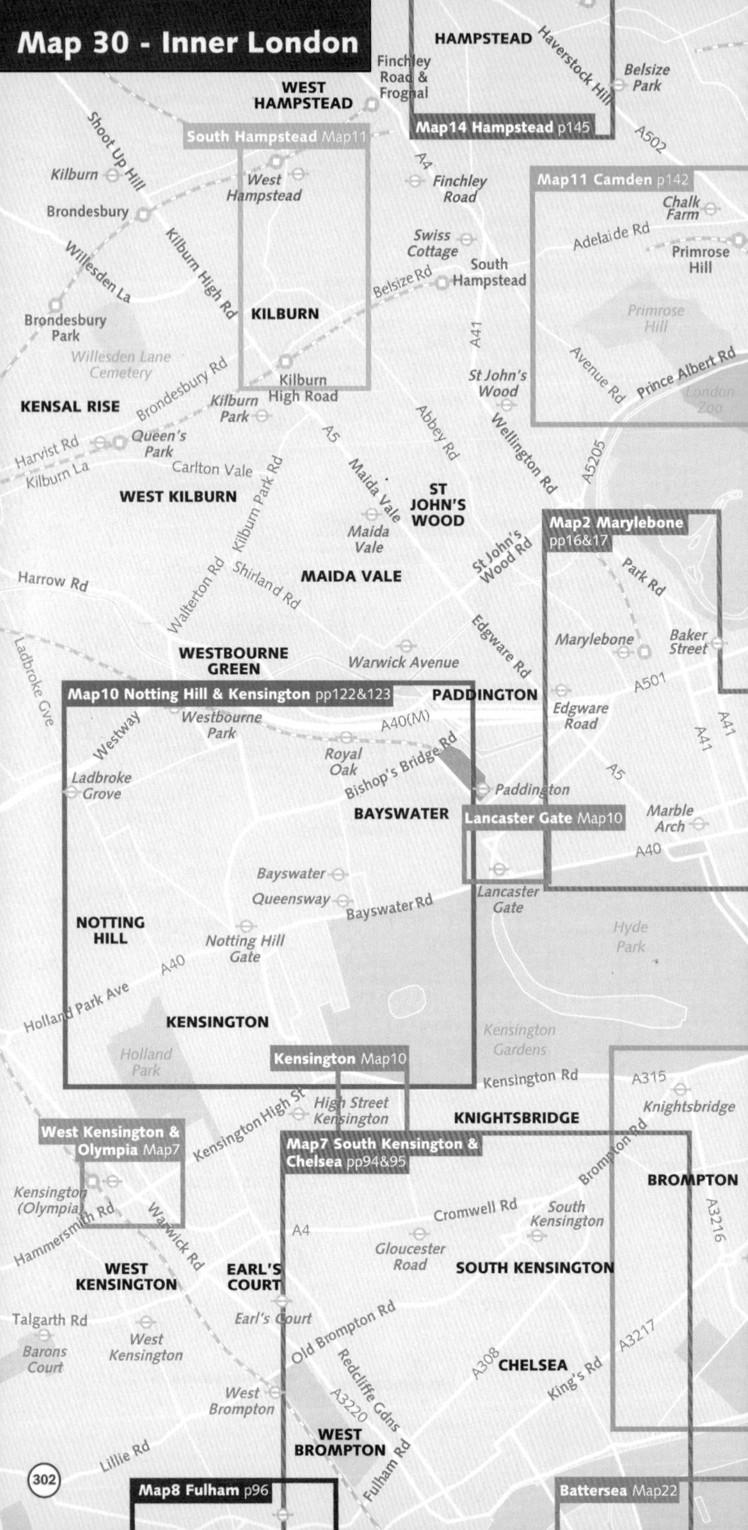
HAMPSTEAD
Haverstock Hill
Belsize Park
Finchley Road & Frognal
WEST HAMPSTEAD
Map14 Hampstead p145
A502
South Hampstead Map11
Shoot Up Hill
Kilburn
West Hampstead
A4
Finchley Road
Map11 Camden p142
Chalk Farm
Brondesbury
Kilburn High Rd
Swiss Cottage
Adelaide Rd
Primrose Hill
Willesden La
South Hampstead
Belsize Rd
KILBURN
Brondesbury Park
Willesden Lane Cemetery
A41
Primrose Hill
Avenue Rd
Prince Albert Rd
Kilburn High Road
St John's Wood
London Zoo
KENSAL RISE
Brondesbury Rd
Kilburn Park
Abbey Rd
Wellington Rd
Harvist Rd
Queen's Park
A5
A5205
Kilburn La
Carlton Vale
Maida Vale
Kilburn Park Rd
WEST KILBURN
ST JOHN'S WOOD
Maida Vale
Map2 Marylebone pp16&17
St John's Wood Rd
Park Rd
Harrow Rd
Shirland Rd
MAIDA VALE
Walterton Rd
Edgware Rd
Baker Street
Marylebone
Ladbroke Gve
WESTBOURNE GREEN
Warwick Avenue
A501
Map10 Notting Hill & Kensington pp122&123
PADDINGTON
Edgware Road
Westbourne Park
A40(M)
A41
Westway
Royal Oak
Bishop's Bridge Rd
A41
A5
Ladbroke Grove
Paddington
BAYSWATER
Lancaster Gate Map10
Marble Arch
A40
Bayswater
Lancaster Gate
Queensway
Bayswater Rd
NOTTING HILL
Hyde Park
Notting Hill Gate
A40
Holland Park Ave
KENSINGTON
Kensington Gardens
Holland Park
Kensington Map10
Kensington Rd
A315
High Street Kensington
Knightsbridge
Kensington High St
KNIGHTSBRIDGE
West Kensington & Olympia Map7
Map7 South Kensington & Chelsea pp94&95
Brompton Rd
BROMPTON
Kensington (Olympia)
Cromwell Rd
South Kensington
A3216
Hammersmith Rd
Warwick Rd
A4
Gloucester Road
WEST KENSINGTON
EARL'S COURT
SOUTH KENSINGTON
Talgarth Rd
Earl's Court
Old Brompton Rd
Barons Court
West Kensington
A3217
Redcliffe Gdns
A308
CHELSEA
King's Rd
West Brompton
A3220
WEST BROMPTON
Lillie Rd
Fulham Rd
Map8 Fulham p96
Battersea Map22

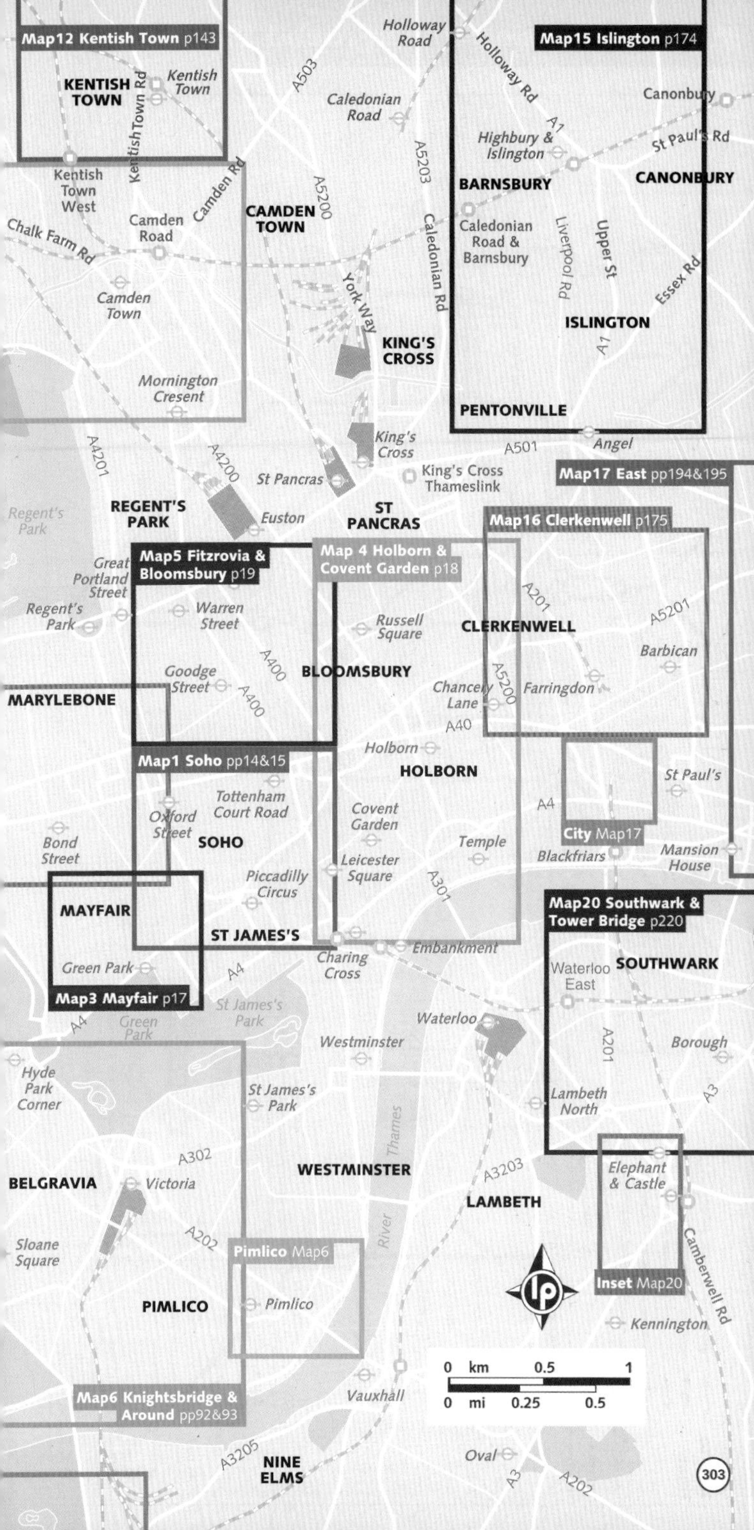

Map12 Kentish Town p143
KENTISH TOWN
Kentish Town
Kentish Town Rd
Kentish Town West
Camden Road
Camden Rd
CAMDEN TOWN
Chalk Farm Rd
Camden Town
Mornington Cresent
Holloway Road
Holloway Rd
A503
Caledonian Road
A5200
A5203
Caledonian Rd
York Way
KING'S CROSS
Map15 Islington p174
Canonbury
St Paul's Rd
Highbury & Islington
A1
BARNSBURY
CANONBURY
Caledonian Road & Barnsbury
Liverpool Rd
Upper St
Essex Rd
ISLINGTON
PENTONVILLE
Angel
A501
King's Cross
King's Cross Thameslink
St Pancras
A4201
A4200
REGENT'S PARK
Regent's Park
Euston
ST PANCRAS
Map17 East pp194&195
Map16 Clerkenwell p175
Map5 Fitzrovia & Bloomsbury p19
Map 4 Holborn & Covent Garden p18
Great Portland Street
Regent's Park
Warren Street
Russell Square
CLERKENWELL
A201
A5201
Barbican
A400
BLOOMSBURY
Goodge Street
Chancery Lane
A5200
Farringdon
MARYLEBONE
A40
Holborn
Map1 Soho pp14&15
HOLBORN
St Paul's
Tottenham Court Road
Oxford Street
Covent Garden
A4
Bond Street
SOHO
Temple
City Map17
Blackfriars
Mansion House
Leicester Square
Piccadilly Circus
A301
MAYFAIR
Map20 Southwark & Tower Bridge p220
ST JAMES'S
Embankment
Charing Cross
SOUTHWARK
Green Park
Waterloo East
Map3 Mayfair p17
A4
St James's Park
Green Park
Waterloo
Westminster
A201
Borough
Hyde Park Corner
St James's Park
Thames
Lambeth North
A3
A302
WESTMINSTER
A3203
Elephant & Castle
BELGRAVIA
Victoria
LAMBETH
A202
River
Sloane Square
Pimlico Map6
Camberwell Rd
Inset Map20
PIMLICO
Pimlico
Kennington
0 km 0.5 1
0 mi 0.25 0.5
Map6 Knightsbridge & Around pp92&93
Vauxhall
A3205
NINE ELMS
Oval
A3
A202

Map 31 - London Underground

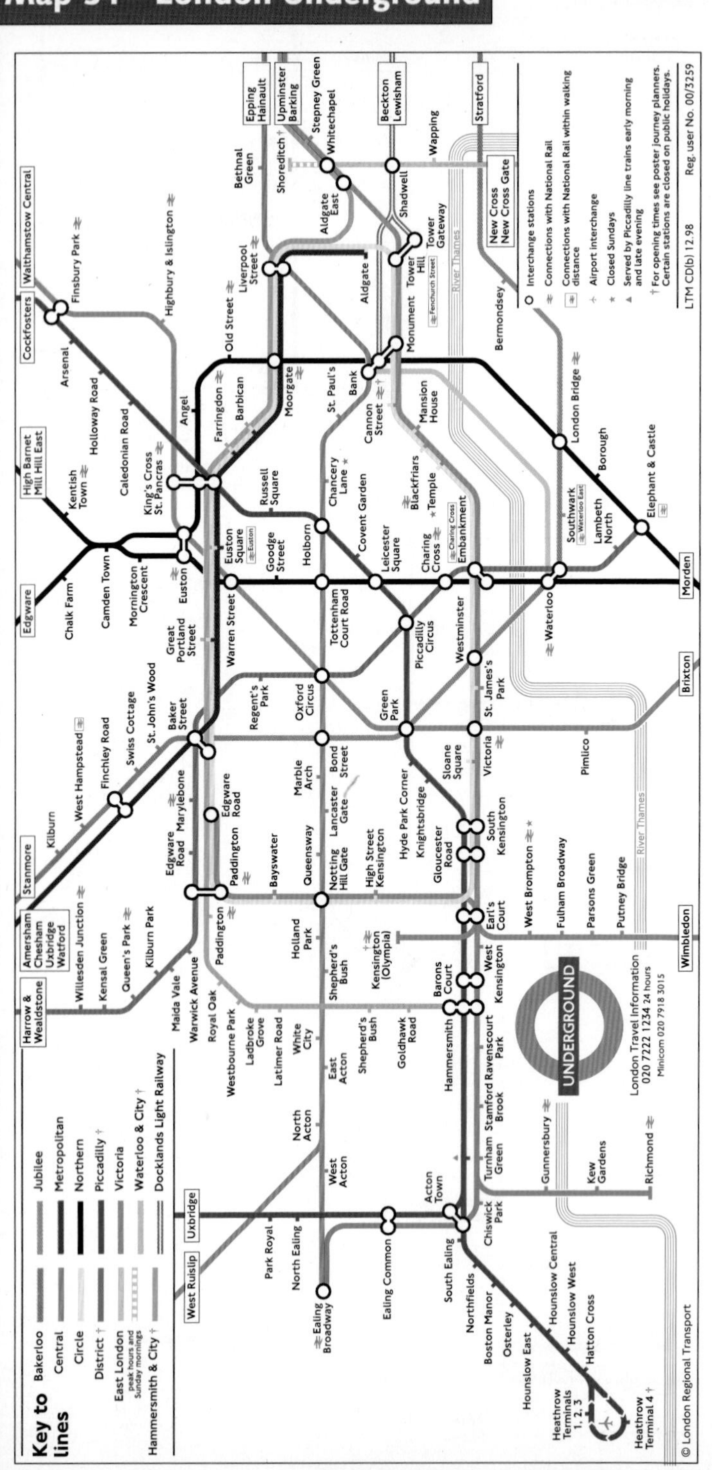